Agriculture and a Changing Environment in Northeastern India

Transition in Northeastern India

Series Editor: Sumi Krishna, Independent scholar, Bangalore

The uniquely diverse landscapes, societies and cultures of northeastern India, forged through complex bio-geographic and socio-political forces, are now facing rapid transition. Yet, popular and academic perceptions tend to be limited primarily to the various conflicts in the region. This series, therefore, aims to broaden the focus to the processes and practices that have shaped, and are shaping, the peoples' identities, outlook, institutions and economy. Eschewing the homogenising term 'North East', which was imposed on the region in a particular political context half a century ago, the series title refers to the 'north eastern' region to more accurately reflect its heterogeneity and the varied issues confronting its diverse peoples. The series will encompass a broad rubric of themes related to culture, social relations, human and economic development, the environment, technology, governance and juridical systems.

Seeking to explore how the 'mainstream' and the 'margins' impact each other, the series will foreground both historical and contemporary research on the northeastern region including the Eastern Himalaya, the adjoining hills and valleys, the states of Arunachal Pradesh, Assam, Manipur, Meghalaya, Mizoram, Nagaland, Sikkim and Tripura. It will publish original, reflective studies that draw upon different disciplines and approaches, and combine empirical and theoretical insights. The monographs and the occasional edited volumes are intended to make scholarship accessible for a wide spectrum of general readers and to help deepen the understanding of academics, policy-makers and practitioners.

Also in this Series

Education and Society in a Changing Mizoram: The Practice of Pedagogy
Lakshmi Bhatia
978-0-415-58920-8

Becoming a Borderland: The Politics of Space and Identity in Colonial Northeastern India
Sanghamitra Misra
978-0-415-61253-1

Unfolding Crisis in Assam's Tea Plantations: Employment and Occupational Mobility
Deepak K. Mishra, Vandana Upadhyay and Atul Sarma
978-0-415-52308-0

Agriculture and a Changing Environment in Northeastern India

Editor

Sumi Krishna

Routledge
Taylor & Francis Group
LONDON NEW YORK NEW DELHI

First published 2012 in India
by Routledge
912 Tolstoy House, 15–17 Tolstoy Marg, Connaught Place, New Delhi 110 001

Simultaneously published in the UK
by Routledge
2 Park Square, Milton Park, Abingdon, Oxfordshire OX14 4RN

First issued in paperback 2015

Routledge is an imprint of the Taylor & Francis Group, an informa business

© 2012 Sumi Krishna

Typeset by
Star Compugraphics Private Limited
5, CSC, Near City Apartments
Vasundhara Enclave
Delhi 110 096

British Library Cataloguing-in-Publication Data
A catalogue record of this book is available from the British Library

ISBN-13: 978-1-138-66291-9 (pbk)
ISBN-13: 978-0-415-63289-8 (hbk)

Contents

List of Tables

List of Figures

Preface

This collection of essays has been a long time in the making. The idea emerged in mid-2007 during a conversation in Shillong when I tried to persuade Vincent Darlong to undertake a work on agriculture and resource management in northeastern India. Most of the available literature on agriculture tended to follow a conventional 'developmentalist' approach to farming and allied activities in the region and did not deal holistically with the changing environment. Vincent agreed that there was need for a critical and nuanced perspective on the theme but rightly pointed out that it would be very difficult for any one person to undertake such a study. I then began contacting others who shared similar concerns and had researched issues relevant to agricultural change in the region.

Not surprisingly this was a slow process, more so because it was entirely unfunded; yet, eventually, several persons agreed to contribute. Many of the essays in this book were originally written for different purposes, but almost all of these have been revisited, reworked and edited afresh for this collection. The authors include scientists and social scientists, academics and development practitioners trained in varied disciplines and using different methodologies. Indeed, it is fairly unusual for essays by conservation scientists, botanists, geographers, economists, historians, journalists, and so on to all appear together in one volume.

The contributors to the book have a common interest in the region and share certain approaches and concerns. The 14 chapters are grouped into three broad sections. Part I deals with selected aspects of agriculture and a changing environment, interweaving historical and socio-political trends with the people's economic choices. Part II uses a gendered lens to bring a fresh perspective to farming, forests, conservation and livelihoods. Part III includes grounded analyses of alternative income-generating interventions that women and men farmers are beginning to explore for improved livelihoods and conservation. Some of the chapters focus on one or more states; others deal with the region as a whole. The Appendix is the synthesis of a detailed study by the North Eastern Social Research Centre, Guwahati, on changing land relations among six tribal groups and one non-tribal group. Possibly the only study of its kind, its authors also discuss policy directions for the future. The grid on the following page gives the chapter-wise coverage of states and the northeastern region (NER).

It is difficult to name all those who have helped to shape this volume in one way or the other, especially the many northeastern women and men farmers and the cross-section of professionals who have generously provided hospitality and shared valuable information and insights. In particular, I would like to thank all my co-contributors for making this book possible. Special thanks are due to the family of the late U. A. Shimray and Rajesh Mall (Jawaharlal Nehru University alumni) for putting me in touch with them; Apurba Baruah and Manorama Sharma, North Eastern Hill University, Shillong, editors of *North East India Studies* for the article by Audrey Laldinpuii and Laithangpuii, and for much else; the North Eastern Social Research Centre, Guwahati, and Walter Fernandes for permission to include his essays and for inspiration over the years; Infochange for allowing Thingnam Anjulika Samom to rework a series of articles into a chapter for this book; Vandana Upadhyay, Rajiv Gandhi University, formerly known as Arunachal University, Itanagar, for her keen interest and timely support; Sanghamitra Misra, University of Delhi for pertinent suggestions; and finally, Omita Goyal, formerly with Routledge, for initiating this series and the present team for taking it forward.

Sumi Krishna
Bangalore
January 2012

Figure 1: Chapter-wise Coverage of States in the Region

Chapter	Arunachal Pradesh	Assam	Manipur	Meghalaya	Mizoram	Nagaland	Sikkim	Tripura	Northeastern Region (NER)
Part I									
1		+							+
2			+						
3				+					+
4			+						
5	+								+
Part II									
6	+								+
7						+	+		
8								+	
9					+				
10	+	+	+	+	+	+	+	+	+
Part III									
11		+		+				+	
12									+
13	+	+			+			+	+
14	+	+	+	+	+	+		+	+
Appendix									
	+	+	+	+					+

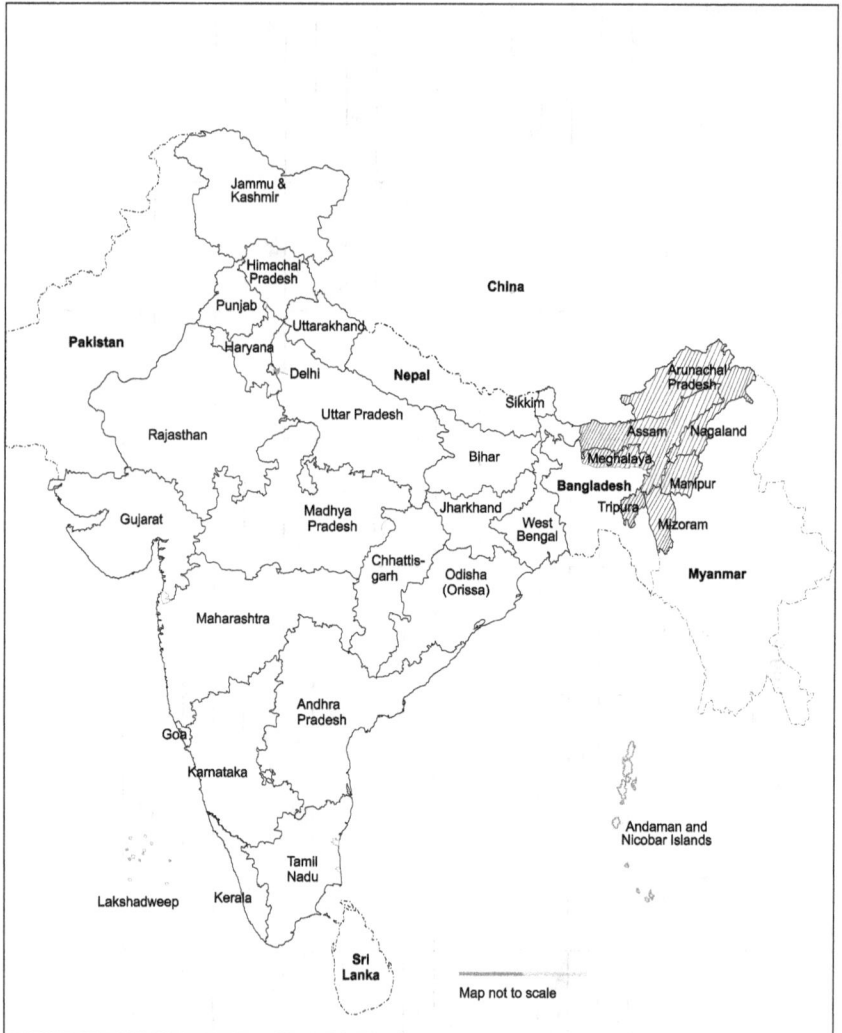

States of India and the Northeastern Region

Source: Prepared by the editor. The boundaries do not imply official endorsement.

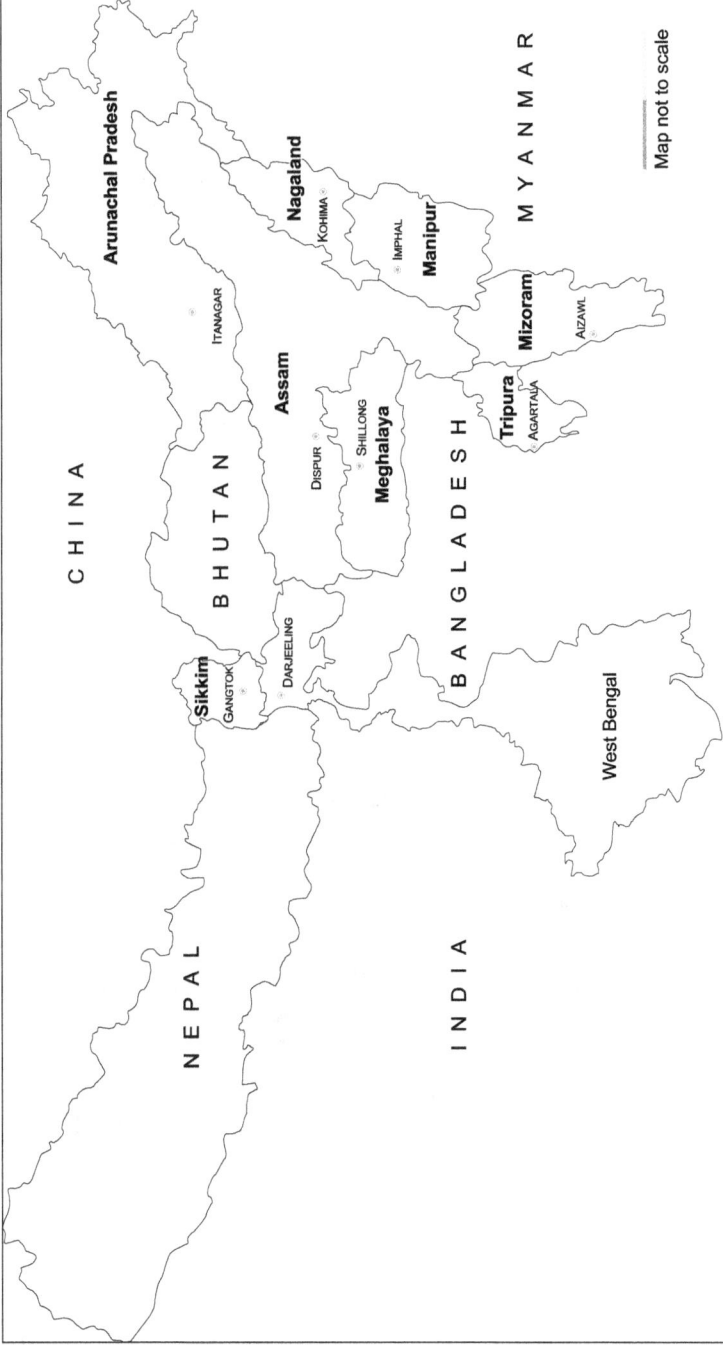

Northeastern India

Source: Prepared by the editor. The boundaries do not imply official endorsement.

Jhum (Shifting Cultivation) Fields, West Siang District, Arunachal Pradesh

Source: Courtesy of Sandeep Krishna

Introduction

SUMI KRISHNA

India's northeastern region (henceforth NER), forged by a unique geological history and peopled by several waves of migration, is extraordinarily complex both ecologically and socio-culturally. It stretches from north Bengal through the eastern Himalaya to what were once 'Greater Assam' and the independent kingdoms of Manipur and Tripura, bordering on Southeast Asia. It is dominated by the eastern Himalaya which extends across a thousand kilometres from Sikkim and the Darjeeling hills through Bhutan and southern China to Arunachal Pradesh. A continuously changing web of geological and bio-geographic factors shape the region's varied topography and local climates. Its diverse peoples are an integral part of the dynamic environment of forests, wetlands and fields. In earlier times, farming served multiple functions and mixed land-use was a safeguard against environmental and economic hazards. During the last century, however, despite relative isolation, external economic and socio-political processes have deeply impacted agrarian and livelihood practices in the region.

Heterogeneity

The northeastern Himalaya has a unique bio-geography (see Mani 1974). This is the region where the pre-tertiary Tethys Sea first began to close with the collision of the Indian (Deccan) and Eurasian continental plates. The Himalayan uplift began around 50–55 million years ago and the mountains are still rising. In the extreme west of Arunachal Pradesh, the ranges lie in an east–west direction; thereafter, they are wrenched into a north–south axis, making a sharp u-turn in the easternmost corner of Assam at the tri-junction of India, China and Myanmar (formerly Burma), and extending in a continuous curve to form the Patkoi and Naga Hills and the broad Manipur plateau. One branch curves back into Assam to form the Jaintia, Khasi and Garo hills of

Meghalaya; another branch bends southwards as the low but steep Lushai hills of Mizoram. The highest peak in the eastern Himalaya is Kanchenjunga at 8,586 m in Sikkim, along the Indo-Nepal border. Further east in western and central Arunachal the peaks are between 6,000 and 7,000 m high. In the extreme east the crests are lower, at 4,000–5,000 m, and in the Patkoi Hills they are below 2,000 m. The mountains are geologically young and fragile, composed almost entirely of sedimentary and metamorphic rock, mainly shale, schist and conglomerates. In the valleys, the derived soils are sandy to clayey-loam. The organic content of the soil is high, making it nitrogenous and acidic like other mountain soils. The NER lies in a seismically sensitive zone and has experienced several earthquakes of high magnitudes. The worst was in 1950, when the eastern-most parts of the region were devastated by an earthquake with its epicentre in Tibet; most recently, in September 2011, an earthquake with its epicentre in north Sikkim hit many regions of the NER and Nepal.

The mountains in the region are dissected by geologically older rivers and their tributaries in a complex hydrological system from the northern watershed to its drainage into the Brahmaputra, Barak and Imphal rivers. From Tibet, the Tsangpo swerves into Arunachal, where it is called the Dihang (or Siang), and becomes the Brahmaputra as it enters the Assam valley. Arunachal's Kameng-Bharali, Subansiri, Dihang and Dibang flow southwards; the Lohit flows in a southwesterly direction, and the lesser Nao Dihing flows northeast. Even in a small state like Mizoram, the terrain is geologically distinctive — low steep hills, sandwiched in a north–south direction with deep narrow gorges and rivers that run in opposite directions. The Tlawang flows northwards into the Barak in Cachar, but the Mat on its east and the Dei on its west flow southwards. The Chhimtuipui river (also called Kaladyne or Kaladam) flows westwards from Myanmar, south through Mizoram and into Myanmar again. The Khawthhlangtuipui (or Karnaphulli) flows west into Bangladesh. The rivers in the NER change course frequently: in eastern Assam a continuously meandering river is aptly named Pagla (mad); in the foothills of eastern Arunachal a not-so-old bridge stands amidst paddy fields, a minor river that it once spanned now nowhere in sight (Krishna 1998a, 1998b)!

With an annual rainfall of 4,500 mm in the foothills, the eastern Himalaya is much wetter and hotter than the western Himalaya of Garhwal and Kumaon, with temperatures rising to 38 degrees in summer. This is why the 'tree-line' here is higher. Tempestuous pre-monsoon showers in March precede the heavy, incessant southwest monsoon through June and July, tapering off in September–October. Arunachal has an average annual rainfall of 3,000 mm but the higher ranges are relatively drier (800 mm a year) and the north-facing slopes too get less rain. The middle altitudes have a 'temperate' climate but certain locations are chilling even in spring as the wind tears through deep gorges. There is less snow in the higher reaches than at similar altitudes in the western Himalaya but winter can be extremely cold. The valleys and the plateaus within the mountains experience a diversity of micro-climates.

The NER is extraordinarily verdant and fertile. The flora and fauna is yet to be comprehensively surveyed and documented. The available records show high species richness and plant endemism. The massive changes that occurred with the subduction of the Indian continental plate and the rise of the Himalaya opened up land connections and migratory routes in different directions. The confluence of biota from regions that are now Tibet, India, China, Malaya and Myanmar made the eastern Himalaya 'a crucible for the evolution of new species complexes' — over 1,800 endemics, more than elsewhere in the Himalaya (Nayar 1996: 9–11). This is one of the world's 18 biodiversity hotspots (Arora and Pandey 1996; Myers et al. 2000; Nayar 1996) and is now classified as an ecoregion (see Olson et al. 2001).

The altitudinal bands of vegetation in the NER correspond only roughly to the conventional 19th-century European classification of alpine, temperate, subtropical evergreen, tropical evergreen and semi-evergreen forests. The northern-most limits of the tropical rain forest can be found here (Proctor et al. 1998). Indeed, as Arnold (2005: 195–96) has noted, the British botanist-explorer Joseph Hooker had to deepen his understanding of the 'tropics' when he travelled through the Darjeeling and Sikkim hills in 1848–49. Hooker's *Himalayan Journals* (1854) record 'temperate' vegetation characteristic of an 'English spring' flourishing at the same altitude of 5,000 ft (1,524 m) as typically 'tropical' plants:

rhododendrons blooming amidst forests of oak; 'tropical' tree ferns, wild banana, palm, fig, bamboo, epiphytic orchids and climbing vines growing beside 'temperate' birch, fir, willow, alder and walnut. 'The paradox of finding tropical and temperate plants nestling in close proximity was not lost on Hooker' (ibid.: 195). The diversity was remarkable and unique. 'At times the representative flora of the tropical, temperate, and alpine zones, instead of being geographically distant and distinct, could be seen simultaneously from a single vantage point or found entangled in jungles that were, botanically speaking, tropical and temperate at the same time' (ibid.: 196). Arnold points out that this complexity did not lead Hooker to abandon the tropical-temperate-alpine classification but it did help to extend the idea of the tropics to an extreme.

The complex geo-morphological processes, which have shaped the rivers and water bodies of the NER, are also responsible for the continuous alluvial deposition forming temporary sandbars and *chars* (river islands) in the Brahmaputra. Some 1,000 of these alluvial formations are almost 'permanent' and are occupied and farmed in winter. Within the chars too, there are distinct water-bodies, all of which are inundated when the river is in flood in summer (Bhagabati and Goswami 2000: 152). The very diverse land-water-wetland formations of the NER, both along the Brahmaputra and in lake systems such as that of the Manipur valley, form unique ecologies that deepen our concept of wetlands.

This physiographic heterogeneity in a small geographic area is paralleled by the complex human diversity. The region has been peopled by several waves of migration. It is surmised that about 2,000–2,500 years ago, the first of the Mongoloid tribes may have come into the area (at about the time that proto-Indo-Aryans were moving into northwest India). There is evidence that a major route into India was through the northeastern corridor and recent genomic research indicates that Tibeto-Burman and some Austro-Asiatic elements entered through this way (Basu et al. 2003). The topography kept tribal clans in virtual isolation. There may have been intermittent inter-tribal warfare but no dominant groups emerged. Hence, instead of homogenisation, there seems to have been a process of diversification into smaller sub-groups having their own belief systems, life styles and languages. The river valleys, low hills and high ranges were, thus, peopled by a great number of ethnic groups that continued to retain considerable fluidity. Indeed, before the British annexation of Assam in the early 19th century 'the tribes were not as sharply defined social formations as they came to be in the subsequent years' (Bhagabati 1988: 2). Colonial rule hastened the demarcation of tribe and non-tribe and the consolidation of each tribe.[1]

In Arunachal alone there are more than 125 enumerated tribes and sub-tribes but barely 15 with a population of over 5,000. In Nagaland linguists recognise as many as 23 language groups. Even the four Tanghul Naga villages studied by Shimray (2007 and in this volume) in a small area of Manipur's Ukhrul district speak four different Tanghul dialects although they also share a common language. The Nagas joke about their layered identity. Four Nagas of different tribes met at a crossroads and sat down to lunch. Each named what he had brought differently, but when they began to eat, they all had the same food, rice and chillies. A Naga legend explains the origin of this babble of tongues: when humans began to climb the stairway to heaven, God (a woman) was afraid she would not have enough gifts for them all and so caused them to speak different languages, thwarting their attempt to work together to reach her (Krishna 1991)!

Development

Given this complex diversity, it is not surprising that the development of the NER is a special challenge. Administratively, the NER includes eight ecologically and socio-politically different states: Sikkim and the 'seven sisters', Arunachal, Assam, Manipur, Meghalaya, Mizoram, Nagaland and Tripura. These states came into existence (often controversially) at different stages and under varying constitutional arrangements.[2] Despite its longitudinal distance east of the Indian meridian (which runs through Ujjain in central India), northeastern India follows Indian Standard Time. Because of this disjunction between 'clock' time and 'real' time, the day appears to break early in the region. This is reflected in the name Arunachal Pradesh, the land of the rising sun (formerly the North East Frontier Agency). The NER constitutes about 8 per cent of the area of the country (Table 1); over 70 per cent of the region is rugged mountain terrain, a considerable proportion being snow-bound and inaccessible. In 2001, it accounted for about 4 per cent

Table 1: Land Area of Northeastern States

State	Land area (sq km)	Population density (persons per sq km)
Arunachal Pradesh	83,743	13
Assam	78,438	340
Manipur	22,327	103
Meghalaya	22,429	103
Mizoram	21,087	42
Nagaland	16,579	120
Sikkim	7,096	76
Tripura	10,486	305
NER	**262,185**	**149**
All-India	3,287,263	313

Source: NEDFi. 2006. *Databank Quarterly.* Guwahati: North Eastern Development Finance Corporation Ltd., p. 2.

of India's population with a marginally higher decadal growth rate than in the rest of the country. Seven out of 10 people live in the plains of the Brahmaputra and Barak valleys (that constitute 80 per cent of Assam), the plains of Tripura (nearly half of the state) and the small Manipur valley. Tribal groups are a majority in four states: Mizoram, Meghalaya, Nagaland and Arunachal (NEDFi 2006).

India's policy for the NER has for long hinged around idealising its remote allure and being apprehensive of its peoples and their aspirations but ever ready to exploit its rich natural endowment.[3] The dual approach of isolation and selective engagement for resource extraction, begun by the British, was continued after independence. For decades, the marginalisation and economic 'backwardness' of the NER co-existed with the extraction and export of oil, tea and timber, mainly from Assam. Few benefits reached the people in the hinterland. Assam, once among the states with the highest incomes in India, became one of the poorest mainly due to unfair resource exploitation and failures of governance.

After the India–China war of 1962, the region's strategic importance made 'integration' with the rest of India the fulcrum of state policy. Local instability was fuelled by economic deprivation and political struggles for identity. The state dealt with uprisings in various parts of the NER militarily but political solutions were also found. New political entities, the states of Nagaland, Mizoram and Meghalaya were created and substantial central government funds began to be allocated for 'developing' the region. While the various struggles for autonomy led to an acknowledgement of the peoples' political and cultural interests, the preoccupation of policy makers was mainly with national security concerns. The formation of the North East Council in 1972 and special plans for tribal and hill areas were attempts to focus on economic development but a coherent and democratic strategy for development, and the institutions of local governance, were missing.

The development of timber markets and the commercial demand for non-timber forest products led to the privatisation of community forests in parts of the NER. Certain sections of society benefitted from this trade but privatisation also led to extensive deforestation. In December 1996, the Supreme Court banned the inter-state movement of timber and the associated tree-felling. Some view the legislation as the imposition of a dominant 'mainstream' society that does not recognise the cultural role of forests and forest products in northeastern life (Nathan 2000; Nongbri 2001). The ban did not stop the burning of trees for charcoal but it does seem to have helped to curtail deforestation.

Since the late 1990s, India's economic liberalisation policy has resulted in rapid changes in the NER, reopening trade and commerce across the region's international borders and paving the way for more aggressive inflows of private capital. The S. P. Shukla Commission Report on 'Transforming the Northeast' (Planning Commission 1997) recommended improving the infrastructure and opening up the region for trade. The establishment in 2001 of the department, which later became the ministry, responsible for the development of the northeastern region (DONER) has provided the institutional framework and a common budget for regional planning, especially for power, irrigation, roads and communication. The 'Vision 2020' document prepared by the National Institute for Public Finance and Policy provided the thrust for the government's policy to 'look east' towards Southeast Asia (DONER 2007).

River waters are the region's greatest resource; the Brahmaputra is part of the great Ganga–Brahmaputra basin with enormous potential (Verghese 2004; Verghese and Ramaswamy 1993).

There is, however, a sharp debate on how the rivers should be used and for whose benefit (Vagholikar and Das 2010). In 2001, the Central Electricity Authority identified the NER as India's future powerhouse, listing some 168 potential locations for large hydroelectric projects, mainly in Sikkim and Arunachal Pradesh with a cumulative installed capacity of 63,000 MW (Kalpavriksh 2005). But in a seismically active and geologically fragile zone there is deep concern about a hydropower policy based on large dams rather than on smaller dams and run-of-the river projects. Although under Indian law, environment impact assessments are mandatory, it is well-known that these are done cursorily with a view to produce an assessment favouring dam-building and without taking into account the social and ecological impacts. Changes in the flow patterns of the Brahmaputra and its tributaries are already affecting local fisheries and peoples' livelihoods. Open-cast mining for coal in parts of the region, the extraction of limestone, and the controversies over uranium mining in Meghalaya (see Karlsson 2011; Shimray and Ramana 2007) also impact on the environment. Das (2010) points out that climate change adds another layer of uncertainty.

All the NER states receive 90 per cent of their budget as grant and 10 per cent as loan from the central government. This inflow of development funding and several special schemes seem to have intensified the on-going process of stratification both within and among the states. Literacy is high in some states; there is relatively better access to schooling than elsewhere in India, particularly in areas which have a history of educational institutions that were established by European and American missionaries. But the absence of industry and a largely subsistence agriculture have restricted people's livelihood choices to service occupations. Government jobs are highly prized and often become conduits for making 'easy money' through a parallel economy.

In a region where two out of three people are engaged in agriculture and whatever industry exists is based on forest and agricultural produce, there is little understanding at the policy level of the heterogeneity of the agricultural resource base in the hills, the foothills and the valleys and its multifarious linkages with the lives of the people. The contemporary policy 'vision' for the region revolves simply around increasing the income of the eight states and their integration with the larger polity. This is being done through developing hydropower primarily for export to the rest of India, improving local infrastructure for the movement of goods, and emphasising improved agricultural productivity by expanding the market for horticultural crops. Several state governments in the region have declared their intention to move towards organic farming.

Farming

Throughout the NER, farming is much more than a matter of raising animals and growing crops. It is a way of life, interwoven with culture and belief systems. Farming families are involved in a cluster of activities including dairy and livestock (sheep, goat, pig), poultry, fish, *jhum*, sericulture, and the conservation of watersheds. Changes in farming practices are taking place because of the growing density of people and settlements around the cultivated areas (Burman 2002) and because of government policies that restrict *jhuming* (shifting cultivation) in order to promote settled wet-rice cultivation.

The per capita availability of land (0.66 ha) in the NER is twice that in the rest of India but because of the mountainous terrain only a quarter is cultivable compared to nearly 60 per cent for the rest of India (North Eastern Development Finance Corporation Ltd. [NEDFi] 2006). Moreover, jhum farming (shifting slash-and-burn cultivation) in the hills requires a larger area for rotation. About a sixth of jhum land is estimated to be under cultivation at a time, as jhum fields are cyclically left fallow for the forest vegetation to naturally re-establish itself. Both settled cultivation (in hill terraces and the valleys) and jhum are characterised by a wide variety of crops that require low inputs and offer a buffer against failures. A small jhum field in the hills may have as many as 35 different crops. Conventional measures of agricultural productivity, however, undervalue the output of multiple land-use, and especially of jhum fields. The significance of jhum fallows is not appreciated. Agrarian diversity is recognised and promoted as an exhibit for tourists but not as a central feature of the region's development.

Since the 1970s, one of the goals of development policy in the NER has been to stop shifting cultivation and substantial funding has been allocated to achieve this. Yet, jhum persists. The Shukla Commission (Planning Commission 1997) noted that while hill farming was largely under jhum, terrace cultivation and 'wet rice' (generally rain-fed) were expanding. Jhum was becoming less productive because of a shorter cycle; in some areas this inhibited the regeneration of forests and led to soil erosion. The report observed (in an understatement, one might add) that not all resettlement schemes for families involved in jhum had worked well. Jhuming could not be ended 'all at once' and sensitivity was required because this was 'a way of life'. It noted that the Indian Council of Agricultural Research (ICAR) had a hill farming programme that combined forestry, horticulture or tree-farming and terraced cultivation at different elevations. Others have advocated improving jhum practices. The best known example of higher productivity from jhum is from Nagaland, where jhum crops are being combined with fast-growing trees of economic value, notably alder. Formerly, jhuming met people's subsistence needs but all over the NER increasing aspirations for cash incomes means that *jhumias* have to earn profits from farming. Hence, farmers are switching to cash crops such as pineapple and arecanut, despite difficulties with managing horticultural crops. Tea, rubber and other plantation crops are also being tried. But farmers have to deal with increasing labour requirements and the intricacies of the open market for which they are not adequately prepared.

Land tenure in the NER varies depending on the traditional land-use practices in the hills and plains, as well as the settlement patterns and social structures.[4] As there has been no cadastral survey or land settlement across the NER, there are few records of ownership. Tripura is exceptional in having defined a land-ownership regime under the Tripura Land Revenue and Land Reforms Act, 1969, which applies to the entire state, including the hill areas. In Tripura, all land that is not privately owned is vested with the government, whereas in other northeastern states different forms of community control of land management continue. Generally, among tribal groups in the hills, the lands used for shifting cultivation are communally held. Valley land, terraced land, homestead land and short fallows are privately owned. (See also Ganguly 1993; Jamir and Nongkynrih 2002; Nongkynrih 2008.)

Across the NER, in places which are becoming urbanised, land markets have developed leading to a shift from communal to individual holdings, but this is usually only within the local tribal group. Individually owned terraces in the hills have also been cultivated for several decades. With the stratification of society and the emergence of new social formations because of the spread of education and some diversification of employment, land-holding patterns and agrarian relations are changing, as also gender relations. Women's representation in traditional and modern governance structures is negligible (see Krishna 2004) and they and poorer sections of society are being increasingly marginalised. Consider Mizoram, a state which is relatively well-developed by conventional indicators. Mizoram's Agricultural Land Act of 1955 has facilitated individual land rights and the transfer of communally held land to individuals. Thangchungmunga (1998) argues that this has resulted in fertile and more easily accessible lands being concentrated in the hands of a new elite and has impoverished others, intensifying the migration of rural people to urban areas.

Credit for farming is especially complicated because of the variety of land tenure systems and the lack of documentation of ownership, which is an essential feature of conventional bank lending procedures. In a report to the Reserve Bank of India (RBI 2006), Usha Thorat, then a deputy governor, made the innovative point that banks should seek evidence of the prospective borrower being a farmer rather than insisting that the person be a land holder. Her report recommended that banks should accept community and social guarantees as collateral for bank finance. In Nagaland, there are now cases of village bodies providing such guarantees.

The Themes of the Book

The contributions to this volume bring a fresh perspective to agricultural transition in the context of a changing environment. The book is structured in three parts. Part I discusses the complex processes of agrarian change, highlighting the impact of policies and people's own aspirations on the closely intertwined ecology and economy in the region. Part II is specifically concerned with the gender dimensions of agricultural change in an environment where forestry, biodiversity and farming are intimately interrelated, and the responsibility for food production is borne mainly by women.

Part III covers some of the alternative farming and livelihood options that are being propagated and the community-based initiatives that could help conserve and sustainably manage the environment and farming systems.

ASPECTS OF A CHANGING ENVIRONMENT

The opening chapter in Part I, Ritupan Goswami's historical study of floods and fields in the Brahmaputra valley, examines the role of the 'life-giving' river in the farming cycle. In earlier times, farming practices and settlement patterns had been in keeping with the characteristics of the three zones in the valley: the flooding river banks, the plains further inland suitable for transplanted rice, and the sub-montane tracts in the foothills occupied by indigenous tribes. The rice cultivation areas were the most densely populated and the relatively better-off people would also cultivate the river banks and the temporary island chars of the Brahmaputra. Seasonal flooding was essential for soil fertility. But in the 20th century, British colonial policy altered the relationship between the people and the river. The colonial government did not distinguish between a shifting population of temporary settlers on flood-prone land and the permanent cultivation in the interior. Indeed, the perception was of vast lands waiting to be occupied. British policy encouraged the immigration of peasants from East Bengal and settlements in the flood zone for enhancing colonial revenue. This began its transformation into a 'problem' river of sorrow, especially for the poor peasants. Goswami argues that the destructive flooding that left the peasants homeless, landless or destitute, was not a problem because the floods suddenly became more severe, but because of more people and property to be destroyed, even when the floods were of the same intensity and scale as before.

As in the plains, so too in the hills; the late U. A. Shimray points out that colonial rule altered both the geography and the politics of the Naga Hills. The contiguous Naga area now falls within four states in India (Nagaland, Manipur, Arunachal Pradesh, and Assam) and also northern Myanmar. For centuries, Naga livelihood practices were intertwined with their understanding of the local ecology; their traditional economic system, based on their knowledge of agriculture and natural resource management, provided food and conserved the ecology. Over time, the spread of education and the state's development projects have hastened the privatisation of community land and eroded customary concepts of exchanging and sharing labour that had underpinned the community economy. Changes in land-use and ownership created new social disparities. Ancestral and acquired properties are now being divided among male siblings, even as the expansion of terraced fields is constrained by the topography. As children become educated, both household and farm labour is shifting to elders. Without viable alternatives, jhum continues, has even increased; households that do not own forest lands are particularly affected. The disintegration of traditional institutions and customs of resource management together with the penetration of the urban economy through indiscriminate commercial logging and individualised hunting and fishing threatens the ecology. Shimray argues for building the tribal economy based on the customary knowledge and methods of forestry and farming.

This resonates with Dhrupad Choudhury's detailed analysis of upland communities, as in Meghalaya. Asking why jhumias jhum, he points out that jhum farmers do not view traditional land-use systems as contradictory to agricultural development. Indeed, jhum farmers too aspire to better incomes from farming. But plantations and terraced cultivation, which have been promoted by the government, deprive the poor of access and reduce the land available for shifting cultivation and the duration of fallow periods, reducing productivity. This has marginalised the poor and may also dispossess the matrilineal Khasi and Garo women of Meghalaya of their assets in land. Choudhury argues that it is possible to safeguard common property by adapting traditional systems to prevent privatisation and land transfers, as some groups have done, and that 'government policies and approaches need to understand, acknowledge and honour such frameworks'.

On the ground, however, government policies seem far removed from such an understanding. At the world-famous Loktak Lake in Manipur, in March 2009, I was startled by a painted sign on a hillock overlooking the water that read 'Shoot to Kill'.[5] The lake is guarded by paramilitary personnel, very young men from distant parts of the country trained to flush out extremists from the *phumdis*, the floating islands of vegetation that characterise this unique wetland. Thingnam Anjulika Samom's many-layered account of Loktak's history and culture highlights its vital role in ensuring food security, and the people's anguish over its destruction by the Loktak hydropower project, the Ithai barrage and urbanisation of the catchment. Ineffective drainage and solid waste management in Manipur's swiftly growing urban areas are polluting its rivers and water bodies, including Loktak. This is compounded by the run-off of agricultural chemicals. She urges: 'harmonise using the waters of Loktak to fulfil human demands for food security, livelihood and hydropower, along with effective ecological management of the lake's resources.'

In his overview of the linkages between land, environmental degradation and conflict, Walter Fernandes argues that changes in land relations are related to cultures and that the 'imposition of another culture on a traditional group' is detrimental to the community and to women in particular. As he says, the solution is neither reverting to tradition nor accepting it absolutely. While individual ownership of land and resources cannot be prevented, alternatives have to be found that also draw upon traditional community values, thus, modernising tradition rather than replacing it entirely. This approach is substantiated by the detailed study (outlined in the Appendix) by Fernandes and Melvil Pereira, who point out that 'changing land relations, especially land alienation cannot be attributed to any one cause but takes many forms', including the 'individual orientation of the administration, modernisation of the customary laws often supported by elite aspirations, and displacement by development projects'. Therefore, solutions too cannot be simplistic.

GENDER DIMENSIONS OF FARMING

Many of these concerns are taken forward in Part II, which brings a gendered perspective to farming, forestry and agro-forestry in the NER. Deepak Mishra makes the pertinent point that the diversification of livelihoods by individuals and households, whether due to distress or in response to new possibilities, is part of a contested process of acquiring and using resources. In Arunachal Pradesh and elsewhere in the region, the integration of relatively isolated communities with a collective subsistence economy into an individual-based commercial economy leads to socio-economic differentiation of the community and impacts upon traditional institutions. In particular, this undermines women's resource rights, use and ownership, while increasing their work burden. Indeed, the recent history of the NER reflects the rapidity with which relative gender egalitarianism is being overtaken by male dominance.

Chanda Gurung Goodrich focuses on the tribal communities of Sikkim and Nagaland, where men have come to be seen as 'providers', superior to women 'caretakers'. As agrarian-forest dwellers, both the Lepcha women of Sikkim and Naga women play a key role in agro-biodiversity management and conservation. Their authority over three levels of agriculture — the ecosystem, species and gene — is based on their knowledge (particularly of seeds and plant breeding) and their labour. But, women's work and knowledge are now being undermined by a market economy that undervalues all non-market transactions. The women's adaptive livelihood practices are threatened by both global and regional market economies, land tenure issues, and a rapidly increasing population. In a 'surcharged clash of identities', women are being sidelined and 'it is difficult to predict how gender relations, land-related stewardship and sustainable agro-biodiversity conservation will play out'.

The northeastern woman's contribution remains largely invis-ible in economic analysis, policy formulation and project design say Vincent Darlong, S. K. Hore and S. Deb Barma. Documenting women's role in food production in Tripura, where food security is a distant goal, they argue that women must be viewed as producers, consumers and preservers of rice germplasm. There are many areas that need to be addressed through a gendered lens: the household livelihood status, time allocation of members of the household, the control over resources and income, women's post-harvest and marketing activities, and their role in the labour market. Such information would strengthen the database related to women's responsibilities, needs and constraints in the rice-farming economy and programmes to increase rice production and food security in Tripura. Similarly, Audrey Laldinpuii and Laithangpuii in their nuanced study of the rice economy and gender relations in Mizoram, also urge a deeper understanding of women's role in rice farming. Mizo men's involvement in farming declined in British times partly due to administrative policy that required men's voluntary or forced labour in public works. Women began to take on more farming duties, along with their household chores, and there was little respite from farm labour even during pregnancy or after giving birth. Younger women are now more concerned about their health but the gendered division of labour continues. The new technology of irrigated rice cultivation using farm machinery is accessible mainly to men. Moreover, under the prevailing values of Mizo society, the women's position is dependent on their acceptance of its patriarchal norms.

Looking at the NER as a whole, Krishna discusses the linkages between gender ideology and rice farming. A comparative analysis of the states in the region reveals that positive indicators of women's status, such as higher rates of literacy, work participation and greater autonomy are not sufficient safeguards against the erosion of women's traditional knowledge and skills, increase in their labour, and regressive changes in gender relations. Even moderate levels of food sustainability seem to be associated with high levels of gender disparity, pointing to the 'gendered price' of rice. Gender disparities in customary practices are reinforced by conventional development and agricultural policies, which together advance new forms of patriarchy. There is evidence of greater control over women's sexuality, increasing violence against women and a declining sex ratio in some states. Krishna argues that these are major social changes forming the substratum, the power structure, upon which the rice-farming system rests and that the adverse gender outcome of conventional development in northeastern India is, in this respect, similar to trends in the rest of the country.

ALTERNATIVE LIVELIHOOD INTERVENTIONS

Many of the contributions seem to point to the need for an integrated farming systems approach in the NER. The question is whether and how new commercial crops can be integrated into sustainable farming strategies to improve livelihoods and incomes (Sharma, Jianchu and Sharma 2007). P. K. Viswanathan analyses the significance of introducing rubber into an integrated farm livelihood system. He shows that small land holders can combine rubber with food crops in various ways, reducing a household's need to buy essential foods, pulses and vegetables from the market. Rubber is a crucial raw material grown extensively in Southeast Asia but the plantation mode of production in these countries needs to be restructured in the context of the NER, so that there are sufficient institutional, financial and technical support mechanisms for farmers. The experience with rubber in Assam, Meghalaya, and Tripura 'shows that the sustainability of the rubber smallholders largely depends on their access to secure property rights, and efficient and transparent rubber marketing systems'.

Recognising the constraints of a fertiliser-based Green Revolution mode of agriculture in the NER, Nilabja Ghosh suggests alternative strategies that are in keeping with the rich agro-ecology of the region and the emerging market potential. She argues that it is not land scarcity so much as the ability to make the best use of the land that is a major constraint in enhancing agricultural productivity. Given the availability of fertile rain-fed lands (albeit in difficult terrains), tribal systems of land tenure and the widespread ownership of livestock, 'organic farming seems a promising avenue'. Ghosh notes the advantages of organically grown vegetable and fodder crops, which can also be recycled as biomass or used to add value through processing activities.

Horticulture, in conjunction with organic farming, is being most vigorously promoted in the NER to reduce shifting cultivation, control soil erosion, enhance livelihoods and prevent out-migration. The rich and varied topography, soils and agro-climates are well suited to the cultivation of vegetables, fruits, flowers, spices and medicinal plants, especially on lands where other food crops cannot be grown. The three cases described by Krishna of a fruit (pineapple), a vegetable (*Sechium edule*, squash or 'chow-chow'), and a flower (orchid) cultivation in different states reveal the potential of horticulture, and also the challenge. Programmes need to incorporate local traditions of mixed home-garden farming and to strengthen linkages in the chain not just from lab to land but from land to market. In their detailed case study from Arunachal, K. M. Jayahari and Monalisa Sen demonstrate how an innovative intervention has helped to convert an indigenous and threatened species, *Rhododendron arboreum*, into a horticultural species. Rhododendrons dominate the temperate and timberline ecosystems in the eastern Himalaya but are facing extinction due to over extraction. Many hybrid species of ornamental rhododendrons are in demand in the global market but the *Rhododendron arboreum* has not been considered a horticultural species in India. Using participatory processes, the intervention succeeded in involving local people in conserving the rhododendron ecosystem and improving local livelihoods through the production and sale of rhododendron squash. A similar point is made in a different context by Vincent Darlong and S. K. Barik who hold that community forestry initiatives need to be strongly linked to people's livelihoods, reinforcing local knowledge and management systems. They argue that the present policies have led to breaking up communities and hardening ethnic identities and resource conflicts. Communities need to be rebuilt on the basis of their own culture. Control of land is not the only issue, because the economy of production and marketing is in the hands of middle-men and outsiders. Local people have to be empowered to add value to their farming by processing and marketing their produce, shifting the focus from individual production to community marketing.

Seeking Sustainability

Farming systems in northeastern India are embedded in a dynamic heterogeneous environment that has been shaped over centuries by nature and people. In today's globalising India, the environment and the economy are undergoing rapid transformation with a far-reaching impact on peoples' lives and livelihoods. As Fernandes and Pereira point out (Appendix, this volume), complex problems require many-pronged solutions. Sustainable alternative farming systems (see Mishra and Misra 2006) and livelihood interventions that combine traditional and modern methods are still in a nascent stage but do show the way forward. The productivity focus of the 'Green Revolution' approach cannot just be grafted onto existing farming systems without sensitivity to the known social and ecological problems of intensive agriculture (Krishna 1996). Communities and cultures cannot be flattened in the quest for economic growth and individual profit. Food and livelihood security cannot be 'engendered' without addressing the structural aspects of development and of patriarchy (Krishna 2009). This varied collection is itself a reflection of the diversity of issues that need to be encompassed in evolving an approach to agricultural development in the NER. Four threads run through the chapters: the first is the recognition of the dynamic social and ecological heterogeneity of the region. Second is the understanding that agriculture is embedded in myriad contexts in the social and ecological fabric of people's lives. The third is the need to combine perspectives that are grounded in local contexts with broader frameworks of analysis, tracing the linkages between external political and socio-economic pressures and agrarian and livelihood changes at the village level. The fourth is the need to base policy on a historical understanding and critique of the assumptions in the prevailing mainstream approach to agriculture and the changing environment of the region.

Notes

1. The Constitution of India recognises 'Scheduled Tribes' as a category but does not define it. The term 'tribe' has negative connotations related to its conceptualisation in evolutionary anthropology as a primitive stage and by its use by the British colonial administration. In much of India, the term 'adivasi' has replaced 'tribe' in the people's own conceptualisation of their identity. In northeastern India, however, the preferred term is 'indigenous' because adivasi refers specifically to plantation labourers, who are tribal migrants from north, south and east India.

2. The political and administrative structure of the northeastern states emerged in response to the particular needs of the region and was governed by different 'peace agreements' with the union government and by special overriding provisions of the Constitution for Nagaland, Assam, Manipur, Mizoram and Arunachal Pradesh. Special provisions for these states provide that no Act of Parliament in respect to religious and social practices, customary law and procedure shall apply unless adopted by a resolution of the respective Legislative Assembly. A separate schedule of the Constitution also provides for District and Regional Councils, which have considerable independence but no financial power to deal with local administrative and legislative matters.

3. Stuart Blackburn (2003) writes of the 'romance of isolation, the presumption that tribal cultures, especially in the peripheral north east are timeless, or live in an eternal present'. He notes that trade routes from Tibet to Assam passed through even the relatively more remote parts of the northeast frontier, now Arunachal Pradesh, and that oral testimonies record armed conflicts with the British (see also Blackburn 2008).

4. In Mizoram where about half the population lives in urban areas, land settlement certificates are in use but transfers are only permissible to tribals and government agencies. Communally held land, especially

in the hills, is distributed by the village chief to families settled in the village. In Tripura the Forest Department gives land holding certificates to individual jhum farmers. In Arunachal Pradesh land possession certificates are available through a long and cumbersome process. In Arunachal's Khonsa and Changland areas community land is now rapidly being converted into tea plantations. In Nagaland, terrace cultivators may have permanent ownership rights but land holding practices vary from one Naga tribe to another. In Meghalaya, there are no possession certificates but land may be mortgaged to banks as collateral. Land holding certificates are available in the Manipur valley. In Assam, regulations amended in 2002 permit mortgaging of land to banks (see Chakrabarti 2003).

5. The controversial Armed Forces (Special Powers) Act, 1958 gives special powers and legal immunity to the armed forces to act in notified 'disturbed areas'. These powers include the right to search, arrest and even to open fire against persons suspected to be acting against the law.

References

Arnold, David. 2005. *The Tropics and the Travelling Gaze: India, Landscape and Science 1800–1856*. Delhi: Permanent Black.

Arora, R. K. 1996. 'Indian Region Provides Treasure of Wild Plant Genetic Resources', *Diversity*, 12(3): 22–23.

Arora, R. K. and Anjula Pandey. 1996. *Wild Edible Plants of India: Diversity, Conservation and Use*. New Delhi: National Bureau of Plant Genetic Resources, Indian Council of Agricultural Research.

Basu, Analabha, Namita Mukherjee, Sangita Roy, Sanghamitra Sengupta, Sanat Banerjee, Madan Chakraborty, Badal Dey, Monami Roy, Bidyut Roy, Nitai P. Bhattacharyya, Susanta Roychoudhury, and Partha P. Majumder. 2003. 'Ethnic India: A Genomic View with Special Reference to Peopling and Structure', *Genome Research*, 13: 2277–90

Bhagabati, A. C. 1988. 'Tribal Transformation in Assam and North-East India: An Appraisal of Emerging Ideological Dimensions', Presidential Address to Anthropology and Archaeology Group, Pune: 75th Indian Science Congress.

Bhagabati, Abani Kumar and A. K. Goswami. 2000. 'Some Aspects of Biodiversity and its Conservation in the River Islands of the Brahmaputra', in Shekhar Singh, A. R. K. Sastry, Raman Mehta and S. Uppal (eds), *Setting Biodiversity Conservation Priorities for India: Summary of the Findings and Conclusions of the Biodiversity Conservation Prioritisation Project*, Vol. 1. New Delhi: World Wide Fund for Nature — India, pp. 152–53.

Blackburn, Stuart. 2003. 'Colonial Contact in the "Hidden Land": Oral History among the Apatanis of Arunachal Pradesh', *The Indian*

Economic and Social History Review, 40(3): 335–65. Revised version available at http://www.soas.ac.uk/tribaltransitions/publications/file32488.pdf (accessed 17 September 2011).

Blackburn, Stuart. 2008. *Himalayan Tribal Tales: Oral Tradition and Culture in the Apatani Valley*. Boston: Brill.

Burman, B. K. Roy. 2002. 'Demographic Profile of the Hill Areas of North East India', in Sarthak Sengupta (ed.), *Tribal Studies in North East India*. Delhi: Mittal Publications, pp. 1–9.

Chakrabarti, S. B. 2003. 'Agrarian Relations in the Tribal Milieu', in T. R. Subba and G. C. Ghosh (eds), *The Anthropology of North-East India*. Hyderabad: Orient Longman, pp. 242–57.

Das, Partha J. 2010. 'The Hydropower–Climate Change Nexus: Myth, Science and Risk for Northeast India', in Neeraj Vagholikar and Partha J. Das, *Damning Northeast India*. Kalpavriksh, Aaranyak and Action Aid, pp. 10–11. Available at http://www.kalpavriksh.org/images/EnvironmentandDevelopment/NorthEastDams/Damming%20Northeast%20India_Single%20page%20format.pdf (accessed 17 September 2011).

DONER. 2007. *North Eastern Region Vision 2020*. New Delhi: Ministry of Development of North Eastern Region, Government of India.

Ganguly, J. B. 1993. 'Development of Peasant Farming in the North-Eastern Tribal Region', in Mrinal Miri (ed.), *Continuity and Change in Tribal Society*. Shimla: Indian Institute of Advanced Study, pp. 298–313.

Hooker, Joseph Dalton. 1854. *Himalayan Journals or Notes of a Naturalist* (Two Volumes). London: John Murray. E-book available at http://www.gutenberg.org/cache/epub/6478/pg6478.txt (accessed 17 September 2011).

Jamir, Amba and A. K. Nongkynrih. 2002. *Understanding Land Ownership and Management Systems of the Khasi, Jaintia and Garo Societies of Meghalaya*. Rome: International Fund for Agricultural Development.

Kalpavriksh. 2005. *Dossier on Large Dams for Hydropower in Northeast India*. Compiled by Manju Menon with Kanchi Kohli. New Delhi: Kalpavriksh, Pune and South Asia Network on Dams, Rivers and People.

Karlsson, Bengt G. 2011. *Unruly Hills: Nature and Nation in India's Northeast*. New Delhi: Social Science Press.

Krishna, Sumi. 1991. *India's Living Languages*. New Delhi: Allied.

———. 1996. *Environmental Politics: People's Lives and Development Choices*. New Delhi: Sage.

———. 1998a. 'Arunachal Pradesh', in M. S. Swaminathan (ed.), *Gender Dimensions in Biodiversity Management*. New Delhi: Konark, pp. 148–81.

Krishna, Sumi.1998b. 'Mizoram', in M. S. Swaminathan (ed.), *Gender Dimensions in Biodiversity Management*. New Delhi: Konark, pp. 182–210.

———. 2004. 'Gender, Tribe and Political Participation: Control of Natural Resources in North-Eastern India', in Sumi Krishna (ed.), *Livelihood and Gender: Equity in Community Resource Management*. New Delhi: Sage, pp. 375–96.

———. 2009. *Genderscapes: Revisioning Natural Resource Management*. New Delhi: Zubaan.

Mani, M. S. 1974. 'Biogeography of the Himalaya', in M. S. Mani (ed.), *Ecology and Biogeography in India*, The Hague: W. Junk Publishers, pp. 664–81.

Mishra, A. K. and J. P. Misra. 2006. 'Sustainable Development of Agriculture in Northeastern India: A Quest for More Economical and Resourceful Sustainable Alternatives', *ENVIS Bulletin*, Himalayan Ecology, 14(2): 4–14.

Myers, N., R. A. Mittermeier, C. G. Mittermeier, G. A. B. da Fonesca, and J. Kent. 2000. 'Biodiversity Hotspots for Conservation Priorities', *Nature*, 403: 853–58.

NEDFi. 2006. *Databank Quarterly*. Guwahati: North Eastern Development Finance Corporation Ltd.

Nathan, Dev. 2000. 'Timber in Meghalaya', *Economic and Political Weekly*, 25(4): 182–86.

Nayar, M. P. 1996. *'Hot Spots' of Endemic Plants of India, Nepal and Bhutan*. Thiruvanthapuram: Tropical Botanic Garden and Research Institute.

Nongbri, Tiplut. 2001. 'Timber Ban in North-East India: Effects on Livelihood and Gender', *Economic and Political Weekly*, 36(21): 1893–900.

Nongkynrih, A. K. 2008. 'Privatisation of Community Land of the Tribes of North East India', in Walter Fernandes and Sanjay Barbora (eds), *Land, People and Politics: Contest over Tribal Land in North East India*. Guwahati: North East Social Research Centre, pp. 16–37.

Olson, David M., Eric Dinerstein, E. D. Wickramanayake, E. D. Burgess, G. V. N. Powell, E. C. Underwood, J. A. D'amico, I. Itoua, H. E. Strand, J. C. Morrison, C. J. Loucks, T. F. Allnut, T. H. Rickets, Y. Kura, J. F. Lamoreaux, W. W. Wettengel, P. Hedao and K. R. Kassem. 2001. 'Terrestrial Ecoregions of the World: A New Map of the Earth', *Bioscience*, 51(11): 933–38.

Planning Commission. 1997. *'Transforming the North-East: Tackling Backlogs in Basic Minimum Services and Infrastructural Needs'*, High Level Commission Report to the Prime Minister (Chaired by S. P. Shukla). New Delhi: Planning Commission.

Proctor, J., K. Haridasan and G. W. Smith. 1998. 'How Far North does Lowland Evergreen Tropical Rain Forest Go?' *Global Ecology and Biogeography Letters*, 7: 141–46.

RBI. 2006. *Report of the Committee for Financial Sector Plan for North Eastern Region* (Usha Thorat Report). New Delhi: Reserve Bank of India.

Sharma, Rita, Jianchu Zu and G. Sharma. 2007. 'Traditional Agro-forestry in the Eastern Himalayan Region: Land Management System Supporting Ecosystem Services', *Tropical Ecology*, 48(2): 1–12.

Shimray, U. A. 2007. *Ecology and Economic Systems: A Case of the Naga Community*. New Delhi: Regency Publications.

Shimray, U. A. and M. V. Ramanna. 2007. 'Uranium Mining in Meghalaya: Simmering Problem', *Economic and Political Weekly*, 42(52): 13–17.

Thangchungmunga. 1998. 'Agrarian Change and Social Transformation among the Mizo (the Tribal State in North-East India)', *International Journal of Social Economics*, 25(2/3/4): 261–66.

Vagholikar, Neeraj and Partha J. Das. 2010. *Damning Northeast India*. Kalpavriksh, Aaranyak and Action Aid. Available at http://www.kalpavriksh.org/images/EnvironmentandDevelopment/North EastDams/Damming%20Northeast%20India_Single%20page%20 format.pdf (accessed 17 September 2011).

Verghese, B. G. 2004. *India's Northeast Resurgent: Ethnicity, Insurgency, Governance, Development*. New Delhi: Konark.

Verghese, B. G. and Ramaswamy Iyer (eds). 1993. *Harnessing the Eastern Rivers*. New Delhi: Konark.

World Bank. 2007. *Development and Growth in Northeast India: The Natural Resources, Water, and Environment Nexus*. World Bank Report No. 36397-IN. Washington DC: The International Bank for Reconstruction and Development/The World Bank.

PART I

ASPECTS OF A CHANGING ENVIRONMENT

1

Floods and Fields in the Brahmaputra Valley: 20th-century Changes in Historical Perspective

RITUPAN GOSWAMI

River Brahmaputra — the principal river of Asom — is today widely considered a 'problem' for agricultural development and a cause of sorrow for the peasants who inhabit its fertile valley. Statistics of flood damage and erosion in the last 50 years show that the losses to the peasantry are indeed enormous. But how is it that while just a century ago the floods were generally considered to be a part of the agrarian cycle and complementary to cultivation, they are now posited in opposition to agriculture? This essay is an attempt to historically examine the metamorphosis of this benevolent river, which made cultivation possible by fertilising the land with the silt it bore, into a 'problem' river. It is argued that a major factor underlying this metamorphosis was the fundamental change in the nature of agriculture carried out in the riverine zone along the banks of the Brahmaputra as per the immigration and settlement policy of the British colonial state.

The Three Ecological Zones

The agricultural and settlement pattern of the Brahmaputra valley was attuned to its natural geophysical divisions, but also reflected social divisions. Three ecological zones with specific characteristics could be distinguished on each bank of the river. The first zone was the closest to the river starting from its banks to a few kilometres inland, from where the second zone began, extending further inland for another few kilometres, an area of flood-immune plains with fertile soil, where transplanted rice cultivation, the most important crop in the valley, was extensively carried out. This gave way to the third zone — the submontane tract — which was at the foot of the hill ranges that surround the valley from three sides. Referring specifically to the Kamrup district but applicable to the other districts as well, the *Report of the Assam Provincial Banking Enquiry Committee* of 1930 (hereafter *RAPBEC*) noted: 'On both banks we have three natural divisions — low land near the river, liable to flood (called the *chaporis*), a higher belt inland where transplanted paddy is grown (on the north bank this is known as the *rupit mahal*) and the submontane tract near the hills' (GOA 1930: 23). The most densely populated and predominantly rice-producing *rupit* land cultivated by 'Assamese cultivators' was in the middle tract. The population density could exceed 800 per square kilometre in this tract, as in south Nalbari. Here the standard of living was higher than in either the *chaporis* or the submontane tracts. Conditions in the chaporis were far less favourable, paddy cultivation being more uncertain, communications less easy, and opportunities for subsidiary occupations more limited than in the rupit mahal or the transplanted-rice lands. The submontane tract in the foothills likewise was less favourably situated for cultivation and avenues for disposing of the surplus produce. These parts were also considered unhealthy. The inhabitants belonged mainly to the 'backward tribes', and these factors altogether led to a lower living standard than on the rupit mahal (ibid.).

The Brahmaputra's riverine islands or *chars* and the chaporis on its banks with their own peculiarities constituted one such natural division in the valley. The British categorised this as 'fluctuating cultivation' because the river caused extreme changes in the area and output from year-to-year. This fluctuating cultivation, known as *pam*, supplemented the peasant's permanent rice cultivation with mustard, pulses and other high-value winter crops. Till the end of the 19th century, the chars and chaporis were permanently inhabited by only a few communities of Mishings, Kaivartas or Nadiyals, whom the dominant-caste villagers inhabiting the middle-rupit zone considered to be of lowly status. Others stayed on the chars and chaporis — whether they were *pamuas* or graziers — only temporarily, cultivating on the river banks, though to a smaller extent than the people of the other two tracts. In the period under review, it was common for the people of the rupit zone to take up land for temporary cultivation in the chars and chaporis, but the reverse was not the case; the riverine people hardly owned land in the submontane region where permanent habitation and cultivation existed, and even if they did, the land was relatively inferior to that of their more prosperous neighbours. The chapori lands which were classified uniformly as *faringati* or wasteland in government revenue records were not necessarily uniform in soil quality or crops grown. As the chief commissioner of Assam noted in 1904, 'There are differences of soil. But they are not constant, as the annual floods effect great changes by the deposition of soil and sand. And a dense growth of high grass entirely obscures the natural features of the surface soil, so long as it is uncultivated' (Monahan 1904).

On the extensive inundated lowland chaporis, the cultivators grew 'early' rice for home consumption, and pulse and mustard for sale. The cash income thus obtained provided the land revenue payable not only upon these chapori lands, but also upon some portion of the established rice lands. 'Peasants cultivated some amounts of *chapori* land in addition to their permanent village holdings. . . . In well-established villages relinquishments [of land] were few in number. But in the *chaporis*, where the land was generally given up after two or three years' of cropping, [relinquishment requests] were annually filed by thousands' (Anon. 1904). In such tracts, since the production of winter rice, mustard and pulses during the dry season was highly variable, the occupants had to pay the land revenue six weeks before the date of payment was normally due in the early 20th century.

One flood a year was considered normal in these low-lying tracts. Generally the floods occur from the middle of June to September in the Brahmaputra and the north bank rivers, and up to October in some south-bank tributaries. If the floods came relatively early, in June or early July but did not recur again in the later months, it harmed the *ahu* crops and the *sali* seedlings, but time was still available in the season to grow the sali seedlings once again for transplant during August and September. If a flood took place between mid-July and mid-August, not much damage was done to the ahu crop, as most of it was already harvested. Such floods however destroyed the sali seedlings, leaving no time to grow them again and also damaged the *bao* crop to various degrees. If the flood came very late, i.e., in September or October, it generally did great damage to the standing sali crop (GOA 1955). Thus, cultivation in the valley had to be carried out according to the opportunities and constraints of the climate, floods and the soil, making use of the advantages while trying to negate the ill-effects.

Over the centuries, the riverine communities formed the most intimate relations with the Brahmaputra and its major tributaries. Indeed, it is said that these communities were more dependent on the River Brahmaputra than on the land. They developed a thorough, deep knowledge and understanding of the river while engaging in productive activities. Their knowledge of the terrain and the Brahmaputra's character equipped them to inhabit the river and its banks with relative safety. They looked upon the river with awe and reverence; it was at the centre of their lives, culture and society. Before the riverine tracts were permanently settled by great numbers of immigrant peasants from East Bengal by the beginning of the 20th century, these were predominantly inhabited by the poorest, most marginalised classes, that is, various tribal communities as well as the oppressed castes, including the outcastes and Untouchables of Hindu society, as was noted by the *Assessment Report of Central Jorhat Group* of 1905.

Till the first decades of the 20th century, when heavy floods occurred it was common practice for the residents of the chars to leave their houses for a few days and take shelter with their cattle on high lands further inland. It is reported that they seldom lost their cattle or store of paddy, though it was known and expected that the standing crops of ahu and sali would suffer from floods to some extent almost every year. During 1891–1901 the population of this fluctuating group with predominantly temporary cultivation increased considerably. In fact, the villages in the group grew from 1,254 to 1,650 under Sibsagar subdivision and from 3,950 to 6,079 in Jorhat subdivision. Though the corresponding data for Golaghat subdivision in 1891 was not available, by 1901 the number of villages stood at 11,481, and it was assumed that the increase was in proportion to the other two subdivisions.

In the South Bank Fluctuating Group, the inhabitants were said to be 'half Hindus and half Miris', and the Hindu pamuas included all classes of people from the 'established' or permanent villages which were separated from the riverine pam tract by a line of embanked roads. The Miris or the Mishing community, on the other hand, were its permanent inhabitants, and in 1901, had more than a thousand villages on the riverine tract. They generally did not own land in the permanently settled villages and therefore had no option of temporarily leaving their homes during high floods unlike the 'Hindu' pam cultivators, who cultivated '*chapori* land only to supplement the cultivation which they have in their own villages, either because they have not enough land or in order to obtain a surplus.' As such, their way of living was attuned to the floods. For instance, their houses (unlike that of the pamuas) were constructed on elevated platforms made of bamboo and reed. The other occupations in this tract were 'fishing and lime-making by Doms, pottery by Kumars, and eri-silk weaving by the women of all Hindu castes' (GEBA 1906).

The rupit mahal rice-field settlements between the riverine and submontane tracts were the most populous in the Brahmaputra valley. Most of the permanent rice cultivation was undertaken here. During the nearly 600 years of Ahom rule in the region, the area under settled rice cultivation grew extensively; forest areas were brought under cultivation and new grounds lying unused were broken for transplanted paddy cultivation, around which grew the culture of mustard, pulses, sugarcane, opium, garden produce, and so on. These rice-producing regions with their dense population and high revenue generation were the mainstay of Ahom political power, while for the majority of the working people agriculture was at the subsistence level, as the region entered the phase of colonial occupation in the early 19th century.

Settling the River: The East Bengal Peasants

The 1881 Census of Asom counted 280,000 persons who were born outside the province and had subsequently immigrated to Asom: immigrant tea garden labourers constituted 170,000, 'temporary visitors' to the province 50,000, and settlers engaged in agriculture, trade and services 60,000. The figures, even though approximate and of doubtful accuracy, showed that while 40,000 persons born in Asom resided in Bengal according to the Bengal Census of 1881, around 30,000 Bengal-born persons resided in the Brahmaputra valley. The exchange of population between the two neighbouring colonial provinces seemed mutual and near-equal in the 1880s, if one excludes the tea garden workers (GOA 1883: 29). The official perception of a scanty population and abundant unutilised land, and the state's attempts to bring about an externally induced transformation through immigration, was to change this equation in the next few decades.

Tea was a much-celebrated runaway success story, but the expansion of the area under food crops by Asom's peasants was less than satisfactory for the state. The slow agricultural growth in the province was often attributed to the lack of enterprise among the Asom peasants, and the colonial dream of seeing a class of agricultural capitalists was yet unrealised. A prevalent stereotype within the colonial bureaucracy was that a numerically large peasantry would lead to more land being brought under cultivation. Since the colonial state considered the growth rate of the valley's population during the late 19th century to be quite slow, infusing a migrant population into the province was actively considered from the beginning of the 20th century. This commonly held perception was expressed in an official communication in 1905, 'The lower portion of the valley has lost population owing to the mortality from *kala-azar*', while in the government's calculations, 'the growth of the purely Assamese population in the upper portion has been exceedingly slow' (Kershaw 1905). The most widely cited and appreciated model of success in the 'reclamation' of forests for rice production so far was provided by the colonial experience of Burma, and given its proximity to Asom, it was presented by the provincial government as the ideal model for Asom to emulate.

It was, of course, admitted by the state that though the 'wasteland' that Asom could offer to the immigrant settlers was supposedly quite extensive, it was by no means so large as was sometimes claimed by over-enthusiastic official opinion. A very large proportion of the area of uncultivated land in the plains districts of Asom was considered by the native population to be permanently uninhabitable, riverine lands deeply submerged during a part of the year. Only certain forms of temporary habitation were considered to be attuned to the amphibious environs of the rivers. Conditions in the extensive chars and chapori lands were 'obviously not suited to permanent colonisation', as even the government admitted in the early 20th century (Kershaw 1905). Moreover, some parts of the valley, particularly in Darrang district, were endowed with stretches of savannah land between the riverine and forest tracts along the foothills; the fertility of the soil being poorer and the altitude too high, this was not favourable for rice or for crops that required a fertile soil and a regular supply of water.

The colonial state contended that what remained for future reclamation, after excluding these apparently unfavourable tracts, was still a very large area available for permanent cultivation, sparsely inhabited by 'Cacharis and similar tribes of Indo-Tibetan stock, whose neighbourhood is shunned by Hindus' (Kershaw 1905). Two great difficulties still awaited the future immigrants, the government concluded. First, the initial cost of reclamation was very high, and second, the jungles of Asom were considered exceedingly unhealthy and dangerous to those who ventured to clear it. The high mortality from dysentery and anaemia among the labour force employed by the tea gardens to clear land (during the decades of rapid extension of tea cultivation in the second half of the 19th century) was presented as testimony to this.

During the last quarter of the 19th century, the area under cultivation in five districts of the Asom valley had expanded by 'only 24 per cent', and about a third of this increase was attributed to the reclamation by the tea garden workers who had been brought in by tea planters, and had subsequently migrated from their tea gardens to village settlements. Disappointingly for the state, there was no rapid development comparable to what had been achieved in the districts of Lower Burma. Some colonial administrators held that cultivation would have advanced with greater pace had 'colonists' been encouraged to take up land by the offer of revenue-free tenure during the earlier years of their leases. This concession was enjoyed by peasants who applied for land in Burma. The government regretted that though the rules prevalent in Asom did not prevent its chief commissioner from granting land on revenue-free terms or at nominal rates, as indeed was done in leasing out land for tea cultivation, very little use had, however, been made of this power for the cause of extending ordinary cultivation. Thus, it was always the practice in the Brahmaputra valley during the colonial period to levy full revenue on newly broken land from the first year of occupancy itself. The reasons for this are not difficult to ascertain, and were also admitted by the colonial government (Kershaw 1905).

First, the revenue procedure of the province did not recognise the difference between the shifting cultivation carried out in the riverine zone and the permanent cultivation of the rupit zone that was free from deep inundation, with the result that a single set of rules had been applied to both the ecological zones. As the secretary to the commissioner of Assam explained to the Government of India, 'Since in the Valley a large proportion of the total ordinary cultivation was under fluctuating system under which fields shifted every two or three years, the government feared that the grant of an initial revenue-free tenure of a few years in such lands would exempt the *raiyats* from the payment of any revenue whatever' (Kershaw 1905). Second, and more importantly, the state admitted that such concessions could have the 'highly undesirable outcome' of inducing the tea garden workers who had served out their initial contracts to take up cultivation as peasant proprietors in large numbers, undermining the tea planters' interests and depleting their labour force.

Though the prevailing labour laws formally allowed the garden workers to leave their garden after the expiry of four years, coercive practices of the plantation owners stringently prevented even the legally 'free' labourers from leaving. The provincial colonial government was, it was claimed, 'while anxious to secure fair treatment and reasonable prospect to immigrants who owe their footing in the province to the initiation of the tea industry, would be reluctant to see action taken, in the interest either of government revenue or of philanthropy, which would be at the expense of the capital that is invested in tea' (Kershaw 1905). In 1888 when the plantation owners suspected that the government was initiating a scheme to offer revenue-free land to 'time-expired' tea garden workers, tea garden managers in the valley had already 'assured' the colonial government that 'the general offer of land with a revenue-free period would deplete their labour forces' (ibid.). The government conceded that 'any attempt actively to encourage tea-garden coolies to abandon their service for ryoti cultivation would be greatly resented by the planters as involving unfair competition between their legitimate interests' (ibid.).

The flow of immigration from Eastern Bengal districts picked up in the 1910s and 1920s. As it turned out, a majority of them were made to inhabit the chaporis and chars of the Brahmaputra for permanent cultivation and settlement. It was an environment which they were arguably familiar with because of the similarities with the conditions in their home district of Mymensingh, but this pattern of settlement had far-reaching and unforeseeable implications, encompassing all aspects of social life in Asom, including the political, economic, social and cultural spheres in the late 20th century (Baruah 1999; Hussain 1993; Weiner 1978).

There were many significant characteristics of this latest flow of immigration and settlement, which distinguished it from the earlier instance of migration to Asom, that of the tea garden labourers. The East Bengal immigrants settled primarily on the riverine tract, not only because they were accustomed to this environment and it was highly productive, but also because colonial policy allowed them to take up only this type of land. Apart from cultivating rice, they also introduced jute, a high-value cash crop, which grew steadily in the first half of the 20th century. The connectivity provided by the Brahmaputra and its numerous tributaries played an important role in jute processing, transport and trade.

During the first few decades of the 20th century, the settlement of East Bengal peasants expanded to cover the riverine tracts on the north and the south banks and the chars and chaporis from the westernmost district of Goalpara through Darrang, Kamrup and Nowgong to parts of Lakhimpur. Along with the introduction of changes in the agrarian production process by the new peasants, there was also a marked change in the way the riverine landscape was put to use. The administrative integration of Eastern Bengal with the province of Asom and the emergence of the new province of Eastern Bengal and Assam in 1905 played a catalytic role in the initial phase of this process. Not only did the administrative set up change in this period, but also the usual landscape of the riverine chaporis, which were now showing signs of permanence. *The Report of the Banking Enquiry Committee* noted in 1930 that in the previous 20 years a unique feature of Asom had been 'the continuous stream of immigrants, mainly from Mymensingh in Eastern Bengal — who have spread out in large tracts of land in Assam Valley' (GOA 1930: 7). In their home districts, the peasants found the exactions under the oppressive zamindari system and the pressure on the land too severe, and were attracted to Asom by reports of wide expansion of government wasteland under relatively lower revenue assessment. The changes brought in by the new settlers to the demographic pattern of the valley were summed up as follows:

> Before the immigrants from Eastern Bengal came to the province, there were large areas of waste lands in all districts. The indigenous Assamese, prior to that time, used to take up much land for cold weather crops, preferably near the bank of the Brahmaputra, on annual lease. These he would cultivate for three years or so and then throw them up, seeking fresh pastures of which there was [sic] abundance. After some years, he would go back to the previous lands, knowing that probably no body would have taken them up, as there was enough spare land for all. This was in addition to his permanent rice land in or near his village. The coming of the Mymensingh people has changed all that. They have occupied most of those waste lands (frequently buying them at an exorbitant price from the Assamese who had them under annual lease) and brought them under permanent cultivation (GOA 1930: 16).

In the westernmost district of Goalpara too, there was a steady growth of the immigrant population. It was noted that 57,000 immigrants from East Bengal came to settle before 1911. The 1921 census showed that 150,000 settlers made up nearly 20 per cent of the total population. 'Since then immigration has extended especially on the low lands adjoining the Brahmaputra. There has also been expansion by Santals and others in the submontane tracts in the north of the district' (GOA 1930: 25). The chaporis of Barpeta subdivision showed a 700 per cent increase in the area under settlement in the previous two decades. This shows that the practice of fluctuating cultivation and temporary settlement gradually gave way to permanent cultivation and habitation on the riverine tract.

Indeed, the Brahmaputra chars of Goalpara district were not only cultivated but also permanently inhabited by the Eastern Bengal peasants in 'a very large proportion'. Their cultivation included ahu (transplanted rice) and jute, the out-turn and productivity being highly dependent on the nature and timing of the annual floods. As the then deputy commissioner of the district noted, 'if the floods are late and not extraordinary in height no particular damage is done. If on the contrary, the floods occur early in June before the crops are harvested, or very high so as to damage Amon [transplanted rice] and jute, the position of the people becomes very precarious' (Playfield 1922a). The floods of 1921, however, took a destructive form, as 'this year the floods came very early, before the ashu [ahu] crop had been reaped. It died down after having done great damage and rose again higher than ever to complete the destruction of the first crop and the "Amon" crop as well' (Playfield 1922b). A subdivisional officer termed it an 'abnormal flood, the like of which the people here have not seen for the last twenty years'; it had brought 'untold miseries to thousands of people and cattle and has rendered many families homeless' (Rahaman 1922). He reported, 'Ninety percent of the sufferers are Bhatia Mussalmans. They could not sow their Ashu crop in time owing to the first flood which took place in the middle of *Jaisto* [early June] last and the crops they sowed after that flood have been damaged by the present flood. The same remark applies to the jute crop also' (ibid.).

The Colonisation Scheme

Padma hoitē ailam ami asāmeri chor
Barramputroi bhanglo amār shēina sonār ghor;
shei ghor chariya jabo kothāy upāy bolona
shara jibon dukhē gelo ārto shohēna

— Song of immigrant peasants[1]

The 'Colonisation Scheme' was initiated by the colonial government in the second decade of the 20th century in the western and central Asom districts, aimed at an organised settlement of the ongoing immigration from Eastern Bengal to the riverine tracts of the Brahmaputra. The scheme was initiated when in a conference of the members of the Assam Legislative Council in 1928, certain representatives objected to the manner in which the colonial government had so far been 'allowing immigrants to settle anywhere they liked causing great disturbance to indigenous people' (Desai 1931b).

In Nowgong district, the scheme 'started in November 1928 with approximately 28,000 *bighas* of land comprised in 29 villages along the bank of the Brahmaputra in Laharighat and Bokani mauzas. Almost the whole area suitable for cultivation has been settled' (Datta 1931e). The land brought under the scheme was excluded from settlement under the existing ordinary rules. It was not surprising that the whole area under this 'immigrant group' of villages was chapori land. As the settlement officer of Nowgong observed, 'The entire area of the group partakes of chapari character and is a formation by the action of the Brahmaputra' (Anon. 1931b). For the state, this type of land was perfectly suited to the needs of the eastern Bengal peasants and the crops they were to cultivate. The settlement officer in charge of the Nowgong colonisation scheme explained:

> Generally speaking the soil in the villages nearest the Brahmaputra is sandy. . . . In such areas the Assamese used to practice their *pam* cultivation. The immigrants prefer this kind of soil for growing jute. The area is annually submerged by the Brahmaputra flood and the soil which gives its best to jute cultivation comes out of water with its richness restored after the rains. Unless the floods are untimely, i.e., occur before the jute is high enough not to go completely under water or after the sali crop has been transplanted late in the season, the annual inundations are a natural process of fertilisation and most welcome. Without a normal flood even the steeping of jute for extracting the fibre becomes difficult in many places (Anon. 1931b).

The kind of land to be cleared by the immigrant peasants under the scheme varied in different localities and tracts. The nature of the overgrowth was a factor, although the material conditions of the peasants played a more important role in determining their pace and ability to turn forests into fields. While the grass jungle on the chapori tracts was easier to clear, the *ekra* — reed jungle in the riverine lands — took much longer and more effort to be made cultivable. More importantly, a poor or marginal peasant took a longer time to clear and cultivate lands than those with cash and food.[2] Subsequent developments in the settlement of the East Bengal peasants in Asom were to demonstrate that the social and not the natural conditions played a more decisive role in determining the pace and pattern of the ongoing 'reclamation'. As it turned out, the 'Majority of the colonists have little ready cash or grain for their maintenance, while carrying on clearance of [their] allotted land. There are a number of cases in which the colonists have to work on other people's lands for their maintenance, while engaged in clearing their own land in the colonisation area' (Anon. 1931c).

While touring the new settlement villages under the Colonisation Scheme in Nowgong in May 1929, the settlement officer noted exuberantly in his official diary that the scheme was going to be a success, as large numbers of applications for land were received both from immigrants from the East Bengal district of Mymensingh and the Indian mainland (also termed 'Hindustani'). A beginning had been made, he proclaimed, though the new settlers turned out to be 'not typical of what we want', that is, peasants with wherewithal, ownership of means of production and cash to take up large amounts of land, and who could undertake rapid agrarian expansion. Due to the vulnerable financial condition of the majority of the immigrants having land in these colonisation blocks, they generally owned no more than 15 *bighas* of land per family on average, considered by the government to be not of large-enough size (Pritchard 1931). Though the settlement officers earmarked some additional land for each immigrant family residing in the newly settled villages to be taken up in the future, the transfer of land deeds was contingent upon their ability to pay a premium to the government and fulfilling of other terms and conditions of colonisation, including the permanent residence on the area they till, which effectively meant permanently inhabiting the riverine and flood-prone tract (ibid.).[3] Even if immigrant families wished to take up more land, their inability to pay the premium was a major impediment. At the commencement of the scheme, the rates of premium charged by the government were, 'In the first year only Rs 2 per *bigha* is taken as premium from the colonists, the total receipt up to date being Rs 12,636. The second installment of premium at Rs 3 per *bigha* is due in the third year, and then the main Installment of Rs 20 not until the fifth year' (Gimson 1931b). As per the colonisation rules, the East Bengal peasant who failed to pay the premium was liable to be evicted from his land (Rhodes 1931).

But the demand for land by the immigrant peasants was growing. In his report to the commissioner of the Assam Valley Division, the settlement officer of Nowgong proposed that 29,976 *bighas* of land belonging to a block of 16 villages in the Mayang *mauza* be added to the present scheme, in addition to the original 28,000 *bighas*, which had nearly been occupied in entirety, 'except for some land which has been washed away by the Brahmaputra and some which is unsuitable for cultivation'. A part of the proposed chapori land on the Brahmaputra, in Mayang, was under fluctuating pam cultivation by the native peasants mostly belonging to various tribal communities, and primarily growing mustard (Gimson 1931a). On inspection of the settlements, it was found that at Jhargaon in the newly included block of Mayang, 'there were some protests from Assamese villagers on the ground that the land was required for them for their *pam* cultivation' (Anon. 1931a). However, the objections were rejected by the authorities on the plea that 'there is plenty of waste land left in the neighbourhood for the Assamese' (Anon. 1931a). But the tension prevailing due to the conflict over land forced the district settlement officer to call a halt to any addition of land to the Colonisation Scheme in Nowgong for a few years, if not permanently (GOA 1943b).[4]

Nevertheless, the results of the work put in by the immigrants in clearing the riverine chapori tract and bringing it under cultivation and habitation seemed startling. Significantly, not only did the extent of cultivated land expand dramatically in some of the immigrant blocks, but its quality and character was also changed. As one settlement officer noted in October 1930, 'The immigrants who have taken up land within the last few years have cleared and regularly cultivated their lands from the very beginning and no land has remained as *faringati* from any deceptive appearance' (Datta 1931c). Two aspects of the agrarian life of the valley demonstrated more than any other that the nature of the land on the river was changing; first, the rate of relinquishment of cultivated land in general and in the chapori tracts in particular showed a gradual decline, and second, the area under transplanted rice grown in permanently held rupit lands grew replacing broadcast rice which was a major crop of the faringati land (Desai 1931a). While the acreage under ahu, sali and bao varieties of rice in the chapori group in 1906 was 40.93 per cent, 4.52 per cent and 6.48 per cent respectively, in 1929 the same changed to 13.35 per cent, 11.73 per cent and 37.51 per cent. On the other hand, while 37.11 per cent of the land was under mustard cultivation in 1906, it declined to 20.32 per cent in 1929. As has been noted, 'In the increase in the *sali* there is a clear indication that the country is changing from fluctuating towards permanent cultivation' and the 'falling off in the percentage of mustard (as well as of *ahu*) is a clear indication of a move towards settled cultivation' (ibid.). The colonisation officers argued, 'The settlement of immigrants and the Colonisation Scheme has recently been a potent influence, both by example and by raising the fear of a possible danger' (Desai 1931a). Though the evidence of this transition presented here is only from one group of chapori villages, a similar trend could be witnessed in other groups of villages and regions settled by the East Bengal peasants as well (Datta 1931c).[5]

In Nowgong district, the Census of 1931 registered a significant increase of the population in Khathowal, Juria, Laokhowa, Dhing, Bokani and Lahorijan *mauzas*, which was considered to be due to large-scale immigration of settlers mainly from Mymensingh. The East Bengal peasants cleared tracts of dense jungle along the south bank of the Brahmaputra and occupied nearly all the lands which were open for settlement in the riverine tract. The outcome of this process and its contribution to a rapid enhancement of colonial revenue was greatly appreciated by the colonial government. The government was all praise for the newcomers,

> These people have brought in their wake wealth, industry, and general prosperity to the whole district. They have improved the health of the countryside by clearing the jungles and converting the wilderness into prosperous villages. Their industry as agriculturists has become almost proverbial and they extract from their fields the utmost that they can yield. Their love and care of cattle is also an object lesson to others. Government revenue has increased. Trade and commerce have prospered (GOA 1932: 45).

The immigrant's inclination to undertake hard labour and to survive difficult conditions was well appreciated, but though their efforts enhanced colonial revenue, the peasants could hardly improve their lot in their new home. If the objective of leaving their homeland was to escape the excruciatingly exploitative environs in search of a life of economic security, dignity and freedom, it is doubtful that the majority of them found it in Asom.

Floods and the New Settlements

With the advent of the East Bengal immigrants the whole face of the country along the Brahmaputra . . . has undergone a tremendous transformation from 'chapari' and fluctuating into a permanent regular jute-growing area.

S. N. Datta, settlement officer of
Nowgong District (Datta 1931c)

By the 1930s the number of immigrants from Bengal to Asom was said to be around 500,000 (Guha 1977: 206). Permanent cultivation on the banks of the Brahmaputra regularly resulted in losses due to floods and erosion. The *Report of the Line System Committee* (GOA 1938, hereafter *RLSC*), notes that according to the colonisation officer of Nowgong, of 159,839 *bighas* in the scheme only 64,000 *bighas* had been settled, the rest having been made unfit for cultivation by erosion.

Still, the government preferred to settle the immigrant peasants in the vicinity of the Brahmaputra, because allowing the immigrants to take up land on the submontane tract could lead to clashes with the indigenous tribal communities. As the sub-deputy collector of Kalaigaon Circle in Mangaldai subdivision of Darrang district noted in the context of expanding the Mangaldai Colonisation Scheme, 'I want to take this 10,000 *bighas* [of the Orang Reserve Forest] because it is fairly high land and near the Brahmaputra' (GOA 1938, Vol. II: 79). The same officer observed that from the colonial government's point of view, the riverine tract was preferable to land further inland and between the riverine and submontane tracts. This was argued primarily on two grounds. First, it was claimed that such tracts were preferred by the migrants themselves, and second, that clashes with the indigenous people were less likely if settlements were allowed in the riverine tract, as these were sparsely populated. The stereotypical perception that Bengal peasants preferred the riverine belt, the tribal communities favoured the submontane tracts close to the hills, while the 'Assamese' wanted to stay put on the tract in-between the two, had already crystallised within the colonial bureaucracy, which was reflected in the colonial settlement policy.

The process and pattern of settlement bears particular significance to the present study, because it becomes evident that as permanent habitation grew and settled cultivation expanded on or close to the rivers — primarily the Brahmaputra — the annual floods as well as the high floods started to adversely affect their lives. This is not because the floods had become increasingly more severe, but because of more people and property to be destroyed, even by the floods with similar or lesser intensity and scale as in the past. The crucial significance of this transformation in the pattern of settlement from fluctuating to permanence had much to do with the changing relations with the rivers and the floods, and therefore this process requires a close historical scrutiny.

Barely two years after the Nowgong Colonisation Scheme was initiated in the predominantly riverine tract, the inundations of the Brahmaputra started to make their presence felt. Sand deposits brought down by the flood-waters covered 850 *bighas* of land belonging to 59 immigrant families in 1930 in the mauzas of Laharighat and Bokani, rendering it uncultivable (Datta 1931a). Though the land made unusable for cultivation in this way was less than 2 per cent of the total land under the scheme, the significance of the damage lies in the fact that it occurred in spite of the colonial officials' claims that 'The water level seems to have fallen over the whole area since the last settlement [in 1906] and inundations are neither so frequent nor so serious as before' (Desai 1931a). This assurance turned out to be badly out of tune with reality, and one can arguably infer that the colonial authorities deliberately undermined and downplayed the possible effects of floods on the permanent inhabitants of the riverine tracts to hard-sell the plots of land under the scheme.

Moreover, though it was assumed and assured by the government that the East Bengal peasants were adapted to a riverine life, the new conditions of an alien country were against the fast adoption of the ways of the natives who had a better knowledge of the terrain. Therefore, when the destruction struck, the government was forced to provide fresh land to the affected families because many had already paid the premium for the land. As the already scarce government 'wastelands' were unavailable in the vicinity, 1,297 *bighas* of the Dumkura Professional Grazing Reserve was added to the Colonisation Scheme in July 1930. Though the inclusion of this land in the Colonisation Scheme had multiple claimants from the graziers and villagers, it was 'opened up' with the familiar argument that there was still enough land around for such purposes.

Migration of peasants in search of new land from one place of the valley to another after their own was washed away by floods was becoming a common phenomenon in the 1930s. It was reported that around a hundred families migrated from Kamrup district to Darrang after they lost their land to the floods (GOA 1938, Vol. III: 88). Likewise, the mauzadar of Bogribari in Barpeta subdivision of Kamrup district reported that in villages Lakhipur, Maheshkuthi, Marchakandi, Damdamia, washed away by the

Brahmaputra, there were 1,000 to 2,000 landless families. While half of them migrated to other places, the remaining sustained themselves by working as *kamlas* or agricultural labourers (GOA 1938, Vol. III: 124). Thus, the Bengal peasants who lost their land and belongings to the floods or erosion aggravated the problem of landlessness and destitution in the region. A large number of the Bengal peasants who came to the valley in the late 1930s and 1940s could not own land due to the near-full occupancy of the tracts under the Colonisation Scheme, which substantiates the inference that even in the riverine tracts, land was increasingly becoming scarce. By 1938, in the Samaguri Circle of Nowgong district alone, for instance, there were more than 20,000 such landless cultivators of East Bengal origin, even going by the conservative government estimates. These peasants were forced to work as agricultural labourers or cultivated on both immigrant and indigenous landowner's fields as tenants and as sharecroppers on *adhi* terms (ibid.: 12). With the kind of exploitative system in which the eastern Bengal peasants were forced to work in the Brahmaputra valley, it was not unusual to find them utterly impoverished and destitute when floods frequently swept over their lands and crops. The settlement officer of Nowgong reported in August 1931 that

> the recent Brahmaputra flood, which is said to be the highest on record since 1907, has hit the people of the Immigrant and Chapori groups very hard. These areas suffered also from the last years' flood. . . . The general fall in the price of agricultural products — specially that of jute — have struck at people's economic vitality; on the top of this, these two successive floods with the attendant loss of crops, house, property etc., have rendered most of them, without at least a year's time to recuperate, unable to meet the increased demand of land revenue, which has been proposed for the Immigrant group, and which has been sanctioned already for the Chapori group (Anon. 1931d).

Mayang mauza, to a part of which the Nowgong Colonisation Scheme was extended, was known to fall under a low-lying tract, often inundated by floods of the Brahmaputra. Six villages under ordinary cultivation were reported to be 'completely washed away by the Brahmaputra' in the mauza between the years 1906 and 1930, while the area in another seven decreased due to erosion (Datta 1931b). Likewise, in Nowgong district, 'About 13,000 *bighas* in Laharighat and Bokani notified as Colonisation area has either been washed away by the Brahmaputra or spoilt by sand deposit' (Datta 1931d). The same wave of floods also affected the immigrant group comprising the Juria, Laokhowa, Dhing, Lahorighat and Bokani mauzas in Nowgong, in which 'wide tracts of country covered by reed and grass jungle have been converted into open, clear, excellent cultivated fields' by the Bengal peasants (ibid.). Though the settlement officer claimed that 'Floods of old days are now a rare occurrence' and that 'The ordinary annual Brahmaputra flood enriches the soil and the methods of cultivation of new-comers take advantage of it', he also admitted that 'Never within the last 20–25 years was there a flood of such magnitude as that of September 1930' (Datta 1931e). He further remarked, 'It came at a time when jute had not yet been harvested fully and gathered in. *The Assamese* bastis *occupy generally high lands, but the immigrants have settled in any available area.* In Laokhowa, Juria and Bokani the bastis went and remained under water for several days causing untold suffering' (ibid.).

As a result of the floods, the colonial state was forced to consider postponing new rates of land revenue in the immigrant settlements of Nowgong district. The state rued the loss of land revenue and premium on land that was to be collected from the East Bengal peasants. For the state, the series of destructive floods was a throwback from the path of development and success of the Colonisation Scheme it envisaged for the immigrants. In what was termed as a 'reversal' of the scheme in Nowgong due to floods, the commissioner of Assam Valley Division observed,

> The abnormal flood of last year has thrown things back badly just when the scheme was developing rapidly. In a normal year it is probable that Rs 25,000 would have been realised as premium, in addition to the second installment [of land revenue] . . . nearly a quarter of the total area reserved for colonisation was either washed away by the last flood or damaged for greater or less periods by sand deposits (Bentinck 1931).

The crisis of the immigrants was accentuated by their near-complete dependence on the jute market, which was under the control of the Marwari trader, generally also a moneylender.

The destructive flood of September 1930 was accompanied by a 'trade depression' and consequent 'abnormal' fall in the price of jute to a low ₹3 per *maund*, which was even below the actual cost of production (Datta 1931c). The price of mustard, grown as a second crop by many peasants, also experienced a downward spiral. To add to it was the reassessed rates of land revenue, through which the colonial state sought to increase the collection by as much as 50 per cent in the immigration groups of mauzas. For instance, the total land revenue assessment of the Nowgong immigration group was increased from ₹204,574 to ₹303,816 in November 1931, a steep hike of 48.51 per cent (Datta 1931d). In a somewhat ironic portrayal of the situation, the settlement officer observed,

> The immigrant has been hit much harder than the Assamese. The former keeps no stock of paddy, takes heavy advances from the Marwaris or other Mahajans and grows jute which requires much outlay. Without a good price for jute, his domestic economy has got out of gear; he is out of pocket, has no money to pay his Mahajan and finds it difficult to raise a loan. The Assamese has got his *bharal* (granary); he is in no difficulty about food, though he has to deny himself a little of the ordinary amenities of life. The immigrant is a hard, tough man and no fatalist and is patiently working and waiting for better days; with the return of normal trade conditions his present distress will disappear (Datta 1931d).

An appreciable hope, perhaps, but too distant from the reality, as more settlers came into the valley in search of land to face even harder economic, social and political challenges than the early East Bengal settlers whose path they followed, not to talk of the challenges thrown up by the landscape. The government was also now doubtful of the success of the Colonisation Scheme, once the initial euphoria of land reclamation slowly died down, or in any case was tempered by serious concerns after confronting the hard realities. As the Retrenchment Committee of the Assam Legislative Council admitted in July 1931,

> Progress of colonisation was not up to expectation on account of the unprecedented drop in the prices of jute which was the money crop of these people [East Bengal immigrants]. Government were considering whether they should not extend the scheme of *salami* to the ex-tea garden coolies who were now settling in large numbers

in Nambor colonisation area, and whether they should not charge the same premium from immigrants from the Surma Valley who came and settled in the Assam Valley (Desai 1931a).

Table 1.1 shows the total area of land settled with indigenous and immigrant peasants in the five years between 1938 and 1943, with the indigenous peasants owning land predominantly in the clayey 'rupit mahal' tract and the submontane tract, while the immigrants in general possessing the sandy riverine tract on and around the Brahmpautra.

Table 1.1: Total Land Settled with Indigenous and Immigrant Peasants in Brahmaputra Valley, 1938–39 to 1942–43 (All Figures in Acres)

Year	Settled with indigenous peasants	Settled with immigrant peasants
1938–39	775,046	193,795
1939–40	784,125	199,608
1940–41	790,386	206,275
1941–42	835,801	206,593
1942–43	849,499	209,345

Source: Government of Assam (GOA). 1943. 'Reservation and Settlement of Land with Professional Graziers, Immigrants and Indigenous People', Assam Legislative Assembly Debates, 30 November 1943, pp. 1055–57, ASA.

As can be seen from a comparison of the figures in the table, though almost one-fifth of the total land in the valley, primarily in the low-lying tracts, was settled by the immigrants by the early 1940s, the rate of agrarian expansion in this zone was not as dramatically high as it was at the beginning of the Colonisation Scheme in the early 1930s. This also falls short when compared to the rate of growth in the land settled with the indigenous population, mostly in the clayey rupit lands as well as the submontane zone. While the land settled by the indigenous people grew by 74,453 acres or 9.6 per cent between 1938–39 and 1942–43, that settled by immigrants grew only by 15,550 acres or 8 per cent in the same period.

For the colonial government, the importance of the Colonisation Scheme thereby declined within almost a decade of its initiation, as it failed to continue the high rate of agrarian expansion as distinct from indigenous agriculture (Tucker 1988).[6] But the dynamics of demographic distribution, settlement pattern and the nature of agriculture changed drastically as a result, ushering in a new and primarily a conflicting relation with the Brahmaputra. These developments are a strong pointer that the by-now familiar and oft-repeated imagery of floods in the Brahmaputra valley, replete with the invocations of 'disaster', 'destruction', 'problem', etc., are neither ahistorical nor an eternally present 'curse' of nature. Though natural factors could and did play a significant role in influencing the experiences and perceptions of a phenomenon like flood, and by extension the relation to the river, it would not perhaps be wrong to conclude that in the final analysis, it is the social factors that played a more decisive role in forging a particular form of society–nature relationship.

The experience of the immigrant peasants in Asom indicates that the emergence of the floods as a destructive force particularly to the peasants, which rendered them homeless, landless or destitute, was not just contingent upon a sudden and simple spurt in the river's waters, as might at first appear. It is often ignored that the floods were known to be an old and expected visitor in the riverine tracts of the Brahmaputra, and often a welcome one, until its turbulent course was transformed into homes and hearths as a result of the policies of the incumbent ruling power. The apparent contradiction in the moods and emotions in the songs sung by the East Bengal peasant addressing the river in many ways expresses this dichotomy of our perception of the river with its double-life as a creator and a destroyer, one that helps reproduce life but also extinguishes it. The need therefore is to turn to the existing production relations within society no less than the river to find the factors that could turn a benevolent river malevolent, and its fertile floods a disaster.

Notes

1. 'From the banks of Padma I came to the river-islands of Asom/ The Brahmaputra also destroyed my golden home/Where do I go from here, can some one tell me?/I can't bear this lifelong pain any more' (Hossain 2002: 18). I am grateful to Banojyotsna Lahiri for the translation.

2. Poor peasants here are meant to denote those who have small amounts of land and other necessary means of production which are not sufficient for the sustenance of the family for the entire year, often forcing them to take up additional land on rent as tenant cultivators, or

work as hired agricultural labourers. Marginal peasants on the other hand are those who are landless, and entirely dependent on tenant cultivation or agricultural work on other's fields for their sustenance.

3. 'The settlers are not yet actually resident in these blocks. I have told the colonisation officer that the residence is a condition of settlement, unless a special exemption is granted . . . they will not be allowed to stay unless they accept the colonisation conditions, and have given them one month in which to pay their first premium', wrote the settlement officer of the Nowgong Colonisation Scheme (Pritchard 1931).

4. The indigenous tribal communities continued to complain against immigrant peasants in the decades to follow, and also at times demanded their eviction, as was demanded by Nagendra Chandra Baro and others for 'eviction of immigrants from tribal localities in Kamrup' (GOA 1943b).

5. A similar trend was visible in the northwestern group in Nowgong district. Whereas in 1914–15 the percentage of relinquished land to the total settled area was 9.11 per cent, it came down to a negligible .08 per cent in 1929–30. 'Assessment Report on the North-Western Group (Nowgong District)' (Datta 1931c).

6. Even though the rate of agrarian expansion carried out by the immigrant peasants progressively came down, the overall area they cleared and brought under cultivation in the Brahmaputra valley was by no means inconsiderable. It has been pointed out that 'In the twenty years ending in 1950 the immigrants turned some 1,508,000 acres of forest into settled agriculture' (Tucker 1988: 126).

References

Anon. 1904. Secretary to the Chief Commissioner of Assam, to the Secretary to the Government of India, Department of Revenue and Agriculture, No. 406R-1051R, Shillong 16 April 1903, January 1904, Proceedings of the Chief Commissioner of Assam, ASA.

———. 1931a. 'Inspection Note', 1 February 1930, Rev. A, March 1931, Proceeding No. 112, Assam Secretariat Proceedings, ASA.

———. 1931b. Memo by Settlement Officer, 'Assessment Report on the Immigrant Group (Nowgong District)', No. 727S, Nowgong 19 February 1931, Rev. A, December 1931, Proceeding Nos 248–251, Proceedings of the Chief Commissioner of Assam, ASA.

———. 1931c. Settlement Officer of Nowgong, to the Commissioner of Assam Valley Division, No. 227S, 7 August 1930, Rev. A, Assam Secretariat Proceedings, March 1931, ASA.

Anon. 1931d. Settlement Officer, Nowgong, to the Director of Land Records, No. 357S, 28 August 1931, Rev. A, December 1931, Proceeding Nos 248–251, Proceedings of the Chief Commissioner of Assam, ASA.

Baruah, Sanjib 1999. *India Against Itself: Assam and the Politics of Nationality.* New Delhi: Oxford University Press.

Bentinck, A. H. W. 1931. Commissioner of Assam Valley Division, to the Secretary to the Government of Assam in Revenue Department, No. 349R, Gauhati 29 June 1931, Rev. A, December 1931, Proceeding Nos 220–244, Proceedings of the Chief Commissioner of Assam, ASA.

Datta, S. N. 1931a. Settlement Officer of Nowgong, to the Commissioner of Assam Valley Division, 'Extension of Colonisation Scheme', No. 615S, Nowgong 20 January 1931, Rev. A, March 1931, Proceeding No. 133, Assam Secretariat Proceedings, ASA.

———. 1931b. Settlement Officer of Nowgong, to the Director of Land Records, Assam, No. 205S, Nowgong 23 July 1930, Rev. A, June 1931, Proceeding No. 59, Assam Secretariat Proceedings, ASA.

———. 1931c. Settlement Officer, Nowgong to the Director of Land Records, Assam, 'Assessment Report on the North-Western Group (Nowgong District)', No. 393S, Nowgong 31 October 1930, Rev. A, September 1931, Proceeding Nos 140–155, Assam Secretariat Proceedings, ASA.

———. 1931d. Settlement Officer, Nowgong, 'Assessment Report on the Immigrant Group (Nowgong District), 1931', No. 727S, Nowgong 19 February 1931, Rev. A, December 1931, Proceeding Nos 331–350, Assam Secretariat Proceedings, ASA.

———. 1931e. Settlement Officer, Nowgong, 'Assessment Report on the Immigrant Group (Nowgong District) 1931', No. 727S, 19 February 1931, Rev. A, December 1931, Proceeding Nos 331–350, Assam Secretariat Proceedings, ASA.

———. 1931f. Settlement Officer, Nowgong, to the Deputy Commissioner, Nowgong, No. 123S, 12 May 1931, Rev. A, December 1931, Proceeding Nos 248–251, Proceedings of the Chief Commissioner of Assam, ASA.

Desai, S. P. 1931a. Officiating Director of Land Records, Assam, to the Secretary to the Government of Assam, Revenue Department, No. 33/57, Shillong 13 October 1930, Rev. A, June 1931, Proceeding No. 55, Assam Secretariat Proceedings, ASA.

———. 1931b. Officiating Secretary to the Government of Assam, Revenue Department to the Commissioner of Assam Valley Division, 'Extract from the Recommendation of the Retrenchment Committee', No. 2306R, Shillong 24 July 1931, Rev. A, December 1931, Proceeding Nos 220–244, Assam Secretariat Proceedings, ASA.

Gimson, C. 1931a. Settlement Officer of Nowgong, to Commissioner of Assam Valley Division, No. 500S, 22 October 1929, Rev. A, March 1931, Assam Secretariat Proceedings, Revenue Department, ASA.

———. 1931b. Settlement Officer of Nowgong, to the Commissioner, Assam Valley Division, No. 399S, 10 September 1929, Rev. A, March 1931, Proceeding No. 92, Assam Secretariat Proceedings, ASA.

Government of Assam (GOA). 1883. *Report on the Census of Assam, 1881.* Shillong: Office of the Superintendent of Government Printing.

———. 1905. *Assessment Report of the Central Jorhat Group,* June 1905. Revenue Department, Assam Secretariat Proceedings, ASA.

———. 1930. *Report of the Assam Provincial Banking Enquiry Committee,* 1929–30, Vols I–III. Shillong: Government of Assam Press.

———. 1932. Census of India 1931, Vol. III, Assam, Part I: Report. Shillong: Office of the Superintendent of Government Printing.

———. 1938. *Report of the Line System Enquiry Committee (RLSC),* Vols. II–III. Shillong: Government of Assam Press.

———. 1943a. 'Reservation and Settlement of Land with Professional Graziers, Immigrants and Indigenous People', Assam Legislative Assembly Debates, 30 November 1943, pp. 1055–57, ASA.

———. 1943b. File No. RS 19 of 1943, Assam Secretariat Proceedings, ASA.

———. 1955. *Note on Assam Floods of 1954.* Shillong: Assam Government Press.

Government of Eastern Bengal and Assam (GEBA) 1906. 'Assessment Report: South Bank Fluctuating Group', February 1906, Proceedings of the Lieutenant Governor of Bengal, ASA.

Guha, Amalendu 1977. *Planter-Raj to Swaraj: Freedom Struggle and Electoral Politics in Assam 1826–1947.* New Delhi: Peoples' Publishing House.

Hossain, Ismail (ed.). 2002. *Asomor Chor-Chaporir Loka-Sahitya.* Guwahati: Banalata.

Hussain, Monirul 1993. *The Assam Movement: Class, Ideology and Identity.* New Delhi: Manak Publication.

Kershaw, L. J. 1905. Officiating Secretary to the Chief Commissioner of Assam, to the Secretary to the Government of India, Department of Revenue and Agriculture, No.2531R, Shillong 5 June 1905, Rev. A, June 1905, Assam Secretariat Proceedings, ASA.

Monahan, F. J. 1904. Secretary to the Chief Commissioner of Assam, to the Secretary to the Department of Revenue and Agriculture, Government of India, Shillong, 4 December 1903, 'Reassessment of the Assam Valley Districts', Rev. A, June 1904, Assam Secretariat Proceedings, Government of Assam, ASA.

Playfield, A. 1922a. Deputy Commissioner of Goalpara, 'Flood in North Lakhimpur', Extract from File No. Rev/878/21, No. 736R, Dhubri 20 July 1921, File Nos 110–123, Rev. B, January 1922, Assam Secretariat Proceedings, ASA.

Playfield, A. 1922b. Deputy Commissioner of Goalpara, to the Commissioner of Assam Valley Division, 'Flood in North Lakhimpur', No. 782R, Dhubri 23 July 1921, File Nos 110-123, Rev. B, January 1922, Assam Secretariat Proceedings, ASA.

Pritchard, H. M. 1931. 'Note on Colonisation Scheme', Extract from the Tour Dairy of the Settlement Officer, Nowgong, for February and May 1929, in letter from H. M. Pritchard, Secretary to the Government of Bengal, Revenue Department, to the Commissioner, Assam Valley Division, No. 1125R, Shillong 3 April 1929, Rev. A, April 1931, Proceeding No. 83, Assam Secretariat Proceedings, Revenue Department, March 1931, ASA.

Rahaman, A. 1922. Subdivisional Officer to the Deputy Commissioner, 'Flood in North Lakhimpur', Goalpara, 21 July 1921, File Nos 110-123, Rev. B, January 1922, Assam Secretariat Proceedings, ASA.

Rhodes, C. K. 1931. Secretary to the Government of Assam, Revenue Department, to the Co mmissioner of Assam Valley Division, No. 3670R, Shillong 24 October 1929, Rev. A, March 1931, Proceeding No. 94, Assam Secretariat Proceedings, ASA.

Tucker, Richard P. 1988. 'The Depletion of India's Forests under British Imperialism: Planters, Foresters and Peasants in Assam and Kerala', in Donald Worster, *The Ends of the Earth: Perspectives on Modern Environmental History*. Cambridge: Cambridge University Press.

Weiner, Myron 1978. *Sons of the Soil: Migration and Ethnic Conflict in India*, Princeton: Princeton University Press.

2

Relation of the Traditional Economic System and Ecology: The Case of a Naga Community*

LATE U. A. SHIMRAY

The Naga community is one of the largest ethnic groups in the northeastern region, with more than 40 sub-communities. Their agrarian economic system is at an early stage of development largely dependent on the local environment. Land is the nucleus of household production and consumption. Jhum (shifting cultivation) is the dominant land-use system, along with sedentary terraced wet rice cultivation and forestry. Major Naga groups like the Ao, Sema and Lotha practise jhum; the Angami are noted for skilled terrace cultivation. Other groups like the Tanghul, Mao, Chakhesang, Zeliangrong and Maring practise both jhum and wet rice cultivation. This study is focused on the Tanghul Nagas in Ukhrul district of Manipur state, occupying the hill region near the Myanmar border.

The Tanghul area was traditionally divided into eight zones which were not administrative or political divisions but characterised in former times by occupations like pot-making, salt-making or weaving. The introduction of modern education and Christianity (95 per cent of Tanghul Nagas are Christian, mainly American Baptist) changed the morphology and structure of the community, transforming traditional institutions. The chief now shares power with the Church. New Village Development Boards (more or less like panchayats) are also being formed which are parallel governance institutions alongside the traditional *awunga*.

This essay seeks to understand the relation of the traditional economic system to the ecology; it draws upon a micro-level study conducted in four Tangkhul Naga villages to better understand the relationship of the ecology, population and economic system. Four villages were purposely selected for study based on certain criteria: their practising of sedentary terraced cultivation, or only shifting cultivation, and being distant from or near the district headquarters, Ukhrul town. The survey methodology included both household questionnaires and qualitative methods like participant observation, focus group discussions and personal interviews.

A Naga village — often an irregular settlement on a hilltop or the shoulder of a spur — consists of several households of different clans. The village functioned as a compact and well-knit society which enjoyed sovereign rights. Its economy was local and self-sufficient and its customary laws were to be feared and respected. Village sites were rarely shifted and it is only in recent times that new villages have been established. Hitherto, spatial ties of marriage, politics and trade created an extensive network of relations among the villages. The Naga society is patriarchal; households are nuclear and extended households are not encouraged. The hereditary village chief is the nominal owner of village land and forests, which in practice belong to the whole community, each household having the right to possess homestead, kitchen (home) gardens, paddy fields, gardens, fishponds, and woodland.

The Naga understanding of ecology is manifested through their livelihoods. The land is more than a habitat or political boundary. The land and local environment, particularly the forests, are the basis of the Nagas' social, cultural and economic system. The land-use system, the ownership and transfer of land, and the method of cultivation relate to community and clan land, forests and settlements. Community land and ownership of land have undergone changes, education being the most important factor in the transition along with population pressure. Education has led to a money economy and changes in the barter system. The shrinking of village community land has resulted due to the emergence of private ownership and state-sponsored development projects.

Julian (1990: 69) states: 'Naga communities are organised very strongly around the principle of the village as a unit, ruled over by an autocratic chief.' The villages are sovereign states in nature and always a social, political and religious unit. The village community is a compact well-knit society where the customs and traditions are regulated accordingly. Interestingly, all the Tangkhul Naga villages have their own village dialect which is mostly not intelligible to Nagas of other villages. The four study villages also have their own dialects. But the whole community understands the common language Tangkhul tui.

There is no official record (nor village authority's record) of the exact measurement of village territory and land-use. Even the area of the sub-divisional blocks is not available. Naga villages do not pay land revenue, except house tax. 'There is no land settlement system. As the government is not the landholder, the Naga do not pay tax for holding land. As the government does not procure tax, there is no measurement' says Saikia (1987: 206). The size and settlement area of a Naga village depend on the number of households. Ukhrul is the exception being the district headquarters.

This essay examines the interrelationship of various ecological parameters — the structural parameters, that is, village land and forest, and the functional parameters including land-use for economic purposes. The first two sections examine the demographic and social composition of the village and the nature of the agricultural system. The next sections analyse and discuss the ecological and economic interrelationship.

Demographic and Socio-economic Characteristics

Table 2.1 shows that with the exception of Ukhrul, the other villages are considerably smaller and reflect the average size of Tangkhul Naga villages which range from 30 to 250 households.

The average family size varies from four to seven persons per household. The sex ratio is measured as females per 100 instead of 1,000 males because of the small population. A reason for the lower sex ratio in Ukhrul and Kamjong could be migration of males from nearby villages. A high literacy rate is observed in Halang and Ukhrul; however, it is only 59 per cent in Chingjaroi and 47.5 per cent in Kamjong.

Table 2.I: Demographic Characteristics of Tanghul Naga Study Villages

Demographic characters	Ukhrul	Halang	Chingjaroi	Kamjong
No. of households	1,764.00	256.00	158.00	199.00
Population	10,440.00	1,876.00	917.00	903.00
Males	5,781.00	956.00	470.00	510.00
Females	4,659.00	924.00	447.00	393.00
Sex ratio (per 100 males)	80.00	96.00	95.00	77.00
Family size	5.90	7.20	5.80	4.50
Literacy rate (%)	68.65	74.73	58.88	47.50
Male literacy rate (%)	74.71	80.12	63.19	52.15
Female literacy rate %)	61.15	68.83	54.36	31.96

Source: Office of the Registrar and Census Commissioner. 1991. *District Census Handbook: Ukhrul.* Manipur: Office of the Registrar and Census Commissioner.

The Naga economy is basically one of household production and consumption. Under such conditions, domestic work remains significant for household sustenance. In Naga society, understanding the concept of 'work' is essential to examine the nature of the economic system and livelihoods. Equally important is to understand how the Nagas perceive work in relation to their social and cultural practices. Work is a basic element of common humanity. It is defined as any activity, or expenditure of energy, that produces services and products of value. Indeed, work is a defining force in people's livelihoods.

In the Naga society, the work performed in the household — cooking meals, cleaning, fetching water, collecting firewood, looking after children, drying paddy, pounding and husking of rice — is considered an important economic activity. The household activities can be classified into those that are performed within or outside the homestead. The latter could be further classified into regular or occasional household work (see Figure 2.1).

In discussions, the participants opined that work denotes 'livelihood' and 'survival of the household', and that 'work is duty'. Interestingly, a school teacher from Kamjong village who spends most of his time in the teaching profession, considered agriculture as his primary work and said: 'Life is hard in the hills and there is no alternative to hard work. Otherwise our household will not get enough paddies to sustain till the next harvest. Life is hard for others though I am lucky to be in a government

Figure 2.1: Categorisation of Household Activities

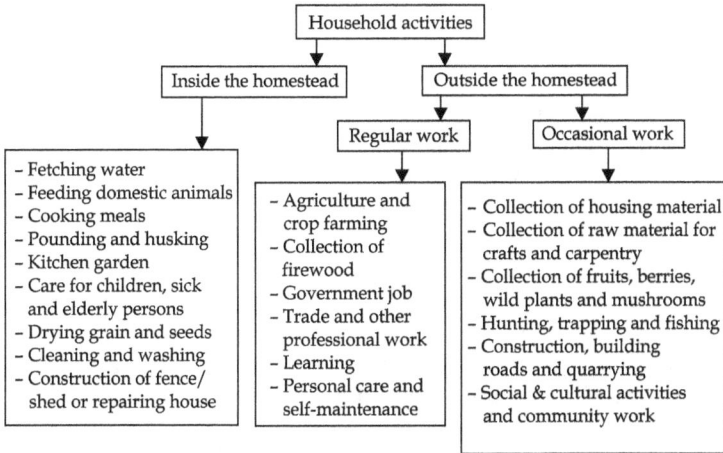

```
                    ┌─────────────────────┐
                    │ Household activities │
                    └─────────────────────┘
                ┌──────────────┴──────────────┐
        ┌───────────────────┐        ┌────────────────────┐
        │ Inside the homestead │     │ Outside the homestead │
        └───────────────────┘        └────────────────────┘
                                      ┌──────────┴──────────┐
                              ┌──────────────┐   ┌──────────────────┐
                              │ Regular work │   │ Occasional work  │
                              └──────────────┘   └──────────────────┘
```

Inside the homestead	Regular work	Occasional work
– Fetching water – Feeding domestic animals – Cooking meals – Pounding and husking – Kitchen garden – Care for children, sick and elderly persons – Drying grain and seeds – Cleaning and washing – Construction of fence/shed or repairing house	– Agriculture and crop farming – Collection of firewood – Government job – Trade and other professional work – Learning – Personal care and self-maintenance	– Collection of housing material – Collection of raw material for crafts and carpentry – Collection of fruits, berries, wild plants and mushrooms – Hunting, trapping and fishing – Construction, building roads and quarrying – Social & cultural activities and community work

Source: Shimray, U. A. 2007. *Ecology and Economic Systems: A Case of the Naga Community.* New Delhi: Regency Publications, p. 96.

job, getting a salary every month.'[1] Their arguments seem to substantiate the philosophy of 'work harder, get more harvest', and the Naga principle, 'He who does not work, neither shall he eat'. The participants emphasised that hard work enhances their position on the social ladder and thereby draws respect in the community. It was noted that many youth court a woman who is hard working. A youth in his mid-20s, a school dropout, said, 'such a hard working maiden is precious; we all need a wife who works hard and is diligent.' Children also begin to take part in household work from the age of about 11; both girls and boys help in activities like fetching water, collecting firewood, husking, cleaning, and looking after the baby and domestic animals.[2] Indeed, work is a virtue for the Nagas.

An important social phenomenon that shapes the household economy is the cooperation and labour exchange among relatives, clan and neighbours. Such reciprocal arrangements, the exchange of labour, and the barter system makes the household's economic pursuit less burdensome. The exchange of labour in Naga society involves *giving* and *receiving*. As in traditional societies, economic behaviour can hardly be separated from the social and cultural system. Economic exchanges provide more space for cultural interaction and sustain the values of social responsibility.

The Nagas' livelihoods evolved around community and incorporated participation; the spirit of oneness making them good citizens of the village. 'The Naga community life was the index of their political, economic and social life' (Shimray 1985: 131). One way to look at the interplay of social groups is to examine the individual's life cycle and the routine of daily life (Julian 1990). From an early age, children are expected to help with basic household and agricultural tasks and are incorporated into work groups based on the age cohort, or *yarnao*. This cohort works on a rotational basis, called *yar-kathui*. Most of the agricultural activities are performed in groups including those of children and youth, the clan members, relatives and neighbours. The other mode of exchange involves paddy and sometimes money. However, exchange of labour with monetary compensation is rather rare. In most cases, labour and services are paid in paddy. In the sphere of labour exchange, more importance is given to the fulfillment of social obligations, thereby perpetuating the social order. They are aware of the value of money but do not consider it an essential medium of exchange. Cooperative approaches in agricultural works are the common feature in Naga society.

A cycle of work starts in winter, that is, after the November harvest. Men collect housing materials and women store food items. Normally, the houses are renovated or rebuilt in the dry season, January and February. The houses are built turn-by-turn by relatives or clans or friends, free of cost. On average, each thatch house takes a week to build. In return, the house owner gives a feast in the evening to the people who participated in the construction work. Such practices enhance the solidarity of the society, and the sense of collective responsibility in social and economic activities. After this comes seed-sowing, plantation, weeding, and ultimately the harvest. If a household could not complete the cultivation or harvest on time, the relatives or neighbours had to help them.

Apart from the main economic activities, there are large numbers of people who participate in other household work. These activities substantively supplement the main economic work. Such subsidiary activities somewhat resemble that of 'marginal workers' in the Indian population census. (The census defines marginal workers as those who have worked at any time in the year preceding the enumeration but have not worked for the major part of the year.) Various types of subsidiary activities are weaving, carpentry, hunting and trapping, food gathering, basketry, woodcarving, making charcoal, and fishing.

Agricultural System

Traditionally, the southeastern region of Ukhrul district (including the Phungyar, Kamjong and Kasom sub-divisional blocks) practise shifting cultivation. These regions are mountainous; the rivers are quite small and run through many gorges and steep valleys. Dun (1981) specified certain reasons for the practice of shifting cultivation in this area and sedentary cultivation in the northern area — the length and period of settlement, pressure on land, availability of water supply and favourable slopes/valleys may have led to this difference in the agricultural practices.

Indeed, shifting cultivation is one of the oldest forms of mixed cropping agricultural activities, and can be the primary, secondary or tertiary cultivation of an area. Primary cultivation villages traditionally depend only on shifting cultivation for their livelihood. Secondary cultivation villages practise sedentary terraced cultivation as well as shifting cultivation. In these two types of shifting cultivation the product of the land is used mainly for domestic consumption. The tertiary cultivation villages use the produce for commercial purposes.

Shifting cultivation is a multi-cropping system, that is, varieties of crops and vegetables are grown but the main crop is rice. Primary shifting cultivation is characteristically done on the slope of the hill where there is little or no scope for development of terraced fields as the slope is very steep and the stream or river basin is very narrow. Hence, these villages 'lack' the skill of terraced cultivation. The fallow period of the shifting cycle varies from village to village depending on the given topographic conditions, size and area of village territory, village population and household numbers. The people in these villages usually do not domesticate buffaloes. There is community land and forests. But shifting cultivation areas are owned by the household. Normally kitchen gardens are absent.

In searching for new sites for shifting cultivation, the villagers observe the tree trunks and branches that indicate soil fertility. If the bark of the tree trunk is mature, the soil is considered fit for cultivation. The trees in the selected area are not randomly slashed but certain stumps are preserved. Depending on the species and variety, some trees require a height of about 1 m, others require 1.5–2 m for proper sprouting of new coppices. When the tree is cut, care is taken to avoid cross-section splitting. And after every cut, a slab of stone or a lump of earth is kept on the freshly cut stump to protect it from frost and direct sunlight, which may result in failure to regenerate new shoots.

One essential procedure in shifting cultivation is constructing a 'fire line' or fire path around the sites on the eve of the burning so that the burning of slashed trees may not spread to the adjoining village forests. If it rains just after burning the jhum fields, it is considered a good 'sign' since the burnt ashes will remain in the soil to provide natural manure with nutrients like potassium. Studies (NEPD and IIRR 1999) show that the high temperatures during jhum burning enhance the release of other native soil nutrient elements. Burning soil microorganisms accelerates the process of nutrient release to the plant. This is further justified by Ramakrishnan (1992: 170) who says, 'An important change that would occur as a consequence to burning the slash is a rapid increase in soil pH with implications on soil biological activities and nutrient availability.'

Traditionally, Nagas practise alder (*Alnus nepalensis*) tree-based shifting cultivation (see Sharma and Ambasht 1988).[3] The greater portion of the alder stem is left uncut and at the same time, the trees are pollarded.[4] The species is a successful coloniser of landslide-affected or freshly exposed rocky and eroded slopes. Its root nodules with the endophyte *Frankia* are effective in biological nitrogen fixation. The production of nitrogen-rich litter and mineralisation also contributes to a biological build-up of soil fertility. NEPD and IIRD (1999: 30) studied the use of alder in the Naga jhuming system and found that after hundreds of years of pollarding the yields of crops are still sustained.

Villages that primarily depend on sedentary terraced cultivation practise secondary shifting cultivation, growing seasonal crops and vegetables on a small scale for household consumption, but not rice. The general characteristics of the secondary shifting cultivation are that it is done on gentle hill slopes, on small areas, as compared to primary shifting cultivation. Once the farmed areas are abandoned by the household they automatically revert back as community land. The villages in northern and central Ukhrul district (including Chingai and Ukhrul sub-divisional blocks) practise both sedentary terraced cultivation and secondary shifting cultivation and also maintain kitchen gardens. Sedentary terraced fields are usually located on gentle hill slopes and river valleys, with paddy being cultivated as a monocrop. Some crops are grown on the raised earth bunds of the paddy fields.

Every individual household owns sedentary terraced fields. In the Tangkhul Naga region, there are two types of terraced cultivations: *rayi-lui*, permanent wet-terraced cultivation in the narrow river valleys or flood areas on the river bank; and *akang-lui*, dry rain-fed terraces in areas where the soil is capable of retaining water. In rayi-lui, the water is constantly supplied from the nearby rivers or streams through a small canal, whether it is the agricultural season or not. In the akang-lui, the rain and springs are the only sources of water. The practice of sedentary terraced cultivation is determined by the ecological structural parameters. The terrace can be constructed only when the terrain permits, preferably on flat land between hill slopes. Sedentary terraced cultivation is an intensive agricultural system. Nagas do not use biofertilisers and other chemicals but maintain the soil fertility by using traditional methods.[5] Water is channelled from the nearby stream or river allowing continuous in-and-out flow in the terraced fields. Circulation of water from the channels is essential to keep a sufficient amount of water in the fields. Also, flood water from the stream or river contains an enormous amount of nutrients. The soil in the river valley is fertile due to nutrients being washed out from the hill slopes during the rainy season. These processes of in-and-out flow of water supply enough nutrients.

Controlling weeds in agro-ecosystems, both shifting cultivation and sedentary terraced cultivation, is an important task in the cultivation process. Weeds are often considered to be competing with crops for the limited resources that are available in the system (see King 1966). But, according to Ramakrishnan (1992: 123): 'In the north-eastern Indian jhum system, the traditional farmer conserves about 20 per cent of the total weeds in their plots. The farmer on the basis of his empirical knowledge is able to discern when a "weed" becomes a "non-weed" in the system. Therefore, they only carry out a partial weeding rather than total weeding, since they have important nutrient conservation roles in the system.' The method of controlling soil erosion in shifting cultivation is maintained through simple techniques. The half-burnt logs are arranged in a horizontal manner on the slope with the support of tree stumps. Bunds are also built to control the soil during the rainy season. Weeding is conducted twice in shifting cultivation and once in terraced cultivation.

Today, sporadic tertiary shifting cultivation is practised in many villages in the community land mainly for commercial purposes. Only one or two varieties of crops are grown, commonly potato, garlic, muster leaf, soyabean, and cabbage. The household that is engaged in such activity sells the produce in the nearby market, that is, the district headquarters or the state capital, or sometimes within the village. The other type of tertiary cultivation is of commercial plants like teak and tea.

Hunting and fishing are among the old traditional practices in Naga society. Hunting is strictly for the men. The Nagas' hunting gear is simple; the traditional spear and knife and hunting dog.[6] Guns like musket and shotgun are recent introductions. Both individual and community hunting are practised. Community hunting is very common but confined to the dry season. Over-hunting is not allowed. Men seldom hunt during the agricultural season. Like hunting, fishing is also done as individuals or as a community. Community fishing too is a dry season activity. A particular bark of creeper is used as fish 'poison'. The creepers are beaten, pulverised and the sap is washed into the dammed-up river, causing the fish to float to the surface. This is not a real poison, since the sap deoxygenates and stuns the fish momentarily, rather than poisons the water. This form of traditional community fishing does not affect the river ecosystem.

Ecological and Economic Interface

The ecological dimensions include both structural and functional parameters; the former are static and unchanged whereas the latter are dynamic and change with time. The functional parameters include various land-use systems and the ownership of land and forest, which are important for the livelihood system and economic sustenance. Hence, functional parameters focus on agricultural land-use and forestry. The relationship between the economic system and human activities in respect to ecological parameters needs critical examination in the context of the present changing social and economic system. Due to the transition in the social and economic system, the relationship among the various ecological parameters is also eventually changing. This study focuses on both endogenous changes as well as exogenous influences. The changes in structural parameters could be due to the increase of household numbers, population and expansion of the village settlement area within the village territory. Another factor is the village social system, which is traditionally regulated by the institution of village authority. Functional parameters, being dynamic in nature, have an impact on land and forest land. Besides, physical encroachments associated with urbanisation and market forces intensify various functional parameters.

To understand the interrelationship between ecological parameters and the economic system of the Nagas, a micro-level study was conducted. Figure 2.2 broadly depicts the interrelationships between the various ecological parameters and economic systems of the Nagas. Agricultural activities are performed within the given village ecological setting. The nature of cultivation and land-use are determined by the topographical situation of the region. Therefore, the village land and forest land are the only natural source of village economic sustenance. Moreover, the Nagas observe their traditional knowledge system in order to sustain their agricultural system, forestry and the village ecosystem.

Land-use Systems and Ownership of Land and Forest

The land-use system in those villages that practise only shifting cultivation may be applied on village community land and forests owned by the village community; and on forest land owned by the individual household. The village chief is the nominal head of community land and forests. Forest land within the periphery of the village settlement area (measuring roughly 2 to 3 km in radius) is divided into several 'blocks' which, for convenience, are referred to as mountain ranges or hill-blocks, called *luipam*. Shifting cultivation is practised in these areas on a rotational basis.

Figure 2.2: Inter-relationship between Ecological and Economic Systems

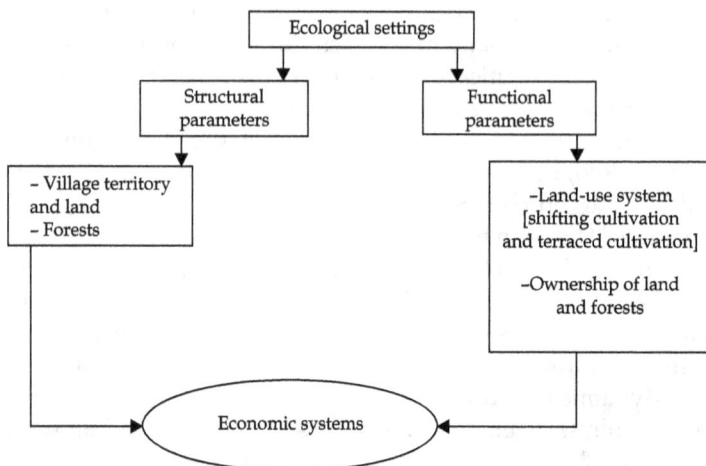

Source: Shimray, U. A. 2007. *Ecology and Economic Systems: A Case of the Naga Community.* New Delhi: Regency Publications, p. 106

Each block is further subdivided into smaller plots of land called *ram/lampuk.* Each lampuk is owned by the individual household. Some households have many plots of lampuk. However, the size of plots varies. When a particular block becomes too small for the whole village to practise shifting cultivation, two or more blocks are cleared for cultivation. Individual household plots are demarcated by rivulets, terrain or by raising stone slabs. It is interesting that the owners can easily identify their plots of forest land after several years of fallow. Also, they seem to have no problem in identifying their plots even when they are covered by vegetation. The lampuk land belonging to different individual households is inherited from their ancestors. In case a household does not own even a single plot of forest land, they may request a plot from their relatives or friends. The main crops are rice, maize, local varieties of pulses, mustard, sesamum, tobacco, yam, garlic, gourd, onion, cucumber, beans, chilli, and pumpkin. Home gardens are not maintained because in shifting cultivation there is multiple, mixed farming and a household grows the required crops and vegetables in the jhum area.

SEDENTARY CULTIVATION

Some villages traditionally practise both sedentary terraced cultivation and secondary shifting cultivation. The whole village land and forests are managed and controlled by the village community under the supervision of the village authority. Any bonafide village member can undertake any kind of agricultural activities in the community land. Households who wish to carry out secondary shifting cultivation coordinate among themselves and look for a suitable site. Collective cultivation maintains a feasible sustainable cycle; such utilisation of land is monitored by the village authority. The main crops grown in such cultivation are millet (*Eleusine coracana*), corn, potato, yam, and chilli.

Sedentary terraced cultivation, managed by the individual household, depends on the topographic features of the given village land, that is, availability of arable land that can be cut into terraces, and the possibility of channelling water without much topographic negotiation. In the survey, villagers practised both dry and wet sedentary terraced cultivation. A village has several terraced field areas, the luipam are situated in the river basin and valley. They are sub-divided into many smaller plots, *rakhong*, belonging to individual households, demarcated by stones erected at terraced bunds.[7] An average plot is 0.5–1 ha. Some households own more than four plots.

Maintaining the kitchen garden is an important subsidiary economic activity of the household. The home garden includes both annual and perennial crops and vegetables, which reduces dependency on secondary shifting cultivation. The size of the garden varies depending on the availability of space. Maintaining a kitchen garden depends on how much time and labour the household members can spare. The common cereal crop is maize; vegetables and spices include pumpkin, cucumber, mustard leaf, chilli, cabbage, brinjal, spring onion, bean, garlic; fruits include orange, mango, banana, plum, peach, passion fruit, and sugar cane.[8]

Home gardens have been intensively used and are maintained throughout the year. In the garden, household waste and decomposed kitchen scraps are used as manure to keep the soil fertile. The household waste includes firewood ash from the hearth, pig dung, cow dung, husk, and decomposed weeds. Not only does this provide natural nutrients to the soil, but the home garden also helps in recycling household and kitchen waste. This complementary recycle system maintains the healthy ecosystem of the household. There is also a supply of fresh vegetables to the households. The NEPD and IIRD (1999) report suggests that in Naga villages, home gardens have proved to be a profitable venture not only in terms of an assured supply of fresh, nutritious vegetables for home consumption, but also as a means of supplementing income. Vegetables from home gardens are increasingly finding their way to markets in town and roadside stalls as the people prefer locally grown fresh and nutritious vegetables and fruits.

When asked in the survey about why the villagers were not able to maintain home gardens on a larger scale, it was reported that most of their time and labour was engaged in agricultural activities. A kitchen garden needs constant attention because the crops and vegetables are often destroyed by domestic animals.[9]

ANIMAL HUSBANDRY

Domesticating animals is an important activity. The pigs generally live at the ground level along with the humans in huts constructed on stilts. The normal frequency of pig slaughter in the village is once a month. The Nagas consume pigs not only as a part of their normal diet but also make a feast of it during certain celebrations. Swine husbandry is based on the efficient recycling of resources with the agricultural system (Ramakrishnan 1985). The waste biomass from agriculture, including food that is left over or unfit for human consumption, is recycled through swine husbandry. Waste crops and vegetables from jhum and kitchen gardens are also used as swine-feed. Although this makes swine husbandry cheap, it involves intensive care and labour.

The Nagas also keep cattle, including the semi-domesticated *mithun* and buffaloes, normally kept in large forested areas. Mithun is solely for consumption. The buffaloes are employed only during the agricultural season for ploughing the terraced paddy fields. After the sowing season is over, the buffaloes are set free in the forest.[10] Traditionally, the Nagas also keep fowl, especially for meat for household consumption, and to sell.

Changes in the Traditional Systems

The land-use system and ownership of land and forests differs slightly in the study villages. However, the concept of ecological structure, that is, the village territory, land and forest is the same and these ecological parameters form the foundation of the Naga way of life. Whether in shifting cultivation or sedentary terraced cultivation, the agricultural activity is traditionally conducted in cooperation with the village community. For instance, slashing of forests is done collectively. In sedentary terraced cultivation it requires the cooperation of several farmers and communal work to maintain and improve the water delivery system. Table 2.2 shows the different types of land-use systems in the region.

In the survey, it was found that these traditional land-use systems are undergoing considerable strain due to demographic

Table 2.2: Land-use Systems and Ownership of Land and Forest Land in the Study Villages

Village	Community land and forest land	Forest land/ woodland	Sedentary terraced fields	Homestead
Kamjong	Village chief is the nominal head but managed by the community	Owned by the individual household and shifting cultivation operates in such forest land		Owned by the individual household
Chingjaroi	Village chief is the nominal head but managed by the community		Owned by the individual household	Owned by the individual household
Ukhrul and Halang	Village chief is the nominal head but managed by the community	Owned by the individual household and shifting cultivation operates in such forest land	Owned by the individual household	Owned by the individual household

Source: Shimray, U. A. 2007. *Ecology and Economic Systems: A Case of the Naga Community.* New Delhi: Regency Publications, p. 111.

and socio-economic changes. Within the Naga villages, population is increasing. Both the village authority and the Church maintain the record of the village population and households, including the annual number of births and deaths. However, the information of the Church authorities is more reliable.[11] Every newborn is 'dedicated' to the church at the age of four or five months, for the 'Christian Birth Registration'. The survey found that the number of children being 'dedicated' is very high in all the villages but the annual number of deaths is much lower. The birth rate seems alarming in proportion to the total population of the village.

As mentioned earlier, the average family size is six to seven members. A recent social phenomenon observed in the villages is the decreasing age at marriage. Respondents in the studied villages categorically mentioned that the age at which boys and girls get married is decreasing, on average 20 to 24 years for boys and 18 to 22 years for girls. Traditionally, early marriage had been discouraged in Naga society, for marriage determined one's maturity. In earlier days, the Naga *morung* (dormitory) culture played an important role in shaping one's personality and social outlook. It was compulsory for all the young boys and girls to become members of the morung. The boys slept in the boys' morung and the girls in the girls' morung. The senior morung members generally administered the morung on the advice of the village elders (Shimray 1985). The juniors were taught manners, obedience and discipline. They were also taught various arts and crafts, ranging from basket-making and wood-carving, to folk songs, dances and narrating village folktales and history. The morung discipline and teachings enabled the young people to turn out as perfect mature citizens. After making themselves 'perfect persons' in the morung, the young men could court and select partners for marriage. It was in keeping with this tradition that the Nagas maintained a higher age of marriage. Marriage was a sign of maturity, making one eligible to become a member of the village authority, and gain recognition in the clan organisation. However, the recent trend of early marriage is due to early school dropouts and unemployment. It is found that the reasons for dropping out of school are lack of financial support, negligence in studies and voluntarily giving up education to help their parents in cultivation and household activities.

On average, every year, there are two to three marriages taking place in the study villages. One marriage means the addition of one household in the village. As soon as the son is married, the parents move out to another newly built house leaving the former house as well as landed properties, which they inherited. Since the Naga economic system (production and consumption) is mainly household-based, more households in the village system exert more pressure on land and forest. Therefore, the increase of household numbers in the village has a direct impact on the village land and forests.

In the recent past, till about two decades ago, the jhum cycle used to be 15 years. The increase of population has resulted in shortening the jhum cycle and the extensive use of forest land. But it is not possible to pinpoint the exact time when the changes occurred. Because of the shorter rotation, jhuming is now carried out on the fallow land before it is fully re-vegetated. This adversely affects the economic yield which gradually declines. Ramakrishnan (1992), who analysed the economic and energy aspects of the jhum system, concludes that a 10-year jhum cycle is the minimum cycle length, if jhum in the present form is to be sustained. Shortening the cycle is distorting the land-use system and disrupting the traditional linkages between the people and the forest ecosystem. Indeed, this also leads to land degradation resulting in loss of nutrients, invasion of weeds and retarding the growth of the secondary forest. This necessitates bringing larger areas of forest land under jhum cultivation.

In the study area, the length of the jhum cycle is still nine–11 years. This is still a 'feasible' cycle as per Ramakrishnan's criteria. However, there is a declining trend, as the cycle length used to be 15 to 20 years. Recently, land-use for shifting cultivation has become more intensified and more blocks of luipam (forest land) that could have been left fallow, are being required to meet the demand. Earlier, the village managed with only one luipam but in recent times, the village uses two luipams. The productivity of the land is also declining, and so, households often operate larger areas in order to sustain themselves for a year. The main reason for the demand for a bigger area is the unprecedented increase of population and household numbers in the village.

As in the case of shifting cultivation, the population practising sedentary terraced cultivation has also increased, resulting in detrimental effects to the ecology. In sedentary terraced cultivation, where the topographic features determine the availability of arable land for terracing, there is no evidence of new luipams in the river valley in the last decade. From the survey it may be observed that this is because the area suitable for terracing has been exhausted; terracing also requires human labour and involves monetary cost. Moreover, the terrace construction requires community cooperation. Even when the village has a vast area for terracing, not all of this may be cultivable because water channels are also required. Therefore, the expansion of terraced fields is very limited because terracing depends on the nature of the topographic features and the availability of water sources. In many villages, such lands are becoming rather scarce and are being exhausted. Households have not made much improvement or expanded terraced fields since they inherited land from their parents. It is also learned that many households could not sustain themselves on the yearly rice harvest.[12] One reason is division of the household's terraced fields among the married sons.

Lack of 'labour' in the village is a recent phenomenon. Today, most children are sent to the local school, to the district headquarters, or to Imphal to study. As the economically productive age groups are engaged in pursuing education, this increases the burden on parents. Even if the children contribute to the household labour, it would be for a short period, that is, the summer break which coincides with the agricultural season.

Because the joint family system is absent, the increase of household members increases the need for food, firewood and forest produce. An average yield of paddy per hectare is 50–60 baskets, traditional conical bamboo baskets that contain about 25 kilograms each. Two to three hectares are required to sustain a household of six members till the next harvest. The survey showed that many households do not own any forest land, either because of fragmentation or because the land has been sold. Sometimes the youngest son does not get any share of the forest land and depends on the eldest to give some portion of his property. The sale of family forest land started with the appearance of the money economy and the emergence of 'elite-households'. However, selling, transfer or mortgage of individual forest land has to take place only within the village community. Non-residents cannot purchase any forest land. Land is sold mainly because of indebtedness. The majority of the households do not have a regular income except for those in government service or private teaching or trade.

So, when the need for money arises, they are compelled to sell their properties.[13] This is the last resort for most of the cultivator households. Therefore, inequality in land holdings is more visible in recent times.

The village economic activities have also expanded due to external influence. For instance, commercial activities like logging and the firewood business, and commercial cropping on village land is increasing. Uncontrolled and sporadic commercial shifting cultivation on community lands has started in many villages. This 'abortive' cultivation is a relatively recent development, since the early 1990s. This kind of cultivation is mainly for commercial purposes, growing commercial cash crops like potato, cabbage and soyabean, and is entirely a monocrop system. Forest land is rampantly used. Exogenous market forces encourage such activity. Certainly, commercial cultivation is far from the traditional ways and also causes a lot of pressure on the cultivatable land and considerable damage to the surrounding forest. This results in the depletion of forest land and affects the length of the shifting cultivation cycle.

The dynamics of population growth and the expansion of economic activities affect the village ecological parameters. Village territory is an important ecological structural parameter and it determines the limits of the economic activities. Hence, it is important to examine the dynamic functional parameters also.

The Naga tradition envisages that no land is to be sold, mortgaged, leased, bartered, gifted, or otherwise transferred to non-residents of the village. Selling of landed properties like homestead, sedentary terraced paddy fields and household-owned forests should be done only within the village. For selling such immovable landed properties, one has to ensure that the prospective buyer(s) is a bonafide member of the village. In case any outsider wishes to buy the land he or she must first become a bonafide member of the village.[14] But the landed properties, sedentary terraced fields and forest land are not equally distributed among the households. There are households having more landed properties like sedentary terraced cultivation as well as forest land. Disparity in the land holding/ownership is not recent and depends on traditional lineage inheritance. For instance, some households inherited large agricultural land from their parents and grandparents. These can be termed as traditionally rich households. On the other hand, the households (especially government servants and traders) that are economically sound acquire the properties through their economic wealth. Therefore, the existence of selling, mortgage and barter systems contributes to and widens the economic disparity in the village.

To sum up, the traditional practices are being slowly eroded in the midst of the changing socio-economic system in the village. Subsequently, this leads to changes in perception and attitudes towards the community land and forest land. The community-based resource management of village land is an example that needs to be emulated. However, the emergence of individualism in community land and forest land poses a serious threat to the ecological parameters as well as affecting the social system. Moreover, such an approach is expected to generate incentives for greater internalisation and carefree husbanding of resources by any individual. The straightforward individualism of community land and forests will have serious distributional implications in the future and divide the society. Also, it will encourage a trend of 'rich and poor'. Ultimately, the result will be marginalising the poor in the village. Indeed, the transition of community land to individual household ownership is one way of strengthening the patriarchal system of the Nagas.

The effect of external influences on Naga society is more noticeable now. The external influence is pushing for a greater integration with the urban-based and market economy. The trend of market forces is encouraging the villages to aim for cash income and extensive commercial cropping. However, the fundamental concept underlying the traditional economic system has not changed. The principle is still focused primarily on self-sufficiency.

FORESTRY

The forests and forest products constitute important components of the economy and livelihood pattern. These include timber, used both for household and commercial purposes, and non-timber products like firewood, bamboo, cane, wild plants, fruits, mushroom, honey, creepers and climbers, herbs, and tube-roots. The common timber produce in the village is in the form of planks and round logs. Pine or teak wood is used for making furniture and housing materials. Almost all the houses in the villages are built of wood, especially pine wood planks. In Naga society, non-timber forest produce (NTFP) constitutes a significant household economic component. Grasses are mainly used for thatch roofs. Creepers and climbers are good for making ropes. NTFP, including wild plants, mushrooms, honey, herbs, and shrubs may be collected by anyone belonging to the village and are used for household consumption.

The Nagas consume large amounts of firewood. Every household uses firewood for cooking as well as heating; hearths are kept burning on an average for seven to nine hours a day. Earlier, firewood was carried home from the forest by women and children in a *sopkai* (conical bamboo basket) that weighs about 25 kg when fully loaded. Cutting down trees for firewood is mostly done by men. Today, the firewood is ferried by truck. Bamboo is widely utilised in different kinds of activities such as roofing, fencing and making baskets and mats. Also, the bamboo-shoot is a Naga delicacy and is largely consumed in the household. Bamboo products have a market value but the avenue for marketing is very restricted.

It can be said that everything concerning the survival of the Nagas rests within ecological parameters. But large-scale destruction of forests results in disordering the ecology. Commercial forestry is one ecological threat in the region. The Chingai and Kamjong blocks of Ukhrul district, in which the present study was conducted, are known for logging and commercial activities. Round wood logs are supplied to sawmills and wooden planks used for furniture. The logging activities and firewood business in the region started during the early 1980s, mainly due to the improvement of road construction in these two blocks near the border roads by the General Reserve Engineering Force (GREF). As a result of commercialisation of forest products during the mid-1980s and early 1990s, forest goods were ferried outside the district. The ideal route for smuggling forest products is via the Ukhrul-Jessami village border road in Chingai block, which is connected to the Melori-Kohima road in Nagaland. The goods would later reach Dimapur, the commercial town of Nagaland, and then be sent by railway outside the state. With the introduction of sawmills, the Nagas were lured into this business and they became the suppliers of timber to the cities. Logging led to rampant cutting of primary forests. Such activities drastically shrunk the space for shifting cultivation. Moreover, it destroyed the habitat of wild fauna and flora. The increasing need for money is a major driving force for the community resorting to logging.

However, timber logging drastically declined in the mid-1990s due to the intervention of Tangkhul Naga social organisations and students' organisations. The apex community organisation, the Tangkhul Naga Long (TNL), banned commercial logging activity. There was general awareness of the value of the forest and that commercial activities were depleting the local forest resources, resulting in the local populace facing scarcity of forest resources. Moreover, the commercial activities were affecting traditional local self-sustenance and livelihoods. Therefore, the Naga organisations took steps to regulate and stop the selling of forest products outside the region. But commercial activities within the district are permitted, especially those related to firewood and wooden round logs.[15] This was to meet the local demand and to balance the benefits and costs. Exporting forest goods outside the region is, however, continuing clandestinely, although in low intensity.

Concluding Remarks

Colonial rule significantly modified the politics and geography of the Naga hills. The expansion of the British administration dissected the contiguous Naga hills within rigid boundaries, hitherto unknown in the history of the Nagas. Today, the Naga hills fall into four administrative units in India — Nagaland, Manipur, Arunachal Pradesh, and Assam — and also stretch into northern Myanmar (Burma). Over the centuries, the Nagas have learned how to grow food and survive. For many centuries, their knowledge of agriculture and natural resource management and their traditional economic system has sustainably conserved the ecology.

However, over time the land-use system and ownership pattern has changed, creating social 'disparity'. The expansion of new terraced fields is constrained by topography. With productive age groups going to school or to work in towns, the parents' labour in agriculture and household activities has increased. Both ancestral and acquired properties are getting divided among the male siblings. The increase in the number of households and population leads to a shortage of terraced fields increasing shifting cultivation, and pushes the village settlement towards the forest periphery. Households which own forest land (*thingkham*) may be economically viable but others suffer. The penetration of the urban economy is affecting the ecology through commercial logging and cropping, unregulated forest burning, intense graz-ing, extensive hunting and fishing (indiscriminate individual hunting with shot guns instead of seasonal community hunts), and insect hunting (cutting down trees for edible insects that live in the tree trunks).

The Naga traditional institutions and customs regulate resource use and management. But changes in ecology and its knowledge have been brought about by the community and various 'development' measures, seriously threatening the ecology. It is essential to uphold the customary knowledge system, technologies and innovation related to the agricultural system and forestry. Recognition of customary practices would sustain the tribal economy in the long run.

Notes

* U. A. Shimray had not completed this article when he tragically passed away. We have had to, therefore, draw heavily upon Chapter 5 of his *Ecology and Economic Systems: A Case of the Naga Community* (pp. 92–121). The introductory paragraphs, providing the context of the study, are taken from earlier chapters and the concluding remarks from the book's conclusion. The article is included here with the permission of his family. Special thanks to Waryaola Shimray for facilitating this and to Rajesh Mall for providing the contacts.

— Editor

1. The monetary economy of the village often depends on local government servants, private teachers, traders, and business persons. Otherwise, there is no source of income because it is not viable to market the agricultural products outside the village.

2. The household activities performed by the children cannot be considered as 'child-labour'. It is Naga tradition that young ones must help the parents.

3. The alder, widely distributed in the Naga hills, is a large deciduous tree which is usually found in clusters. It can be easily recognised by its grayish and dark green bark. It is an ecologically pioneering species, a rapid coloniser of degraded land (NEPD and IIRD 1999).

4. The alder has the ability to sprout again when the main trunk is cut, usually at 2 m above the ground. This permits coppicing on the stump which may be subsequently harvested.

5. In sedentary terraced cultivation, the Nagas use traditional methods for enhancing nutrients especially in the wet terraced paddy field. During the process of turning up the soil, the straw is buried in the soil itself. It decomposes when the soil is watered and acts as good natural manure, making the paddy field more fertile.

6. Hunting is strictly for men. Women are forbidden to touch the hunting gears like the gun or musket, spear and *dao* (knife).

7. The demarcated stones cannot be removed from their original position. If this is done without the knowledge of the neighbour, the defaulter will face serious social sanction and the matter will be taken up either by the clans or the village court.

8. Home garden produce is meant for household consumption; surplus produce is often shared with relatives and neighbours, or sold.

9. In Naga society, women are responsible for maintaining the kitchen garden. A young woman mentioned that some households have started growing plants that were traditionally not cultivated, like garlic, cauliflower, pea, radish, carrot, and watermelon.

10. Cow-rearing is a recent phenomena in Naga society. Keeping goat, sheep and duck is not common. The cow was introduced by the plains people, especially the neigbouring Meitei community, and the immigrant Nepalis. The Nepalis own most of the cows and sell milk and meat locally. The cows are kept with the permission of the village authority and on condition of paying compensation to the village. However, recently, the local people have discouraged cow-rearing, because it requires large forest areas for grazing.

11. There are one or two churches in most Tangkhul Naga villages.

12. When households cannot sustain themselves on the store of rice till the next harvest, they often borrow from relatives or neighbours, and return the borrowed rice in the next harvest. Sometimes, rice is exchanged for labour.

13. The need for money is felt and used in the following order of priority: (*i*) school fees/uniform/books, (*ii*) medical care, (*iii*) clothes, (*iv*) festivals, particularly Christmas, (*v*) starting a business.

14. According to tradition, if someone wants to become a bonafide member of the village, he/she must discard the original surname, and be attached to one of the clans of the village. Such adoption is followed by the killing of and feasting on a four-legged domesticated animal.

15. Logging and other commercial activities related to forest produce are totally regulated by the village authority and the TNL at the community level. Sometimes, this regulation faces inevitable loopholes due to the corruption among their members.

References

Dun, E. W. 1981 (reprint). *Gazetteer of Manipur*. New Delhi: Vivek Publishing Company.

Julian, J. 1990. *The Nagas*. London: Thames and Hudson.

King, L. L. 1966. *Weeds of the World: Biology and Control*. London: Leonard Hill Books.

NEPD (Nagaland Environmental Protection and Development), IRRD (International Institution of Rural Development). 1999. *Building upon Traditional Agriculture in Nagaland, India*. New Delhi: IRRD.

Ramakrishnan, P. S. 1985. 'Conversion of Rain Forests in North Eastern India', in J. S. Singh (ed.), *Environmental Regeneration in Himalaya: Concepts and Strategies*. Nainital: Central Environmental Association, pp. 69–84.

———. 1992. *Shifting Cultivation and Sustainable Development: An Interdisciplinary Study from North Eastern India*. Paris: UNESCO and Oxford University Press.

Saikia, Jogamaya. 1987. 'Land Relations in Nagaland', in B. B. Dutta and M. N. Karna (eds), *Land Relations in North-East India: A Sociological Study*. New Delhi: People's Publication House, pp. 201–7.

Sharma, E. and R. S. Ambasht. 1988. 'Nitrogen Accretion and its Energetic in the Himalayan Alder', *Functional Ecology*, 2: 229–35.

Shimray, R. R. 1985. *Origin and Culture of the Nagas*. New Delhi: Pamleiphy Shimray.

Shimray, U. A. 2007. *Ecology and Economic Systems: A Case of the Naga Community*. New Delhi: Regency Publications.

3

Why Do *Jhumiyas Jhum*? Managing Change in Shifting Cultivation Areas in the Uplands of Northeastern India*

DHRUPAD CHOUDHURY

For successive governments, both at the state and the centre, management of shifting cultivation, or jhum as it is locally known, has been — and still remains — a fundamental imperative for agricultural development planning pertaining to the uplands of northeast India. Development planners and policy makers perceive the practice of shifting cultivation as subsistence economically unviable and environmentally destructive and hence, a major hurdle to the development of the region. Governments, therefore, have consistently tried to replace it with settled agriculture, allocating substantial financial outlays through successive Five Year Plans since the early 1970s. Shifting cultivators, too, desire change as much as the governments do and desperately seek options that would help them transgress the practice and move towards attaining their aspiration of assimilation into the mainstream economy. Towards this end, they perceive government programmes as a critical — often the only — means to take them out of poverty and hence, eagerly await opportunities to avail the benefits of such programmes. However, despite the desire of the community and efforts by the government to usher in change, shifting cultivation remains an enigma and persists in large parts of the region even today.

The situation, therefore, demands an objective appraisal to examine the reasons underlying its persistence — without eulogising or condemning either the practice, or government efforts — and thereby, identify concerns that require urgent attention if transformation of upland agriculture is to become a reality for all.

This essay draws predominantly on the West Garo Hills district of Meghalaya, a location ideally suited for such an appraisal given the predominance of shifting cultivation and the rapid change reflective of the process of transformation consequent to government programmes and market influence. The milieu is reflective of other parts of the region as well and hence the findings should broadly hold true for the whole of northeast India.

Agricultural Transformations: The Early Attempts and their Impacts

As long as the upland communities were insular, isolated and unassimilated to the market economy, shifting cultivation was sufficient to meet all their needs, including that of food security. However, as such communities gradually came into the folds of mainstream development bringing accompanying market penetration into these areas, the foremost concern for the average shifting cultivator increasingly turned to cash generation to meet household consumption needs. Some of the agricultural produces from shifting cultivation − maize, vegetables, chillies, sesame, ginger, and cotton − have a good market demand; produce from the fallows and forests − mainly wild edibles, honey, wildlife, and firewood − also finds markets among the urban consumers. Shifting cultivators sell their agricultural products in the weekly markets individually to generate the much needed cash and try to supplement incomes by selling forest produce to urban households. However, they fail to obtain a steady and satisfactory return from either, primarily because of the lack of marketing skills and their unorganised nature of marketing the products. Further, the sale of forest produce though attractive, does not offer regular returns being occasional and unorganised, thus failing to provide a steady income. Not surprisingly, this encourages exploitation by traders from the plains for both agricultural and forest produce and hence fails to offer satisfactory returns. Government programmes with their promise of cash generation, therefore, seem to offer a welcome opportunity to take shifting cultivators out of a desperate situation where income security has become synonymous to survival.

Programmes targeted towards transformation of shifting cultivation were initiated in the 1970s with a thrust on horticulture and cash crop promotion. Coffee, rubber and cashew plantations besides horticultural crops such as pineapple and citrus were established under various government schemes as alternatives to shifting cultivation. Schemes were also launched to encourage terrace cultivation with the twin objectives of expansion of wet rice cultivation (thus reducing the dependency on shifting cultivation for rice) and promoting soil erosion control. The plantations, established by concerned departments under centrally sponsored programmes, were initially meant to have a demonstration effect and were largely planned and maintained by the departments on land made available by participating villages; the involvement of the villagers was limited to providing labour for establishment and maintenance of the plantations during the gestation period, after which the plantations were handed over to villagers to reap the benefits from the crops. To encourage subsequent adoption and expansion of such cash crops, subsidies were made available through specific schemes.

Despite their desperate need, the acceptance of such programmes by the villagers was not very encouraging until recently and few, if any, replicated these options. Factors such as the lack of familiarity with the crops and their management, difficulty in sourcing seed and saplings as well as inadequate access to technical backstopping made farmers hesitant to adopt these crops. The additional labour demand for maintenance was an added deterrence. Farmers were reluctant to take up even horticultural crops such as pineapple and other fruits because of their high perishability; also, given the poor accessibility to road heads and the lack of knowledge about markets, compounded with the absence of storage facilities or any processing options, adopting such crops proved risky and unattractive. Farmers who took up such crops often found themselves vulnerable to exploitative traders and frequently had no recourse but to resort to distress sales, invariably at a loss.

The most critical factors that discouraged farmers from accepting these alternatives, however, were the long gestation period during which no returns could be expected and the near absence of access to market linkages once the crops started maturing. Further, restrictions on the sale of crops such as coffee in the open market during this period — coffee could be sold only to the Coffee Board till the late 1990s — frustrated the farmers to the extent that plantations set up with enthusiasm in many villages were abandoned and allowed to revert back into fallow forests. In many areas, plantations of coffee, cashew and other cash crops were slashed down consequent to poor market linkages and farmers reluctantly reverted back to shifting cultivation.

The Changing Upland Landscape: Transformations in West Garo Hills

Over the years, however, shifting cultivators have slowly revived the process of transformation, often with the active encouragement of different government programmes and the gradual increasing influence of markets. With the rapid penetration of market forces into the uplands of northeast India and the consequent transformation of the subsistence economy into a monetarised, cash-driven system, most upland households have little choice but to accept sedentarised options or rapidly transform conventional shifting cultivation into a 'commodified' form (Choudhury et al. 2003), often complimented with settled agricultural options that allow them a means of cash generation.

The estimates reported by the Task Force on Shifting (Jhum) Cultivation set up by the government of Meghalaya in 2001 seem to suggest the gradual transition of the upland landscape in Meghalaya from shifting cultivation to settled systems. Agricultural statistics for the district of West Garo Hills, covering the period 2000 to 2008, reflect this trend and suggest a gradual reduction in the area under shifting cultivation, albeit at a very modest rate. The figures also show the expansion of sedentary agriculture, particularly the expansion of cash crops. While the expansion of some crops has been gradual and increased steadily over the years, the expansion of arecanut, rubber and tea has been remarkable, particularly between 2004–05 and 2007–08 (Table 3.1). While farmers expanded cashewnut by 2.77 per cent (over 2004–05 figures), the expansion of arecanut, rubber and tea for the corresponding period were 38.09 per cent, 80.06 per cent and 125.15 per cent, respectively. These figures reflect several underlying determinants and are important indicators for managing transformations.

Arecanut is a non-perishable product, with comparatively low labour demands. The crop is common in the neighbouring state

Table 3.1: Changes in Agricultural Land-use, West Garo Hills, Meghalaya (in Ha)

Land-use categories	2001–02	2004–05	2007–08	% change (from 2001–02)
Total arable area	33,911	34,182.00	na	nc
Total jhum area	3,704	3,588.00	3,568	(–) 3.67
Wet rice/terraces	na	13,753.00	7,118	nc
Pineapple	978	997.00	na	nc
Cashew	1,283	1,298.00	1,334	(+) 3.98
Arecanut	1,088	1,108.00	1,530	(+) 40.63
Tea	120	163.00	367	(+) 205.83
Rubber	60	45.54	82	(+) 36.67
Total cash crops	3,529	3,611.54	3,313	(+) 29.87*

Source: Choudhury D., N. S. Jodha and E. Sharma. 2008. 'Policy Approaches in Management of Shifting Cultivation: Compromising Equitable Access, Food Security and Common Property Institutions', Paper presented at International Association for Studies of Commons Conference 'Governing Shared Resources: Connecting Local Experiences to Global Challenges', IASC Conference 2008, Gloucestershire, UK, p. 4.

Notes: *Percentage change calculated excluding area under pineapple; na: data not available; nc: not calculated due to lack of complete time series data.

of Assam (and the bordering districts in Bangladesh) and Garos have been familiar with arecanut, given their betel chewing habit. Thus, apart from markets outside, arecanut also has a local market. Sapling sourcing too is not difficult as the crop has been introduced in the district by farmers themselves many years in the past (as early as the beginning of the century in areas bordering the plains of Assam and Bangladesh). Moreover, market linkages are already established with commission agents and traders collecting the product from the villages, easing the burden of transportation to markets for the producers. The most important reason, however, is the lack of the need for substantial investments making the crop amenable for adoption by even the poor.

Tea and rubber, unlike arecanut, are crops introduced by government departments under various schemes and programmes designed to replace shifting cultivation. The expansion of both these cash crops was slow given that both were alien and unfamiliar crops, there was a need for large land holdings, substantial investments and the absence of processing units, compounded with poor market linkages and uncertain markets. The improvement of market linkages and price stability of rubber has fuelled its expansion. The trend for tea has particularly been exceptional and the establishment of a processing factory at Rongram by the Tea Growers Federation has probably contributed substantially to this impressive growth.

Transition from Shifting Cultivation to Settled Agriculture: Are Transformations Really Taking Root?

While the Task Force estimates and agricultural statistics indicate a gradual transition from shifting cultivation to settled agricultural systems and suggest a resultant reduction on the dependency on shifting cultivation, the results of a field study conducted in six villages of West Garo Hills to get a 'reality check' seem to indicate otherwise and suggest the need for a critical re-examination of the statistics provided by the agencies (Choudhury et al. 2008).[1] The study, covering 81 households in six villages, found that while transformations, particularly the induction of cash crops such as arecanut, were progressively expanding in the uplands, they did not necessarily reduce the dependency of households on shifting cultivation as nearly all the surveyed households continued with the practice (though exceptions did exist in a few villages) (Table 3.2). Contrary to the Task Force report and the agricultural statistics provided by the authorities, shifting cultivation seems to persist in the study villages. An interesting revelation of the survey is the fact that access to shifting cultivation has not changed despite transformations (and a reduction in area under shifting cultivation as suggested by the agricultural statistics), and all households retain their access to shifting cultivation plots (Table 3.2). Moreover, the study also revealed that a growing proportion of households had multiple farming systems managed simultaneously. In other words, while households have started the process of transition into settled agriculture, they continue to retain the practice of shifting cultivation. Thus, agricultural census operations need to quantify this nuanced dimension of agricultural change and revise the assumption that expansion of settled systems automatically signifies the relinquishing of shifting cultivation.

Table 3.2: Agricultural Land-use Profile in Sampled Villages, West Garo Hills

Sl no.	Village	No. of households (HH)		% HH practising jhum	% HH having mixed farming*	% sampled HH having access to				
						Jhum plots				
		Total	Sampled			Annual	Occasional	Orchards	Terraces
1.	Chidoagre	41	20	100.0	35.0	100	0	100.0	33.0
2.	Tapra Alda	35	16	87.0	33.0	100	0	100.0	33.0
3.	Bolsagre	20	10	100.0	12.5	86	14	100.0	12.5
4.	Rongsep Adugre	22	9	100.0	62.5	100	0	100.0	62.5
5.	Adu Klangre	nr	15	66.7	14.0	100	0	100.0	18.0
6.	Boldanngre	nr	11	100.0	0.0	100	0	87.5	0.0

Source: Choudhury D., N. S. Jodha and E. Sharma. 2008. 'Policy Approaches in Management of Shifting Cultivation: Compromising Equitable Access, Food Security and Common Property Institutions', Paper presented at International Association for Studies of Commons Conference 'Governing Shared Resources: Connecting Local Experiences to Global Challenges', IASC Conference 2008, Gloucestershire, UK, pp. 5–6.

Notes: *Mixed farming systems signify households practising jhum, orchards and wet rice terraces; nr – not recorded

Of more interest is the fact that all households reported having access to orchards, including those in the control village. The explanation for this is not far to seek: as the need for cash generation increases and the desperation of villagers becomes more acute, families gradually introduce cash crop saplings — particularly pineapple and arecanut — into the jhum fallows prior to shifting to their next plot. Gradually, the number of saplings in the plots is increased during subsequent years, effectively converting the jhum fallows into a plantation or orchard. This process allows even poorer households to establish their own plantation and as labour demands are minimal (the planting being undertaken in plots under cultivation and preceding fallowing), the proportion of households having orchards is gradually increasing, effectively changing the landscape of the uplands. Overall, agricultural statistics as well as field studies do confirm the gradual diversification of agricultural systems in the upland and while the transition to settled systems seem evident, the reduction of dependency on shifting cultivation seems questionable, requiring more rigorous quantification. Thus, shifting cultivators — and the upland landscape — seem in transition, rather than transformation from shifting cultivation to settled agricultural systems.

Why Do *Jhumiyas Jhum*? Reasons Underlying the Persistence of Shifting Cultivation

While it is clear that agricultural transition is taking roots in the uplands of northeast India, the transformation of shifting cultivators to settled agriculturalists is yet to become a reality. Despite the growing acceptance of alternate options, concerns still remain among a majority of shifting cultivators — in particular the poor — forcing them to persist with the practice. Why do *jhumiyas* (shifting cultivators) jhum? What forces shifting cultivators to persist with the practice despite available alternative options? It is obvious that understanding the underlying compulsions holds the key to transformation of the uplands of northeast India — perhaps even elsewhere where the practice is prevalent. In order to probe the question further, a rapid survey was conducted in early 2009, covering seven villages in three districts of Meghalaya to compliment the earlier study in West Garo Hills and assess emerging concerns in regard to agricultural transformations (see Leduc and Choudhury, forthcoming).[2] The findings from both the studies suggest that the underlying causes for the persistence of shifting cultivation are an admixture of selective and extremely poor access to government programmes, inadequate penetration of government efforts, the lack of easy access to resources and services coupled with the inherent strengths within the practice of shifting cultivation, particularly those that allow upland farmers a certain degree of risk aversion and buffer the vulnerability.

TRANSFORMATIONS, RISK MANAGEMENT AND VULNERABILITY

For shifting cultivators, the practice, despite its subsistence character, allows them a harvest of a wide variety of crops throughout the year, giving confidence to avert risks. Indeed, the diversity of crops within shifting cultivation is a strategy evolved to spread risks and serves as a risk insurance mechanism. The mixed cropping allows sequential harvesting of crops, ensuring food availability throughout the year (Figure 3.1); in the present context, the only crop that is insufficient is rice. The variety of crops (and the various landraces within each crop) ensure that even if crop failures happen due to adversity of weather (unusually heavy monsoon showers, hailstorms or drought) or due to pests and pestilence — which is extremely rare in this system — some of the landraces of each crop type (cereals, legumes, tubers, spices) will have the resilience to perform and hence, farmers will not be faced with a total crop failure. Ensuring crop diversity, therefore, allows shifting cultivators to avoid the risk of complete crop losses and possible starvation. In addition, the regenerating fallows provide them with diverse edibles, meat, medicines as well as several utility products — the most important being fuelwood — and products that generate cash incomes.

In contrast, settled agricultural systems such as wet rice terraces or plantations — systems promoted as alternatives — fail to provide such diversity and allow mixed cropping of a few crops at best; moreover, such systems do not provide for sequential harvesting and harvests are usually limited to a single season (Figure 3.2). Although agricultural transformations hold out the

Figure 3.1: Seasonal Resource Availability from Shifting Cultivation

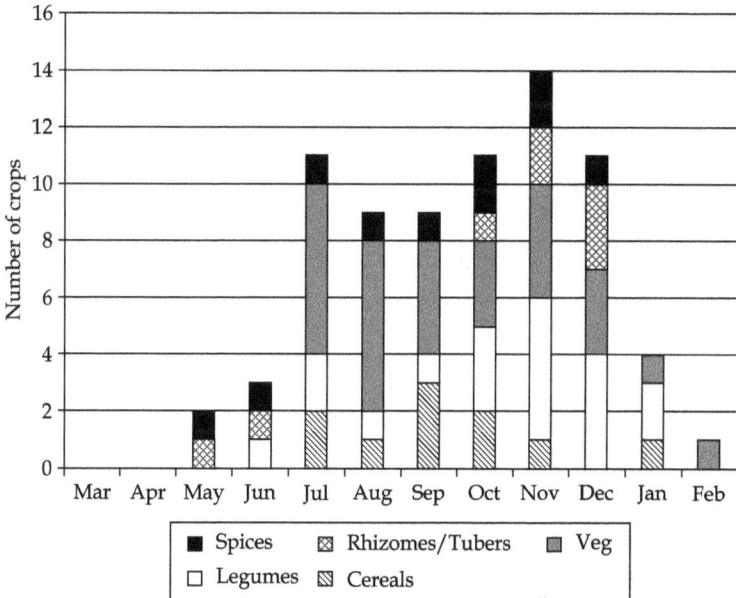

Source: Based on primary survey of eight villages conducted in Ukhrul, Manipur (2002–04).

promise of cash generation and improved incomes, the absence of risk-spreading provisions make shifting cultivators apprehensive about change. The bitter experiences of farmers who have tried to transform to cash crops, the uncertainty of markets and unassured returns undermine the confidence on such options, making farmers hesitant in making the change. Volatile markets, unattractive prices and the exploitation at the hands of traders make shifting cultivators, particularly the poor, extremely wary of the high vulnerability that such transformation could entail. Moreover, the absence of returns from plantations during the initial transition years and the resultant inability to ensure food security make farmers reluctant to change. For shifting cultivators, replacement of the practice with cash crops, despite the promise of cash generation, implies the eradication of their risk management strategy and hence, signifies an increased vulnerability to food insecurity

Figure 3.2: The Diversity of Resources Annually Available to the Upland Farmer from Different Systems

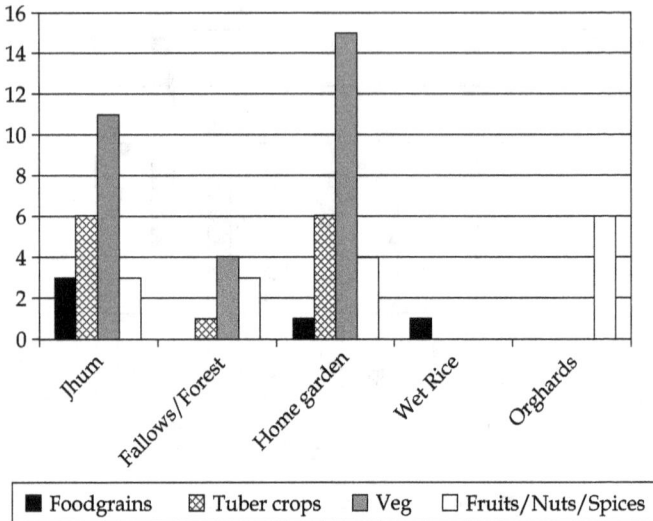

| Foodgrains | Tuber crops | Veg | Fruits/Nuts/Spices |

Source: Based on primary survey conducted in 30 villages across East and West Garo Hills, Ri Bhoi (Meghalaya), Karbi Anglong, (Assam), and Ukhrul (Manipur), 2010.

and poverty. This dilemma is the fundamental cause for the hesitancy among shifting cultivators to change.

ACCESS TO INFORMATION, BENEFITS AND EXTENSION

Notwithstanding the misgivings and concerns about increased vulnerability during transition, shifting cultivators realise that, in the long run, they have to transit to settled agriculture, particularly to cash crops. This, however, requires certain prerequisites — access to information about relevant schemes and programmes, access to the requisite subsidies and inputs as well as tenurial security, subsequently followed by the necessary extension and marketing support. Despite the hype on various programmes promoting transformation, information on modalities and eligibility for availing the benefits from such schemes does not seem to be universally accessible. Programmes designed to encourage transformations — such as the Watershed Management Programme for Shifting Cultivation areas — are not universally applicable and still remain confined to villagers in selected watersheds where the programme is under implementation, thus depriving others from the benefits of the programme. Most farmers opine a selective dissemination of both programmes and the related benefits, perceiving the benefits as going to the elite or well connected.

Cash crops being promoted by different departments — tea, coffee, rubber, cashewnut — require relatively larger land parcels and significant investments. Households wishing to adopt any of these crops require the necessary approval (and a no objection certificate) from the village authorities before they can embark on such plantations sponsored under government schemes. Although in theory it should not be difficult to get an approval, in practice, it is not uncommon to find that such approvals are given mostly to the elite, and the poor (and later migrants) are often left deprived. Without this approval, access to all benefits — subsidies, bank credit — are denied and hence, efforts by poorer households to adopt such cash crops are effectively nipped in the bud.

This bottleneck, however, has not prevented poorer households from adopting cash crops and they have done so by innovative choices of crops that allow reduction of external dependency. In practice, this is reflected in the rapidly increasing introduction of pineapple and arecanut into jhum fallows. The preference for these crops stems from the relatively higher degree of endogenous control possible in adopting both these crops. Adoption of pineapple or arecanut by farmers on their own initiative does not require obtaining prior approval for tenurial access to land from the traditional authority — the *nokma* and *maharis* in the context of Garo villages — as these crops can be grown in successive fallows or the home garden (locally known as *baganbari*). Propagules — areca saplings and pineapple suckers — are relatively easy to procure from other farmers. Information and knowledge on management of the crops are also available with peers and hence the dependency on external agencies — extension agents of the concerned departments — can be dispensed with. Moreover, marketing of such crops is relatively easy as traders and commission agents come to the villages in season. Above all, arecanut is a non-perishable crop and hence allows storage if required, thereby reducing the chances of exploitation by traders and their agents.

This universal access, however, shows a drastic departure in regard to wet rice terraces and it appears that a majority of the households are deprived of having access to this system (Table 3.2). A factor that contributes to this limited access is the attribute of terrain — the limited land suitability given the sloping topography — but given the demands on resources (both human and financial) required for conversion to terraces and valley bottom cultivation and the initial need for importing labour adept in wet rice cultivation, it is not surprising that a large majority of households remain unable to develop this farming system. It is fairly reasonable to assume that the latter would belong to the less well-to-do, particularly the poor and deprived.

LABOUR DEMANDS AND AVAILABILITY — IMPLICATIONS FOR AGRICULTURAL MANAGEMENT

With the increase in agricultural transformation in the uplands of northeast India, the incidence of households having multiple agricultural holdings is also growing. Almost all households have at least one production system in addition to their traditional shifting cultivation fields (Table 3.2). Not surprisingly, the demands on labour for management of the multiple systems have increased proportionately. Labour availability required for managing these systems, however, is woefully inadequate and the majority of households in the uplands find insufficient labour a major concern for managing agriculture (Choudhury et al. 2008). While an increasing proportion of the richer households engage wage labourers for agricultural work, a substantial proportion of upland households still cannot afford to engage wage labourers due to insufficient income, and continue to depend on household labour alone for managing their agricultural systems (Table 3.3).

Household labour availability for agricultural activities has progressively decreased with family members moving out of the village for education or wage-earning opportunities. Often, households are left with the very young, the aging and the women, or only the aging parents. Scarcity of able-bodied labour is becoming an issue in most villages as the young migrate to urban areas for education or to seek employment. With diversification of farming systems, particularly during transition from shifting cultivation into settled systems, demand on labour has become a serious issue affecting the management of the agricultural systems (Choudhury et al. 2008). For households that are in transition, diversification of the farming system has increased

Table 3.3: Labour Requirements, Availability and the Ability to Engage Labour

		% HH reporting			
Sl No.	Village	Insufficient labour	Engage labour	Cannot employ	Household labour only
1.	Chidoagre	64.5	32.0	38.00	29.50
2.	Tapra Alda	73.5	36.5	41.50	21.00
3.	Bolsagre	65.5	58.5	41.50	41.50
4.	Rongsep Adugre	71.0	52.5	25.00	23.00
5.	Adu Klangre	66.0	62.5	31.25	31.25
6.	Boldanngre	73.0	0	100.00	100.00

Source: Choudhury D., N. S. Jodha and E. Sharma. 2008. 'Policy Approaches in Management of Shifting Cultivation: Compromising Equitable Access, Food Security and Common Property Institutions', Paper presented at International Association for Studies of Commons Conference 'Governing Shared Resources: Connecting Local Experiences to Global Challenges', IASC Conference 2008, Gloucestershire, UK, p. 11.

the burden of agricultural workload. While this is true for both men and women, the increase in workload for women is spread throughout the year while that of the men seems more concentrated in one season. Women's workload has worsened with the increasing decline in productivity from shifting cultivation and inadequate returns from other systems. Declining productivity compounds the situation forcing the menfolk to migrate from the village for seasonal work in mines and other wage-earning opportunities. Of late, such migration — though seasonal — has left the burden of agricultural management on women whose workload has increased to levels where the poor and small families are forced to altogether give up agriculture and look for wage earnings as the sole livelihood option. Insufficient labour availability has obvious effects on the management and productivity of the farming systems, and diversification of agricultural systems in a scenario where labour availability is inadequate (or farmers unable to engage labour due to insufficient income) is a situation that requires serious examination and addressing. With diversification of production systems and the persistence of inadequate labour availability, management and a satisfactory productivity from all systems seems questionable. Although the rich and well-off can afford to engage wage labour, particularly for plantations, non-availability of able-bodied household labour limits the ability of the poor to take up plantation crops at a scale that is economically viable, sometimes totally restraining their choice for taking up alternative agricultural practices. This aspect seems to be completely overlooked by agencies promoting transformations and may prove to be counter-productive in the long run, unless the choice of crops is judiciously made and a focus on hardy and non-labour-intensive crops intensified.

ACCESS TO MARKETS: THE NEED FOR ORGANISED MARKETING

Alternatives to shifting cultivation centre around cash crop options whose markets are far away, mostly outside the region. For shifting cultivators, whose experience of markets and trading has, at best, been limited to the local weekly market, establishing market linkages for the cash crops with alien market agents and distant markets has been extremely demanding. A majority of the shifting cultivators who have taken up cash crop plantations have had to depend entirely on traders and commission agents coming to them to buy their produce. More often than not the experiences of the shifting cultivators in this respect has been extremely discouraging with the traders and commission agents frequently exploiting them and on some occasions even coercing them to distress sales. An issue in this regard, which has often been the cause of exploitative practices by the traders, is that of volume. For most of the shifting cultivators, the size of their plantations is, at best, small holdings. The volume of produce from such plantations, therefore, is not sufficient enough to attract traders unless several of the producers bulk their products to ensure a quantity attractive enough for the traders to procure at the farm gate. The absence of access to market information, particularly in regard to quality, demand and pricing has further accentuated their difficulties.

ACCESS TO CREDIT: THE NEED FOR A REAPPRAISAL OF CREDIT POLICY ISSUES

Transformations in agricultural land-use, particularly the establishment of horticulture, cash crop plantations and wet terraces has been fuelled with liberal doses of subsidies made available under various schemes and programmes of the government. With the completion of the project period, all subsidies available for the activities also cease. For farmers who see the benefits of the alternatives offered and desire to venture into such activities, adoption of the options has to be done with investments from their own resources as the concerned department can no longer offer the subsidies supporting such activities. For shifting cultivators, this is beyond their means as they have limited capacities for investments.

Although an option is to approach banks for a loan, the rarity of banking in rural uplands compounded with the unfamiliarity of banking systems and associated transaction norms, as well as the insensitive communication − alien languages, the inability to read and write and the often unhelpful attitude of the staff − makes the effort to even approach banks unattractive to the illiterate, marginalised shifting cultivator. Even if these hurdles are overcome, shifting cultivators cannot avail of this potential option as banks need a land title deed as a collateral against loans. Shifting cultivation is practised under common property regimes and hence, no land titling is available. The inability of shifting cultivators to produce a land title deed has deprived them from availing of any bank loans. Although a recent policy suggestion has been to initiate the land titling process as a solution to this issue, this will not be feasible in the near future given the complications of such an initiative in the context of common property regimes and the lack of understanding on tenurial frameworks within the latter. This is further aggravated by the absence of any cadastral survey in the uplands. An easier solution, perhaps, is to modify the policy to accept institutional guarantees in lieu of land title deeds, in which case the necessary guarantees could be provided by the village council or similar traditional institutions. Till the issue of access to credit in the context of common property situations − the absence of land titles such as that of shifting cultivators − is addressed and suitable policy changes brought about in regard to collaterals, wider acceptance of alternatives and the upscaling of transformations will not progress at desired rates, particularly for the benefit of the poor, frustrating both community aspirations as well as the government's objectives to bring about change.

Fostering an Inclusive Transformation: Facilitating Participation of the Poor and Disadvantaged

Despite government efforts and the aspiration of upland communities, transformation of shifting cultivation into settled agriculture in the uplands of northeast India still remains an elusive goal. It is quite obvious that to translate this goal into reality, transformation has to be inclusive and must ensure the participation and partnership of the entire community, particularly the poor, in the process of change. It is also equally clear that if the poor are to partner in this process, their concerns have to be given immediate and adequate attention and steps taken to enable their active participation. Although addressing the concerns of shifting cultivators requires action at multiple levels (as outlined in the previous section), the fundamental prerequisite is the need for an enabling policy environment, itself entailing reforms in the existing approach to managing shifting cultivation. An enabling policy environment, however, can only be possible when policy makers make a departure from existing approaches and show more empathy and sensitivity to the voices of the practitioners. To set the process in motion, a beginning could be made by addressing the following concerns.

Making Transformations Inclusive: Targeted Programmes

Although several centrally sponsored schemes are under implementation, few, if any, are tailored to address the inclusion of the poor. In addition, as pointed out earlier, most of these programmes continue to be implemented in selective areas leaving the majority of shifting cultivators out of the purview of such schemes. Further, none of the programmes have an exclusive focus on the poor. Consequently, the poor and disadvantaged among the shifting cultivators are deprived of the benefits of such schemes. It is necessary, therefore, to design programmes that exclusively target the poor and the disadvantaged — such an approach would be a critical step in fostering the partnership of the poor in agricultural transformation of shifting cultivation areas.

Incorporating Multi-cropping and Risk Insurance in Upland Agricultural Intensification

Alternatives to shifting cultivation promoted through government programmes encourage the establishment of wet rice cultivation and cash crop plantations. These alternatives are aimed to completely replace shifting cultivation, but by design, do not accommodate the mixed cropping characteristic of shifting cultivation systems. The inability to incorporate mixed cropping deprives the shifting cultivators of sequential harvesting — hence food availability throughout the year — and the accompanying risk spreading that is inherent in the traditional practice. Alternatives to shifting cultivation promoted by government programmes overlook this fundamental attribute and offer options that encourage monocultures. Not surprisingly, shifting cultivators are reluctant to adopt such alternatives.

There is a need for flexibility within the programmes encouraging transformation to allow for diversification of crops with the possibility of sequential harvesting. This would contribute substantially to removing the hesitation for transformation presently shown by farmers. An innovative approach to address this issue has been practised by villagers in Chandigre, West Garo Hills. Chandigre villagers established extended home gardens around their homesteads, incorporating many of the crops found in the shifting cultivation fields together with cash crops such as oranges, tea and coffee (Roy and Choudhury, unpublished). This innovation allowed them to take advantage of government programmes encouraging cash crop plantations while continuing with the traditional practice of mixed cropping and sequential harvesting, but in home gardens. The extended home gardens provided Chandigre villagers with a land-use option that allowed the blending in of traditional practices with the new. Building on this innovation, the North Eastern Region Community Resource Management Project (NERCORMP), a joint project of the government of India and International Fund for Agricultural Development (IFAD), promoted the concept of home gardens across six districts of the region. The success of this innovative approach is evident from the fact that home gardens have become one of the best interventions of NERCORMP and are common throughout the project villages. The experience of Chandigre and of NERCORMP suggests that given the flexibility of crop choices and of opportunities to blend traditional practices, most of the reservations held by shifting cultivators towards transformations can be overcome and thereby, the transformation process made more inclusive. This flexibility in regard to crop choices and land-use needs to be incorporated within programmes designed to address management of shifting cultivation.

Making the Right Choice: The Need for Reorienting Perceptions on Products from Shifting Cultivation and Encouraging Product Promotion and Marketing

Crops in shifting cultivation were normally cultivated for subsistence needs; however, even in the undistorted traditional practice certain crops from shifting cultivation did have a market value — maize, sesame, vegetables, cotton, spices, and certain tuber crops. With the commodification of shifting cultivation, one of the major commodity crops cultivated in the system is ginger. Although ginger is an important commodity crop for most upland areas, there is no recognition of this crop being a product from shifting cultivation or of its *de facto* organic nature. This perception needs to be changed and efforts need to be taken to capitalise on the organic nature of ginger from shifting cultivation fields and promote it as such.

Vegetables from shifting cultivation have a high demand in the local markets and in certain urban areas in the region, thriving markets have developed in recent years specifically trading such products. These products are highly sought after not only for their cultural and culinary values, but are also deemed to be healthy, organic and highly nutritional, thus attracting a premium price often substantially higher than the prices of vegetables imported from the plains. Fallow products — particularly non-timber forest products and wild edibles — have a ready market that is evident from the interest shown by traders from both within and outside the region (and the flourishing trade in many of the produces from fallows). Such products — NTFPs such as bay leaves, cinnamon, broomgrass and bamboo as well as wild edibles such as banana inflorescence, bamboo shoots, mushrooms and wild fruits — are specific to regenerating fallows with an apparently healthy market demand and can potentially offer a comparative advantage for the upland producers. Products from the shifting cultivation — whether crops or from the fallows — are seemingly competitive and can potentially give a comparative edge, unlike the cash crops under promotion. Shifting cultivators therefore, find it difficult to understand why governments do not promote such local products instead of focusing on exotics that are alien to the region and decisively uncompetitive. Shifting cultivators strongly feel that rather than promoting exotic cash crops, government departments should support them in developing markets for the products from their fields and fallows and thus help them exploit the comparative advantage inherent to such products.

TRANSFORMATIONS AND CHANGES IN PROPERTY REGIMES: IMPLICATIONS FOR TENURIAL ACCESS AND SECURITY

Conversion of arable land for wet rice cultivation and cash crop plantations is invariably at the expense of shifting cultivation fallows. As fallows are converted to plantations, such lands become *de facto* privatised. Customary laws allow tenurial rights to community land as long as such land is under cultivation, and reverts back to the common resource pool only if the family declines or is unable to use it and keeps the land unattended for more than a certain period. Plantations established on fallows (which in effect, are community land), thus reduce the total area available for use under a common property regime. Similarly, when rice terraces are established, community rights cease to exist over the land as long as such lands are cultivated. As in the case of plantations, customary laws allow the family tenurial rights as long as the land is under cultivation and therefore, such lands also transform from common property to *de facto* private holdings. Moreover, in the case of terraces, legal provisions under different state legislations provide for the registration and titling of such land. Households holding terraces can get the land registered in their name and attain the right of legal ownership even though the parcel of land was originally a common property. This registration and titling legally changes property rights completely, allowing the owner, if they so desire, to even sell the land to which hitherto, they had only tenurial rights. The provisions under customary laws, buttressed by legal provisions have helped in the conversion of common property to private property. In fact, in some areas of the region, this issue has become so acute that annual access to wet terraces is auctioned to the highest bidder by the new owners, thus effectively depriving the poor from having access to terraces for cultivation.

The promotion of plantations and wet rice cultivation, particularly terraces, has thus not only deprived the poor of opportunities for access to such land, it has also deprived them their endowments, marginalising their shifting cultivation by reducing the land left for the practice and in the process, reducing fallow periods, thereby, ultimately impacting on the productivity and returns from their fields. The poor, therefore, view transformations as a process that increasingly marginalises their cultivation practice and productivity from their fields, thus depriving them of their entitlements for equitable access to productive land and a livelihood. Among matrilineal societies such as the Khasis and Garos of Meghalaya, such trends may also signify the possibility of dispossessment of land assets by women in the not too distant future. As transformations progress and more common property resources get transformed into *de facto* private holdings, the proportion of the deprived will increase, giving rise to a growing proportion of 'tomorrows' poor'.

This trend requires immediate attention and needs to be arrested. Shifting cultivators, particularly the poor, acutely express the need for addressing this issue. Customary norms for access to land ensured universal access to all households within a village. Government programmes promoting settled agricultural practices need to modify guidelines to ensure that access regimes are not changed drastically as a result of such programmes. It is necessary to encourage land zoning within target villages so that (*i*) uncontrolled conversion of fallows to cash crop plantations or wet terraces is regulated, (thereby also ensuring regeneration of fallow forests), and (*ii*) the benefits of such programmes are made more inclusive. This requires an understanding of prevailing customary access regimes and efforts to suitably modify guidelines of programmes so that interventions made are within existing customary land tenure frameworks, thereby ensuring the continuity of universal access by all and hence facilitating the inclusion of the poor in programmes designed to make possible transformations.

Conclusions

The findings of the present study as well as earlier studies conducted in the region (Choudhury and Sundriyal 2003; Choudhury et al. 2003; Choudhury 2006; Roy and Choudhury unpublished) seem to indicate that upland communities have been responding to the needs for change without compromising on common property access regimes. Innovations based on traditional tenurial access frameworks that ensure long-term tenurial security but safeguard ownership patterns, by preventing ownership transfer rights address the needs for transformations without encouraging privatisation. Government policies and approaches need to understand, acknowledge and honour such frameworks. The desire of governments for agricultural change and economic development is shared equally by upland communities; the difference lies in the introduction of such initiatives within traditional land-use and access frameworks as against those of replacement.

Notes

* This essay is based on several years of research on the subject by the author. During the course of these studies, several organisations and individuals have provided support in various forms that have contributed to the understanding of the issue. The author would like to particularly express his gratitude to the villagers in different locations who have shared their time and insights and to the district authorities who provided support, information and access to relevant documents. Logistic support from district teams of NERCORMP and MRDS is gratefully acknowledged.

1. The study was jointly supported by the IFAD Technical Assistance Grant (TAG) at International Centre for Integrated Mountain Development (ICIMOD) and a National Science Foundation grant to Prof. Piers Blaikie and Joshua Muldavin, visiting scientist, ICIMOD.
2. The rapid appraisal was conducted in January–February, 2009 and covered the villages of Warima Chokela in South Garo Hills, Matchurigre and Bikonggre in West Garo Hills, Samanda Chinemgre in East Garo Hills and Mawthawtieng, Tyniar and Warwar in East Khasi Hills.

References

Choudhury, D. 2006. 'Equitable Resource Access under Shifting Cultivation Systems in North East India', in ANGOC and ILC, *Enhancing Access of the Poor to Land and Common Prpoerty Resources: A Resource Book*. Quezon City, Philippines: Asian NGO Coalition for Agrarian Reform and Rural Development (ANGOC), and Rome: The International Land Coalition (ILC), pp. 200–3.

Choudhury, D. and R. Sundriyal. 2003. 'Issues and Options for Improving Livelihoods of Marginal Farmers in Shifting Cultivation Areas of Northeast India', *Outlook in Agriculture*, 32(1): 17–28.

Choudhury, D., D. Ingty and S. Jamir. 2003. 'Managing Marginalisation in Shifting Cultivation Areas of Northeast India: Community Innovations and Initiatives', in Tang Ya and Pradeep M. Tulachan (eds), *Mountain Agriculture in the Hindu Kush Himalayan Region. Proceedings of an International Symposium*. Kathmandu: ICIMOD, pp. 207–12.

Choudhury D., N. S. Jodha and E. Sharma. 2008. 'Policy Approaches in Management of Shifting Cultivation: Compromising Equitable Access, Food Security and Common Property Institutions', Paper presented at International Association for Studies of Commons Conference 'Governing Shared Resources: Connecting Local Experiences to Global Challenges', IASC Conference 2008, Gloucestershire, UK.

Leduc, B. and D. Choudhury. Forthcoming. 'Agricultural Transformations in Shifting Cultivation Areas of Northeast India: Implications for Land Management, Gender and Institutions', in Dev Nathan and Virginius Xaxa (eds), *Social Exclusion and Adverse Inclusion: From Deprivation to Development of Adivasis in India*. New Delhi: Oxford University Press.

Roy, Sangeeta and D. Choudhury unpublished. 'Community Responses to Increasing Marginalisation in Shifting Cultivation: Intensification of Homegardens in Chandigre, West Garo Hills, Meghalaya'. Results of a research study done by NERCORMP, and submitted as a case study for Documenting Farmer's Innovations in Shifting Cultivation, an initiative commissioned by ICIMOD (2003).

4

A Dying Lake: Food Security versus 'Development' — Loktak, Manipur*

THINGNAM ANJULIKA SAMOM

The Lore of Loktak

In the shadows of your footsteps
Many lives exist
On your nature's bounty
Many lives lean
O, beloved mother Loktak
O, beloved mother Loktak . . .
(from Ranbir Thouna's song, *Loktak*)

It might seem rather ironic that a lake that has inspired so many songs and paeans over the centuries should now need songs championing its survival. But Loktak, the largest freshwater lake in northeast India, needs as many champions as it can get if it is to survive, let alone regain its glory. This is where Ranbir Thouna, leading Manipuri singer, composer and ad filmmaker, steps in. From organising concerts and a cycle rally to releasing an album and booklet on the lake, Thouna has been campaigning for the protection of the lake. The musical campaign 'Save Loktak, Our Life' is reminiscent of A. R. Rahman's efforts to save the Taj Mahal. 'I grew up on the banks of Loktak, dependent on it for our vegetables, fish and survival,' he said, adding, 'It is so much part of our history and culture.'

Eighty-one-year-old Maisnam Ningol Ibemhal's life is linked to Loktak in a different way. Though a resident of Singjamei area in Imphal West district, Ibemhal and her family had sought refuge in Thanga during the Second World War, known here as the Japan War. Despite being warned against it after the diagnosis of a heart ailment three months ago, she is adamant about making the 50 km trip to Thanga island from Manipur's capital city of Imphal. 'I must see Thanga, the place which gave us refuge; I want to see if the friends I played with are still there. But above all I want to see the sparkling waters of Loktak from the Thanga hills,' she whispers. As an 11-year-old, she would climb to the Thanga hill to watch the Japanese and RAF bombings of the state. Returning to the Thanga hills and the Loktak after seven decades, Ibemhal eagerly asks our hosts about the people she used to know. Most of them are no longer alive. The *mandap* or religious community hall attached to a temple, where her family was housed as war refugees too wasn't there anymore.

The lake has undergone drastic changes, especially in the last three decades. 'The water used to stretch for miles into the horizon glinting in the sunlight like a giant mirror,' Ibemhal sighs nostalgically, gazing at the green *phumdis* (floating biomass) dotting the lake. It is not only the geographical topography of the lake that has changed in the last few decades. According to environmentalist Kh Shamungou, the lake is also beset by increasing pollution, siltation, rapid proliferation of *phumdis* and the commissioning of the Loktak hydel project in the 1980s. Seventy years ago, when Ibemhal was a child, Loktak Lake was already the keeper of tales and history in Manipur. Said to be formed in times when humankind and the gods frolicked and intrigued together, Loktak Lake has been a reservoir of myths, legends, romances and paeans. The timeless romance of Khamba and Thoibi was interwoven with Loktak Lake, while many of the scenes in Meitei folklore and legends were played out on the shores of the lake.

Located between 24°25′ to 24°42′N latitude and 93°46′ to 93°55′E, the 300 sq km lake is spread over three districts in the valley — Imphal West, Bisnupur and Thoubal. Around 132 plant species found in the lake are used as food, fuel, fodder and medicine. The 54 fish species found here feed the fish-loving people of the state. Besides being the source of livelihood for hundreds of people, Loktak also houses the floating national park Keibul Lamjao, the only home in the world to the endangered Sangai deer.

The Loktak is not only the largest freshwater lake in the northeast but also the largest lake in the Manipur river basin, covering 61 per cent of the total identified wetlands of Manipur. In reality, it comprises about 20 small and large lakes including Loktak,

Takmu, Ungamen, Laphupat, Thammumacha, Khulak, Yena, Sana pat, Utra pat, and Tharopokpi. This topography becomes quite distinct during the lean season. During the monsoons, the lakes are meshed together in a contiguous water body. The parting of the lakes has, however, become another legend connected to Loktak waters. In 1983, the Loktak hydropower project on the Manipur or Imphal river, with the Loktak Lake forming the headwaters to provide regulated storage for power generation, was built. It was a multipurpose project with power generation of 105 MW for power supply to Manipur, Nagaland, Assam, Mizoram, Arunachal Pradesh, Meghalaya and Tripura, and lift irrigation to 23,000 ha (57,000 acres) in the Manipur valley. The project is under the National Hydroelectric Power Corporation (NHPC) Ltd. A major component of the project is the 10.7 m high and 58.8 m long Ithai barrage constructed at the confluence of the Manipur river, the Khuga river and the Ungamel channel near Ithai village, south of Loktak. The water level at the Ithai barrage is maintained throughout the year at 786.5 m to provide adequate supply for the hydro project.

However, this has meant that the lake water is at a permanent high level, not only submerging the identity of the Loktak Lake and the smaller lakes but also changing the hydrological regime, ecosystem and life culture of the people living in and around the lakes.

The Trade-off between Food Security and 'Development'

'The power situation is better now, so are the roads. But today, in Toubul, there are only a few families who do not buy rice from the market,' points out 58-year-old Thoudam Gyaneshor of Manipur's Toubul village. Toubul, with a population of around 4,044, according to the 2001 census, located in Bishnupur district, 34 km from the state capital Imphal, has been one of the worst casualties of the Loktak hydropower project and its constituent Ithai barrage. A case filed by the Loktak Lake Affected Areas Peoples' Action Committee in the Guwahati High Court, Imphal Bench, states that an estimated 80,000 ha of arable land have been destroyed in the subsequent inundation and frequent flash floods that occur through the year. Gyaneshor lost 3 ha of agricultural land to Loktak after the project was commissioned in 1983. It was the same for most families in Toubul. The loss is significant, since Toubul was once known for its production of *taothabi*, a variety of rice grown on wetlands. 'At one time (the people of) Toubul had no dearth of rice in their homes. But after the barrage came, almost every house is compelled to buy rice from the market for consumption,' says Gyaneshor.

Sixty-four-year-old Soraisam Kola used to feed her family of 20 with rice grown on her 1.5 ha of agricultural land. 'The produce was so good that even after we ate and sold some there would be so much left over from each season that some of the rice would eventually get mouldy,' she recalls. Now, she buys rice at Rs 26 a kilo! Oar on her shoulders, as she prepares to go down to the lake for her afternoon fishing trip on Loktak, she says: 'Loktak ate my fields, it ate my cows too now that the fields are no longer there . . . Loktak ate everything.'

Gyaneshor used to harvest 200 phoubot of rice annually from his fields (phoubot is a local measurement amounting to around 50 kg). He would sell around half the harvest, leaving the rest for his family to use. 'I was not rich by rich men's standards, but I was not poor either. I had rice and there was fish from the lake and vegetables from the kitchen garden. There wasn't much I lacked,' he recalls. After losing his agricultural lands, Gyaneshor was forced to convert part of his fields into a fish pond. But not without apprehension: water from the lake often spills into the ponds during the monsoons, carrying away most of the fish. If the floodwaters spare him, he earns around ₹40,000–50,000 annually. 'It is my land and I have to put it to some use, no matter how much I gain or lose,' he says.

Gyaneshor's neighbour, 70-year-old Keisham Brajamani, continues to pay revenue tax for his 1.5-ha field that now lies 'about two men's height' under water. 'If we don't pay, it will become khaasland/wasteland and be lost to us,' he says. Behind his statement is the hope that one day the water will dry up and he will be able to sow paddy again. Brajamani, who used to harvest around 100 sacks of rice annually from his own fields, now farms 1 ha of land on lease. He invests both manual labour and money and gets around 30–40 phoubot of rice; the owner gets around 20 phoubot after each harvest.

Both sides of the 0.5 km stretch of road leading from Toubul market to the banks of Loktak Lake are testimony to how proponents of the Loktak hydropower project failed to take into account the project's effect on the lake's ecosystem and the people and wildlife whose lives are inextricably linked to the lake. What used to be paddy fields have been converted into strips of fish ponds framed by eucalyptus trees on one side and the huge sheet of vegetation-covered water that is the lake on the other.

Considered the lifeline of the people of Manipur, Loktak Lake plays an important role in the socio-economic and cultural life of the state. Around 12 per cent of Manipur's population are directly dependent on the lake for their livelihood. Much of the rest of the population, especially people living in the valley area, depend on the lake's fish and vegetation resources for their nutrition and economic security. Overall, 132 plant and 54 fish species have been identified in the lake. While fish forms a major part of the local cuisine and socio-religious practices of the people, especially the majority Meitei community, plant resources are used as food, fodder, fuel, thatching, fence material, medicines, raw material for handicrafts, and for religious and cultural purposes.

When the 105 MW Loktak hydropower project was first commissioned in 1983, it was in the hope that the project would rapidly usher in an era of industrial, commercial and agricultural prosperity in the otherwise backward state. But the question being asked today is whether the disadvantages outweigh the advantages.

Depleting Resources and Impact on Livelihood

'Earlier, during the winter, when water was low, we would grow paddy and vegetables in the water floor left behind by the retreating lake. So, we had our rice, our own vegetables and fish. Now that there is no seasonal fluctuation in the water level, we buy everything except fish from the mainland,' says 62-year-old Heisnam Sajou of Thanga village. Fish is an important part of the local cuisine in the northeastern state of Manipur, especially for the majority Meitei Hindu community inhabiting the valley. The annual demand for fish in the state is around 25,000 metric tonnes. Most of it comes from Loktak Lake. Fish is not only an important source of protein, it's an inextricable part of indigenous religion and cultural practices. The *ipan thaba* ceremony of the Meiteis, usually conducted on the sixth day of the birth of a child, involves as many as seven fish varieties. *Nga thaba*, which is the release of *ngamu* or *murrel* into a pond, is an important religious rite performed as part of the marriage ceremony. Friends and relatives usually visit the sick with live fish.

Fishery is a vital economic resource in Manipur, contributing approximately 3 per cent to the state's gross domestic product. Both men and women fish; the women use dip nets to catch smaller varieties. The processing and selling of fish is usually done by women. According to the *Economic Survey of Manipur 2009–2010* report (Government of Manipur 2010), fish production in the state for the year 2007–08 was estimated at 18.65 thousand tonnes, as against 18.53 thousand tonnes in 2006–07. The total fish requirement far exceeds indigenous production, therefore large quantities of fish are imported to fill the gap.

Hailing from Sekmaijin Awang Leikai village in Thoubal district, 44-year-old Sorokhaibam Tampak is one of thousands of *unjha* (as local women fish traders are known here) dependent on fish from Loktak and other wetlands in Manipur for their livelihood. She has lived all her life by the banks of Loktak. As a young girl she and her friends would gather aquatic vegetables that grew in the lake for consumption at home. Tampak now supplements her husband Ibopishak's income by selling fish. She makes around ₹200–300 on a lean day, ₹700–800 on a good day. 'Earlier, it was easy to sell two or three *maunds* (one *maund* is 40 kg) of fish in a day. Now it is becoming increasingly difficult to sell fish due to rising prices. Also, the fish catch in Loktak is dwindling rapidly', she says.

The *Loktak Atlas*, co-published by Wetlands International, Loktak Development Authority and India Canada Environment Facility (ICEF), in 2004, reports that at the time of the joint study the fish catch from Loktak accounted for merely 11 per cent of the total fish production in Manipur (Trisal and Manihar 2004). Prior to the 1950s, the lake contributed 60 per cent of total fish production, of which migratory fish from the Chindwin-Irrawady river system contributed 40 per cent of total capture fishery. As many as 54 fish species representing 17 families are found in the lake. 'Loktak is a goldmine. If you go to Loktak you will never come back empty-handed. There's fuel, fish, vegetables . . . even if you just pick tharoi it will become your curry for the night. There's nothing you don't get from Loktak', Tampak insists, heaping escargots into the empty *rasgulla* tin that serves as her measuring cup.

Another popular produce from Loktak Lake is *heikak* whose leaves, stem, roots, and fruits are eaten as a vegetable by local people. For children, heikak has been a nutritious snack for generations. 'When we were younger, my uncle used to bring us sackfuls of heikak, and we would spend hours eating it. Sometimes, my mother would cook heikak with a little bit of rice', says Tombi, whose mother is from Moirang in Bishnupur district, on the banks of the Loktak. But heikak is more than just a snack. 'During the floods of 1966, even during times of food scarcity, many people, especially those from lower economic backgrounds, would come to buy heikak as they could not afford rice', says 62-year-old Heisnam Sajou of Thanga village in Bishnupur district, around 50 km from Manipur's capital city Imphal. Heikak fruit cooked with a little bit of cereal produces enough food to replace the staple diet of the state, rice.

However, both fish and heikak are slowly disappearing from Loktak Lake. 'When we were young children following our father on his fishing trips, what struck us was the mass of heikak stems and fruit in the water that would make rowing almost impossible. Nowadays you don't see them in Loktak; they are bred artificially in farms', says Ramananda. Hailing from Ningthoukhong area in Bishnupur district, Ramananda uses gill nets to fish in Loktak Lake. Water levels in the lake used to rise during the monsoons and recede in winter, allowing the lakeshore inhabitants to use the lake bed for agricultural purposes. The receding waters also allowed heikak seeds to germinate and take root. 'After the Ithai barrage was built and the hydroelectric project started running, the lake water level is always high. So, the germination and growth of heikak plants is reduced. Many fish variety have also disappeared', says Sajou. Loktak Lake used to serve as a breeding and spawning ground for pengba and other migratory fish from the Chindwin-Irrawady river system. However, the Ithai barrage has blocked the migratory pathways of these fish causing a decline in their population and ultimately their disappearance from the state. Both government and individual fish farmers have been trying to revive pengba populations in fish farms in the last few years.

Fish and heikak are not the only produce from Loktak that forms part of the local food economy of Manipur. Overall, 132 plant species have been identified from various parts of the lake. Some of these, including komprek, kolammni, thangjing, ishing kundo, ishing ikaithabi and tharo are not only eaten as vegetables but are also used for medicinal purposes. All 53 settlements in and around Loktak, located in the valley districts of Bishnupur, Imphal East and Thoubal, are directly or indirectly linked to the lake. The total population of these communities in 2001 was 279,935, accounting for 12 per cent of Manipur's total population. According to the *Loktak Atlas*, 33 per cent of lakeshore households harvest aquatic vegetation for use as fuel, 18 per cent for use as vegetables, 2 per cent for use as fodder, and 1 per cent to manufacture handicrafts. Annually, 15,400 MT of plant biomass is harvested for use as fuel, 1,900 MT for use as vegetables, 230 MT for use as fodder, and 40 MT to make handicrafts.

From Owners to 'Occupiers'

Forty-year-old Salam Tamu and her husband Sobha cook, eat, sleep, and dry fish on the roughly 250–300 sq ft of floating biomass, locally known as phumdis, on Loktak Lake. In the evenings, she smokes some of the smaller fish she had caught during the day using her dip net. Her husband goes out fishing most of the day, starting with the first harvest from the trap cages at dawn. Tamu rows out early in the morning in their canoe with the first harvest and the smoked fish to sell in the nearest market. Tamu and Sobha originally hail from Arong Nongmaikhong, in Manipur's Thoubal district, around 52 km from the state capital Imphal. Ten years ago when she first started living on her phumdi hut, she would look at the distant lights on the mainland. 'I would cry, missing my family and neighbours there. Now whenever I go there, I am unable to stay there long. This hut in the middle of the water is more than a source of income, it is my home now', she says.

According to reports by the government implementing agency, Loktak Development Authority (LDA), a census conducted among phum hut-dwellers in 2001 recorded a population of 1,977 fisherfolk living in a total of 733 phum huts. Among them, 84 per cent are permanent dwellers who do not have a house on the mainland. Around 8 per cent, like Tamu, are temporary dwellers who have a house on the mainland where their families live. The rest are migrant fishermen who visit the phums only during the fishing season. 'This is how we have survived for so many years', she says. Her only son, Chaoba, stayed behind with her in-laws in Arong Nongmaikhong to study at the nearby school. About a month ago, he got a job with a security agency. With almost 650,000 educated unemployed looking for jobs there was little scope for Tamu and her husband, who was barely literate, to find proper earning avenues in either the organised or the unorganised sectors. The situation is compounded by the fact that, apart from government jobs, there are very few opportunities in industry or private organisations in Manipur.

Tamu's neighbour on the lake, 39-year-old Ayingbi, also left three of her children behind at her in-laws in Thongam Mondum when she moved with her husband Herachandra and youngest child, four-year-old Thoibi, to eke out a living on Loktak Lake. As Ayingbi and her husband had earlier fished at Pumlen pat, another lake located in the Thoubal-Bishnupur district border area, they were used to the hard work. However, staying on a hut built on a floating island of vegetation in the middle of the lake was a new experience. 'When we were working at Pumlen we could return home in the evening and be with our children. But when our expenses rose with the children's education and rising price of essential commodities, whatever we earned was not enough. We heard that earnings were good on Loktak, so we came here last winter', she says. Life in the floating huts is not idyllic, even if the setting is. Dwindling fish stocks and increasing competition mean that profits depend on how much one can invest. 'For us poor people, even ₹10,000 is a huge sum. But for those investing ₹30,000–40,000 on nets alone, earning ₹1,000 a day is no big deal. We have to make do with ₹100–200', says Tamu. Added to that is having to buy all the essential commodities from the mainland. 'Fish and water are the only freely available items', says Ayingbi, adding, 'but now we have to be careful about the water too'. The water in the lake is becoming increasingly polluted due to the inflow of water from rivers like the Nambul and Nambol that flow through urbanised sectors of the state. Also, the phumdis have no sanitation or drainage system — everything goes straight into the lake. Medical facilities and schools too are on the mainland.

Small children staying with their parents on the lake are confined to the 10 ft × 10 ft one-room huts where they sleep, cook, eat and process their fish. 'When we are at the market selling fish, our hearts are always unsettled thinking about our children back at the lake. Water surrounds them; there have been so many cases of young children drowning in the lake', says Ayingbi. Despite all the shortcomings, however, the lake is their guardian. 'Loktak is our mother. We are able to feed our children and run our family only because of her grace. Where else will we go', asks 27-year-old Salam Pramo of Nongmaikhong, in Thoubal district, who has been living in a phum hut for three years. Pramo and her husband Kabi chose Loktak over Ungamen Lake, located close to their home, because of the better fish catch and earnings.

But insecurity dogs them here too. Legislation passed by the state government, the Manipur Loktak Lake (Protection) Act 2006, defines 'persons who dwell in huts or houses on the phumdis or use the phumdis' as 'occupiers'. An important part of the Act which aims 'to provide for administration, control, protection, improvement, conservation and development of the natural environment of Loktak Lake and for matters connected with as incidental thereto', divides Loktak Lake into two zones — a core zone comprising 70.30 sq km, which is a 'no development zone', or 'totally protected zone', and a buffer zone of other areas of the lake excluding the core zone. A vital aspect of this division is the ban on building huts or houses on phumdis inside the lake, planting *athaphum*, or engaging in athaphum-fishing in the core area. Tamu, Pramo and Ayingbi's phum huts are located inside this core zone.

Fifty-six-year-old Ningthoujam Rakhon, general secretary of the All Loktak Lake Floating Hut-Dwellers Progressive Committee, maintains that the Act is a death knell for the nearly 10,000 people living in phumdi huts. 'We have no agricultural landholdings or homestead on the mainland. For generations we have been staying here. We do not know another way of life. Evicting us in this manner is the same as asking us to commit mass suicide', he says.

Rakhon lives with his family on Champu Khangpok, a phumdi village on Loktak Lake populated by around 1,500 people. 'My great great grandfather lived here, and those before him. How can we fish in the Loktak waters without having the safety of our huts? The high winds and rough weather could kill us anytime', he says. Interestingly, Champu Khangpok is on the state's 2001 census list. Also, many residents of the floating huts are said to be on the electoral lists.

Another aspect of the Act is that athaphum is the only phumdi formation recognised for compensation by the local and state authorities. In a memorandum submitted to Chief Minister Okram Ibobi in January this year, the All Loktak United Phumdao Koitha Owners Welfare Association (ALUPKOWA) requested that *phumdao* — a phumdi formation of between 3 acres and 20 acres in area — be left alone during the LDA's phumdi-removal programme on Loktak. 'There are around 250 households, amounting to more than 3,000 people, dependent on phumdao. They feed their children, educate them, and earn money for other expenses from the phumdao. If the government snatches away this lifeline, how will they live', asks Heisnam Brojen, general secretary of ALUPKOWA. He points out that since the phumdao are not anchored with stones, and stay afloat, they serve as clean-ing agents, crushing loose phumdi formations known as *phumjoi*. 'The government should leave these beneficial phum alone and concentrate on removing the phumjoi instead', he says.

With Chief Minister Ibobi stressing, in his Khongjom Day cele-bration speech on 23 April 2010, that there will be no let-up by the state government in its efforts to remove phumdis from the lake and evicting hut-dwellers, the people of Loktak will surely wit-ness a new cycle of dispossession, displacement and loss of live-lihood. Phumdi management has been an important part of the Loktak Development Authority's activities. It recently commis-sioned New Delhi-based K Pro Infra Works Private Ltd to clean up around 13.29 million cubic metres of phumdis from the lake in a joint venture with Progressive Construction Ltd (PCL) based in Hyderabad. The ₹224 crore–contract, scheduled to be completed in two years and three months, is progressing after its inaugura-tion by Manipur Chief Minister Okram Ibobi on 6 January 2009. The State Planning Commission has also sanctioned an amount of Rs 400 crore to clear the lake of phumdis. The move threat-ens the existence of around 10,000 phumdi hut-dwellers living on Loktak Lake who recently joined forces under the banner of the

All Loktak Lake Floating Hut-Dwellers Progressive Committee to oppose their displacement. 'We have submitted memorandums to the chief minister as well as local MLAs to review the move, but we are yet to hear from them', says Ningthoujam Rakhon, general secretary of the committee.

Scions of a Changing Lake

The smell of smoked fish permeated the air in the courtyard of 86-year-old Heisnam Manik, seated on a reed mat in his front verandah located in Thanga Heisnam village in Bishnupur district on the southern banks of Loktak Lake, around 50 km from the state capital, Imphal. In a corner of the ramshackle outhouse piled with trap cages locally known as lû, his daughter-in-law, 60-year-old Keinahal pokes at the fire and gently turns rows of *ngapai* fish on mesh wires above the fire. Her husband, 61-year-old Momon and eldest son Mangoljaoba squat nearby dexterously weaving bamboo slivers to form the cages that will trap the fish.

Thanga is one of three prominent hills in the southern part of Loktak Lake, with a population of around 13,085 according to the 2001 census. Around 95 per cent of the population are fisherfolk. Manik launched into his tales: 'In my time, the fishing traps would be full every day. Once I could not lift one of my traps and had to seek help. When I counted my catch there were 218 *nga samjet* in just that one trap! If you think I am lying, I'm willing to swear by Goddess Loktak Ereima. Such was the catch then; now it is not so anymore.' Momon and Mangoljaoba agree that the fish harvest from this largest freshwater lake in Manipur, indeed the whole of northeast India, is dwindling rapidly. Both catch around ₹300–500 worth of fish a day, working on the five phumdao they have between them. 'Last year, I earned ₹15,000 in a day. But this is very rare', Momon explains.

It's not just the quantity of fish in Loktak that has declined, but also the system and techniques of fishing. 'Thingom pat, Thingei pat, Loktak pat . . . we'd go to these lakes and fish as we wished. We just had to give around ₹20–50 as tax to the *pat chaba*', Manik recalls. The *pat chaba* was both a post and system under which the king would demarcate certain areas of the many lakes in the state and auction them off on lease for a year. The person who won the bid became the *pat chaba* for the said time period and lake area. In turn, he would let the local fisherfolk fish in the area for a daily rental.

Sixty-three-year-old Heisnam Sajou, another Thanga resident, recalls the practice. 'There was one person from Thanga Salam village whom we addressed as Pebet Ningthou. He was the *pat chaba* of this area during 1967–76. After that the system collapsed.' He says, 'The *pat chaba* would, in turn, pay around ₹2,000–₹3,000 as tax to the government annually. The amount varied. Laishram Amuyaima was the *pat chaba* for Thingom pat area. He paid ₹1,500 every three years as revenue to the government. In turn, he took ₹5 from us.' Sajou was still in his early teens then, running errands for his father, a close friend of Amuyaima. The *pat chaba* system had the added benefit of preventing and resolving conflict. 'You could leave your tools behind without fearing that they would be stolen. If someone encroached on your fishing area, he would be there to mediate so that no conflict arose', he adds.

According to environmentalist Dr Kh Shamungou, the practice of leasing out common property existed not only in the lake but also in the hills. After the monarchy ended, the lake area began to be used by individuals or cooperative societies as farmland or for pisciculture. Ngangom Sanajaoba Meitei, project coordinator of the government implementing agency Loktak Development Authority, explains that the *pat chaba* system was a phenomenon practised during the lean or dry season when water in the lake was confined to pockets.

In the past, migratory fish from Chindwin river used to breed in Loktak lake supporting a large population of fishermen living in and around them. As the monsoon receded, local people would reclaim the shrinking wetlands for seasonal agriculture. Fluctuations in the water regime also allowed the phumdis to regenerate whilst maintaining the quality of water in the lake. However, with the commissioning of the Loktak hydropower project on the Manipur river, the fishing tradition and management of lake resources, which were once wholly dependent and synchronised with the natural seasonal cycles, have changed drastically over the last few decades. 'Loktak goddess always replenished the fish population. No matter how much (fish) we caught, they would never vanish. Now the catch is decreasing', says Manik.

An altered water regime, increasing competition among fishermen, indiscriminate fishing, and the use of sophisticated tools are believed to be factors behind the change. 'My father was there, then me, now my son also fishes in Loktak. So the (numbers of) fishermen are increasing but the fish are decreasing. We are just taking out; no one is putting in.'

'Earlier, we had just the cotton nets, dip nets and trap cages to fish. Now even the nylon nets come in so many varieties of length, breadth and interlock sizes that it is possible to catch anything from minnows to big fish in all seasons', Momon says. Momom has around three phumdaos of between 1 and 3 acres in size. The Ithai barrage has also blocked the migratory pathways of a number of fish species such as *khabak, pengba, ngaton, ngasep, ngaten,* and *sareng,* leading to a decline in their population and ultimate disappearance from the state.

'Ours is a riverine system. Replenishing fish in Loktak and restocking is very much supported by and dependent on the river. The ecosystem was able to sustain them at that time', says LDA Project Director Thokchom Ibobi. Set up by the government of Manipur in 1986 for overall improvement and management of Loktak Lake, the Loktak Development Authority (LDA) aims to check the deteriorating condition of the lake and bring about improvements in the lake ecosystem. It also looks after the development of Loktak and its surroundings, with regard to fisheries, agriculture, tourism and afforestation of catchment areas in collaboration with various departments.

Before the Loktak hydropower project and the Ithai barrage were commissioned, the phumdis in the lake were managed by the community. Every year, a common schedule was worked out wherein all communities were involved in deepening channels and cutting and sending phumdis down through the Khordak channel. In the lean season, when the phumdis were dry, they were burnt. In the post–Ithai barrage scenario, the natural process of cutting and sending phumdis down the channel stopped, leading to a proliferation of phumdi and rapid eutrophication of the lake.

Increasing monetary returns from athaphum fishing brought more people into the occupation, leading to competition amongst the fishermen, exploitation of fishery resources and a decrease in fish catch. An informal jurisdiction over the lake area has also emerged as individuals exercise rights over areas that are used to lay enclosures; others are allowed only after mutual consent. Phumdi management has therefore been an important part of the LDA's activities.

With the passing of the Manipur Loktak Lake (Protection) Act 2006, the LDA became a body constituted under the Act, empowered by it as the 'authority'. The new legislation aims 'to provide for administration, control, protection, improvement, conservation and development of the natural environment of Loktak Lake and for matters connected with as incidental thereto'. Over time, there has been a shift in the LDA's activities. In the early years, it identified problems in the lake area and carried out engineering projects like dredging heavily silted areas. Now, it attempts to address the causes of the problems and develop strategies for sustainable management of the lake through the Sustainable Development and Water Resources Management of Loktak Lake (SDWRML) Project, jointly initiated with Wetlands International South Asia (WISA) in 1997. The LDA has transformed from being an organisation largely engaged in sediment and phumdi management to one that undertakes comprehensive lake management from an ecological and socio-economic perspective, focusing on treating the causes rather than the symptoms of lake degradation.

As early as 2008, the Authority stressed that the conservation and management of Loktak mandates a strategic shift in water management, balancing human needs with the multiple values of the lake, and adopting a stakeholder-driven approach. It also pointed out that water-use within the Manipur river basin for ecological purposes (restoration of Keibul Lamjao National Park, improving water quality, restoration of natural fish recruitment, etc.) needs to be harmonised with human demands for hydropower, agriculture and domestic use. It proposed that a rationalised water-use plan should form the basis of the Ithai barrage and other upstream and downstream hydraulic structures to enable allocation of water for multiple purposes and yet maintain the multi-functionality of the wetlands.

However, it is well-known that the Loktak project has never been able to provide regular power supply even to villages on the periphery of Loktak; there are daily outages of around 16–18 hours in most parts of the state. Manipur gets a share of around 32.01 per cent of the project's power output; the rest is sold by NHPC to Nagaland, Assam, Mizoram, Arunachal Pradesh, Meghalaya, and Tripura. The multipurpose Loktak power station also provides lift irrigation to over 23,000 ha of land in the Manipur valley.

On top of that, there are the issues of compensation, rehabilitation and resettlement of people affected by the Loktak hydropower project. State Forest and Environment Minister Th Devendra Singh clarified in the Manipur legislative assembly on 15 July 2010 that matters relating to the omission of compensation, rehabilitation and resettlement at the time the MoU was signed between the state government and the NHPC were currently being monitored by the state government.

Delays in payment of compensation have added to the people's frustration. Twenty-two cases are still pending in the Guwahati High Court, Imphal Bench, registered by various farmer societies and committees. The Loktak Lake Affected Areas Peoples' Action Committee, which has around 6,000 members, filed a case for crop compensation in the Guwahati High Court, Imphal Bench, in 1994; the petitioners are still awaiting payment even though the court ruled in their favour a few years ago!

Conclusion

The win-win situation that the LDA envisages would involve not just the sincerity of stakeholders but also strong political will to effect changes and adjustments. The need of the hour is to harmonise using the waters of Loktak to fulfill human demands for food security, livelihood and hydropower, along with effective ecological management of the lake's resources.

It should also be noted that the Ithai barrage and the Loktak hydro power projects are not the only factors contributing to the pitiful condition of Loktak Lake. Urbanisation and siltation from catchment areas too have played significant roles.

According to the *Economic Survey of Manipur 2009–2010* (Government of Manipur 2010), Manipur ranks second among the northeastern states in respect of urbanisation. The urban population has increased from 506,000 in 1991 to 576,000 in 2001. However, the drainage and solid waste management system has remained fairly outdated and unorganised, leading to wastes leaching into the water bodies. The rivers Nambul and Nambol flowing through urban stretches of Imphal and Bishnupur, respectively, directly discharge pollutants, nutrient loads, and solid wastes especially plastics, into the Loktak Lake. According to the *State of the Environment Report* (Government of Manipur 2006) of the Manipur Environment and Ecology Department, the Nambul river (which passes through the heart of Imphal city), dumps 4.9 million tonnes of solid waste and 2,121 cu m of sewage into the lake every year. Run-off from agricultural fields has also contributed significantly to siltation in the Loktak and pollution in several water bodies. The *Economic Survey of Manipur, 2009–2010* (Government of Manipur 2010), notes that fertiliser consumption of the state was 67.40 thousand tonnes in 2007–09. All these factors have combined to transform Loktak from 'the lifeline of Manipur' to 'the sick man of Manipur'. However, even as environmentalists, government agencies and the general public try to address the issue of proper management and conservation of Loktak Lake and its associated wetlands, there seems to be no concerted effort between the different stakeholders including the people living on the periphery of the lake who are dependent on its resources for their livelihood.

'If Loktak dies, Manipur and its people will also be extinct. Therefore the *Save Loktak, Our Life* campaign is not just to save Loktak, but through it to reclaim our history and culture,' singer Ranbir Thouna sums up.

Note

* This essay draws upon research undertaken for Infochange (www. infochange.org) where it first appeared as a series of articles as part of the 2010 FES-Infochange Media Fellowships on common property resources.

References

Government of Manipur. 2006. *State of the Environment Report*. Imphal: Manipur Environment and Ecology Department, Government of Manipur.

Government of Manipur. 2010. *Economic Survey of Manipur 2009–2010*. Imphal: The Directorate of Economics & Statistics, Government of Manipur.

Trisal, C. L. and Th. Manihar. 2004. *The Atlas of Loktak Lake*. New Delhi: Wetlands International — South Asia Programme, and Imphal, Manipur: Loktak Development Authority.

5

Land, Environmental Degradation and Conflicts in Northeastern India*

WALTER FERNANDES

The environment is understood in the West and by the Indian urban middle class primarily as 'nature', while traditional communities, particularly those of the poor, view it as their livelihood. The concept of natural resource management differs according to this understanding. There are also differences in the extent of dependence on nature, and that can become the basis of a conflict. Moreover, the use and management of land is closely linked to the extent of dependence on, control over and understanding of one's livelihood. The formal legal system does not recognise the role of land and of other natural resources as the livelihood of the traditional communities. Thus the 'modern' worldview or philosophy on which the formal laws are based belongs to a culture that is different from that on which the traditional resource management system is based. The contradictory worldviews on land, land-use and management systems based on different worldviews, can result in conflicts.

This essay is an attempt to understand the culture around the land and natural resource management systems in India in general and in the northeast in particular and to study the conflicts that emanate from these differences. It is a bird's eye view of four cultures related to land and natural resources. The first two are traditional, that is, those of the tribal (indigenous) and caste-based communities of the past; then come the changes introduced by colonialism with its own interests and culture around land. The colonial legal system continues to be in force even today and has resulted in more changes and a new culture that shows the implications of this interaction between tradition and modernity.

The Stakeholders

To understand the role of land and of other natural resources in people's lives and the thinking behind their use and management, one has to first study the different stakeholders. This can also help one to understand the impact of land loss and of environmental degradation on various classes. The first stakeholder is the urban middle class for whom the environment is 'beautiful trees and tigers' or nature, to be protected, often from the communities that depend on it (Agarwal 1985: 54). Their understanding of land is that it is only a source of cultivation and construction, that is, an economic source of profit. On the other side are the rural poor and other traditional, particularly tribal (indigenous) communities, to whom land is the centre of their identity, economy and social systems and their very sustenance. The environment would then be an ecosystem with human communities at its centre. Because of the extent of their dependence on these resources some (e.g., Gadgil and Guha 1995: 33–35) call them 'ecosystem people' who have established a symbiotic relationship with the land and other environmental resources, and have for centuries managed these as renewable sustenance resources that had come down from their ancestors and have been preserved for posterity (Sachichidananda 2004: 98–102).

The basic principle of their resource management was equity, based mainly on community ownership or the common property resources (CPRs) that provide both tangible and intangible livelihood to their dependants. The CPRs include common grazing land, common land used for jhum (shifting or slash and burn) cultivation, forests that yielded non-timber forest produce such as edible fruits, leaves and vegetables, small timber and medicinal herbs (Bahuguna 2003: 471–76) as well as watersheds, rivulets, rivers, ponds and other community assets. Thus, in general, CPRs refer to resources which are used in common and are difficult to demarcate. Implicit in much of the discourse is their collective management. Thus the CPRs can be described as the resources on which a community sustains itself through equal usufruct rights. This right of being co-owners is conferred by some type of membership of the community or group such as a village or town. Its central purpose is the use, administration and sustenance of the resource that includes people's culture, economy, social systems and identity. Tribes have customary laws on their management, exploitation, protection and benefit-sharing (Ahmad 1998: 253). That culture has changed considerably during the last century because of the intervention of the remaining stakeholders, especially the third stakeholder, that is, the industrialists who treat these resources only as raw materials to manufacture goods for the middle-class consumer and for their own profit. Some call the industrial sector a lobby of miners of nature in general and of land in particular because they use these resources as raw materials with no concern for their renewal. The fourth stakeholders are the official agencies whose task is to control land, forests and other environmental resources and to manage these resources in a sustainable manner. But more often than not they function as the collaborators of industry and commerce in their search for higher profits (Guha and Gadgil 1996: 36–39).

Linked to this raw material orientation of the resources are the land and forest laws that facilitate their 'mining' by treating land only as a source of profit. That symbolises the difference of outlook or philosophy between the 'ecosystem' and the 'modern' communities. These systems are based on different land-use practices or 'varying activities executed by humans to exploit the landscape, such as hunting or ploughing. The land use pattern primarily determines the landscape pattern in areas where land use is intensifying' (Zonneveld 1993: 31). The principles or worldviews on which the land and resource management systems of these societies are based can be called their philosophy. This is what the next sections will explore.

The Traditional Tribal Culture of Land-use

As mentioned earlier, the traditional tribal systems are based on the concept of nature in general and land in particular as community sustenance that has come down from the ancestors and has to be preserved for posterity. Because of this close link between the identity of their community and land and other natural resources, they have for centuries managed the resources according to their unwritten customary laws that treat them as renewable. The community, which was the legitimising factor in their land-use and management systems, built a culture and an economy based on their sustainable use (Shimray 2006: 10–11). Land, in this system, was a resource which is an asset that is meant to be used according to need but not destroyed or exploited for profit.

The tribal traditions of land-use in India, in the northeast in particular, were based on a culture that had three main traits. The first is the sustainable or renewable use of their resources composed of forests, land and water sources that were also their sustenance. Basic to them being renewable were CPRs and community ownership. They did not reject individual ownership completely but combined it with community control. In the northeast, for example, some like the CPR-dependent Aka tribe of Arunachal Pradesh lacked the very concept of individual ownership and had only usufruct rights over the CPRs. In the jhum season every family cultivated as much land as it required for its sustenance. After the harvest or the three-year cycle that plot reverted to the community (Fernandes et al. 2007: 8–9). Others like the Angami of Nagaland combined individual rights with clan and village ownership but all of it was within a community ethos. A family managed its assets according to the tribe's community-based customary law (D'Souza 2001: 11–12).

In these as well as other tribes, the community included not merely the present but also the past and the future generations. That goes with the second feature of the resource being renewable, which too is linked to the community. The belief that guided the resource management for a renewable sustenance was that it had been handed over to them by their ancestors. It had, therefore, to be used according to present needs and environmental imperatives, and preserved for posterity (Sachichidananda 2004: 141–43). That belief itself emanated from the basic principle of sharing and intra- and inter-generational equity. Within each generation, their customary law ensured that every family had enough to eat according to its need. The Aka custom of land reverting to the community after using it for jhum is one example. Such control ensured that the resource was used according to need and preserved for posterity, thus, inter-generational equity (Fernandes et al. 2007: 38–39).

The third feature is the relatively high status of tribal women compared to that of women in caste societies. That too is true more of the northeast than of other regions. However, while attributing a relatively high status to them no tribe treated women as equal to men. The relatively high status too is based on CPR management. As long as the resource is community owned, women exercise partial control over it because of the gender-based division of power between the family and social spheres. In most tribes, the village council, made up of men alone controls the resource and political power. In most tribal traditions, the woman was in charge of the family and controlled its economy and production. The man represented the family in his society. In matrilineal tribes both descent and inheritance are through the woman but their tribe too is patriarchal and man controls society (Nogkynrih 2009).

The working of all these principles is visible in the tribal land ownership and management systems, especially in jhum cultivation on which some 25 per cent of the tribals in India as a whole and 90 per cent in the northeast sustain themselves (Roy Burman 1993: 176–77). Equity is seen in decision-making processes. Traditionally the village council decided which plot to cultivate in a given year, determined the amount of land to be allotted to each family according to the number of mouths to feed and decided which family with an excess of adults would assist which one with a deficit of workers. After this the man of the house chose the plot his family would cultivate and performed religious rites to mark the beginning of jhum. At this stage the woman took charge of cultivation and organised the work. As a result, the division of work was more gender friendly in jhum than in settled agriculture (Menon 1995: 101–2).

The technology used and the spacing of various crops ensured that land was preserved for the future generations. Jhum was practised on slopes of up to 20-degree gradient. To ensure soil preservation, no plough was allowed to be used on it. Only a hoe could be used. The crops planted were spaced. Before the rains began they sowed root crops that protected the soil on the slopes. They sowed paddy and other crops after the rains began. Weeding too was graded. Some weeds that could preserve soil were left behind. Because of spacing in sowing crops, food was available from October to March since harvesting was also spaced. After March summer fruits became available (Gangwar and Ramakrishnan 1992).

Individual Ownership and Settled Agriculture

Basic to the 'modern' or formal system is individual property. This system is closer to the caste society–based settled agriculture of the past than to the tribal jhum or other cultivation. The caste society did keep a community dimension but without equity that is basic to the CPR-based tribal sustenance. One caste owned the land in the village and the rest were service castes that rendered services as priests or barbers, agricultural workers and in other forms. In reality the leaders divided land between various families and each service caste family was attached to a family from the landowning caste. After the harvest the landowning family distributed grains to the service caste families, the quantity depending on its social status (Fernandes 1996: 141–43). There was similar discrimination in water management too. Men from the landowning caste controlled water and ensured equitable distribution among themselves with focus on irrigation for agriculture. So their water management system paid very little attention to subaltern needs or to drinking water that was the woman's domain (Sengupta 1991: 56–58).

But unlike in the tribal societies that maintain a separation between the family and society, in settled agriculture that is practised by the caste society, the man controls both the family and social spheres. He owns land, takes decisions on what crops to grow and determines the division of work. Men do work like ploughing that is considered difficult and allot to women tasks that involve standing in wet fields and bending for a long time (Fernandes and Pereira 2005: 74–77). In that sense its division of work comes nowhere near the tribal shifting cultivation system in which the woman has decision-making power because of her partial control over the CPRs. Because she is in charge of family production the division of labour in this system is somewhat gender-friendly.

However, there were some commonalities too and many differences between the caste-based and tribal systems. Both of them belonged to the informal society. But the caste-based system had some written documents particularly when a king gifted land to a community, a temple or an individual. But village land was managed by the caste that owned it, by and large based on the word of mouth. This caste can be called a community in a broad sense but it was not based on the sort of equity that governed tribal sustenance. Both the caste and the tribal land management systems accorded the central role of ownership to men but the former added the role of the caste and reflected the supremacy of the king who could gift land as he desired. That too negated the equity that the tribes practised. The caste-related system also had some systems of sharing the CPRs such as the water resources and grazing grounds that belonged to many families but this sharing was linked to agriculture, not to equity (Sengupta 1991: 59-61).

Gender equity is one more difference between these systems. As stated earlier, the tribal woman had a relatively high status. The man was in control of the resource and had social power while the woman was in charge of production. Since she controlled family production the division of work reflected some gender equity. Her control over the family economy turned her into an economic asset and provided the basis for her relatively high social status. In the caste-based societies, on the contrary, the man was in charge of the resource as well as of production and controlled both the family and society. Thus her subordinate status both in the economy and in her society resulted in the caste woman being accorded a lower social status.

These two systems were thus based on two contradictory sets of principles that can also be called their cultures. Both were based on communities. But the tribal system depended on an inclusive and equitable community while the caste community was exclusive and was founded on a caste- and gender-based hierarchy. Power was concentrated in the hands of men from one caste while in the tribes it belonged to men of the whole tribe with some share, though not equitable, accorded to women in the form of control over family production. Both organised their land-use system around the concept of sustenance. But the tribes perceived land as the sustenance of the whole community while the caste societies arranged it around the power of men from one caste. The remaining castes had to depend on the landowning caste. In that sense, the caste system ensured the material sustenance of all the castes without societal equality.

Transition to the Formal System

Both the systems made a transition to a formal status in the colonial age but with different power equations. The formal or 'modern' legal system is based on individual property and the written word and is founded on the principle of the state's eminent domain. In this view land is only a commodity for cultivation and construction. This ideology of the formal law ignores the view of land as people's sustenance or part of an ecosystem with the local community at its centre and imposes its own outlook on people's communities. This view became prevalent in the 19th century when the colonial regime enacted land laws to suit its need of exploiting the resources of South Asia to the benefit of the British Industrial Revolution. Though legitimised in the name of the civilising mission of Europe, the objective of colonialism was to change the economy of the colony and turn it into a supplier of capital and raw material and a captive market for the finished products of the Industrial Revolution (Rothermund 1981: 2–4).

Basic to achieving the objective was monopoly over land for schemes like railways, roads, coal mines and plantations. That required laws meant to turn people's livelihood into a commodity and facilitate land transfer to the profit of the capitalist owners. The process began with the Permanent Settlement of 1793 meant to ensure capital flow through land tax, continued in the laws of the 19th century and culminated in the Land Acquisition Act, 1894 (Upadhyay and Bhavani 1998). Through these laws the regime took over power to acquire land to suit its needs. These laws that continue to be in force today, authorise the state to acquire individual land without the owner's consent and pay some compensation. It can appropriate the CPRs without recognising them as the sustenance of their dependants. To these laws should be added others on biodiversity and forests that too were for centuries the sustenance of the 'ecosystem people'. But the laws turned them into state property. Their dependent communities came to be considered encroachers in their own habitat and were deprived of their rights over the resource. That created a disjunction between them and their sustenance (Ramanathan 2008: 28–30).

The principle on which these laws are based is called eminent domain in the USA and *terra nullius* (nobody's land) in Australia. White colonisation of native land in Australia, New Zealand, southern Africa and the Americas was based on this principle that land without an individual title belonged to none, so anyone could occupy it. In 1992 the Australian judiciary declared some land takeover under it unconstitutional (Brennan 1995: 4–5) but India continues to base its laws on the American version. Its first facet is that land without an individual title is state property and the second is that the state alone has the overriding power to define a public purpose and deprive even individuals of their assets in its name (Ramanathan 1999: 19–20).

Land Alienation and Impoverishment

This changeover came without the involvement of the 'ecosystem people' and with no preparation to join the formal society. The colonial state imposed the land laws based on this worldview on the traditional communities. This imposition affected the dominant castes as well as the tribal communities. But many of the former had access to education and other modern inputs. So they had some preparation to deal with the changes. Most traditional tribes, on the contrary, lived on mineral- and forest-rich land that the colonialists required as raw materials. That turned the imposition of the formal system on the informal societies into an unequal encounter. Land alienation from the traditional to 'modern' communities was a consequence since the latter were unable to deal with the changes imposed on them (Bebarta 2004: 63–69).

This unequal encounter continues to be the basis of a disjunction and of conflicts between the two systems because the colonial laws continue to be in force in the country. One of its consequences is environmental degradation. The legal system that recognises only individual ownership is a major cause of land loss and environmental degradation. Since the CPRs are not recognised as their sustenance, the communities depending on them cannot prevent outsiders from encroaching on that land. For example, in Tripura in northeastern India, the tribal proportion has declined from 58 per cent in 1951 to 31 per cent in 2001 because immigrants have encroached on 40 per cent of their community-owned land with the help of individual-based laws (Bhaumik 2003: 85). Equally important is loss of forests which catered to many needs of the tribal and other rural poor communities. The state handed many of them over to industry as raw material. They were treated as sources of profit and destroyed with no concern for their dependants or for conservation. This process impoverished people (Gadgil 1989).

The third source of land loss is acquisition for development projects. The law that empowers the state to acquire land recognises only individual ownership. More than 25 million ha have been used in India for such projects in 1947–2000, around 14 million of them forests and other CPRs. Their inhabitants, most of them tribal and other rural poor like fish and quarry workers, are considered encroachers and are not compensated and often not even counted among the displaced (Fernandes 2008: 92). Often, records of the CPRs are not kept since they are considered state property and their inhabitants are encroachers. For example, according to official accounts, in Assam the state used 159,017.37 ha of land for development projects and displaced 343,262 persons from them in 1947–2000. The reality is 1.9 million persons displaced from 567,281.29 ha (Fernandes and Bharali 2011: 216, 220). More than 1.5 million displaced persons and 410,261 ha were not counted because according to the law these CPRs are state property and their inhabitants are encroachers with no right to live there.

The Vicious Circle

One can mention many other modes of land alienation. These examples are given only to show the processes that lead to alienation of the people's livelihood. Because of the unequal nature of the encounter, the reaction of these systems to the problems that the process causes differs. That too is based on their worldview of land and the natural resources, all of whose dependants feel the negative impact of the transition from the traditional to the modern economy and new values. But the rural poor, particularly the tribes and other forest dwellers feel its impact more than the remaining groups because it is an attack on their tradition of judicious use of resources and on the systems they had developed to manage land, forests and CPRs as their renewable sustenance (Guha and Gadgil 1996: 36–39).

Loss of their sustenance begins the vicious circle of impoverishment that forces the dependants of these resources to overexploit them and cause further environmental degradation and more poverty. As the former Brazilian president Fernando Henrique Cardoso (1998) said, the first danger to the environment from people's impoverishment is loss of biodiversity and linked to it, loss of the values through which the communities depending on it had managed the resource as renewable. Studies show that loss of this value system or ideology is basic to the vicious circle that leads to further environmental degradation. But reaction to this process differs according to the class one belongs to and one's ideology or culture. To the urban middle class land alienation and environmental degradation are a loss of their recreational spaces while to the rural, particularly tribal, communities it results in loss of their livelihood and consequent impoverishment from which follows further land alienation and destruction of more natural resources. Conflicts are a natural consequence of this contradiction (Chopra and Gulati 2001).

The first step of this process is impoverishment of the economic status they are reduced to by the alienation of their sustenance. It begins with landlessness. Then comes joblessness. For example, studies of families displaced by development projects show that in Andhra Pradesh in South India, the proportion of the landless rose from 10.9 per cent before the project to 36.5 per cent after it and in Assam in the northeast from 15.56 to 24.38 per cent. Even among those who retain land, the average area owned declined, for example, in Assam from 1.2 to 0.6 ha per family. In every state most small and marginal farmers became landless, and medium farmers joined the ranks of small and marginal farmers. They also witnessed a decline in the support mechanisms, such as the number of irrigation ponds and wells, poultry, cattle, and draught animals that used to supplement their agricultural income (Bharali 2007).

Joblessness is the next step. The land and other resources that are alienated from them used to provide them work. They lose this resource with no alternative to take its place. Joblessness resulting from it takes two forms. The first is lower access to work and the second is downward occupational mobility. In Andhra Pradesh, for example, 83.72 per cent of the land losers used to work on their land or elsewhere before its loss. After land loss access to work declined to 41.61 per cent. In West Bengal it declined from 91.02

to 53.18 per cent and in Assam from 77.27 to 56.41 per cent. The second is downward occupational mobility. In most states, more than 50 per cent of the land losers who were cultivators before became landless agricultural labourers or daily wage earners after land loss (Fernandes 2008: 112–13).

Also, displacement can continue as a result of environmental degradation. For example, a new industry often forces people to move out of its neighbourood because after its construction environmental or other consequences such as fly ash and dust generated by the thermal, aluminium, nuclear, cement and other plants destroy the land around it and render it unusable. Its dependants cannot sustain themselves on it and are forced to move out (Ganguly Thukral 1999: 11). Also, the noise and dust pollution and constant blasts in the coal mines often force people to leave their homes (Fernandes and Raj 1992: 151).

Absorbing a New Culture

The changes do not remain external but enter the community itself through the internalisation of the dominant culture. The major change is in the culture of the community in general; its elite in particular internalise the viewing of their sustenance as commodity alone. It is seen first in the demand the leaders make that individual ownership become the norm in their communities. For example, in the Garo tribe of East Garo in Meghalaya in northeast India the leaders accepted the culture of individual ownership in the 1980s. A study two decades later shows that 30 per cent of the tribal families in this district had become landless since their elite had monopolised much of their land (Fernandes and Pereira 2005: 138–40).

These changes also have gender implications. As stated earlier, even the matrilineal societies are patriarchal. Their leaders absorb the culture of greater patriarchy and express it in their land relations. That can be seen among the Garo who are a matrilineal tribe but individual ownership is through men. Among the Khasi of Meghalaya who too are a matrilineal tribe, the male leaders who control the village council exploit their power to their own advantage and turn community-owned land into their private property (Mukhim 2009). Such change of gender attitudes is seen in other tribes too in the manner in which men interpret their customary law and property relations in their own favour (Fernandes and Barbora 2002a: 145–50).

Communities thus deprived of their resources absorb the same culture in another form. The first is the vicious circle of viewing their resources as a commodity alone. Once they are deprived of their resource and are impoverished, for sheer survival they over-exploit the same resource for an income. For example, studies in all the tribal areas show that once they lose their land, the deprived families fall back on their forests that they had preserved for centuries and cut trees for sale as firewood or timber, and cause more deforestation (Gadgil 1989).

The second is to view their own bodies as a commodity. For example, 49 per cent of the families displaced by development projects in West Bengal and 56 per cent in Assam pulled their children out of school in order to turn them into child labourers. Women began to view their bodies only as a source of income. Because of it prostitution grew enormously among the families that had lost their land (Fernandes 2008: 96–97). All these instances point to a major change in subaltern culture. These communities lose hope in their future and think only of the present. As a result, children who are an asset for the future become commodities only for the present and are used as a source of income for survival. The same is the view of women's bodies. In other words, women and children become commodities more than men do.

Conclusion

This essay, which is an overview of the changes in land relations, has shown the new culture that has grown as their result. It shows that imposition of another culture on a traditional group can result in a culture that is destructive of a community in general and of women in particular. The solution is not going back to their tradition by opposing modernisation or 'absolutising' the modern system. One cannot prevent all individual ownership either. One has to find an alternative in beginning with the traditional community values and combining them with the traditional community. Tradition has to be modernised and not replaced completely.

Note

* This essay is based on the studies of the North Eastern Social Research Centre (NESRC) by Fernandes and Barbora (2002a and 2002b), Fernandes and Bharali (2002 and 2006), Fernandes and Pereira (2005), and Fernandes et al. (2007).

References

Agarwal, Anil. 1985. 'Ecological Destruction and the Emerging Patterns of Poverty and People's Protests in Rural India', *Social Action*, 35(1): 54–80.

Ahmad, Afroz. 1998. 'Rehabilitation Policy for the Human Population Displacement Due To The Major Development Projects — Environmentalist View Points', Paper presented at a workshop on 'Displacement and Rehabilitation in India: Future Perspectives' organised by Centre for Rural Studies, New Delhi, 1– 3 June .

Bahuguna, Anjali. 2003. 'Non-Timber Products and Tribal Development', in S. Nautiyal and A. K. Kaul (eds.), *Non-Timber Products of India*. Dehradun: Jyothi Publishers and Distributors, pp. 469–77.

Bebarta, Kailash Chandra. 2004. *Forest Resources and Sustainable Development: Principles, Perspectives and Practices*. New Delhi: Concept Publishing Company.

Bharali, Gita. 2007. 'Development-induced Displacement: A History of Transition to Impoverishment and Environmental Degradation', Paper presented at the Seminar on Ecology, Department of History, Dibrugarh University, 27–28 March.

Bhaumik, Subir. 2003. 'Tripura's Gumti Dam Must Go', *The Ecologist Asia*, 11(1): 84–89.

Brennan, Frank. 1995. 'Parliamentary Responses to the Mabo Decision', in M. A. Stephenson (ed.), *Mabo: The Native Title Legislation: A Legislative Response to the High Court Decision*. St Lucia: Queensland University Press, pp. 1–25.

Cardoso, Fernando Henrique. 1998. *Valuing the Global Environment: Actions and Investment for a 21st Century*. Washington, DC: Global Environment Facility.

Chopra, Kanchan and S. C. Gulati. 2001. *Migration, Common Property Resources and Environmental Degradation: Interlinkages in India's Arid and Semi-Arid Region*. New Delhi: Sage.

D'Souza, Alphonsus. 2001. *Traditional Systems of Forest Conservation in North East India: The Angami Tribe of Nagaland*. Guwahati: North Eastern Social Research Centre.

Fernandes, Walter. 1996. 'Conversion to Christianity, Caste Tension and Search for a New Identity in Tamil Nadu', in Walter Fernandes (ed.), *The Emerging Dalit Identity: The Re-Assertion of the Subalterns*. New Delhi: Indian Social Institute, pp. 140–65.

———. 2008. 'Sixty Years of Development-Induced Displacement in India: Impacts and the Search for Alternatives', in Hari Mohan Mathus (ed.), *India—Social Development Report 2008: Development and Displacement*. New Delhi: Council for Social Development and Oxford University Press, pp. 89–102.

Fernandes, Walter and S. Anthony Raj. 1992. *Development, Displacement and Rehabilitation in the Tribal Areas of Orissa*. New Delhi: Indian Social Institute (mimeo).

Fernandes, Walter and Sanjay Barbora. 2002a. *Modernisation and Women's Status in North Eastern India: A Comparative Study of Six Tribes*. Guwahati: North Eastern Social Research Centre.

———. 2002b. *Immigration and Land Alienation in Assam*. Guwahati: North Eastern Social Research Centre.

Fernandes, Walter and Gita Bharali. 2002. *Land Relations and Ethnic Conflicts*. Guwahati, North Eastern Social Research Centre.

———. 2011. *Development-Induced Displacement in Assam 1947–2000. Uprooted for Whose Benefit?* Guwahati: North Eastern Social Research Centre.

Fernandes, Walter and Melville Pereira. 2005. *Land Relations and Ethnic Conflicts: The Case of Northeast India*. Guwahati: North Eastern Social Research Centre.

Fernandes, Walter, Melville Pereira and Vizalenu Khatso. 2007. *Customary Laws in North East India: Impact on Women*. New Delhi: National Commission for Women.

Gadgil, Madhav. 1989. 'Forest Management, Deforestation and People's Impoverishment', *Social Action*, 39(4): 357–83.

Gadgil, Madhav and Ramachandra Guha. 1995. *Ecology and Equity: The Use and Abuse of Nature in Contemporary India*. New Delhi: Penguin Books.

Ganguly Thukral, Enakshi. 1999. 'Bottom-Up', *Humanscape*, 6(11): 10–12.

Gangwar, A. K. and P. S. Ramakrishnan. 1992. 'Agriculture and Animal Husbandry among the Sulungs and Nishis of Arunachal Pradesh', in Walter Fernandes (ed.), *National Development and Tribal Deprivation*. New Delhi: Indian Social Institute, pp. 100–30.

Guha, R. and M. Gadgil. 1996. 'What are Forests For?' in W. Fernandes (ed.), *Drafting a People's Forest Bill: The Forest Dweller-Social Activist Alternative*. New Delhi: Indian Social Institute, pp. 33–67.

Menon, Geeta. 1995. 'The Impact of Migration on the Work and Tribal Women's Status', in Loes Schenken-Sandbergen (ed.), *Women and Seasonal Labour Migration*. New Delhi: Sage, pp. 79–154.

Mukhim, Patricia. 2009. 'Land Ownership Among the Khasis of Meghalaya: A Gender Perspective', in Walter Fernandes and Sanjay Barbora (eds), *Land, People and Politics Contest over Tribal Land in Northeast India*. Guwahati: North Eastern Social Research Centre and IWGIA, pp. 38–52.

Nongkynrih, A. K. 2009. 'Privatisation of Communal Land of the Tribes of North East India: A Sociological Viewpoint', in Walter Fernandes and Sanjay Barbora (eds), *Land, People and Politics Contest over Tribal Land in Northeast India*. Guwahati: North Eastern Social Research Centre and IWGIA, pp. 16–37.

Ramanathan, Usha. 1999. 'Public Purpose: Points for Discussion', in Walter Fernandes (ed.), *The Land Acquisition (Amendment) Bill 1998: For Liberalisation or for the Poor?* New Delhi: Indian Social Institute, pp. 19–24.

———. 2008. 'The Land Acquisition Act 1894: Displacement and State Power', in Hari Mohan Mathus (ed.), *India: Social Development Report 2008: Development and Displacement*. New Delhi: Council for Social Development and Oxford University Press, pp. 27–38.

Rothermund, Dietmar. 1981. *Asian Trade and European Expansion in the Age of Mercantilism*. Delhi: Manohar.

Roy Burman, B. K. 1993. 'Tribal Population: Interface of Historical Ecology and Political Economy', in Mrinal Miri (ed.), *Continuity and Change in Tribal Society*. Shimla: Indian Institute of Advanced Study, pp. 175–216.

Sachichidananda. 2004. *Man, Forest and the State in Middle India*. New Delhi: Serials Publications.

Sengupta, Nirmal. 1991. *Managing Common Property: irrigation in India and the Philippines*. New Delhi: Sage.

Shimray, U. A. 2006. *Tribal Land Alienation in North East India: Laws and Land Relations*. Guwahati: North Eastern Social Research Centre and Indigenous Women's Forum of Northeast India.

Upadhyay, Sanjay and Raman Bhavani. 1998. *Land Acquisition and Public Purpose*. New Delhi: The Other Media.

Zonneveld, Isaak S. 1993. 'What is Meant by Land Use Change?' in Carole L. Jolly and Barbara Boyle Torrey (eds), *Population and Land Use in Developing Countries*. Washington D. C.: National Academy Press, pp. 30–36.

PART II

GENDER DIMENSIONS OF FARMING

6

Livelihood Diversification: Farming, Forest-use and Gender in Northeastern India*

DEEPAK K. MISHRA

The process of livelihoods diversification, particularly by the poor and vulnerable sections of society, has received increasing critical attention. Yet, how the interface between the locally embedded economic processes and the 'choices' exercised by individuals complicates and shifts their 'livelihood portfolios' needs further understanding. The reallocation of economic assets and activities, within and outside households, is shaped by the larger process of changes in the political economy as well as by the micro-realities of power and powerlessness. The conflicts surrounding such processes and the political economy of differential access to resources, institutions and opportunities among and within the households have not received adequate attention. Livelihood diversification by households and individuals has often been described as an additive process with large multiplier effects, as if in a given context all individuals and households can diversify their livelihoods without much contestation. But livelihood diversification, whether under distress or in response to new opportunities, could be a highly complex process, particularly because of the intra-household conflicts of interests between men and women. The gendered nuances of livelihood diversification are intensified in mountain ecology because of the specificities of resources and also because of multiple, overlapping hierarchies, such as between the plains and the hills, among and within the communities, between the state and the communities, and also among men and women. Based on the experiences of the mountain regions of northeast India in general and that of Arunachal Pradesh in particular, this essay analyses livelihood diversification in a forest-dependent hill economy in terms of its interrelations with and impacts on gender relations.

The blanket nomenclature 'northeast' is misleading because the region is characterised by an enormous degree of ecological, cultural and historical diversity, although there is also a great deal of interconnectedness among the economies of the region (Sarma 2001). Livelihoods in the region have undergone considerable transformation, particularly in the past half-century. Gender relations have also been altered in a varied and complex manner. This needs to be analysed in relation to the larger transformations of the political economy, primarily because gender relations are deeply embedded in the economy and the politics of control over resources. At the same time, viewing the economic transformation through the gender lense reveals the socially embedded nature of the economy in clearer terms, an aspect which is often neglected in the mainstream discussions of economic development and change.

This essay starts with selectively reviewing the literature on livelihoods diversification to establish the interconnections between gender relations and the process of livelihood diversification. Then, the livelihoods scenario in the hill economies of the northeastern region is discussed, with specific emphasis on forests as a source of livelihoods. This leads to an analysis of the interrelationship between forests, livelihoods and gender in the region. Largely drawing upon micro-studies by the author and others, the analysis relates to a few critical issues. The nature of ownership and control over forests has been changing; given the involvement of women in collecting a range of forest products, this has significant gender implications. The marketisation of forest products has radically altered the nature of forest-use, which in turn has changed the way forests and forest-related activities are viewed by the forest-dependent population. The shift from family and community labour to wage labour for extraction of marketed forest products changes the intra-family distribution of work as well as opportunities. The gendered nature of forest dependency and its transformation in the context of commercialisation are discussed on the basis of the available evidence. Because of the interdependencies between farming and forest-related activities, some aspects of the gender relations in agriculture become especially relevant, and the impact of deforestation and commercialisation of forest products on women's work burden are also discussed.

Gender and Livelihood Diversification

Ellis (1998) defines a livelihood as 'encompass[ing] income, both in cash and kind, as well as social institutions (kin, family, compound, village and so on), gender relations and property rights to support and to sustain a given standard of living'. Thus, he goes beyond the usual emphasis on income and employment and brings in social institutions, which play a crucial role in determining the constraints and options of individuals and households.[1] Multiplicity of livelihood sources helps rural households to take diverse risks and manage uncertainty through allocating resources across several non-co-varying sectors. In some cases, households, in an attempt to cope with unanticipated shortfalls in production or in earnings tend to diversify their livelihoods. In some other cases, diversification of livelihoods results from responses to opportunities for additional earnings. The strategy is also to build upon complementarities of a range of activities (Start 2001). Livelihood diversification is defined as 'the process by which households construct a diverse portfolio of activities and social support capabilities for survival and in order to improve their standard of living' (Ellis 1998: 4). 'Considerations of risk spreading, consumption smoothing, labour allocation smoothing, credit market failures, and coping with shocks can contribute to the adoption, and adaptation over time, of diverse rural livelihoods' (Ellis 1999: 2). Livelihood diversification strategies are followed both by the poor and those who are not poor. Livelihood diversification positively impacts seasonality, risk, employment, credit and assets. The effect of seasonality is to 'smoothen' labour and consumption by utilising labour and generating alternative earning streams during off-peak periods; the adverse impacts of seasonal fluctuations on farm production (the mismatch between uneven farm production and income and continuous consumption requirements) is mitigated by utilising labour and generating alternative earning streams during off-peak periods.[2] Risk reduction through diversification of activity aims to distribute household resources, such as labour, across a range of activities having different mean-variance combinations (e.g., combining low-mean/low-variance subsistence activities like shifting cultivation with high-mean/high-variance activities like petty trading), or across activities having un-correlated risks, as in farming, where the main source of risk may be unpredictable climate, and urban wage employment where the risks are because of job insecurity.

Shifting the focus from the economy per se to people and their activities, ideally frees the framework from several reductionist trappings and allows us to incorporate many important dimensions of the development process, such as the role of non-tangible assets like trust, cooperation and social networks; the interrelationship between ideology, power and the range of feasible economic choices before individuals and households; the centrality of 'environmental entitlements' for livelihood choices; the importance of participatory approaches to development research and planning, etc. The processes of asset building and livelihoods diversification are deeply social processes but were earlier given inadequate emphasis in some approaches to development. Although 'transforming structures, mediating processes, institutions and organizations appear in all livelihood frameworks', there is a tendency within livelihoods studies to downplay these structural features and to focus on capitals and activities (de Haan and Zoomers 2005: 33). The language of 'multiplier effects' predominates in the discussion on livelihoods choices (Murray 2001), as though it is possible to expand people's 'asset pentagons' in a generalised and incremental fashion. The structures of power and powerlessness as well as the heterogeneity of interests, both within and among 'local' communities are insufficiently recognised. Although 'participation' is stressed in much of the literature, the concept of 'community' implicit in such discussions fails to accommodate the mutually conflicting interests of diverse social groups (Mishra 2004).

The critique of livelihood studies has special relevance for a gender-sensitive analysis of the process of livelihoods diversification. The survival of households crucially depends upon their access to crucial resources and also the utilisation of these resources, both of which are deeply embedded in the local social and institutional structures. The resources to which individuals (and households) can have access depends on the local economy and ecology, and also on the political economy of resource sharing and distribution among the various groups of claimants. As de Haan and Zoomers (2005: 34) point out:

> Failed access and the resultant poverty or social exclusion can also be the result of a mechanism by which some people exclude others from access to resources, with the objective of maximising their own returns. . . . They use property relations or certain social or physical characteristics such as race, gender, language, ethnicity, origin or religion to legitimize this fencing-in of opportunities. Social exclusion and poverty are then consequences of social closure, a form of collective action which gives rise to social categories of eligibles and ineligibles. . . . Livelihood activities are not neutral, but engender process of inclusion and exclusion.

Further, the access of households does not mean automatic and equitable access of all the members of the households. Intra-household distribution of power, privilege and authority determines the disparity in access to these 'available' resources as well as their effective utilisation by the members. Often, the intra-family distribution of resources creates specific barriers for women who want to expand their economic activities or livelihoods options. Such barriers create exclusion from livelihoods sources, or limit the access to livelihoods-supporting assets.

Beyond the access and denial of opportunities, the gender dimension of livelihoods is linked to the gender division of work within the family. Typically, women's share of domestic work and care is greater, which conditions their effective options in pursuing other livelihoods choices that are open to them. This limit is due to the domestic work burden and the demands on their time, and also the restrictions on their mobility, access to social and economic institutions, and lack of participation in public activities as a result of their heavy domestic work burden. These constraints, or the lack of them, make livelihoods diversification a gendered process. As households decide to diversify their sources of livelihoods, there is a reallocation of various assets, responsibilities and risks within the family. Perceptions regarding 'appropriate' gender division of labour and the flexibility in defining such divisions influence the relative share of opportunities and burdens across gender and age. The multiplicity of social hierarchies often reinforces the processes of marginalisation and exclusion for those at the bottom of the social ladder. Entrenched gender hierarchies within the households, intra-community hierarchies based on social status, caste, or class, inter-community disparities in power and influence, as well as the larger dynamics of inequality among nations and regions, may create and sustain an overlapping range of exclusionary and discriminatory livelihood outcomes for some, while simultaneously creating a virtuous cycle of accumulation for some others.

Forests and Livelihoods in Northeastern India

Agriculture continues to be the main source of livelihood for a majority of people in northeastern India, generating about 50 per cent of the region's income. According to the 2001 population census, of the total workers in the region, 55 per cent are agricultural workers. The main features of agriculture in the region are low productivity, attributable to poor irrigation facilities, low mechanisation, limited usage of high-yielding variety (HYV) seeds, and predominance of monocropping and jhuming (Table 6.1; NEDFi 2003: 17). Marginal farmers operating less than 1 ha account for 56 per cent of the total holdings in the region, as against the all-India average of 59 per cent. But small and marginal holdings together constitute around 79 per cent of total holdings in the region. There is also considerable diversity in the agrarian structure of the states (Table 6.2). Peasant differentiation is generally found to be sharper in the case of the densely populated plains than in the hills. But the overall character of the region is that of smallholder peasant agriculture. The level of commercialisation of agriculture in the northeastern states, with the notable exception of the plantation sector, is fairly low. This is partly reflected in the low share of non-food crops in the total cultivated area.[3] The marketisation of agricultural produce is typically low in the hill states, although in some pockets there has been a significant move towards cultivation of fruits and vegetables, spices, and high-value aromatic and medicinal plants. Thus, the overall character of the agrarian economy of the region, notwithstanding some localised or crop-specific exceptions, can still be described as being a predominantly smallholder, partially monetised, low productive, weakly integrated agrarian economy, with a substantial subsistence producing segment (Mishra 2006).

Table 6.1: Shifting Cultivation in the NER

States	Annual area under shifting cultivation (sq km)	Fallow period (y)	Minimum area under shifting cultivation one time or other (sq km)	No. of families practising shifting cultivation
Arunachal Pradesh	700	3–10	2,100	54,000
Assam	696	2–10	1,392	58,000
Manipur	900	4–7	3,600	70,000
Meghalaya	530	5–7	2,650	52,290
Mizoram	630	3–4	1,890	50,000
Nagaland	190	5–8	1,913	116,046
Tripura	223	5–9	1,115	43,000
All NE	3,869		14,660	443,336

Source: 'Task Force on Shifting Cultivation', Ministry of Agriculture (1983), reported in North-Eastern Council. 2006. *Basic Statistics of North Eastern Region, 2006.* Shillong: North-Eastern Council.

Table 6.2: Distribution of Operational Holdings in Northeastern States, 1990–91

States	Marginal (Below 1 ha)	Small (1–2 ha)	Semi-medium (2–4 ha)	Medium (4–10 ha)	Large (10 ha and above)	Average size of holding
Arunachal Pradesh	17.89	18.95	31.58	27.37	4.21	3.62
Assam	59.98	22.57	13.39	3.80	0.25	1.31
Manipur	48.59	34.51	14.79	2.11	0.00	1.24
Meghalaya	36.65	26.09	28.57	8.07	0.62	1.81
Mizoram	46.77	37.10	14.52	1.61	0.00	1.34
Nagaland	9.29	15.00	18.57	33.57	23.57	6.92
Tripura	68.24	21.70	8.81	1.26	0.00	0.97
All NE	55.59	23.01	14.50	5.57	1.32	1.6
India	58.99	18.97	13.21	7.25	1.59	1.57

Source: NEDFi. 2003. *NEDFi Data Bank Quarterly*, 2(1).

At the same time, it is important to note that production for the market is gradually becoming the norm, particularly in the road-side villages and areas having better road connectivity. Studies show that in some contexts, even products from shifting cultivation fields are primarily produced for the markets (Kekhrieseno 2002).

In comparison to the all-India averages, a relatively smaller proportion of workers in the region are dependent on agriculture, yet significantly, the proportion of agricultural labourers is substantially lower in the region than the all-India level.[4] Considerable inter-state differences of agricultural labour also exist in the region, ranging from 3.85 per cent in Arunachal Pradesh and 3.98 per cent in Nagaland to 24.03 per cent in Tripura and 18.09 per cent in Meghalaya (Table 6.3). As studies point out, this process of occupational diversification has not been gender neutral, although the extent of occupational segregation among men and women in the northeastern states tends to be lower than that in India as a whole (A. Mishra 2006).

The forest has always been a significant source of sustenance in the region. Various studies on the livelihoods and employment diversification processes suggest that the crucial drivers of diversification include the natural resource endowments and the institutional structures defining and differentiating the access

Table 6.3: Occupational Structure of Workers in Northeast India, 2001

States		Cultivators			Agricultural labour			HH industry			Other workers		
		M	F	T	M	F	T	M	F	T	M	F	T
Arunachal Pradesh	T	46.77	76.61	58.44	3.44	4.49	3.85	0.73	1.05	0.86	49.06	17.85	36.85
	R	57.7	82.7	68.26	3.99	4.65	4.27	0.57	0.93	0.72	37.75	11.72	26.75
	U	3.44	15.44	6.13	1.24	2.93	1.62	1.39	2.26	1.59	93.93	79.37	90.66
Assam	T	38.66	40.42	39.15	12.34	16.48	13.5	1.71	7.89	3.44	47.29	35.21	43.91
	R	44.36	42.90	43.93	14.14	17.44	15.12	1.69	7.94	3.54	39.81	31.72	37.41
	U	1.74	2.25	1.82	0.68	1.74	0.84	1.83	7.16	2.63	95.74	88.85	94.71
Manipur	T	46.68	45.29	46.06	8.95	14.27	11.31	3.30	16.50	9.16	41.07	23.94	33.47
	R	53.88	53.02	53.49	9.39	14.64	11.76	2.86	14.64	8.17	33.87	17.71	26.58
	U	20.92	13.62	17.87	7.37	12.74	9.62	4.85	24.13	12.9	66.86	49.51	59.61
Meghalaya	T	44.89	51.88	47.80	16.25	20.66	18.09	1.43	2.50	1.88	37.44	24.96	32.23
	R	52.41	57.20	54.47	18.60	22.23	20.16	1.46	2.60	1.95	27.54	17.97	23.42
	U	4.24	7.91	5.46	3.55	7.70	4.92	1.26	1.69	1.40	90.94	82.70	88.22
Mizoram	T	48.77	60.52	53.91	4.93	7.05	5.85	1.20	1.66	1.40	45.11	30.77	38.83
	R	73.03	83.40	77.80	3.45	4.47	3.92	0.79	0.91	0.84	22.74	11.23	17.45
	U	21.78	29.42	24.92	6.57	10.56	8.21	1.66	2.68	2.08	69.99	57.34	64.80
Nagaland	T	55.68	75.32	64.05	3.72	4.34	3.98	1.34	3.19	2.13	39.26	17.15	29.84
	R	67.36	79.51	72.94	4.43	4.48	4.45	1.23	2.89	1.99	26.97	13.13	20.61
	U	3.44	14.93	5.84	0.53	2.31	0.90	1.80	7.52	2.99	94.23	75.24	90.27
Tripura	T	26.61	27.58	26.88	19.72	35.0	24.03	1.63	6.11	2.90	52.04	31.31	46.19
	R	31.78	30.55	31.41	23.40	38.64	27.97	1.74	6.26	3.10	43.08	24.55	37.52
	U	1.82	0.48	1.58	2.04	1.66	1.97	1.10	4.74	1.77	95.03	93.12	94.68
All NE	T	39.83	46.10	41.82	11.97	16.06	13.35	1.72	7.26	3.48	46.36	30.58	41.34
	R	46.26	49.93	47.48	13.96	17.14	15.02	1.68	7.08	3.48	38.10	25.84	34.02
	U	5.27	11.25	6.63	2.01	6.27	2.98	1.95	8.91	3.54	90.77	73.57	86.85
India	T	31.34	32.51	31.71	20.82	39.43	26.69	3.02	6.36	4.07	44.82	21.70	37.52
	R	42.19	36.46	40.14	27.48	43.40	33.20	2.83	5.44	3.77	27.49	14.70	22.90
	U	2.99	4.26	3.21	3.42	11.03	4.71	3.50	12.93	5.10	90.09	71.77	86.98

Source: Government of India. 2001. *Census of India.* New Delhi: Government of India.

and utilisation of such resources, the connectivity status and infrastructural development in the locality, access to education and also the pattern of state intervention in the local economy (Mishra 2007). Being a conflict-prone region, the degree and intensity of these conflicts also constrain and facilitate certain kinds of livelihoods diversification, more so because many of these conflicts are linked to the struggle for land, forest and other sources of livelihoods (Barbora 2002; Fernandes and Pereira 2005: 190–95).

Livelihoods in the northeastern region, as in many less-developed economies, are critically dependent upon 'environmental entitlements'. Environmental entitlements refer to 'alternative sets of utilities derived from environmental goods and services over which social actors have legitimate effective demand and which are instrumental in achieving well-being' (Gasper 1993; Leach et al. 1999: 233). These environmental entitlements play a crucial role in different aspects of livelihood security at the household level, that is, economic security, food security, health security, and empowerment, particularly in fragile ecological contexts (Jodha 2001). A number of case studies show that multiplicity of livelihood sources is a predominant feature in many parts of the region (Fernandes and Pereira 2005: 98; Mishra 2007). The significance of the forest resources lies in their centrality as additional and dependable sources of livelihood, particularly for smoothening consumption.

Mishra (2003), in a field survey in the hill district of West Kameng in Arunachal Pradesh, reported as many as 30 different combinations of livelihoods at the household level (Table 6.4).[5] While the developed villages showed a greater variability in livelihood combinations than the traditional ones, broadly two different kinds of livelihood diversification strategies could be found in this mountainous region. The first one, which concentrates on diversification of livelihoods within and around agriculture, is mostly determined by the survival needs of households living in a high-risk, high diversity ecological setting. Households attempt to combine jhum, terrace and wet rice cultivation with horticulture, animal husbandry, selling of forest products, casual employment in the emerging rural labour market and, in some cases, petty trading. The second kind of diversification is through increasing dependence upon government service, trade and business and large-scale trading in forest products. The latter kind of strategy is generally driven by an accumulative motive of relatively

Table 6.4: Proportion of Area under Forest Cover, Dense Forests and Open Forests in India and Northeastern States, 1999

States	Proportion of forest area to total geographical area	Percentage of dense forest to total area under forest	Percentage of open forest area to total area under forest
Arunachal Pradesh	82.21	83.89	16.11
Assam	30.20	61.28	38.72
Manipur	77.86	34.15	65.85
Meghalaya	69.70	37.90	62.10
Manipur	86.99	20.65	79.35
Nagaland	85.43	36.27	63.73
Tripura	54.79	38.78	61.22
All India	19.38	59.22	40.02

Source: Reddy, V. R., B. Behera and D. Mohan Rao. 2001. 'Forest Degradation in India: Extent and Determinants', *Indian Journal of Agricultural Economics*, 56(4): 631–51.

Notes: (i) Proportion of dense forest area (>40 per cent of crown density) is taken from total forest area.

(ii) Proportion of open forest area (10–40 per cent crown density) is taken from total forest area.

better-placed households. However, the forest plays a central role in either kind of diversification, as a source to mitigate risks and smoothen consumption during seasonal short falls, or as a source of consumables as well as marketable products like timber, and a range of non-timber forest products including medicinal plants.

The entire northeastern region has witnessed a phenomenal degree of environmental degradation over the last few decades (Husain 1996). Although states of the region have a forest cover that is higher than that for the rest of the country, deforestation has been going on at an alarming speed (Table 6.5). The commercial extraction of timber and other forest resources played an important role in transforming the local economy, particularly in hastening the process of monetisation of the exchange process and commercialisation of production relations, even in the relatively inaccessible areas of the state (Mishra 2001). The restrictions imposed in the 1990s by the Supreme Court on commercial extraction of timber have resulted in the closure of timber-based industries and an increase in the area under forest cover as well as loss of employment and income for those dependent on the timber trade (Reddy et al. 2001).

Table 6.5: Distribution of Households According to Household Strategies: West Kameng, Arunachal Pradesh

	Livelihood combinations	Village I	Village II	Village III	Village IV	All Villages
1	Agriculture, forest	1(2.4)	0(0.0)	3(5.0)	1(3.6)	5(3.1)
2	Agriculture, forest, animal husbandry	9(21.4)	4(13.3)	14(23.3)	0(0.0)	27(16.9)
3	Agriculture, forest, wage labour	5(11.9)	2(6.7)	1(1.7)	1(3.6)	9(5.6)
4	Agriculture, forest, government service	2(4.8)	0(0.0)	2(3.3)	3(10.7)	7(4.4)
5	Agriculture, forest, animal husbandry, government service	4(9.5)	4(13.3)	17(20.3)	2(7.1)	27(16.9)
6	Agriculture, forest, animal husbandry, wage labour	14(33.3)	8(26.7)	10(16.7)	9(32.1)	41(25.1)
7	Agriculture, forest, animal husbandry, others	2(4.8)	2(6.7)	2(3.3)	0(0.0)	6(3.8)
8	Agriculture, forest, animal husbandry, trade	0(0.0)	1(3.3)	2(3.3)	0(0.0)	3(1.9)
9	Agriculture, forest, animal husbandry, wage labour, others	1(2.4)	3(10.0)	0(0.0)	0(0.0)	4(2.5)
10	Agriculture, forest, animal husbandry, trade, others	1(2.4)	1(3.3)	2(3.3)	3(10.7)	7(4.4)
11	Agriculture, forest, animal husbandry, trade, services	0(0.0)	0(0.0)	2(3.3)	1(3.6)	3(1.9)
12	Agriculture, forest, animal husbandry, trade, services	0(0.0)	0(0.0)	3(5.0)	0(0.0)	3(1.9)
13	Other combinations	3(7.1)	5(16.7)	2(3.3)	8(28.6)	18(11.3)
	Total	42(100)	30(100)	60(100)	28(100)	160(100)

Source: Deepak K. Mishra. 2003. 'Environmental Degradation and Changing Livelihood Strategies in Rural Arunachal Pradesh', Paper presented at the 45th Annual Conference of the Indian Society of Labour Economics, Kolkata, 15–17 December, pp. 648–49.

Note: While village I and II represent the relatively underdeveloped, isolated rural economies, the other two villages are relatively well-connected.

The impact of commercialisation of forest products on the local economies was substantial. First, commercialisation as a process weakened the property rights regimes in many parts of the region where some form of collective rights over forests and agricultural land had been in existence. The system of 'lease' of forestland by forest contractors led to significant changes in the modes of resource use in Meghalaya (Nathan 2000; Nongbri 2001). In the first phase of commercialisation, Nathan (2000) notes, collective ownership was gradually replaced by the emergence of private (or quasi-private) property rights over forests. In the initial period the emergence of the timber trade led to lease of the forestland for a fixed period, usually to the sawmill owners. This led to wanton clearing of forests, as there was little incentive for the logger to invest in forest regeneration. After some time, many village councils resisted the leasing out of forestland to outsider contractors. This was followed by the gradual emergence of a class of local contractors, who apart from felling trees from their own land also purchased trees from the poorer farmers (Nongbri 2001). Thus, access to timber markets by some led to the differentiation and gradual emergence of a local 'capitalist' class. Some of these contractors emerged as sawmill owners and integrated themselves with the national markets for timber and other forest products.[6]

The livelihoods implications of the restrictions imposed on commercial extraction of timber have been noted by a number of different scholars. Nongbri (2001), for example, has argued that the ban on timber has led to significant shrinkage in livelihoods options for the tribal population. Given the centrality of forests to the livelihoods of tribals, she argued, the ban has virtually resulted in denial of livelihood rights of the indigenous population in the state. Indeed, many organisations and individuals from the north-eastern region viewed this typically as another case of infringement of the local autonomy by an overbearing central authority. Many state governments voiced their opposition and appealed for an early lifting of the ban.[7] Nongbri (2001: 1897) argued that 'the decision was neither a result of ignorance nor oversight, but is symptomatic of the state's attitude to the rights of indigenous people'. In Arunachal Pradesh, the restrictions started a process of deindustrialisation, as most of the industries in the state were wood-based. Mukhim (cited in Saxena undated: 23) on the basis of a study of 10 villages in West Khasi hills, Meghalaya, reported that jhuming 'has resumed with a vengeance after the timber ban since the villagers perceived the forests to be of no value to them while the products of jhumming are'.

However, a field survey in West Kameng district in Arunachal Pradesh (Mishra 2000), which has seen a phenomenal degree of deforestation during the peak years of timber trade, indicated a more complicated picture. First, household level response to the livelihood loss as a result of the restrictions on timber trade included rapid adoption of vegetable cultivation on a commercial basis as well as distress diversification to some non-farm employment. Only a few households reported returning to jhum cultivation, although jhum was not the main cultivation practice in the area. And finally, many among the small and marginal farmers were happy about the restrictions mainly because they thought the destruction of forests had dried up the springs and led to reduced soil fertility.

Diversification as a Gendered Process

The process of livelihoods diversification in the northeastern region has been shaped by the nature and degree to which the local economy has been commercialised as also by the relative access to the expanding service sector, which in many hill economies chiefly consists of the public sector. As already pointed out, whether the shifts in livelihood options occur with agriculture retaining its centrality or there is a movement towards non-agricultural and urban occupations, in the intervening period the forest remains a significant source both for a variety of consumption goods and for alternative earnings. Often it is the last resort of groups uprooted and displaced by conflicts, disasters and debt-induced land alienations. Because the forest plays a significant role in both the survival-induced and accumulative diversification (Mishra 2003), the loss of access to forests has hastened the process of proletarisation in certain contexts. How can we understand the linkages between the shifting forest-livelihoods relations and the changing gender relations in the tribal communities of the northeastern hills? Notwithstanding the limitations of the available information and the inherent difficulties in generalising the results of micro studies in a region characterised by so much diversity, three aspects of the process may be discerned.

First, the question of women's rights over forests and forest products needs to be examined against the backdrop of the conflicts over ownership of forests, not only among the macro-players such as the state, corporate and commercial interests and the community, but also the increasingly complex articulation of collective and individual rights over forests in inter-community and intra-community conflicts. The presence and *de facto* control of a number of non-state agencies and groups further complicates the political economy of forest-use. The nature of forest-use has been observed to change significantly as a 'market' for the products develops; the gender implications of this change in forest-use gets manifested in gender differences in the volume and composition of forest products collected, the marketing of the products and access to the cash income earned through their sale.

Second, given the overlapping and interdependent nature of forest and agricultural activities in many parts of the region, an investigation into the gender implications of the changes in farming systems provides important clues to at least two important aspects of this transition. Since the generally collective ownership of land under jhum is gradually being replaced by permanent cultivation and, by implication, individual property rights over land, women tend to turn into 'disinherited peasants'. Further, as wage labour arrangements are gradually replacing collective labour mobilisation in agriculture, women face new challenges as cultivators and workers.

Third, as forests vanish and the 'nature-based' economy gets integrated into the larger market economy, the gender division of work tends to change, mostly resulting in a greater work burden for women.

Gendered Forest Dependency and Livelihood Strategies

The issue of forest rights in the northeastern region is complex and conflict-ridden. Property rights over forests in the areas that are covered by the Sixth Schedule are mostly in the hands of the local communities, even as there has been a gradual increase in the share of forests under state control. However, community control over forests does not have similar connotations in all parts of the region. For example, in Nagaland, where the ownership of land, including forests, is determined by traditional law as per Article 371A of the Indian Constitution, individual property rights over forests are well recognised. In 1988, 11.7 per cent of the total was state-owned forest, and 88.3 per cent was privately owned (D'Souza 2001: 26). However, even in the forest land owned by village communities and clans, individual property rights are well recognised (ibid.: 44). In Arunachal Pradesh, where nearly 63 per cent of forests categorised as 'unclassified state forest' are in fact in the hands of village communities and clans, the effective control of these forests varies a lot among the communities. Unconstrained individual property rights over land coexist with collective rights in forests. Irrespective of the precise nature of the property rights regime, on the ground there is an unmistakable tendency towards *de facto* privatisation of ownership or at least use rights over forests. Individual ownership rights, particularly in regard to alienation rights, are necessarily subject to community control in many areas (D'Souza 2001: 46; Mishra 2006). Yet, the ethos of collective management was no doubt weakened by the wanton exploitation of 'common' forest resources, particularly timber for private gains in the years before the imposition of the Supreme Court restrictions. Apart from the environmental impact of deforestation, the institutional impact was that the traditional rules of resource-use, which had been designed in a resource-abundant context involving almost zero costs of monitoring, became redundant so rapidly that communities did not have the social capital to address the problem. The emergence of a labour market itself transformed community labour sharing practices and since most of the traditional institutional mechanisms were based upon the implicit assumption of labour-shortage their distributive egalitarianism lost the capacity for conflict-minimisation (Mishra 2002, 2004).

Nathan (2000) has argued that the rise of the timber industry in Meghalaya has been a major factor in the demise of matrilineal property rights among the Khasis. The newly emerging local capitalists have not only taken over the effective management of the forest land owned by their wives and sisters, they have transformed the nature of the property to assert their own ownership rights. Thus, the booming timber trade provided them with the opportunity to accumulate capital by transforming the 'trees on the land into capital in mill accounts', and simultaneously this transformation led to the categorisation of the wealth as 'self-acquired' property, which is outside the matrilineal inheritance system of the Khasis (Nathan 2000). The commercialisation of timber not only resulted in differentiation within the indigenous groups, the nature of differentiation has been such that it has weakened the effective resource ownership positions of women vis-à-vis men.

The extent of forest dependency is particularly high among households living in the mountain areas. A study conducted in 12 villages of Arunachal Pradesh (Mitra and Mishra 2011) concludes that on an average 34.48 per cent of the consumption expenditure of the households of the study area were derived from the community forests. Further, around 37.93 per cent of total consumption expenditure of relatively poor households was derived from community forests. On the other hand, 32.02 per cent and 31.06 per cent of total consumption expenditure were derived from community forests for relatively middle-income and rich households. Thus, in absolute terms the richer sections derive more benefits from the community forest. Another study, on the basis of data collected from three villages in West Kameng district, notes that around 24 per cent of the total income of the households is derived from forests (A. Mishra 2005). The extent of forest dependency does not necessarily change as a consequence of increased levels of earnings, but the nature of forest use and the composition of forest produce collected changes significantly. While poorer households tend to depend on the forest for their survival, better-off households are more concerned with marketed produce. Mitra and Mishra (2011) found that the relatively poor households consumed more fuel wood, bamboo, leafy vegetables etc., and that the consumption of timber was much higher among the rich households. Indeed, the study shows that as the income of the households increased, the percentage consumption of timber also increased but the consumption of minor forest products like bamboo and leafy vegetables reduced.

Thus, moving across the income ladder, the nature of forest consumption changes from dependence for household necessities like food, fuel and fodder, to accumulation. Women are more centrally involved in household consumption than accumulation.

The division of labour in the collection of forest products has been found to be gendered and product-specific. For example, a study in West Kameng, Arunachal Pradesh, notes that women's contribution in the collection of marketed forest products, like timber, bamboo and medicinal plants, was negligible, but that women's labour was more than men's labour in the collection of firewood, grass, leafy vegetables, fruits, and roots. In the collection of house-building materials men's labour was more than women's (A. Mishra 2005). Commercial extraction of forest products has meant that traditional subsistence activities have been turned into income-generating occupations. Commercialisation has also meant greater interaction with traders and dealers and travel to market places. This has led to a situation where either the entire activity has been turned into a predominantly male activity or a division of labour has emerged where women and children join in collecting the forest products and men take over the responsibility of selling the products. In either case, the cash flows get concentrated in male hands. This is exactly what has happened in the Dirang circle of Arunachal Pradesh, where a market for medicinal plants has developed in the past few years. In the neighbouring Nafra circle, with the setting up of pine oil processing units, it is the men who have taken over oil collection, while the women continue to shoulder the responsibility of collecting household consumption items from the forests.

The implications of such privatisation of forest resources for rural women, particularly those belonging to the tribal communities, are at multiple levels and substantial. Many observers, including the early anthropologists, have noted that women in the 'traditional' community management systems had a greater degree of participation in economic activities and hence enjoyed greater freedom than the women of the caste Hindu societies (Elwin 1957; Furer-Haimendrof 1939: 101). Critical scholarship has questioned such a generalised characterisation of gender relations in the tribal communities of the region. However, today, it is evident that the mutually reinforcing impacts of state and market forces, as well as the 'elite capture' of institutional structures of collective control over resource-use, have led to the breakdown of collective management of natural resources leaving women as a group impoverished although individual women belonging to richer sections might have benefited to some extent.

The Transformation of Traditional Agriculture

In northeastern India, the traditional property rights formations exhibited a great deal of tribe-to-tribe variations, but by and large, among the various tribal groups, there has been a gradual shift towards individualisation of property rights over land (Mishra 2001). This process has created a great deal of ambiguity about the *de facto* demarcation of private and communal property as well as about inheritance rights. The evidence from different parts of the world seems to suggest that the transition from collective to private ownership over land generally results in the concentration of private ownership over resources in the hands of men. In some matrilineal tribes women did have rights of inheritance over immovable property, but in many patriarchal societies women had no property rights either over agricultural or homestead land. In some cases, they had partial rights over movable property but generally did not enjoy inheritance rights over agricultural land.[8] Even when women have the right to property, recent studies point out that there is a divergence between ownership and control. Both 'tradition' and the new forces of market and state control work in such a way that the male members of the family exercise effective control over property.

The mere existence of collective property rights over land, not withstanding that such a property rights regime at least guarantees use rights to women, does not necessarily mean more equitable gender outcomes. Fernandes and Pereira (2005: 102), in a comparative assessment of six ethnic groups in northeastern India, find that the status of women among the Akas of Arunachal Pradesh is comparatively low, although property rights over land are collective and the substantial participation of women in shifting cultivation is also the norm. They conclude that the low status is 'probably to be attributed more to the Aka's own tradition than to modernisation or non-recognition of their law'. Several studies note the *de facto* divergence between ownership over property and the right over decision-making concerning the property, even in the communities well known for their relatively egalitarian gender relations (Xaxa 2004). Agarwal (1994: 109), summarising the property rights regimes over land in the case of matrilineal tribes of northeast India, points out that 'customary law vested women with significant rights in land but formal managerial control in land management was vested in man'; according to many, effective male control has been increasing over time (Marak 2002; Mukhim 2005; Nongbri 2003). The process of transformation from shifting cultivation to settled cultivation has been associated with the gradual emergence of individual property rights over land and as a consequence, a move towards consolidation of male ownership over land among many communities. Darlong et al. (2006), in a study in South Tripura, Dhalai and West Tripura districts of Tripura, covering six different ethnic communities, found that in wet rice cultivation the legal rights of ownership were always in the names of the male heads of the family.

There has also been a decline in women's labour contribution in agriculture, but many studies point out significant labour contribution by women even in terrace and wet rice cultivation.[9] The transformation of property relations has hastened the processes of peasant differentiation and landlessness has been increasing among many communities (Fernandes and Pereira 2005; Mishra 2002). Significantly, the shift from what Boserup termed a 'female farming system' to increasing economic and gender differentiation was not primarily because of factors like population growth, but because of state interventions that discouraged shifting cultivation and provided incentives to 'progressive' farmers for growing commercial crops. The institutional strategies of agricultural extension services in these areas are based on the usual assumptions of an individual male, autonomous farmer as the decision maker in agriculture, which in turn has facilitated the recognition of private property rights over land (D. K. Mishra 2006). In Arunachal Pradesh, studies show that the state has not formally recognised private property rights in land but has been a passive observer of the systematic informal transition to private property rights. In this informal transition, women and other marginalised sections tend to lose out (Mishra 2003). On the one hand, the state has facilitated the emergence of private property rights through a series of direct and indirect measures, while on the other hand, by not taking cognisance of the move towards privatisation, it has virtually left the process in the hands of 'traditional' community institutions. These institutions, notwithstanding their other strengths as institutions of decentralised, local-level governance, are hardly 'participatory' when it comes to women (Goswami 2002; Krishna 2004; Mishra and Upadhyay 2007).

Deforestation and Women's Work Burden

As in many other forest-dependent societies, women and children in the hill economies of northeastern India play an important role in gathering forest resources for domestic consumption as well as for commercial use. The declining forest cover, particularly the degradation of forests near the settlements, has meant extra work for many of them. In a field survey in Nepal, Cooke (1998) found that increasing resource scarcity accounts for nearly 80 per cent of the additional time women spend in collection. If environmental conditions deteriorate, women pay more in terms of their higher work burden. In a case study among Thangkul Nagas, Shimray (2004) found that women spend more time in housework than the men. Women have a relatively higher burden of work in activities like fetching water, feeding domestic animals, collecting firewood and crop farming. Environmental degradation in general and deforestation in particular increases the work burden in almost all these activities. Another study in West Kameng district in Arunachal Pradesh points out that, on an average, women spend more time than men in animal husbandry, forestry, fetching water, firewood and fodder, and fruits and vegetables, etc. In villages practising shifting cultivation, women also contribute more time in crop farming, while in villages characterised by settled cultivation and commercial agriculture men contribute more labour than women. The study also notes that women's overall work burden was higher in villages having degraded forests than in villages having relatively dense forests. Interestingly, the study finds that in one of the villages, where a market for forest products has developed, men tend to spend more time in forest-related activities than women, while women continue to contribute more in collecting forest products for self-consumption (A. Mishra 2005). Thus commercialisation paves the way for higher male participation, and probably control over cash inflow, while women bear the burden of extra work as forests get degraded.

Women's significant participation in both food production and food gathering activities could be one of the significant determinants of the relatively egalitarian distribution of food within the households. Analysis of the National Family Health Survey-II data suggests that, contrary to the findings in other parts of India, in the northeastern region, female children have a nutritional edge over male children (Rama Rao et al. 2004). The traditional gender distribution of work in production and consumption of food, however, has been changing very fast, both in rural and urban areas of the state (Krishna 2005). One of the crucial aspects of the food consumption pattern in many parts of the region is the high average consumption of leafy vegetables, roots and tubers as well as fish and meat, in comparison with the national averages. A substantial proportion of these items are collected from forests and jhum fields. Women's nutritional status in the region is not independent of their participation in forest-related activities and access to forest resources, which in turn influences their micro-level strategies for risk minimisation, mutual support, and solidarity in high-risk ecological-economic contexts. Along with gradual privatisation of these resources, the food and nutrition security prospects of households in general, and the access of women and girls to food and nutrition in particular, could worsen further (Mishra and Upadhyay 2007).

Concluding Observations

The process of livelihoods diversification, under distress as well as in response to new opportunities, is not simply the outcome of decisions by individuals and households, but is part of a deeply contested process of acquiring access and utilisation of existing and new resources. As relatively isolated, forest-dependent economies get integrated into the larger economies of resource extraction and commercial exploitation, the mode of resource-use gets transformed from a need-based system to a commercial system. Such a transformation, often leading to differentiation of the peasantry, does not leave the traditional institutions that determine access to resources unchanged. Such changes have been transforming the hill economies of northeastern India in profound ways. As collective institutional structures are being gradually disintegrated, women as a group are facing challenges on diverse fronts. Deforestation and commercialisation of forest products are undermining their use and ownership rights. Moreover, in many of these communities transformation of the agrarian economy from collective/subsistence to individual/commercial agriculture has turned women into peasants without land rights, while increasing their overall work burden. Existing and newly emerging gender differences in access to resources and institutions need to be taken into account while evaluating the implications of livelihoods diversification for women.

Notes

* The author is grateful to Sumi Krishna and Saraswati Raju for their comments on earlier drafts of the article. An earlier version of this article appeared as 'Gender, Forests and Livelihoods: A Note on the Political Economy on Transition in North-east India', *Social Change*, 2007, 39(4), pp. 65–90.
1. Income refers to cash earnings of the household plus payments in kind that can be valued at market prices. In the case of rural households, for example, the cash earnings typically include crop and livestock sales, wages, rents, and remittances. The kind component of income refers to consumption of own-farm produce, payments in kind, and transfers or exchanges of consumption items that accrue between households in rural communities (Ellis 1998).

   Social institutions, which include rules of conduct, norms and expected behavioural outcomes, critically condition the access of households to land, CPRs and other tangible and non-tangible resources. Social norms on permissible courses of action of women, for example, may influence the livelihood options available for women compared to men (Ellis 1998).
2. Household living strategies often involve a variety of different activities like home gardening, exploiting common property resources, share-rearing livestock, family splitting, and stinting, which may not be captured by large-scale surveys.
3. In 1998–99, of the total cropped area in the region, 67.57 per cent was under food crops.
4. According to the 2001 population census figures, of the total workers in the region 41.82 per cent were cultivators, 13.35 per cent were agricultural labourers, 3.48 per cent were household industry workers and the rest 41.34 per cent were other workers. At the all-India level the share of cultivators and agricultural labourers were 31.71 and 26.69 per cent respectively, while household industries provided employment to 4.07 per cent of workers.
5. The results of this survey indicate that the livelihood combination having the highest frequency is agriculture, combined with forest-based activities, animal husbandry and wage labour. The simpler combination of agriculture, forest and animal husbandry also has a significant presence. So has the livelihood combination of agriculture, forest,

animal husbandry and government service. Together, these three combinations explain the diversification strategy of around 60 per cent of all the households (Table 6.5).

6. Nathan (2001) draws a distinction between accumulation of surplus from timber trade by the local (indigenous) capitalist class and that by the capitalists from outside the region, mainly on two counts. First, he argues that the profits of the local capitalist class are likely to be reinvested locally and hence would boost the local economy, whereas profits by the capitalists from outside the region are likely to be siphoned off to other parts of the country. The latter would mean draining of resources from the region. Second, being local stakeholders and part of the indigenous community, the local entrepreneurs are more likely to be prudent in their resource extraction activities in comparison to their counterparts from outside the region. This reasoning tries to de-emphasise the fact that both the local and the 'national' capitalist are part of the same process of surplus accumulation and they have been instrumental in the emergence and survival of each other, at least in the context of timber trade. Again, given the low productive base of the region, much of the profits earned by the local capitalist class are spent on luxury goods produced elsewhere. So the expected benefit to the local economy is less than what is expected. The nature of alliance between this local elite and the timber traders from outside has been such that it is difficult to categorise many among the newly emerging elite as 'capitalists' or entrepreneurs. In many cases, timber trade has generated a local 'rentier' class rather than enterprising capitalists. The extent to which this class of indigenous capitalists are bound by their concerns for the local environment is difficult to ascertain. Available evidence from the region suggests that these local elites, more often than not, used their identity and membership of the local institutions to subvert these institutions and also to convert common property into private property. Many of the local institutional structures did not have the necessary social capital to counter these elites. That inequality adversely affects the community-based natural resource management system has been noted by many studies across the world.

7. The timber trade was also an important source of revenue for the states of the region. Given the overall dependence of these special-category states in central government aid and loans, this decline in revenue generation had significant implications for many of these governments. In Arunachal Pradesh, for example, revenue from forests declined by 84 per cent as a result of the ban (Ramnath 2002).

8. Case studies in various parts of the hilly states of northeast India confirm this. In Arunachal Pradesh, inheritance rights, wherever they exist, are always in favour of sons (Pandey et al. 1997: 202). In

Mizoram, even in the absence of a male child landed property went to the nearest male relative (Nunthara 2004; Laldinpuii and Laithangpuii 2006).

9. In the Southern Angami areas of Nagaland, where both terrace and shifting cultivation is practised, women play a dominant role in both types of cultivation. 'They not only contribute the major portion of labour but also exercise control over different stages of cultivation and the final produce' (Kekhrieseno 2002: 187) so much so that researchers point out that 'Angami terrace cultivation may be termed as female farming system' (D'Souza 2001). Darlong et al. (2006), in a study in South Tripura, Dhalai and West Tripura districts of Tripura, report that in wet rice cultivation, the share of women's work burden was nearly 70 per cent and in the case of upland rice cultivation it was as high as 80 per cent.

References

Adams, R.H. 1994. 'Non-Farm Income and Inequality in Rural Pakistan', *Journal of Development Studies*, 31(1): 110–33.

Agarwal, Bina. 1992. 'The Gender and Environment Debate: Lessons from India', *Feminist Studies*, 18(1): 119–58.

———. 1994. *A Field of One's Own: Gender and Land Rights in South Asia*. Cambridge: Cambridge University Press.

———. 2001. 'Participatory Exclusions, Community Forestry, and Gender: An Analysis for South Asia and a Conceptual Framework', *World Development*, 29(10): 1623–648.

Barbora, Sanjay. 2002. 'Ethnic Politics and Land Use: Genesis of Conflicts in India's North-East', *Economic and Political Weekly*, 37(13): 1285–292.

Boserup, E. 1970. *Women's Role in Economic Development*. London: George Allen and Unwin Ltd.

Brown, David and K. Schreckenberg. 1998. 'Shifting Cultivators as Agents of Deforestation', *Natural Resource Perspectives*, 29. London: ODI available from http://www.oneworld.org/odi/nrp/29.html (accessed 5 February 2012).

Byres, Elizabeth and M. Sainju. 1994. 'Mountain Ecosystems and Women: Opportunities for Sustainable Development and Conservation', *Mountain Research and Development*, 14(3): 213–28.

Carney, D. (ed.). 1998. *Sustainable Rural Livelihoods: What Contributions Can We Make?* London: DFID.

Cooke, Priscilla A. 1998. 'Intrahousehold Labour Allocation Responses to Environmental Goods Scarcity: A Case Study from the Hills of Nepal', *Economic Development and Cultural Change*, 46(4): 807–30.

D'Souza, A. 2001. *Traditional Systems of Forest Conservation in North East India: The Angami Tribe of Nagaland*. Guwahati: North-Eastern Social Research Centre.

Darlong, V. T., D. K. Hore and S. Deb Barma. 2006. 'Gender Concern and Food Security in Rice Farming System in North-east India: A Case-Study of Tripura', *North East India Studies*, 1(2): 40–79.

Das, G. 1995. *Tribes of Arunachal Pradesh in Transition*. New Delhi: Vikas.

Das, J. N. 1989. *Land Systems in Arunachal Pradesh*. Guwahati: Law Research Institute.

de Haan, Leo and Annelies Zoomers. 2005. 'Exploring the Frontier of Livelihoods Research', *Development and Change*, 36(1): 27–47.

Ellis, F. 1998. 'Households Strategies and Rural Livelihood Diversification', *Journal of Development Studies*, 35(1): 1–35.

———. 1999. 'Rural Livelihood Diversity in Developing Countries: Evidence and Policy Implications', *Natural Resource Perspectives* 40, London: ODI. Available from http://www.odi.org.uk/resources/docs/2881.pdf (accessed 5 February 2012).

Elwin, V. 1957. *A Philosophy for NEFA*. Shillong: North-East Frontier Agency.

———. 1965. *Democracy in NEFA*. Shillong: North-East Frontier Agency.

Fernandes, Walter. undated. 'Tribal Customary and Formal Law Interface in North Eastern India: Implications for Land Relations', available at siteresources.worldbank.org/INTINDIA/Resources/walter_fernandes_paper.doc (accessed 5 September 2007).

Fernandes, Walter and Sanjay Barbora. 2002. *Modernisation and Women's Status in North Eastern India: A Comparative Study of Six Tribes*. Guwahati: North Eastern Social Research Centre.

Fernandes, Walter and Melville Pereira. 2005. *Land Relations and Ethnic Conflicts: The Case of Northeast India*. Guwahati: North Eastern Social Research Centre.

Furer-Haimendrof, C. von. 1939. *The Naked Nagas*. London: Routledge and Kegan Paul.

———. 1980. *A Himalayan Tribe: From Cattle to Cash*. New Delhi: Vikas.

———. 1982. *Highlanders of Arunachal Pradesh*. New Delhi: Vikas.

Gasper, D. 1993. 'Entitlement Analysis: Relating Concepts and Contexts', *Development and Change*, 24(4): 679–718.

Goswami, A. 2002. 'Introduction', in A. Goswami (ed.), *Traditional Self-governing Institutions among the Hill Tribes of North-east India*. New Delhi: Akansha, pp. 1–19.

Husain, Zahid. 1996. 'Degradation and Development of Environment in North-East India', in Z. Hussain (ed.), *Environmental Degradation and Conservation in North-East India*. Delhi: Omsons, pp. 1–28.

———. 2003. 'Development Strategy for the North-Eastern Hills', in A. C. Mohapatra and C. R. Pathak (eds), *Economic Liberalization and Regional*

Disparities in India: Special Focus on North Eastern Region. Shillong: Star Publishing House, pp. 169–78.

Hussain, M. 2000. 'State, Identity Movements and Internal Displacement in the North East', *Economic and Political Weekly*, 16 December, 35(51): 4519–523.

Jodha, N. S. 2001. *Life on the Edge: Sustaining Agriculture and Community Resources in Fragile Environment*. Delhi: Oxford University Press.

Kar, P. C. 1982. *The Garos in Transition*. New Delhi: Cosmo Publication.

Kekhrieseno, Chriestina. 2002. 'Changing Property Rights and Women's Control Over Livelihood in Nagaland', in Walter Fernandes and Sanjay Barbora (eds), *Changing Women's Status in India: Focus on the North-East*. Guwahati: North-Eastern Social Research Centre, pp. 183–92.

Krishna, S. 2004. 'Gender, Tribe and Political Participation: Control of Natural Resources in North-Eastern India', in Sumi Krishna (ed.), *Livelihood and Gender: Equity in Community Resource Management*. New Delhi: Sage.

———. 2005. 'Gendered Price of Rice in North-Eastern India', *Economic and Political Weekly*, 40(25): 2555–562.

Laldinpuii, A. and Laithangpuii. 2006. 'Rice Economy and Gender Concerns in Mizoram', *North East India Studies*, 1(2): 40–79.

Leach, M., R. Mearns and I. Scoones. 1999). 'Environment Entitlements: Dynamics and Institutions in Community-Based Natural Resource Management', *World Development*, 27(2): 225–47.

Lipton, Michael. 1980. 'Migration from Rural Areas of Poor Countries: The Impact on Rural Productivity and Income Distribution', *World Development*, 8(1): 1–24.

Low, A. 1986. *Agricultural Development in Southern Africa: Farm Household Theory and the Food Crisis*. London: James Currey.

Marak, Caroline. 2002. 'Matriliny and Education among the Garo', in Walter Fernandes and Sanjay Barbora (eds), *Changing Women's Status in India: Focus on the North East*. Guwahati: North Eastern Social Research Centre, pp. 159–65.

Mishra, A. 2005. 'A Study of Economic Transformation, Environmental Degradation and Female Work Participation in Arunachal Pradesh', Ph.D. Thesis submitted to Rajiv Gandhi University, Itanagar.

———. 2006. 'Occupational Structure and Gender-based Segregation in North-East India: The Case of Arunachal Pradesh', *Social Change and Development*. 4(1): 125–45.

Mishra, Deepak K. 2000. 'Agrarian Relations in Arunachal Pradesh: A Case Study of West Kameng District', Project Report submitted to University Grants Commission.

———. 2001. 'Political Economy of Agrarian Change in Arunachal', *Man and Development*, 23(3): 40–50.

————. 2002. 'Institutional Arrangements and Agrarian Structure during periods of Transition: Evidences from Rural Arunachal Pradesh', in S. S. Acharya et al. (eds), *Sustainable Agriculture, Poverty and Food Security: Agenda for Asian Economies*, Vol. 2. Jaipur: Rawat Publications, pp. 891–902.

————. 2003. 'Environmental Degradation and Changing Livelihood Strategies in Rural Arunachal Pradesh', Paper presented at the 45th Annual Conference of the Indian Society of Labour Economics, Kolkata, 15–17 December.

————. 2004. 'Institutional Sustainability in Natural Resource Management: A Study on Arunachal Pradesh (India)', *Asian Profile*, 32(6): 583–94.

————. 2006. 'Institutional Realities and Agrarian Transformation in Arunachal Pradesh: Changing Realities and Emerging Challenges', *Indian Journal of Agricultural Economics*, 61(3): 314–27.

————. 2007. 'Rural Non-farm Employment in Arunachal Pradesh: Growth, Composition and Determinants', NLI Research Studies Series, No. 075/2007, Noida: V. V. Giri National Labour Institute.

Mishra, Deepak K. and V. Upadhyay. 2007. 'In the Name of the Community: Gender, Development and Governance in Arunachal Pradesh', in Sumi Krishna (ed.), *Women's Livelihood Rights: Recasting Citizenship for Development*. New Delhi: Sage, pp. 167–208.

Misra, B. P. 1979. 'Kirata Karyokinesis: Mode of Production in Tribal Communities of North East India', in A. N. Das and V. Nilakanth (eds), *Agrarian Relations in India*. Delhi: Manohar.

Mitra, Amitava and Deepak K. Mishra. 2011. 'Environmental Resource Consumption Pattern in Rural Arunachal Pradesh', *Forest Policy and Economics*, 13(3): 166–70.

Mukhim, Patricia. 2005. 'Gender Concerns and Food Security in Rice Farming Systems of North-East India', *Dialogue*, 7(1): 126–54.

Murray, Colin. 2001. *Livelihoods Research: Some Conceptual and Methodological Issues*, Background Paper 5, Chronic Poverty Research Centre, University of Manchester.

Nathan, Deb. 2000. 'Timber in Meghalaya', *Economic and Political Weekly*, 35(4): 182–86.

Nongbri, Tiplut. 2001. 'Timber Ban in North-East India: Effects on Livelihood and Gender', *Economic and Political Weekly*, 36(21):1890–900.

————. 2003. *Development, Ethnicity and Gender: Selected Essays on Tribes in India*. New Delhi: Rawat.

North-Eastern Council. 2006. *Basic Statistics of North Eastern Region, 2006*. Shillong: North-Eastern Council.

North Eastern Development Finance Corporation Ltd. (NEDFi). 2003. *NEDFi Data Bank Quarterly*, 2(1).

Nunthara, C. 2004. 'Land Control, Land Use and Kinship Structure in "Lushai" Hills', in Mignonette Momin and Cecile A. Mawlong (eds), *State and Economy in North East India*, Vol. 1. New Delhi: Regency, pp. 74–75.

Pandey, B. B. (ed.). 1997. *Status of Women in Tribal Society: Arunachal Pradesh*. Itanagar: Directorate of Research, Government of Arunachal Pradesh.

Rama Rao, G., L. Ladusingh and R. Pritamjit. 2004. 'Nutritional Status of Children in North East India', *Asia-Pacific Population Journal*, 19(3): 39–56.

Ramakrishnan, P. S. 1992. *Shifting Agriculture and Sustainable Development of North-Eastern India*. Paris: UNESCOMB series, Carnforth: Parthenon Publications. Reprint, Delhi: Oxford University Press, 1993.

Ramnath, M. 2002. 'Meghalaya: Impact of Ban on Timber Felling', *Economic and Political Weekly*, 37(48): 4774–777.

Reddy, V. R., B. Behera and D. Mohan Rao. 2001. 'Forest Degradation in India: Extent and Determinants', *Indian Journal of Agricultural Economics*, 56(4): 631–51.

Sarma, Atul. 2001. 'Economic Development of the Northeastern States in the Context of Globalisation', *Strategic Analysis*, 25(2): 293–312.

Saxena, N. C. undated. 'Rural Poverty in Meghalaya: Its Nature, Dimensions and Possible Options'. Available at http://planning-commission.nic.in/reports/articles/ncsxna/ncrural.pdf (accessed 5 February 2012).

Shimray, U. A. 2004. 'Women's Work in Naga Society: Household Work, Workforce Participation and Division of Labour', *Economic and Political Weekly*, 39(17): 1698–711.

Start, D. 2001. 'The Rise and Fall of the Rural Non-farm Economy: Poverty Impacts and Policy Options', *Development Policy Review*, 19(4): 491–505.

Ullah, Mahbub. 1996. *Land, Livelihood and Change in Rural Bangladesh*. Dhaka: University Press.

Upadhyay, Vandana and Deepak K. Mishra. 2004. 'Micro Enterprises in Hill Economies: A Study on Arunachal Pradesh', *The Indian Journal of Labour Economics*, 47(4): 1027–38.

Valentine, T. R. 1993. 'Drought, Transfer Entitlements and Income Distribution: The Bostwana Experience', *World Development*, 21(1): 109–26.

Visaria, P. and R. Basant (ed.). 1994. *Non-agricultural Employment in India: Trends and Prospects*. Delhi: Sage.

Xaxa, V. 2004. 'Women and Gender in the Study of Tribes in India', *Indian Journal of Gender Studies*, 11(3): 345–67.

7

Gender Dynamics in Agro-biodiversity Conservation in Sikkim and Nagaland*

CHANDA GURUNG GOODRICH

Subsistence farmers all over the world, and especially in environments where high-yielding crops and livestock do not prosper, play a major role in maintaining agro-biodiversity by cultivating a large variety of crop species. The Convention on Biodiversity defines agro-biodiversity as 'the diversity at all levels of the biological hierarchy, from genes to ecosystems, that is involved in agriculture and food production . . . the fundamental and distinct property of agricultural biodiversity is that it is largely created, maintained and managed by humans' (Secretariat of the Convention on Biological Diversity 2001). Thus, agro-biodiversity is the biological diversity of agriculture-related species and their wild varieties which occurs at the levels of the agro-ecosystem, species and gene. Today, agro-biodiversity is being seriously depleted due to genetic erosion, which is one of the most alarming threats to world food security. It is known that 75 per cent of the world's food is generated from just 12 plant and five animal species. Only 200 out of 10,000 edible plant species are used by humans, and of these, rice, maize and wheat contribute nearly 60 per cent of the calories and proteins obtained by humans from plants (Lambrou and Laub 2006). The importance of biodiversity and plant genetic resources in human survival and food security makes it vital to maintain crop diversity on farmers' fields, especially in 'hot spots' of plant genetic diversity. Indeed, this is considered a 'global life insurance policy' by the Convention on Biology Diversity (Secretariat of the Convention on Biological Diversity 2001). In such a scenario, the contribution of the farmers of the eastern Himalaya and the northeastern hills in conserving and maintaining agro-biodiversity is of immense value. Conservation practices in the region are traditionally adaptive strategies based on indigenous knowledge. This essay draws upon research conducted in three sites — in Sikkim and Nagaland in India and Sankhuwasabha in Nepal — to understand the causal links between ethnicity and gender, and how these affect agro-biodiversity management practices. The essay, however, focuses on the research findings from Nagaland and Sikkim concerning how social and agricultural practices in some of the indigenous ethnic communities of this region have evolved to conserve and maintain crop diversity, and examines the criticality of gender for agro-biodiversity conservation.

Social and Gender Systems and Livelihood Practices

Humans have lived in this region for several millennia, adapting their custom, lifestyles and livelihoods to the local environments. Historically, the region and its people have been exposed to various external influences — transhumance of people due to war and conquest, trade, out-migration, and immigration. More contemporarily, development interventions have considerably broadened the range and nature of encounters. As a consequence, the cultural discourse of the region's societies has evolved through a process of mediation, negotiation and resistance to external influences (Gurung 1999). All this movement and inter-mixing of communities in the rugged terrain is reflected by the diversity of ethnic and religious groups across the region. Their survival depends on subsistence farming and necessitates the extensive use and management of natural resources. Besides producing many types of crops (mostly landraces), farmers rely extensively on wild plants to meet their needs for fiber, shelter, food, medicine, tools, and household implements.

Among the numerous ethnic communities of this region are the Lepchas of Sikkim and the Nagas of Nagaland. For the last half-century, like other ethnic groups that inhabit the middle mountain ranges, these communities too have been exposed to a myriad influences. The Lepchas have been exposed to the Lamaist culture of Tibetan-Buddhism, the caste system of Hinduism brought by the Nepalis, and the greater 'egalitarianism' of Christianity.

Similarly, the Nagas have been exposed to the British, the Christian doctrines brought by the British and American missionaries and to the low-landers of India. The process of interaction with and influence of these external hegemonies was based on relations of inequity. Stratification on the basis of class, caste, wealth, religion, and gender became the norm. Prior to this, the divisions and/ or stratifications were based on clan and tribe affiliation rather than these parameters. In such a context, the external and more powerful groups came to be ranked higher in status, while the ethnic communities became 'second-class' citizens in their own land. Such encounters led to Hindu and Christian gender ideologies that follow patriarchal practices having a major influence over the communities' way of life. This had a strong impact on the ways gendered spaces and gender relations came to be conceptualised in the culture and practice of these ethnic groups. Adding to such historically embedded asymmetries are the present centre/periphery relations and lowland/highland dichotomies. All these have led to transforming the sustainable lifestyles of the people, their socio-cultural values and systems as well as subsistence practices.

The traditional subsistence systems and livelihood practices of the Lepchas and the Nagas were hunting-gathering, considered 'men's domain', and slash and burn cultivation, considered 'women's domain'. This gender division of labour and spaces was based on the cultural belief derived from biological attributes that women were the symbols of fertility, 'caretakers and nurturers', and men the 'active providers'. This was more a matter of convenience and physical endurance than power and control. However, due to the external encounters and hegemonies, the traditional livelihood practices have undergone transformation as private property tenure was introduced leading to settled agricultural practices, which gradually began to replace traditional subsistence systems of hunting-gathering and slash and burn cultivation. Traditional social and gender systems too underwent changes because social and gender systems of a community, although linked to religion and ethnic identities, are also strongly influenced by external forces (Gurung and Gurung 2006). As these traditional societies faced new influences and practices, the social, and more particularly, gender relations were reinterpreted and renegotiated (Gurung 1999). With the transformation in livelihood practices — which included not only new technologies and crops but also new beliefs and value systems that were attached to these activities — traditional gendered spaces in the livelihood systems too underwent transformation: agricultural space gradually came under the control and domain of men. Farming systems and what goes on within them came to be seen as 'the work place', where production for the market occurs; it is a domain or area that is spatially and socially distinct from 'the home', therefore a 'public' domain. This 'public' world of work and production tended to be seen, and ideologically constructed, as the world of men (Zwarteveen 2008). Thus, women lost their control over this sphere of activity and came to be considered merely as 'helpers'. However, their workload in this sphere of activity in no way decreased.

Today, agriculture is the mainstay of the region and 70 per cent of the people depend on it. The climate and seasons are conducive for growing a large number of crops — cereals, fruits and vegetables — and the region's geographical characteristics allow farmers to cultivate subtropical and sub-temperate crops simultaneously and in the same location with comparative ease. Most of the famers cultivate crops under natural conditions with no external inputs such as chemical fertilisers.

Even today, two land-use types are extremely important for these communities: forests and agriculture. Despite the degradation and loss of two-thirds of the eastern Himalayan forests due to indiscriminate felling of trees over the last few decades, the forests harbour over 9,000 species of flora and fauna (Myers 1988) and are still of great significance to the people. For the peoples of these communities, the forests are not only sources of timber, fuel wood, other non-timber forest products (NTFPs), such as medicinal herbs, edible fruits and plants, but are also the sites for grazing, foraging and slash and burn cultivation. Within the agro-forestry system, agriculture combined with livestock provides the main subsistence for the majority as hunting was abandoned years ago. Land holdings are highly differentiated but marginal and small holdings form the bulk of the total.

Gender and Agro-biodiversity Conservation

As with most of the ethnic communities inhabiting the eastern Himalaya and the northeastern hills, for the Lepchas and Nagas too the conservation of agro-biodiversity developed as a strategy for survival and is not seen by the people themselves as conservation per se. The roles and responsibilities of men and women in conserving agro-ecosystems, species and genes are defined on the basis of the different skills and knowledge that they have acquired and the socio-cultural norms and practices that have shaped them. Furthermore, dominant and accepted cultural symbolism informed by a powerful spatial imagery carries strongly gendered ideological connotations that men should be the 'providers' whereas women should be nurturers and caretakers. Added to this are the ideologies and notions of women as symbols of fertility, the impurity of women, etc. Consequently, men and women are associated with different crops and spaces/domains. Thus, distinct gender roles in agricultural labour and spatial divisions in gendered domains of authority between the different agro-ecosystems and crops mean that women and men have unique relationships to agro-biodiversity (see also Oakley and Momsen 2005). The work done and knowledge held by men and women are also valued differently based on the social and gender systems of the communities.

AGRO-ECOSYSTEM MAINTENANCE

Traditionally, the Lepchas and Nagas practised only one type of land-use — slash and burn cultivation — where they cultivated all their crops: the Lepchas cultivated upland rice, millet, buckwheat and maize; the Nagas cultivated upland rice, job's tears (*Coix lacryma-jobi*), millet and maize. Women were in complete control of this type of cultivation and they did almost all the work, with men helping them only in the felling of trees and cutting or lopping bigger branches.

However, with external influences, new technologies in agriculture were introduced in the early 19th century, the most significant being terracing. Thus, several types of land-use were practised: swidden cultivation along with home gardens and wet terrace fields, and, in the case of the Lepchas, agro-forestry areas where the cash crop cardamom was extensively cultivated. These agro-ecosystems came to be divided and classified into 'male' and 'female' domains on the basis of the social and gender systems that had come to be dominant. Each of these agro-ecosystems came under the control of either men or women based on reasons pertaining to power, importance, value — both in terms of cash and prestige or status in the given social and gender system. Among both the Lepchas and Nagas the wet terrace fields are prized possessions of the families for their fertile soils and proximity to water sources and they are usually reserved for wetland paddy. These are classified as a 'male domain' because wet rice is considered a major crop and additionally the area is usually large as compared to the other agro-ecosystems. Although women provide the bulk of the work here in sowing, transplanting, weeding, harvesting, and seed selection, their contribution is not established and they are considered merely as 'helpers'.

Lepchas have two types of terraces: (*a*) the *ari/yong* irrigated terraces are located in the lower elevations and marshy areas. Crops grown here include wet land paddy (15 varieties), maize (six varieties), potato (four varieties), wheat (two varieties), pulses (four varieties) and soyabean. (*b*) rain-fed *sukha bari* where upland rice (three varieties), maize, buckwheat (two varieties), barley (four varieties), millet (four varieties) including *kaguni/kamdak* (in Nepali/Lepcha), sorghum, mustard (two varieties), and numerous tuber crops are cultivated.

Nagas (Angami tribe) have various types of terraces: (*i*) *Dsuzo* rain-fed terraces, (*ii*) *dzutsu* irrigated terraces, (*iii*) *waluli* partially irrigated terraces near homesteads, (*iv*) *dzutse* terraces near streams, which are irrigated throughout the year, (*v*) *khuso* terraces located far away from the homestead and water sources, and (*vi*) *wakhra* dry terraces located near the dzutse and khuso, where approximately 50 varieties of paddy are cultivated. Apart from this, other crops like maize (seven varieties), several varieties of millet and potatoes are also grown here.

Among both the communities home gardens (called *leeden sing* by the Lepchas) are considered part of the 'female domain' because these are usually small in size and the crops grown are all subsistence or 'minor' crops like vegetables, herbs and traditional crops only for home consumption. This agro-ecosystem has the highest diversity of crop species and varieties. Being 'caretakers' and 'nurturers', women are responsible for feeding their families and caring for their health. Therefore, they cultivate a variety of crops, vegetables and medicinal plants in the home gardens for family consumption and use. For instance, Lepcha women cultivate 24 vegetables (and many more varieties), seven types of spices and eight types of fruit crops in their home gardens; Naga women grow 30–40 varieties of beans, 30 varieties of squash, two varieties of mustard leaves, two varieties of cabbage, three varieties of garlic, two species and two varieties of tomatoes, three varieties of solanum, and several other vegetables like carrot, mint, spring onion, etc.

To optimise diversity with maximum yield, women of both communities try to utilise land as much, and in as many ways, as possible. As most of the farmers have small landholdings, women practise various crop combinations and crop rotation methods. Home gardens are also the area where women experiment with new crop species and varieties that they get from their different seed networks and also from the forests. Home gardens not only maintain but also sustainably improve crop diversity, thus making these extremely significant areas for the use and conservation of agro-biodiversity. The women carry out all the work in this area with the men rarely helping.

Slash and burn has been classified differently by the two communities: the Lepchas consider the *sadlium* area a 'joint domain' of men and women, while the Nagas consider jhum as a female farming system and thus a 'female domain'. The difference is largely based on the extent and type of interaction with and the policy adopted by the influencing or ruling powers. The history of the Lepchas shows that they were exposed to both the Tibetan-Buddhist and the Hindu-Nepali cultures over a long period. The Tibetan-Buddhist influence lasted longer as the ruling power, but was concentrated only in the cultural and religious sphere. The Hindu-Nepalis came to Sikkim to make a living; they were not rulers and mixed freely with the Lepchas. The close interaction between the two groups led to the Lepchas adopting a combination of the livelihood practices and values. The *sadlium* agro-eco-system, which was completely under the control of women, is now considered a 'joint domain' of both men and women because work in this area is considered 'outside' work, within the men's sphere, but the crops cultivated here are minor crops which are associated with women. Hence, this is regarded as a joint domain.

Among the Nagas, the influence of and interaction with the Christian missionaries was concentrated only on the religious sphere while the influence of the lowlands is fairly recent. Therefore, the impact of both has not been felt so much in the livelihood systems and practices. Furthermore, the British policy of non-intervention in internal and personal matters, which allowed the Nagas to follow their own traditional customary laws and practices, is another reason for the traditional gender spaces/spheres of control being still relatively strong. Therefore, jhum cultivation is still very much a woman's farming system and the swidden plots are exclusively 'women's domain'. Women cultivate a mix of about 70 crops that include 34 varieties of upland rice, seven varieties of maize, and four varieties of job's tears, several varieties of millet, taro, ginger, chilies and cotton. Thus, there is an intimate link between jhum cultivation and crop biodiversity (Nakro and Kikhi 2006).

Despite the different ways in which slash and burn areas are viewed and categorised, the work done by women and men in this agro-ecosystem is almost equal and similar. Men do the 'heavy' work (this categorisation of 'heavy' and 'light' work is again based on the conventional gender ideology) of cutting trees and branches, while women clear the undergrowth; burning is done by both depending on whoever is free; sowing and weeding are done mostly by women, although the Lepcha men do help sometimes, but among the Nagas, this work is done solely by the women; harvesting is done by both women and men.

The *punzok* agro-forestry area is unique to the Lepchas. These are areas within the forest which are considered a male domain and an extension of the forest where traditionally men hunted game. In addition, six varieties of cardamom, a major cash crop and so under men's control, is cultivated here. Women have no control over this area. Men do all the work of planting, weeding, pruning, harvesting, curing, and marketing. Women are rarely involved and only serve as helpers when there is a shortage of male labour.

SPECIES CONSERVATION

Formerly, the Lepchas and Nagas cultivated only the traditional crop species of which there were numerous varieties. All the crops were of equal value and importance. External influences, the introduction of new crops and new forms of patriarchy, have altered farming practices and gender relations. The most significant of these new crops is wetland rice. The irrigated rice and wheat became major crops and were associated with men. With other traditional crops beginning to lose their use value, specific crops came to be seen as men's crops or women's crops on the basis of their economic importance, food value and cultural significance. Men were more involved with the production of major crops (rice, millet, maize and cardamom) and women with minor subsistence crops and vegetables. Crop varieties also declined as farmers preferred exotic seeds and high-yielding hybrids.

As traditional crops lost their importance, a higher value was given to fruits and cash crops which are important to the cash economy. All these changes occurred with the introduction and development of new and improved seed varieties without community control and by ignoring the empowerment of mountain farmers and their ability and freedom to choose in the context of local knowledge. These introduced crops affected the agro-biodiversity and the consequences were alarming in the long term. The Lepchas who used to cultivate 27 varieties of dry rice (Gorer 1938) and 12 varieties of millet (Siiger 1967), now cultivate only two varieties of dry or upland rice (that too only in the remote areas), and four varieties of millet. Of several traditional crops, only millet is considered a major crop now because of its cultural and religious value and because its use in the making of the traditional brew, beer, is a pre-requisite in all religious and cultural functions; it is also the main offering to the gods and to guests. Similarly, the Nagas traditionally used to cultivate 30 varieties of millet and job's tears but the number of varieties of these crops has been decreasing gradually, while the number of irrigated paddy varieties is increasing. Now there are approximately 30 varieties of wet rice being cultivated even in the one small village, Viswema, which was one of the research sites of the study.

Thus, at the species level, the major crops, which are associated with and are under the control of men, have far fewer varieties. On the other hand, the traditional and subsistence crops that are now considered minor crops, and associated with and cultivated by women, have a huge diversity of species and varieties. Unfortunately, the way gender relations operate today, women benefit very little from their major role in the conservation of agro-biodiversity. This despite the fact that women are doing most of the work in the cultivation of the 'major' crops also as they are involved in all the stages of work (sowing, transplanting, weeding, manuring, harvesting, storage, seed selection, seed keeping and also seed exchange to some extent).

GENETIC MANAGEMENT

The linkage between agro-biodiversity and distinct gender roles is particularly in relation to seed management which involves seed selection, seed saving and seed exchange (Howard 2003; Howard-Borjas 2001; Momsen 2004; Rocheleau et al. 1996; Sachs et al. 1997; Zimmerer 1996). Traditionally, as well as in the present context, this sphere falls under the 'women's domain' among both the Nagas and the Lepchas. Thus, this is the only sphere where there has been no change in the gender roles and authority. Women select and store seed of all crops, major and minor, except cardamom, the Lepchas' cash crop. The older women in particular do this work because of their experience and because the tasks require less physical effort. Such a role is legitimised by culture and gender ideology as women are considered the symbols of fertility. The women have exclusive control of decision-making processes and the practice of seed management. Thus, women are the knowledge holders of genetic management at the household level, which is crucial not only for conserving agro-biodiversity but also for their livelihood. This knowledge is obtained from first-hand experience beginning at a very young age. Information is passed down and learnt from female relatives through observation, demonstration and participation.

Seed management systems involve selection, storage and supply/exchange. Seed selection is done on the basis of several morphological criteria such as health, freedom from disease, drought resistance, resistance to wind and rain, and grain quality. Besides, women also have certain preferences. For instance, they select for early ripening, palatability, ease in grinding, preparation and processing time, and suitability for fodder, etc. It was found that they rarely look for market value. Women also have various traditional and indigenous methods of saving and storing seeds.

The major source of seeds for most farmers among both the Lepchas and the Nagas is their own household, which accounts for approximately 90 per cent of the seed supply. In addition, there are elaborate terms of exchange between family members, neighbours and neighbouring villagers. Within villages, exchange is an important means by which seed quality is retained within communities. Women are the decision-makers and are directly involved in the exchange of seeds within the village, sharing views and information on how the seed is selected and stored, and what varieties and seed qualities others have. In this way, they serve as seed conservers. Seed swapping within a village is occasionally done by men under the guidance of women. Visiting female relatives, especially married daughters, always carry seeds to and from their husbands' villages. During such visits women also exchange views and information regarding seed selection and storage.

Box 7.1: Example from the Chekasang Tribe of Nagas

Among the Chekasang Nagas, it was not uncommon for a daughter married and living in another village to carry seeds when visiting her natal home. Traditionally, in times of war between tribes, the daughters were known to carry seeds hidden in the goiter of chickens. Also, it was not unusual for some girls to be sent off in marriage to enemy tribes to learn the secrets of seed management. While preparing to come home, such women are known to have fed the choicest grains to chickens that they would carry with them and which would then be slain in their natal village. New seed sources were maintained in this way.

Source: Field notes.

Seeds purchased from the market are considered 'external' because men as 'providers' conduct 'outside' work where women have no control over these sources.

Thus, women's distinct social networks and their higher dependence on these networks (Agarwal 2000) are a backbone to agrobiodiversity conservation. Women have played and continue to play a key role as indigenous breeders, knowledge managers and seed distributrs (Inhetveen 1998). As women have a better understanding of how seed exchange networks are maintained, genetic losses are avoided through years of learning and oral tradition.

Although there has been no change in the gender role and authority in the gendered space of agro-biodiversity, there has been a drastic change as regards the valuation and importance of the work and knowledge held. Previously, this work and knowledge was given its due importance, but once agriculture became the domain of men and women lost control over it, and the market economy also came to be dominant, women's work as well as knowledge of genetic resource management was undervalued.

Neither men nor women give importance to such a vital task. Both men and women view women's work with seed management as a socially constructed role of convenience: women work near the home whereas men are in the fields, and seed management is considered to be a home-based activity (Oakley and Momsen 2005). In the words of the Lepcha women it is *'basi biyalo garne kaam'* meaning work that is to be done at leisure. Indeed, women's contributions to agro-biodiversity management (seed selection and storage, pruning and tending plants, etc.) are not considered activities in their own right, but rather an extension of women's reproductive chores (Padmanabhan 2005). Thus, seed management work and knowledge is in the 'women's sphere' and considered 'inside' work, not of much importance in the context of gender relations in the contemporary cash economy.

However, it is also not unusual for men to become involved in seed selection and saving activities, especially when physical disabilities hamper them from doing other heavy agricultural tasks. Interestingly, their knowledge is passed to their daughters and not sons, thus such role change is temporary, based on the current practical needs of the family. When due to whatever circumstances a man takes over seed work, the value and importance immediately increases and his status in the society too rises. This is very clear in a case where a man belonging to the Lepcha community had taken up this work as he was physically too weak to carry out other 'heavy' work ascribed to men. He had acquired the knowledge of seed selection and storage from his mother and wife. His role as a man gave him wider mobility whereby he could go out and get new varieties and also more information. Besides, as a man he was free of the daily household and reproductive chores, thus giving him the time to experiment in the fields with new crop varieties. As a result he had introduced several new varieties of maize, rice and vegetables in his village. Thus, he acquired the position of a seed expert not only in this village but also in the neighbouring villages, gaining him immense prestige and status. The case distinctly shows that what is actually an intellectual and manual task becomes invisible when done by women, as then transactions take place away from the market in the realm of another reproductive task and so are considered as an extension of 'women's nature'. Whereas when this same task is performed by a man and takes place in the realm of the cash economy then additional value is added to it. As pointed out by Padmanabhan (2005) the misconceptualisation of women's work as their essential character and not as part of their labour is still a powerful tool to dilute women's contributions and respective claims.

FOOD HABITS, FOOD PREFERENCES AND PREPARATION METHODS

Another extremely important factor that contributes to the conservation of crop species and varieties is that of its utilisation. The specific crop species and varieties are conserved through their utilisation, which is ultimately linked to a lifestyle (Padmanabhan 2005) including food habits and food preferences. With the introduction of new crops, especially white rice cultivated in wet terraces, and the external influences that have transformed social and gender systems, food habits, preferences and preparation methods too have changed having a direct impact on how agro-biodiversity is maintained and conserved. Thus, crop diversity is inextricably linked to the numerous food habits of the ethnic groups. Because women have to take care of food preferences and preparation, they possess extensive knowledge of the particular characteristics of different varieties of 'minor' and subsistence crops. Men too possess such knowledge but with regard to the major crops and other cash crops.

Women continually experiment and try out new varieties with the preferred traits in their 'domains' so that they can have more options. For instance, Naga women first try out new varieties in small plots near the field hut where they can observe their growth regularly, and if this meets all the characteristics they require to fulfil the food habits, the variety is accepted and cultivated in their home gardens and swidden fields.

Conclusion

Past events in the eastern Himalaya and the northeastern region and the human populations of neighbouring states and countries had an enormous impact on the gender relations of the communities whereby 'providers' (men) have become more dominant than 'caretakers' (women). Now, the dynamics and complexities of gender-segregated power relations within households and

Box 7.2: Some Examples

White rice grown in wet terraces is now the most important crop in terms of taste as well as social prestige. There are numerous ways of preparing rice — Lepchas do this in five different ways and the Nagas have seven ways. The number of varieties cultivated is also the highest as compared to other cereal crops like maize, wheat, millet, upland rice, etc.

Due to the significance of wetland rice, *ghaiya*, the traditional upland rice has gradually lost its importance, especially among the Lepchas, leading to a drastic decrease in the varieties cultivated. However, among the Nagas, this crop is still an important food and they have many ways of preparation, so even today 34 varieties of upland rice are cultivated.

Maize is an important crop especially as it is an alternate source of food during scarce periods. It is prepared in numerous ways. However, since this crop is not considered of social and cultural value, but only for 'filling the stomach', the number of varieties is the same as that of wetland rice.

Millet, a traditionally important crop has lost much of its food value. It is still of religious and cultural importance to the Lepchas. However, as they use this crop only for religious rituals and social ceremonies in the form of *chi* (a fermented alcoholic brew) the number of varieties of millet has decreased drastically.

Among the Nagas, job's tears is a traditionally important crop associated with feasts of merit (offered to the ritual specialist who conducts the rituals related to all agricultural activities, along with rice and meat) but has lost its importance, as feasts of merit are rarely, if ever, given and the crop is also not eaten as food these days. It is only used as fodder for pigs. As such the number of varieties has decreased.

Among both the groups, the traditional crops that have lost their importance as food have now given way to various vegetables, spices and fruit crops. These have become important accompaniments to rice and other major food, resulting in an increase in the number of species and varieties of such crops. This can be seen in the home gardens and swidden plots maintained by women.

Source: Field notes.

communities influence the systems of, and are reflected in, the agro-biodiversity management of the communities.

By virtue of their gender roles, both Naga and Lepcha women have played and continue to play a key role in the management and conservation of agro-biodiversity as indigenous breeders, knowledge managers and holders, and seed distributors (Inhetveen 1998). This study shows that women's distinct roles in agricultural labour and their authority over the three levels (agro-ecosystem, species and gene) based on their gender, places women in a position of managing and conserving agro-biodiversity more directly.

Traditional systems of seed management, food habits, food preferences and preparation methods, the ritual and socio-cultural significance attached to certain crops, are all factors on which crop diversity depends. In such a system, women are the principal custodians of agro-biodiversity. However, what appear as pure conservation strategies are culturally embedded activities, making sense for the actors only from a livelihood perspective (Padmanabhan 2005). In addition, as the market economy views all transactions in the non-market realm as of no value, women's work and knowledge are not seen as conservation strategies in any way.

As incidences of poverty and low household incomes are fairly easy to measure in today's world, poverty has become the standard yardstick for development. While measuring the success of development in the eastern Himalaya and the northeastern region, perhaps the indigenous native communities of the region rank lowest and rarest of all. As the true ends of development are not incomes but freedom to choose a way of life (Sen 1999) and ability to adapt in the ever-changing landscape, the livelihood practices of these peoples are adaptive by enduring external changes that influence their livelihood and society. This inclusive societal arrangement had always benefited them as agrarian forest dwellers. However, such a lifestyle has also isolated them, so they remain marginalised from the mainstream development. At the same time, the increasing influences of both global and regional market economies, land tenure issues, and a rapidly increasing population have combined to create and intensify socio-ecological as well as political conflicts. The overall spin-off of these occurrences is that major parts of this region are undergoing movements for cultural and political rights and recognition resulting in clashes not only with the government(s) in power, but in many instances among the various communities themselves. In this surcharged clash of identities in the region, women's contributions, their equitable recognition and economic reward are all but diluted despite these being key issues in the sustainable management of agro-biodiversity. Bearing in mind the changing times and history of the region and its peoples, it is difficult to predict how gender relations, land-related stewardship and sustainable agro-biodiversity conservation will play out.

Note

* This essay draws upon the findings from the Project 'Gender, Ethnicity and Agro-biodiversity Management in the Eastern Himalayas', funded by the International Development Research Centre (IDRC), Canada. The research team included Chanda Gurung Goodrich, Sion Lepcha, Chozule Kiki, and Aneugla Aier.

  Previous and different versions of this essay have appeared in *Habitat Himalaya – A Resources Himalaya Factfile*, 8(1), 2001; *Agrobiodiversity Conservation and the Role of Rural Women, Expert Consultation Report*, 2002, FAO, Regional Office for Asia and the Pacific, Bangkok, Thailand; International Potato Center-Users' Perspectives with Agriculture Research and Development (CIP-UPWARD), Los Banos, Laguna, Philippines; SEAMEO South-east Asia Regional Center for Graduate Study and Research in Agriculture (SEAMEO-SEARCA) RAP Publication 2002/07; *Mountain Agriculture in the Hindu Kush-Himalayan Region*, 2003, Tang Ya and Pradeep M. Tulachan (eds), Proceedings of an International Symposium held 21–24 May 2001 in Kathmandu, Nepal.,ICIMOD, Kathmandu, Nepal.

References

Agarwal, B. 2000. 'Conceptualising Environmental Collective Action: Why Gender Matters', *Cambridge Journal of Economics*, 24(3): 283–310.

Gorer, Geoffery. 1938 (1987). *The Lepchas of Sikkim*. Delhi: Gian Publishing House.

Gurung, Chanda and Nawraj Gurung. 2006. 'The Social and Gendered Nature of Ginger Production and Commercialization: A Case Study of the Rai, Lepcha and Brahmin-Chhetri in Sikkim and Kalimpong, West Bengal, India', in R. Vernooy (ed.), *Social and Gender Analysis in Natural Resource Management. Learning Studies and Lessons from Asia*. New Delhi: Sage; International Development Research Centre, Canada; China Agriculture Press, Beijing, China, pp. 37–64.

Gurung, Jeannette D. (ed.). 1999. *Searching for Women's Voices in the Hindukush-Himalayas.* Kathmandu: International Centre for Integrated Mountain Development.

Howard, P. L. 2003. *Women and Plants: Gender Relations in Biodiversity Management & Conservation.* London and New York: Zed Press.

Howard-Borjas, P. 2001. 'Women in the Plant World: The Significance of Women and Gender Bias for Botany and Biological Diversity', Inaugural Address, University of Wageningen, Wageningen.

Inhetveen, H. 1998. 'Women Pioneers in Farming: Gendered History of Agricultural Progress', *Sociologia Ruralis,* 38(3): 265–84.

Lambrou, Yianna and Regina Laub. 2006. 'Gender, Local Knowledge, and Lesson Learnt in Documenting and Conserving Agrobiodiversity', Research paper No. 2006/69), United Nations University, UNU-WIDER.

Momsen, J. H. 2004. *Gender and Development.* London and New York: Routledge.

Myers, N. 1988. 'Threatened Biotas: Hot Spots in Tropical Forests', *The Environmentalist,* 8(3): 187–208.

Nakro, Vengota and Chozule Kikhi. 2006. 'Strengthening Market Linkages for Women Vegetable Vendors', in R. Vernooy (ed.), *Social and Gender Analysis in Natural Resource Management. Learning Studies and Lessons from Asia.* New Delhi: Sage; International Development Research Centre, Canada; China Agriculture Press, Beijing, China, pp. 65–94.

Oakley, Emily and Janet Henshall Momsen. 2005. 'Gender and Agrobiodiversity: A Case Study from Bangladesh', *The Geographical Journal,* 177(3): 195–208.

Padmanabhan, Martina Aruna. 2005. 'Institutional Innovations towards Gender Equity in Agrobiodiversity Management — Collective Action in Kerela, South India'. CAPRi Working Paper # 9. International Food Policy Research Institute (IFPRI).

Rocheleau, D., E. Wangari and B. Thomas-Slayter. 1996. *Feminist Political Ecology: Global Issues and Local Experience.* London and New York: Routledge.

Sachs, C. E., K. Gajural and M. Bianco. 1997. 'Gender, Seeds and Biodiversity', in C. E. Sachs (ed.), *Women Working in the Environment.* London and Washington DC: Taylor & Francis.

Secretariat of the Convention on Biological Diversity. 2001. *Assessment and Management of Alien Species that Threaten Ecosystems, Habitats and Species.* CBD Technical Series, No. 1, Montreal, Canada.

Sen, A. 1999 *Development as Freedom.* London: Oxford University Press.

Siiger, Halfden. 1967. *The Lepchas — Culture and Religion of a Himalayan People: Part I.* Copenhagen: The National Museum of Denmark.

Zimmerer, K. S. 1996. *Changing Fortunes: Biodiversity and Peasant Livelihood in the Peruvian Andes*. Berkeley: University of California Press.

Zwarteveen, Margreet. 2008. 'Seeing Women and Questioning Gender in Water Management'. Paper submitted for the panel 'Engendering Water Governance in South Asia: Re-thinking Policy and Practice', International Conference on Water Resources Policy in South Asia (SaciWaters, 18–20 December 2008, Colombo, Sri Lanka).

8

Gender, Food Security and Rice Farming in Tripura*

VINCENT DARLONG, D. K. HORE AND S. DEB BARMA

India's northeastern region (NER), encompassing the states of Arunachal Pradesh, Assam, Manipur, Meghalaya, Mizoram, Nagaland, Sikkim, and Tripura, is a region of unique landscapes. Predominantly mountainous and upland but interspersed with valleys and rivers, this picturesque region is endowed with biodiverse forests and ethno-diverse tribal and non-tribal communities. Many hills across the region are dotted with remnants of agricultural footprints in the form of shifting cultivation (jhum), while the valleys are characterised by settled agriculture.[1] Agriculture with allied activities is the mainstay of the economy in the NER, which provides livelihood support to more than 70 per cent of the population. The effective area of NER under productive agriculture is 40–50 per cent, compared to the all-India average of 64 per cent (Agarwal 2003). The pattern of agricultural growth has remained uneven across the region and crops. The NER covers 7.7 per cent of India's total geographical area, but being hilly terrain it produces only 1.5 per cent of the country's total food grain and, therefore, the region continues to be a net importer of food grains.

Tripura is among India's poorest states in per capita State Domestic Product (De 2007). For many years, the state was known for its escalating insurgency problems. Nearly 85 per cent of the population live in rural areas and earn their livelihood mainly from agricultural activities. In spite of several measures undertaken, poverty, especially rural poverty, has not appreciably reduced. Estimates of the Government of Tripura show that the present extent of poverty is much more than that of other states in the NER.

The Department of Agriculture estimated that about 24.3 per cent of the geographical area is available for agricultural use in the state. Agriculture in Tripura is mostly rice production. Wet rice cultivation (WRC) is the most common practice, while the upland rice cultivation (URC), also known as shifting cultivation or jhum cultivation, is still prevalent in pockets. It is estimated that nearly 90 per cent of agricultural operations are related to rice farming. However, only half of the available agricultural land is effectively utilised; optimal use of agricultural lands is constrained by the lack of irrigation facilities, credit and financial support, non-mechanised agricultural operations and weak market linkages for agricultural produce. Large numbers of women work as agricultural labourers. Although women play a dominant role in rice farming operations in all the rice-producing communities and countries (FAO 1996, 1997), agricultural development efforts have not been sensitive to the needs of women farmers because of the general premise that 'farmers' are usually men.

This essay uses a gender focus, looking at the roles, responsibilities, problems, and priorities of women and men, to understand the extent of the changing roles of women of tribal and other communities engaged in rice farming in Tripura.[2] The structural relationship of gender inequality and disparity is manifested in labour markets and political structures as well as in households. Therefore, we seek to examine the disparities, disadvantages and obstacles faced by women in terms of access and control over resources, welfare and development relating to rice farming and food self-sufficiency. We specifically focus on: (*a*) women's access to land and land tenure systems, and their role in decisions relating to choice and marketing of crops; (*b*) the nature of women's labour in the rice economy, the impact on their health, and the economic organisation in terms of wages; (*c*) women's present status as preservers of agricultural knowledge in the traditional rice economies; (*d*) women's drudgery-prone activities in rice farming, including their indigenous knowledge vis-à-vis the improved tools and implements and their involvement in the introduction and spread of new technology; (*e*) women's contribution to shifting cultivation (jhum) and whether their voices have been heard while proposing alternative systems to jhuming or in introducing new varieties of rice seeds; (*f*) their role in conserving rice diversities; and (*g*) women's concerns in relation to agrarian policy-making processes, particularly regarding rice farming in Tripura. The essay draws upon case studies from seven locations or sites involving seven different tribal communities. In two of the locations both the WRC and URC (jhum) were practised, while in the remaining sites only WRC was seen. Thus, a total of six WRC sites and three URC sites were studied.

The essay starts with a profile of the state, briefly outlines trends in agriculture and agricultural policies, and then discusses aspects of rice farming, production and rice germplasm. We then analyse gender concerns in rice farming through case studies, leading to suggestions and general conclusions.

Profile of Tripura

Only 10,492 sq km in area, Tripura is among the smallest states in India. Nearly 70 per cent of the state is hilly (locally known as *tilla*) giving rise to a number of rain-fed rivers and streams that flow into Bangladesh. About 59 per cent of Tripura is classified as forest (and is under the ambit of the Forest Conservation Act); about 90 per cent of this is actually covered with various categories of forest. About 39 per cent of the forest area is classified as 'reserved'. Therefore, only a small area of land (between 24 and 27 per cent) is available for agriculture. Despite its small size, Tripura is one of the most populous states, with a density of 305 per sq km. The state merged with the Indian Union in 1949 and attained statehood in 1972. Formerly, tribal communities formed the major part of the population but with the changing geopolitical situation, the demographic character has changed rapidly. Consequently, the tribal population reduced to 31.13 per cent in 2001 from about 93 per cent in 1947 (Kapur 2007). The majority of the rural people are poor and face serious food and nutritional insecurity.

Physiographically, Tripura has three distinct terrains: the north–south oriented hill ranges (designated as Zone I); undulating plateau lands (Zone II); and low-lying alluvial plains (Zone III). Each of these zones has its own characteristics in terms of agricultural growth, particularly for rice farming. Five major hill ranges, separated by narrow valleys 20 to 30 km wide extend southward into the Chittagong Hill Tracts of Bangladesh. Between the easternmost range Jampui and the Baramura-Debtamura hills in the west are the Sakhantlang, Longtarai and Atharamura ranges. The highest peak in Tripura is the Betliangchhip (3,600 ft) in North Tripura, with a panoramic view of neighbouring Mizoram. Many of the hill ranges are under shifting cultivation, but the valleys (called *lunga*) with alluvial soils are productive agricultural areas, particularly for paddy. The population density in the alluvial valleys is also the highest, though such areas are fairly limited.

Administratively, the state has four districts (North Tripura, Dhalai, West and South Tripura), 17 sub-divisions, 40 development blocks, 13 urban areas, besides the Tripura Tribal Areas Autonomous District Council (TTAADC or ADC) under the Sixth Schedule of the Constitution, which has its own administrative and functional jurisdiction. Tripura has 60 members in its legislative assembly and 30 members (including two nominated) in the district council. The Panchayati Raj institutions in Tripura are well developed and integrated with four Zilla Parishads; there are 82 elected members of Zilla Parishads (including 28 women) and as many as 23 Panchayat Samities (with 299 elected members including 106 women), 513 Gram Panchayats (outside ADC) and 527 Village Committees (within ADC).

Tripura has 19 major tribes. However, based on the socio-cultural and linguistic affinities, these tribes can be categorised into two major groups, that is, the Borok group (mainly the Tripuris, Reang, Jamatia, Mog, Noatia, and also including the Koloi, Rupini and Murasing) and the Halam-Kuki-Lushai group (comprising the Lushai, Kuki and Halam tribes and their sub-tribes). The Munda, Santal, Oraon, and Bhil tribes of central India were brought into the state by the colonial tea industry as labourers in tea plantations and are considered to be 'migrant' tribes. Other tribes, like the Garos, Khasis, Lepchas, and Bhutias, migrated to the state on their own for economic and livelihood reasons. In general, the tribals in Tripura are economically backward, socially vulnerable, ethnically threatened, and educationally weak. Of the 19 tribes in Tripura, the Reangs/Riangs are categorised as a 'primitive tribal group' (PTG).[3] Upland rice cultivation, jhum, continues to be identified with the tribal communities in the state.

Trends in Agriculture and Agrarian Policy

The economy of Tripura is primarily agrarian and more than 70 per cent of the people depend on agriculture for their livelihood.

The terrain with low hills and criss-crossing valleys, the monsoon climatic conditions and soil characteristics, are fairly favourable for agri-horticultural species. After forests, agriculture is the major land-use, with cultivation of both traditional crops and newer horticultural species which are gaining popularity. Agriculture contributes 42 per cent of the State Domestic Product (SDP) and 64 per cent of employment, with small and marginal farmers constituting 90 per cent of the total farmers. There has been a steady rise in the contribution of the tertiary sector to the SDP but the secondary sector has remained almost static at about 7 per cent. The net sown area constitutes about 24 per cent of the total area; only 19.6 per cent of the total cultivable area receives assured irrigation. About 75 per cent of the net sown area is generally double cropped. Due to the high population density, the average size of operational holdings of 0.97 ha is much smaller than the all-India average of 1.68 ha (Government of Tripura 2009a).

Tripura's agricultural performance, particularly in rice and food grain production in the last 50 years, indicates a gradual but significant improvement. For example, the area for rice production increased from 164,630 ha in 1955–56 to 245,780 ha in 2001–2; production increased from 137,670 MT in 1955–56 to 608,770 MT in 2001–02, and productivity increased from 835 per ha in 1955–56 to 2,477 per ha in 2001–02 (Government of Tripura 2007). This clearly shows the efforts of the government in technological intervention along with improved seed quality and management practices. During the same period, the number of agricultural labourers increased in rice farming systems, as also their skills.

Jhum (Shifting Cultivation)

Jhum continues to be the predominant livelihood occupation of a large number of tribal peoples in Tripura, especially among the Tripuri, Reang, Jamatia, Kuki, Garo, Noatia, Halam, Mag, Chakma, and Lushai. Of the 55,049 households (with a population of 288,390) who are practising jhum, 21,677 households are entirely dependent on jhum while the rest are partly dependent. Though jhum cultivation was common in the past, now about 50 per cent of the tribals have turned to settled cultivation. Jhuming is mainly for food crops, though some religious functions are associated with the practice, particularly among the Reang. Due to the low productivity and low incomes, as also deforestation and soil erosion, the government policy is to win people away from shifting cultivation by providing alternatives. Although the jhum practices vary among the different tribes in Tripura, there is negligible variability in cropping patterns and the use of fallows. Rice cultivation remains the main objective of jhuming but the varieties of crops cultivated in the jhum fields have generally reduced over the years. Jhum has been the principal means of conservation, cultivation and propagation of upland rice germplasm varieties. According to the studies done by Sharma and Hore (1990), Tripura had at least 30 rice landraces cultivated in the upland jhum farming system until the mid-1980s. With the reducing area under jhum, there has also been genetic erosion of the upland landraces of rice in most parts of Tripura. Today, jhum is no longer done in the systematic manner of the by-gone years. Most jhum fields are in forest lands, which are under the control of the Forest Department. The 'protected' forests have now been re-designated as unclassified state forests (USFs) and jhum is now mostly carried out in such forests. On the other hand, due to the state government's vigorous jhum control efforts, there are some positive results as many of the traditional jhum lands have been converted into horticultural crop lands such as those under pineapple cultivation in the North Tripura and Dhalai districts.

In spite of the official policy of doing away with jhum, the Government of Tripura has taken rather a rational view on the matter. About 15,000 ha is under jhum cultivation. The state government has deemed more appropriate to provide a package of practices for improving the productivity of existing jhum crops while encouraging the farmers to take up settled cultivation practices. With these objectives in view, the Department of Agriculture developed a 'Package of Practices' for improving the production and productivity of jhum crops, with a special thrust for improving the economic condition of poor jhumias.[4]

AGRICULTURAL PERSPECTIVE PLAN (2001–10)

Tripura has brought out a Perspective Plan of Agriculture for the period 2001–10. Its main vision as a food-deficit state is achieving self-sufficiency in food grain production, including rice and other pulses. The amount spent on importing food grains would then be used for developing infrastructure. The Plan takes the per capita daily rice requirement as 500 gm, amounting to an annual deficit of 218,000 tonnes. By 2010, it was expected to be in surplus of 18,000 tonnes. For pulses the target was to increase production to make possible a daily consumption of 17 gm per capita per day in 2010.

For achieving its aims, the irrigation potential would be increased from the present 51,000 ha to 116,867 ha, and the cropping intensity for rice would go up from 169 per cent to 283 per cent. The area under low-yielding local varieties is to be replaced gradually with short duration high-yielding variety (HYV) rice as the first kharif (summer) crop. Medium-duration HYVs yielding at least 3,000 kg per ha are to be grown as the second kharif crop. Rice varieties with the potential of at least 3,500 kg per ha are to be grown in the rabi (winter) season. So, 58,000 ha (42 per cent of the second kharif rice area) and 50,000 ha (50 per cent of the rabi rice area) were to be put under hybrid rice by the year 2010. The area under pulses will be increased from the present level of 9,800 ha to 34,000 ha. The productivity of jhum rice is to be raised from the present level of 600 kg per ha by adopting a package of improved practices. The area under potato is to be increased from 5,000 ha to 10,000 ha. The plan considers agriculture an economic activity and not merely subsistence farming but its goals can only be achieved by the adequate flow of investment through credit institutes.

Having ascertained the availability of land and requirement of food for the projected population, the Perspective Plan suggests various strategies to ensure food security: increasing irrigation potential and cropping intensity to the maximum possible extent; seed and varietal replacement; enhancing consumption of plant nutrients; incorporation of bio-fertilisers in conjunction with inorganic fertilisers; integrated pest management; and research support. It also emphasises the need for adequate farm power, credit, extension support, and ensuring people's participation. The state government expects wholehearted cooperation and active participation from people from all walks of life, specially the representatives of the three-tier Panchayat and Autonomous District Council as well as the concerned government officials.

RICE FARMING AND PRODUCTION SCENARIO

Rice, the main staple in Tripura, is grown in three seasons — *Aus, Aman* (winter) and *Boro* (summer) — and many areas also practise jhum. Tripura is an important rice-producing state although its share of India's rice production has been rather insignificant (0.51 per cent in 1955–56; 0.76 per cent in 1975–76; 0.61 per cent in 1995–96 and 0.57 per cent in 1999–2000), but the yield of 2.2 tonnes/ha is slightly higher than the all-India average of 2.0 tonnes/ha. The area under rice production in Tripura has always been above 90 per cent of the total area under food grains production. Singha (2003) has observed that the first two decades (1950s and 1960s) of high performance were due to the expansion of area under agriculture, and from the 1970s high production is directly correlated with the increasing irrigation, fertilisers (NPK) and the introduction of HYVs. There has also been significant increase in farm mechanisation in recent years; more tractors, power tillers and water pump sets are being utilised. The mechanisation in rice farming is particularly in the vicinity of the state capital Agartala. Farm labour, both male and female, has also increased.

In terms of the food self-sufficiency ratio, Tripura represents an interesting situation. Among the northeastern states, the population density of Tripura is second to Assam; it also has the second lowest human–land ratio and ranks fourth in percentage area under cultivation. Yet, interestingly, Tripura has the highest food self-sufficiency ratio, assuming an average rice requirement of 500 gm/day/person, and also by the government's estimate of requirements as 618 gm/day/person. Though the data has been deduced from the production figures of 1990–91, it is assumed that the data generally reflects the current scenario. Yet, in practice, Tripura remains a rice-deficit state.

In recent years Tripura has increasingly adopted the system of rice intensification (SRI) to improve the rice yield. Various assessments of SRI in Tripura showed an average rice yield of 4.3 tonnes/ha against the average yield of 2.2 tonnes/ha under traditional rice cultivation (Prasad 2007). Currently, Tripura has about 45,000 ha under SRI benefiting more than 100,000 farmers. A report of the World Wide Fund for Nature (WWF) and ICRISAT on Tripura's experiences with the SRI method projects that the state can easily achieve its target of producing 130,000 tonnes of paddy, which is equivalent to about 90,000 MT of milled rice, by 2015 (WWF 2007).

RICE GERMPLASM

Tripura has a very rich resource of rice germplasm diversity. Our knowledge of the rice germplasm is primarily from the works of Sasikumar and Sardana (1987) and Sharma and Hore (1990), though other studies from northeastern India in general also include information on the state (Asthana and Majumder 1981; Seetharaman et al. 1974; Srivastava 1978).

Based on extensive field work, Sharma and Hore (1990) recorded over a hundred landraces or varieties, classified as per their habitat and quality.[5] These are: wetland rice that generally require some amount of standing water in the field, though most of these can grow well under normal rain-fed conditions; upland (jhum) rice that are resistant to drought or low rain conditions, and adapt to low phosphorus and potash soils; deep-water rice that either require or can tolerate continuous submerged or flood water conditions; soft rice preferred for quick cooking, preparation of local snacks and savouries, and also for brewing 'rice beer'; and scented rice used for preparing local delicacies, snacks, sweets, and savouries, particularly during festivals and marriages.

Sharma and Hore (1990) also report the alarmingly rapid genetic erosion of rice germplasm; the recorded 42 indigenous varieties in 1986 were reduced to 32 by 1990, within just four years. The primary reason for this genetic erosion is the modernisation of agriculture with the introduction of HYVs to meet the growing need of the increasing population.[6] According to their study, while rice production increased, the rate of loss of landraces varied from 12.5 per cent to over 73 per cent in 1990.

Preliminary Assessment of Impacts of the Agriculture Perspective Plan

A preliminary assessment of the impacts of the Perspective Plan of Agriculture was carried out during 2007. As per the report, there had been significant indicators of change in the agriculture scenario. Quality HYV certified seed production increased from 28 MT in 1999 to 5,000 MT in 2007. Production of hybrid paddy seeds increased from 10 tonnes in 2004 to 50 tonnes in 2007. Balanced use of fertiliser rose from 25 kg/ha in 2000 to 47 kg/ha in 2007. Similarly production and use of bio-fertilisers increased from 1.4 kg/ha in 2000 to 20 kg/ha in 2007. Agricultural credit to farmers adopting SRI increased paddy yields by 40–45 per cent (in some cases even 50 per cent) over 12,992 ha in 2007. The number of farmers trained increased from 7,150 in 2000 to 65,475 in 2007. Farm mechanisation has also been significantly achieved.

The number of power tillers made available increased from 300 in 2002 to 444 in 2007; other improved farm implements like paddy reaper/harvester, weeder and paddle thresher also significantly increased from 112 in 2002 to 12,521 units in 2007 (Government of Tripura 2009b). However, no impact assessment seemed to have been done for jhum.

Overall, the state's economy is characterised by high incidence of poverty, low per capita income, low capital formation, inadequate infrastructural facilities, geographical isolation, communication bottlenecks, low industrial progress and high un-employment problems. Lack of infrastructure has made the process of economic development extremely difficult (Government of Tripura 2009c). This in turns affects the overall low progress of agriculture in the state.

Gender Issues in Rice Farming: Case Study Analysis

Field studies to understand gender issues in rice farming were done in selected villages and communities in Tripura. These study sites were Kathalcherra, Kukicherra, Chow Manu, and Gandacherra (Dhalai District), Champaknagar (West Tripura), Dasda (North Tripura), and Killa (South Tripura). Initial field studies were done in 2005–6 but were revisited during 2009–10 in order to capture changes. While wet rice cultivation (WRC) dominated in all the study sites, upland rice cultivation (URC) or jhum were still prevalent in three sites, that is, Chow Manu, Kukicherra and Gandacherra. In this study six different tribes or communities were covered who were traditionally shifting cultivators and had taken up WRC over the past 30–40 years. Due to small sample sizes (five to 23 households in each site), the findings may be taken as indicative, not conclusive. Information on the study sites and the communities are given in Table 8.1.

GENDER ISSUES AND PARAMETERS

The present study forms part of an extended study initiated earlier in the state on (*a*) status of tribal women and (*b*) community forestry. In these studies, data were collected using a combination of what is generally known as Rapid Rural Appraisal (RRA) and Participatory Rural Appraisal (PRA).[7] Selected indicator parameters were studied as outlined in the following paragraphs.

Table 8.1: Basic Information on the Case Study Sites and Communities Involved, Tripura

Category of rice farming	Village/study sites	District	Community	Land ownership
WRC	Kathalcherra	Dhalai	Darlong Kuki	Owner cultivator
	Kukicherra	Dhalai	Halam & Reang	Owner cultivator
	Gandacherra	Dhalai	Reang & Chakma	Owner cultivator
	Dasda	North Tripura	Chakma	Owner cultivator
	Champaknagar	West Tripura	Deb Barma	Owner cultivator
	Killa	South Tripura	Jamatia	Owner cultivator
URC or Jhum	Chowmanu	Dhalai	Tripura	Traditional jhum land
	Kukicherra	Dhalai	Halam & Reang	
	Gandacherra	Dhalai	Reang & Chakma	

Source: Compiled from the field study by the authors.

Land Ownership

All the communities in the study are patriarchal and patrilineal. Therefore, all land *pattas* (legal land ownership documents) for WRC were in men's names. Generally, women do not own any land and significantly none of the women thought it necessary to have land in their own names, except a few who were literate. Across the tribes, most women view the land as family-owned although registered in the husband's name. The women said that socially they have equal rights over the use of such lands for farming. Also, husbands consult with their wives to dispose of lands; most communities consider this 'good social practice'. Among the Darlongs, some families indicated that uplands (orchards, pineapple cultivation or home gardens) were customarily recognised as the women's but there were no legal documents of ownership. Indeed, among the Darlongs, gifting land by brothers to their sisters at the time of land distribution or succession of inheritance (usually after the death of parents) is considered good practice. In the upland jhum areas, the land ownership was not clear. Such lands were not in the name of the men or the women. While the families consider the jhumland as common village land, legally this is Unclassified State Forest (USF), treated as government or *khas* land.

Access to Land

It was observed that men and women have equal access to family land or fields and ownership was not the issue. Generally,

Darlong, Jamatia and Chakma women consult their men particularly when they want to grow off-season and winter vegetables, and secure men's support in fencing the vegetable field and purchasing seeds or seedlings. Men also help in irrigating vegetable crops.

Seeds and Varietal Ownership or Custodianship

Across the tribes, women are considered custodians of seeds. Most of the men interviewed felt that the women were better able and trusted to look after rice seeds. They acknowledged the women's expertise and skill of preserving and storing various types of seeds, and deciding the sowing time for jhum.

Decisions about Rice Varieties and Other Crops for Cultivation

The choice of crops or rice varieties for WRC is made by both men and women, across the tribes, although largely it depends on the availability of seeds preserved by the women from the previous season/year. Among the Reangs of Gandacherra the men made most of these decisions as the women felt that they did not know much about the WRC rice varieties. However, when it came to URC or jhum, across the tribes and particularly among the Reangs, Tripura, Jamatia, and Halam, women took the lead. They clearly played the major role in seed sowing and maintaining jhum fields, weeding, guarding, and harvesting. Women were also responsible for post-harvest activities.

Decisions about Post-harvest Storage, Processing for Consumption and Sale of Rice

In all WRC systems, both men and women take care of the post-harvest storage, though women are specially concerned with seed storage. Men construct the storage house or weave special storage bamboo baskets; women decide the quantity of seeds to be stored, and maintain the seeds to prevent insect infestation. Men take the decisions on the sale of rice, but often consult the women. Processing the rice for household consumption is women's responsibility. In the jhum system, sale of rice is jointly decided by the women and men. Among the Reang and Tripura tribes, jhum rice is seldom sold, but used for brewing traditional rice beer. Occasionally, if jhum rice is sold, it is to buy a larger quantity of cheaper rice for consumption or brewing rice beer.

Decisions about the Use of Income from Rice and Sale of other Commodities

Among all the communities in this study, the men generally keep the earning from the sale of rice, although women do get a share for their requirements (such as purchasing new clothing for themselves and children during festivals). As most women farmers in the present study were illiterate or had a low level of general awareness, they felt the money was more secure with the men. But there were also families who felt that women were better keepers of household money than the men. In most cases it was observed that the families traditionally consulted before any major expenditure was made from the money earned from the sale of rice or any other products. Among jhuming communities, the women collect vegetables from jhum fields for sale in the local market and use the proceeds to buy weekly household requirements.

Role and Nature of Labour Contributed by Women in Rice Farming

The issues examined were: (*a*) the nature and dimension of labour contributed by women farmers in rice farming, (*b*) relative work burden of the women, (*c*) impact on health of the women in rice farming and (*d*) economic organisation in terms of wages of women in rice farming. The WRC system has different stages of activities, including land preparation for rice nurseries, land preparation and field levelling for transplanting rice, and activities relating to pre-harvest, post-harvest and processing. In the WRC system men do most of the farm work that requires strenuous physical labour or strength; women participate in most other activities in addition to other household work. The nature, dimension and extent of participation by women and men farmers among the different tribes appear to be more or less the same with women participating in a larger number of activities than the men. Thus, the relative 'work burden' (percentage of time spent or labour hours contributed) by men and women among these communities has been estimated as 45:65. Similarly, in URC or jhum cultivation, the proportion of labour by men and women is 25:75, more or less similar across the tribes.

In both kinds of rice production systems in Tripura, women's work burden is higher than that of men; 65 per cent in WRC and 75 per cent in jhum. This indicates the extent of rural women farmers' involvement in rice farming in Tripura's owner-cultivator land holding system. Among the landless farm workers, however, both women and men spent an equal amount of time in rice production, though men are preferred for specific jobs such as ploughing and land preparation, and women for transplantation, weeding and harvesting activities.

Women's Wages

The wages of agricultural farm workers differ from place to place and tribe to tribe. Most women farm workers were, however, paid less than the men, though they effectively had longer working hours. In our preliminary observations of farm workers among the Darlongs of Kathalcherra, men average five-and-a-half hours of work compared to women's six-and-a-half hours. Yet, the women's average daily wage was ₹90 compared to the men's ₹100. This is justified as a *convention, rather than discrimination*, as women farm workers may leave (or have the choice to leave) the field a little earlier than the men as women are expected to fetch water and cook food at home. Similarly, the women may also begin their work a little later than the men. This is generally an accepted norm among this community and the women do not feel discriminated against.

Drudgery in Rice Farming

In all the study sites, the women continue to use only the indigenous tools and implements in rice farming. These include the spade and hoe for preparing the land and cutting water channels for irrigation, the sickle for harvesting, traditional baskets for transporting rice seedlings and harvested paddy, locally fabricated implements of tin and bamboo for lifting water for irrigation. Women appear to be comfortable with these tools and technology across the communities engaged in WRC. The jhuming women were acquainted only with indigenous technology for upland rice farming. This included the *dao* (a machete) for cutting bamboo and small trees, the bent dao for weeding, the sickle for cutting rice stalk, headstrap-supported baskets and hand-pounding tools for de-husking. Nowadays, most women take their paddy for de-husking to mini rice mills that have spread in most market places and larger villages of Tripura.

The limited use of improved tools and implements such as power tillers, water pump sets and insecticide sprayers was studied in some of the rice farming (WRC) areas. Generally, women knew about these tools/implements and would like to use them but none of the women were found to be operating these implements. The women in Champaknagar area have used the foot-operated thresher machine for separating paddy from stalk and some of them were already practising SRI technology. Drudgery reduction for women in rice farming should be a priority for agricultural policy and planning. Further study and detailed data are necessary; the Krishi Vigyan Kendras and the extension wings of the State Agriculture Department could help to understand the extent of women's involvement in the introduction and spread of new technology.

Women's Health

As women are involved in so many other labour-intensive activities, besides farming, such as collecting and carrying head-loads of firewood and drawing water for household needs, it was difficult to correlate between women's work in rice farming and their health status. In the owner-cultivator farming system, pregnant women worked on their own time and space, with other family members supplementing their share of work. Among the landless farm workers too, pregnant women continue to work whenever work is available, mostly in the fields of relatives or neighbours within the village itself. None reported discrimination by anyone on this account. Even among the shifting cultivator communities, pregnant women preferred to go to the jhum field, performing any chore at their own pace and ability, which keeps them rather healthy, agile and energetic. Women interviewed in the present study said that they do get sick, not because they work in rice farming, but because of seasonal diseases. We noticed that anaemic conditions, perhaps related to malnutrition and poverty, appeared to be significant among the women in the study.

Agricultural Indebtedness Relief

The Tripura Agricultural Indebtedness Relief Act, 1979 includes provisions for the relief of agricultural indebtedness of farmers including livestock farmers, landless agricultural workers and tribal shifting cultivators (jhumias). The Act has brought relief to women farmers in many rural areas of the state.

WOMEN IN OTHER FARMING SECTORS: HORTICULTURE AND LIVESTOCK REARING

The present study collected information on women's role and participation in horticulture and livestock rearing. Among the Darlong communities of Kathalcherra, pineapple cultivation is mainly undertaken by women, with men initially clearing the fields, erecting fencing and planting saplings. Women do periodic weeding, thinning or removal of young suckers (for planting in new areas), and harvesting. Women and children guard the plantation during fruiting. The pineapple fruits attract animals such as porcupines and monkeys; jungle crows peck the ripened fruits; domestic animals feed on the young leaves; and wild boars frequently dislodge the roots and feed on them. It was estimated that typically, Darlong women bear 80 per cent of the work burden in maintaining pineapple fields.

Livestock, particularly pig rearing and poultry, are traditional activities of all rural tribal groups under this study. All these communities consider this the woman's domain. Men construct livestock shelters but all other activities, 95 per cent of the work burden, are the women's responsibility. Women regularly collect feeds and feed the pigs, take care of the piglets, do the cleaning, etc. In recent years, however, men have also started taking an interest in vaccinating the pigs, and selling piglets or pig meat in the market.

WOMEN AS PRESERVERS AND COMMUNICATORS OF AGRICULTURAL KNOWLEDGE

It was difficult to assess women's agricultural knowledge in the WRC system perhaps because many of these communities were shifting cultivators till recently. While women did store the seeds in the WRC system, it was the men who actually selected the seeds that needed to be preserved. Women were generally aware of the stages of activities of the farming calendar but could not really do much without the participation of men, particularly in land preparation involving ploughing. Women are most skilled in rice transplantation, weeding, harvesting, and a few aspects of post-harvest processing such as drying of paddy, parboiling for dehusking, etc.

However, in the traditional farming system of jhum, women farmers among the Reangs, Halam, Tripura, and Chakmas were well acquainted with the farming calendar, seed selection, the combination of seeds for sowing, and sowing practices. They were also well versed in assessing which crops would be good in which gradients of jhum land, and the harvesting cycle (i.e., which crop to harvest when and how) and so on. They could also identify the maturity of tuber crops based on the condition/appearance of the stem/stalk or looking at the nature of the soil just above the tuber crops. Selections of fruit and other economic trees in the jhum field were usually done by the women, and such trees were properly marked with appropriate signs (e.g., bamboo-cross on the stem of the tree, or partial removal of the bark of the trees, etc.) so that everyone knew that these trees should not be harvested until maturity.

Besides, in the typical jhum system, the women took the initiative for collecting rice seeds for the following year's cultivation. The women usually make careful selections by collecting the right types of panicles with maximum numbers of grains per panicle. These are carefully harvested and kept separately for the following year's seeds. On an average, a woman stores about 25 kg of paddy seed for an area of 1 ha. Our study showed that such careful collections of panicles could take between five and seven days or more.

The women were also well acquainted with post-harvest methods of seed preservation based on species. They knew exactly how to preserve seeds of various crops for the following years. Indeed, the communities recognise such knowledge as the women's domain. The men's major contribution in upland rice farming is in selecting and preparing the land, slashing and burning vegetation, demarcating the boundary, constructing 'jhum huts' in the fields.

WOMEN AND AGRARIAN POLICY IN TRIPURA

Tripura and Assam were among the first states in NE India to adopt a policy for rehabilitation of shifting cultivators through providing alternative means of livelihood. Many programmes were initiated as early as the mid-1950s. Today, different departments and programmes of the Government of Tripura and the Tripura Tribal Areas Autonomous District Council are addressing the issues of alternatives to shifting cultivation and jhumia rehabilitation. The Agriculture Department encourages land terracing for permanent food crop production, and improved crop varieties for shifting cultivation areas. The Horticulture Department introduces fruit and nut crops such as pineapple and cashew. The Forest Department emphasises cultivation of tree and forest species as alternative economic activities. The Tribal Rehabilitation Plantation Corporation has supported rubber plantations as alternatives to shifting cultivation. The Fishery Department provides subsidy and grant for the development of fish farms for alternative livelihoods.

These initiatives are paralleled by funding for various schemes related to health and education by the Tribal Welfare Department. Occasionally, houses for the resettled jhumias have also been provided. But during the present field study, it was learnt that houses constructed and provided by the government agencies through jhumia rehabilitation schemes are often not occupied or are abandoned by the jhumias after a short period. The houses have been designed and constructed in the style of general semi-urban dwelling houses, without consulting the jhumias and keeping their requirements in mind.

The Rural Development Department has provided assistance for the integrated development of areas inhabited by jhumias. There are state programmes specially designed for the 'upliftment' of the 'primitive' or most backward communities (tribals) of the state, which have benefited the Reang, many of whom continue to be shifting cultivators. The Tripura Tribal Areas Autonomous District Council also executes a number of programmes and projects for the tribals in general and the shifting cultivators in particular. In recent years, many of the departmental programmes have become gender sensitive, and there are specific programmes designed for rural women, through women's Self-help Groups (SHGs), for micro-enterprises, which are intended to discourage jhuming and improve their economic opportunities.

In addition, Tripura has an ambitious policy document for planning and development, *Approach to People's Plan in Tripura*. Initiated at the dawn of the new millennium, the document includes the concerns on shifting cultivation and jhumia rehabilitation, though not specifically the needs of the women.[8] It states:

All primary sector departments will coordinate with each other to draw up the programmes for the economic uplift of jhumias. These programmes will have strong market focus and be subsidy based. The Tribal Welfare Department will monitor the proper implementation of the programmes and insist that a significant portion of the departmental resources should target jhumias. Apart from jhumias, there are a large number of tribal cultivators who, while not primarily dependent on jhum, live in upland areas. The focus in upland areas will be significantly on forestry, horticulture and animal husbandry. All primary sector departments will target the upland areas through specific programmes framed keeping in mind the special needs of the tribals and the tribal areas. The Tribal Welfare Department will monitor the proper implementation of the programme (Government of Tripura 2000: 8–9).

The Tripura government had also initiated a 37-Point 'Special Package for Development of Scheduled Tribes for the Period 2003–04 to 2006–07', which includes the development of women and shifting cultivators. It says (Point No. 26) that 'rubber plantation will be taken up for the benefit of the Scheduled Tribe (S.T.) jhumia families in 3,000 hectares to benefit 3,000 families to increase their income. Assistance will also be provided to eligible S.T. families for taking up Tea and Coffee plantation in suitable areas' (Government of Tripura 2003: 2). It emphasises training and inputs in improved farming practices for at least 10,000 jhumias (Point No. 27). And it also says that at least 1,000 tribal SHGs will be set up with an emphasis on women's groups (Point No. 33). It must, however, be noted that although Tripura has a long history of jhumia rehabilitation and jhum control programmes, careful analysis of these programmes does not indicate that the women have particularly benefited. There is also no conclusive evidence that the voice of women has been sufficiently heard or accommodated while designing and proposing alternative systems to shifting cultivation or while introducing new varieties of rice for jhum cultivation.

Both the important policy documents, the *Perspective Plan for Agriculture for the Period 2001–2010* (Government of Tripura 2009b) and the *Approach to People's Plan in Tripura* (Government of Tripura 2000), do not directly indicate any vision and strategy, which can be said to be gender-sensitive or women-oriented. However, recent approaches of various government departments and agencies involved in integrated rural development, improvement of rural livelihood and employment opportunities, jhumia rehabilitation and development of alternative livelihood activities, are increasingly adopting schemes and projects which are gender sensitive and address the concerns of the women. In many of these programmes, it has now become mandatory to focus on gender-sensitive policies, programmes, and projects, and constitute women-exclusive SHGs. Some of the successes have also been documented by the State Institute of Public Administration and Rural Development (SIPARD) and others.

In addition, Tripura also has an industrial policy, which specifically encourages development of women entrepreneurships, though mainly in the consumer industry, not specifically in the agricultural sphere. However, within the industrial policy of Tripura there is an ambitious development policy for agro-based industries, though again not specifically gender-sensitive or women-oriented. However, many of these policy statements can be translated into policy actions to benefit women and towards an overall policy of food security. The policy reads,

> As is known, Tripura's economy is predominantly agricultural. A large section of our tribal people still practise shifting cultivation. Because of the influx in population and tremendous pressure on the plain land, there is massive unemployment in the agricultural sector. To overcome this, modern horticultural practices — under the Rehabilitation programme for providing productive employment to the marginal farmers and shifting cultivators — will be continued vigorously. Tripura grows one of the finest varieties of pine apple, jackfruit, orange, guava etc. Recently, the tribal population has taken up vegetable cultivation also. The food and fruit products have a very wide market, provided these are scientifically preserved and processed. With adequate training programme, with the active assistance of nutrition experts from the Government of India, food and fruit processing and ventures will be given all encouragement. The existing training centres will be strengthened and training facilities at new places will be created. In consultation with the Agriculture, Horticulture, Fisheries and Forest Departments, Special projects will be formulated for production of more food-stuff for canning purposes. Preservation of fruits, fish, bamboo shoots and other fruit products will be taken up under this programme. (See Industrial Policy of North Eastern States — Tripura, available at www.lexuniverse.com/industrial-policy [accessed 24 February 2011]).

It may be mentioned that Tripura is currently implementing two important externally aided projects, that is, the Indo-German Development Cooperation for Participatory Natural Resource Management and the Japan Bank for International Cooperation (JBIC) funded project for sustainable management of the forest wealth of the state through improvement of the density and quality of the forest cover. Both these programmes are gender sensitive. Similarly, the National Bamboo Mission includes initiatives to benefit rural women in Tripura.

Suggestions and Concluding Remarks

Agricultural growth in northeastern India, particularly self-sufficiency in food grain production, will continue to be a challenge for farmers, agricultural scientists and agricultural policy planners. There are inherent problems and numerous untapped potentials for agricultural development. Strategies for agricultural research and development in the region need to take advantage of the region's rich natural resources and biodiversity; congenial climate for crop diversification, particularly horticultural crops; rich soil suitable for agriculture; and the communities who are well acquainted with both upland and lowland farming (Barah 2006; NAAS 2001). Tripura envisaged achieving food grain self-sufficiency by 2010 through its 10-Year Perspective Plan that was initiated in 2000. While improving significantly in rice production, the state is yet to achieve food security for its people, with enough food for an active and healthy life. The present study clearly shows that women in Tripura contribute a very significant share of work and bear the burden of rice farming, particularly among the rural communities and in both the wet rice and upland jhum cultivation systems. Women could be much more effective with more equitable physical and economic access to productive resources.

Food security for Tripura primarily means sustainable production of rice in all farming systems. This requires conservation of the state's rice germplasm, particularly the traditional high yielding varieties and those having potential for developing into hybrid varieties through vigorous research and development programmes. As women play a predominant role in the rice farming operations in Tripura, sustainable rice-based food security and, thereby, rice germplasm conservation through upland and wet rice cultivation can be more effectively achieved only if gender concerns are recognised and actively promoted in the various resource planning and financial management programmes related to rice farming processes. Also, economic and welfare activities need to be more gender-responsive. What may be needed is a series of women-oriented projects to be executed by the women for their benefit and upliftment.

Women's contribution to food production and security is of paramount importance to the sustainability of Tripura. As clearly seen in the present study, women are often the main food producers, income earners and guardians of family health and nutrition. Unfortunately, particularly in rural areas, their contribution has not yet been sufficiently recognised to overcome the constraints they face. Therefore, any effort to increase rice production and raise the food security of marginal and underprivileged rural households must address the needs of women as producers, consumers and preservers of rice germplasm.

Development programmes and implementation strategies must address and accommodate the concerns of rural women, particularly the women farmers. Experience showed that it is not sufficient to target benefits for the underprivileged in the hope that women will automatically gain. Women must be targeted directly, either through specific projects or through project components especially designed for the rural women. Such projects should be integrated into the overall development process and elicit the support of the society as a whole. Gender concerns ought to be the hallmarks of policy initiatives in a new paradigm of development planning and discourse.

Self-sufficiency in rice production and food security can be achieved only if all stakeholders are considered in policy-making processes, programme and project designs and implementation. The roles, responsibilities, needs, and constraints of women, who carry out a considerable part of rice production, and hence contribute to food security, generally remain invisible in economic analysis, policy formulation and project design components; this is particularly so in Tripura. Moreover, one of the major constraints is that there are no reliable and unbiased data available on women and men's different roles in various rice farming systems among different communities of the state. It must be clearly understood that without adequate inputs and suggestions from women and men farmers, technology interventions alone cannot ensure sustainable rice production, distribution, consumption, and preservation of rice germplasm. The involvement of women in all stages of research and development, policy making and planning is essential to ensure that the most productive and effective use of limited land resources meets the present and future food security demands from household to state to national level.

Tripura has yet to achieve food security as per its ambitious agricultural perspectives plan. Recent results and achievements of SRI give ample hope and possibilities for Tripura in realising its food security ambition. Emerging conducive policy environment along with political will as well as appropriate interventions through internally designed and externally aided projects could also add to increased opportunities of rural food security in the state. However, the good policies must be translated into action programmes in every corner of the state incorporating all the rice-producing areas, both WRC and URC. Together with these programmes, there must also be a strong component for human resource development, particularly development of women. Any programme for food security and increased productivity should also be strongly linked with other welfare activities and basic requirements such as education of women, family planning, health care, access to clean drinking water, and nutrition programmes.

Notes

* The authors are grateful to Dr Baharul Islam Majumdar, agronomist, State Agricultural Research Station, Directorate of Agriculture, Tripura, Agartala, Tripura who provided us valuable information during the first phase of the field study. The authors are also thankful to Mr Amar Das, the former director of agriculture, Government of Tripura who shared his valuable experiences to enrich the present study during the first phase of field studies.

   Much appreciation is also expressed to Shri M. Chakma, TCS for facilitating and conducting the field studies at Gandacherra while he was the zonal development officer, TTAADC, Gandacherra, Dhalai District, Tripura.

   The present study could not have been completed without the valued participation of the farmers and rice cultivators, particularly the women farmers, who were always eager to reply to our numerous queries with patience and curiosity. They have enriched us much and to them we express our deepest gratitude.

Finally, the keen interest taken by Dr Sumi Krishna for editing the original draft study report in its present form and encouragement offered by her to update the available information and revisit the case studies during 2009–10 is gratefully acknowledged.

1. 'Jhum' is a local word in northeast India for shifting cultivation. In upland areas of northeast India, including in Tripura, a family cultivates a plot of land by slash and burn method to grow mixed crops for a year or two, and then leaves it as fallow for forest and land regeneration. The jhum cycles (the intervening periods after which the same plot is cultivated) traditionally were 10 years or more, but have now reduced to 4–5 years in most cases, thereby reducing the productivity of jhum cultivation and at the same time increasing the environmental consequences. Although often considered as a way of life for the shifting cultivators by many sociologist and anthropologists, jhum in recent years has drawn the attention of government, development planners, foresters and environmentalist as a cause of forest depletion, environmental degradation and biodiversity loss. In Tripura, the shifting cultivators are some of the poorest.
2. Gender refers to the socially constructed and culturally variable roles that women and men play in their daily lives, which may be reinforced by the prevailing customs, laws and specific development policies of the state, region or nation.
3. PTG is an abbreviation for Primitive Tribal Group, now rephrased as Particularly Vulnerable Tribal Group. Notified by the Government of India, the PTGs have a low rate of population growth or declining population, pre-agricultural level of technology and extremely low literacy rates. There are 75 PTGs across 17 states and Union Territories in India. In Tripura, the Reangs are notified as the PTGs. In 2001, the Reangs were approximately 16.6 per cent of the tribal population of Tripura.
4. *Jhumia* refers to a shifting cultivator or a farmer or a household or a family dependent on jhum.
5. Varieties of rice according to Sharma and Hore (1990):

   Wetland rice: *Khalisatiya, Chanmouri, Rangoon Buh, Binni (white), Sonamukhi, Meli, Rangagellong, Sarendyama, Chrui, Billrong, Dulakanrong, Gheegoj, Bandosal, Manlotoi, Nadirsail, Latasal, Chaplaish, Jhikot, Lalmoti, Kushari, Malhail, Bowelia, Garcha, Binny Rongmala, Katikalam, Motori, Basa, Koshari, Sengamuri, Chewomuri, Jhingot, Chambi, Phultengri, Tilak Cachhari, Hailchinal, Chankunia, Lingchikon, Rongichawal, Gochalati,*

Corchasada, Chalmuni, Mulai, Pakla, Jhingar, Kalpaha, Nagarasail, Biron, Kartik-kalam, Mainnasal, Binny (red), Gorasal, Maluti, Kalamkati, Chikansal, aichaha, Seroy (red), *Jotinidhan, Laichha, Murai, Beti, Maichrom, Phakang* and *Maidani.*

Upland (jhum) rice: *Badia, Maisai-ningha, Marao, Maima, Gelong, Binny* (white), *Bhadois, Lankapora, Kamranga, Lumuru, Kanaktara, Koprok, Maiasaw, Jhum maloti, Saroidhan, Sonamukhi, Betti, Seroy, Kanchali, Garo maloti, Tripura chinar, Bhajrah, Bidi kaprov, Rang kaprov, Kala kaprov, Badiya, Salungens, Sereh, Sutu Bhadity* and *Misini.* The Tripura Agricultural Research Station is conducting research on these upland varieties of rice, viz., *Maidan, Godiamma, Kamrang, Aduma, Garu Malati* and *Jhum Malati.*

Deep-water rice: *Aus dhan, Batisar, Pares dhan, Nalbajal* and *Marabajal.*

Soft rice: *Baljuri, Pipralaish, Bindi* and *Manoharsali.*

Scented rice: *Govind bhog* (black), *Khasa Govind bhog* and *Koliajiri*

6. The popular high-yielding rice varieties introduced in Tripura include DR 92, IR 8, IR 20, Jaya, masuri, JR 9, JR 11, Jalaj, Kalinga-2, Basudev, Shyamali, Sona, Sonali, Ratna, Rasi, Bala, TRC Borodhan-1, NDR-97, TRC-87-251, Vandana, etc.

7. PRA methods used included: *Direct observation*: The study villages were visited for first-hand information and understanding of the place, people and various other aspects relating to the study objectives. Observations and findings were noted down. *Semi-structured interviewing*: A checklist of topics was prepared earlier based on experiences, and informal interviews and interactions were held at the household level both with the men and women. *Interviews with key persons*: Key persons of the village, viz., headman, members of village councils, teacher(s), retired government servants, women group members and leaders were interviewed and interacted with, often individually or in groups (e.g., members of the village council, members of women organisations, etc.). Key points, findings and observations were noted. *Group interviews*: Group interviews were also conducted often consisting of men and women, youth, students and retired service personnel. Such group interviews often led to discussion and expressions of opinion, though most often women were prompted or encouraged to speak out. *Transect walks*: Transect walks as part of the direct observations was carried out in the study villages and in their paddy fields. Various types of rice farming related activities, particularly post-harvest hulling, milling, drying, storage, husking facilities, etc. were observed during such walks.

8. With the beginning of the new millennium, Tripura launched an ambitious plan and vision for all-round development (Government

of Tripura 2000). The section on 'Agriculture' outlines the agrarian policy of the state.

'The target for Agriculture Department is to increase the production of field crops by 50 per cent and double the production of fruits and vegetables, within next 5 years. This will require the following consequential actions:

(i) Agriculture Department will set up a certification programme supported by supply of requisite technical guidance and the supply of breeder seeds;

(ii) At least double of the existing irrigated area would be brought under irrigation in the next 5 years. Water harvesting technology, to avoid the huge run-off loss of rain water, would be resorted to wherever possible;

(iii) Soil testing, treatment and conservation would be taken up for increasing productivity;

(iv) Tissue culture and nursery programmes would be taken up for plantation crops;

(v) CD ratio needs to be improved by restoring both bankers' and cultivators' confidence;

(vi) Agriculture Department will launch a separate programme for cultivation of spices in view of their good potential in Tripura;

(vii) Drawing up of special programmes targeted solely for tribal cultivators in recognition of the special needs of upland areas;

(viii) Tribals would be motivated for cultivation of vegetable and special schemes may be taken up for them.

In achieving the above targets the State would also target commercialisation of agriculture and develop specialisation within Tripura, in food processing, storage, marketing and agricultural research.

Production of horticultural crops, like pineapple, would be staggered over a longer duration using modern technologies so that the growers get income and the processing units are fed over a larger period' (ibid.: 15–16).

References

Agarwal, A. K. 2003. 'Economic Reforms and Agricultural Development in North East India: Some Issues', in K. Sengupta and N. Roy (eds), *Economic Reforms and Agricultural Development in North-East India*, New Delhi: Mittal Publications, pp. 3–12.

Asthana, A. N. and N. D. Majumder. 1981. 'Studies in Rice Germplasm of North Eastern Hill Region'. Research Bulletin No. 11, ICAR, India.

Barah, B. C. 2006. *Agricultural Development in North-East India: Challenges and Opportunities*. New Delhi: National Centre for Agricultural Economics and Policy Research.

De, U. K. 2007. 'Food Security and PDS in Tripura: A Policy Intervention'. MPRA Paper No. 6292, 2007.

Food and Agriculture Organisation (FAO). 1996. *Women: The Key to Food Security*. Fact sheets prepared for the occasion of the World Food Summit, Food and Agriculture Organisation, Rome.

———. 1997. *Gender: Key to Sustainability and Food Security. Illustrated Plan of Action for Women in Development*. Rome: Food and Agriculture Organisation.

Government of India. 2002. *Census of India (2001): Tripura*. New Delhi: Government of India.

Government of Tripura. 1987. *Survey Report on the Jhumias of Tripura 1987*. Agartala: Tribal Welfare Department, Government of Tripura.

———. 2000. *Approach to People's Plan in Tripura*. Agartala: Government of Tripura.

———. 2003. *Special Package for Development of Scheduled Tribes for the Period 2003–04 to 2006–07*. Agartala: Government of Tripura.

———. 2007. *50 Years of Development of Agriculture in Tripura*. Agartala: Department of Agriculture.

———. 2009a. *Some Basic Statistics of Tripura 2009*. Agartala: Directorate of Economics & Statistics, Government of Tripura.

———. 2009b. *Major Achievements After Implementation of Perspective Plan: Agriculture*. Agartala: Department of Agriculture, Government of Tripura.

———. 2009c. *Economic Review of Tripura (2008–2009)*. Agartala: Government of Tripura.

———. 2010. *Tripura at a Glance 2009*. Agartala: Government of Tripura.

Kapur, A. 2007. 'Demographic Invasion of India from the North East', *Indian Defence Review*, 22(2). Available at www.indiandefencereview. com/search.php?...Vol%2022.2 (accessed 20 October 2010).

NAAS. 2001. *Strategies for Agricultural Research in North-East*. New Delhi: National Academy of Agricultural Sciences.

Prasad, C. S. 2007. *SRI Success Story in Tripura. Dams, Rivers & People*. New Delhi: SANDRP.

Sasikumar, B. and S. Sardana. 1987. 'Evaluation of Rice Germplasm in Tripura', *Plant Genet. Res. Newsl.*, 71: 31–33.

Seetharaman, R., D. P. Srivastava and D. P. Ghorai. 1974. 'Preliminary Studies in Rice Cultivars from North East India', *Ind. J. Genet. & Plant Breed*, 34(2): 143–49.

Sharma, B. D. and D. K. Hore. 1990. 'Rice Germplasm Collection in Tripura State', *Indian J. Pl. Genet. Resources*, 3(2): 71–74.

Singha, A. 2003. 'Rice Production in Tripura — 1955–2000', in K. Sengupta and N. Roy (eds), *Economic Reforms and Agricultural Development in North-East India*. New Delhi: Mittal Publications, pp. 105–14.

Srivastava, D. P. 1978. 'Diversity in the Late Duration Rice Cultivars from North East India', *Oryza*, 15(1): 26–33.

WWF. 2007. *More Rice, Less Water: Small State, Big Results — Experiences of SRI in Tripura, India*. Hyderabad: WWF-ICRISAT Project.

9

Mizoram's Rice Economy and Gender Relations*

AUDREY LALDINPUII AND LAITHANGPUII

This essay attempts to highlight the allocation of gender roles in the agricultural economy in Mizo society. It also tries to bring out the value of the unpaid or unwaged labour of women in rice production in particular and in various economic activities in general. We began this work with a small field study in August–September 2004 to get primary data on gender relations in the rice economy in present-day Mizoram. The results of the study made us aware of some striking developments in the ground reality.

Field Study

To assess the impact of government policies, the position of rice economy and the role of women in it, a small sample was studied. A team comprising Lalbiakthangi Rokhum, Vanlalsangi and Hmingthanchhunga surveyed Thingsulthliah village and Champhai town where jhum and wet rice cultivation, respectively, were practised; 76 women cultivators were interviewed, 29 from Thingsulthliah and 47 from Champhai. Time and fund constraints restricted the data collection for this study. However, the areas selected have their own specific importance for rice farming as Thingsulthliah is one of the agricultural circles of Aizawl district and Champhai is a main centre for wet rice cultivation and among the first places where wet rice was introduced. The findings from this limited study bring out at least some significant information and give us a fair idea of the present condition of the rice economy in relation to gender in Mizoram.

The major findings are discussed here. As regards land ownership, of the 76 respondents only 14 (18.42 per cent) women have land registered in their name. Of these 14, it is important to note that eight are single, five inherited the land from their parents and only one bought the land. Though 62 women (over 80 per cent) do not own land, the major work in the field like sowing, weeding and harvesting is done by women. Besides working in the field 43 of the respondents have *leipui* or vegetable gardens where they do most of the work.

As shown in Table 9.1, because the yield is not very high and the land-holding is generally small, 55 (72.36 per cent) of the respondents could not produce enough rice to last them a year. Only 21 of them produced enough rice to sell in the market. So, in addition to working in their own field and in *leipui*, 36 (47.36 per cent) respondents have to work as daily wage earners (DWE) in others' fields to sustain their family. Women are discriminated against in daily wage work, paid less for the same kind of work that men do; men are paid ₹90 a day in Thingsulthliah and ₹100 in Champhai, while women are paid ₹80 in both places.

Tables 9.2 and 9.3 throw light on the nature of work participation and decision-making roles. Both men and women preserve seeds: 34 (44.74 per cent) of the respondents single-handedly carry out the work of preserving the seeds; 24 (31.57 per cent) said that they never had anything to do with this work, while 18 (23.68 per cent) said that seed preservation was carried out together with their male counterparts.

Table 9.1: Production and Labour Input in Leipui, Mizoram

	Thingsulthliah			Champhai			
	Yes	No	Total	Yes	No	Total	Grand total
Having surplus produce	3	26	29	18	29	47	76
Working in others' *leipui* as DWE	15	14	29	21	26	47	76

Source: Authors' field study, 2004.

Table 9.2: Work Participation

	Thingsulthliah				Champhai				
	Male	Female	Mutual	Total	Male	Female	Mutual	Total	Total
Preservation of seeds	5	23	1	59	19	11	17	47	76
Labour in leipui	0	17	1	18	1	21	3	25	43

Source: Authors' field study, 2004.
Note: The total labour in the leipui is less, as not all the respondents own leipui.

Table 9.3: Decision-making

	Thingsulthliah					Champhai					Grand
	Male	Female	Mutual	Market price	Total	Male	Female	Mutual	Market price	Total	Total
Choice of rice to grow	10	16	3	0	29	20	19	8	0	47	76
Choice of plot	12	15	2	0	29	25	15	7	0	47	76
Choice of rice to sell	0	3	0	0	3	6	7	5	0	20	23
Amount of rice to sell	0	3	0	0	3	2	7	9	0	20	23
Fixing of price	0	3	0	1	3	6	4	5	2	20	23

Source: Authors' field study, 2004.

In matters relating to decision making, of the 76 respondents, 35 (46.05 per cent) have a say in the kind of rice to grow and 11 (14.47 per cent) decide this mutually with male family members. The remaining 30 (39.47 per cent) have no say, with their male counterparts having the sole authority to make the decision. Of the 35 women who do have a say, six are single or widows. The data in Table 9.3 points to the conclusion that in matters relating to decision making, women's role is minimal. Yet, 79 per cent of the respondents work for an average of five to eight hours a day. Some even worked for 10 hours a day. The kind of implements they used like hoe, sickle, etc. are light and easy to handle and do not seem to give them much problem. But, it is often the nature of the work, which involves continuous bending, that causes headaches, fever, back aches and stomach problems.

To increase production and to improve the living condition of the cultivators, the government had introduced new technologies and adopted a number of measures. However, the impact of these efforts is very dismal (Table 9.4): 51 (67.10 per cent) are not aware of the new technology introduced by the government; 10 are aware of it but do not have access; very few, only 15, were able to access and benefit from the new technology. Regarding the government's Mahni Intodelh (Self-sufficiency) Project, of the 76 respondents, only 34 (44.74 per cent) are aware of it and only 18 found it beneficial (Table 9.5).

Table 9.4: New Technology

	Thingsulthliah			Champhai			
	Yes	No	Total	Yes	No	Total	Grand Total
Aware	4	25	29	21	26	47	76
Have access	3	26	29	12	35	47	76

Source: Authors' field study, 2004.

Table 9.5: Mahni Intodelh (Self-sufficieny) Project

	Thingsulthliah			Champhai			
	Yes	No	Total	Yes	No	Total	Grand Total
Aware	16	13	29	18	29	47	76
Benefit from it	3	26	29	15	32	47	76

Source: Authors' field study, 2004.

It is clear from this study that women are still among the disadvantaged groups so far as rights to land, decision making in the agricultural arena and use of modern technology are concerned. To understand this situation we researched the traditional agrarian system, land relations, government policies in both pre-independence and post-independence periods, besides gender relations in Mizo society to see where women stood then and where they stand today. We also examined the underlying forces that operate in gender relations in the process of the development of modern Mizoram. An investigation of the historical roots is needed to understand the present socio-economic condition of women. So, the history and the migratory process of the Mizo as recorded by historians and other social scientists needs to be looked into for a better understanding of the existing gender relations in the agrarian economy of Mizoram.

Society and Migration of the Mizos

The Mizos belong to a Mongoloid stock, speaking Tibeto-Burman language. 'Mizo' is a generic term for tribes like the Lusei, Hmar, Mara (Lakher), Lai (Pawi), Fanai, etc. living in the present state of Mizoram and the adjoining areas. In the earlier European records these people are referred to as Kuki, Lushai and Chin. Using the term Mizo for all the tribes of this state and for some tribes of the adjoining areas touches upon identity questions. However, in the present context, for convenience sake, the term Mizo is being used to refer to these tribes who have a more or less similar traditional social, economic and political structure, all following a patriarchal system. Legends tell us that the Mizos emerged from a rock called *'chhinlung'* which is taken by many of the writers and Mizo historians to be the Great Wall of China. From there they moved southwards and settled in the Kabaw Valley for sometime, after which they moved further west and came to the present state of Mizoram.[1]

Rice Cultivation amongst the Mizo

During the course of their migration towards the present homeland (Mizoram), the Mizos must have lived a subsistence life. Their main food crops probably included maize, millet and yam.

The form of agriculture practised was jhuming. There was also a significant absence of iron implements for agricultural tools. As they migrated from place to place they were unlikely to use rice as their staple food as rice cultivation would have entailed settlement in a particular place for at least a particular period of time. One of the most acceptable views regarding the beginning of the cultivation of rice amongst these tribes is that they got acquainted with this food crop only after they came in contact with outsiders, probably the people from Burma, after reaching the Kabaw Valley. However, at this time rice might have been a part of their diet, but not the staple food, which was maize. They would have also consumed *mimzu* (maize beer). Indeed, for many of the tribes who remained in present-day Myanmar rice was not their staple food until the mid-20th century (Lehman 1963).

From the Kabaw Valley, one after the other, the clans moved towards the Chin Hills. Later they seem to have dispersed in different directions. Villages emerged as temporary clan settlements in different places. It appears that these developed their own customs and traditions, as each village was an independent entity. According to some writers (Lalthangliana 2001; Liangkhaia 1951; Nunthara 1995) migration towards the west and settlement at places like Thantlang and Lentlang mountain ranges in the 16th c,entury coincided with the starting of rice cultivation amongst the various tribes.

From Thantlang and Lentlang they migrated further west, making both friends and enemies, often fighting over land. They faced inter-village, intra-tribal and inter-tribal wars. Constant war brought the question of security of the village to the forefront giving rise to the need for a leader who could lead the clan in such an unstable situation. It was around this time that the different clans began selecting a headman of the village. Later this evolved into hereditary chieftainship. At a time when 'might was right', men who were physically strong helped protect the village from all adversaries, humans and wild animals. They often slept together in the *zawlbuk* or boys' dormitory. The chief and the zawlbuk became indispensable and an important institution of decision-making. Women were not allowed in the zawlbuk, and were absent in the decision-making bodies like the council of elders.[2] Thus, the then existing situation, which led to the increasing societal demand of male power based on physical strength seems to have relegated the role of women to the background. Moreover, constant feuds and vulnerability to wild animals which demanded physical strength seems to have led to the rising control of females by the males. As the men often had to devote themselves to the work of defence the major labour in the field/ agriculture seems to have become the duty of the women. The traditional division of labour within the family as well as within the contained village, based on sex and age must have been disturbed too because of these changes.

Settlements in Mizoram: Society and Economy

By the time the different tribes reached the present homeland the Sailo chiefs more or less established their domination over almost all the other clans and were mainly concentrated in the northern part. However, they could not withstand their most formidable enemy, the Pawi tribe. A constant threat from the Pawi led to the coming together of the seven Sailo chiefs who formed a bigger village with a stronger force at Selesih, known as *Selesih Sangsarih* (Selesih village with 7,000 households). The formation of this confederacy under the chieftainship of the Sailo clan brought to an end the large-scale migration of the tribes (Lalthangliana 2001).

The position of women in society may have begun to decline during the Sailo rule, as the position of women in the southern areas not under Sailo dominion appeared to be relatively much better. This may be inferred from the derogatory sayings about women in northern Mizoram during Sailo rule:

hmeichhe finin tuikhur ral a kai lo (women's wisdom does not reach beyond the public water point),

chakai sa sa ni suh, hmeichhe thu thu ni suh (as crab meat cannot really be considered a meat, so the words of women cannot be considered wise),

hmeichhia leh palchhia a thlak theih (old fences and wives can be changed), and

vau sam loh leh hmeichhe vau loh chu an pawng tual tual (unthreatened women become unbearable like uncut grass fences in the jhum field).[3]

Such derogatory remarks about women were virtually absent among the Lakhers and the Pawis, who settled in the southern part of Mizoram. There is also a saying in the north that women from the south are more 'idle' compared to women of the north. But the case seems to be that southern women have more free time and occupy a better position in society. The concept of the *thaibawih* (henpecked husband) is also found among the Sailos/ Lushais. If a man helps a woman in the household or with chores considered women's work, he is referred to contemptuously as a *thaibawih*. Hence, girls who are submissive, hardworking and 'feminine', not questioning male authority, are highly sought after as wives. Examining the sayings and terms indicates the male bias in gender roles and that patriarchal values and norms became more deeply entrenched in society from the time of Sailo rule.

The Sailo chiefs dispersed from Selesih in different directions, as jhuming did not let them remain in a particular place for a very long time. The chiefs became more concerned with the local administration and elders were appointed to help. The number of chiefs depended on the village size and the chief's choice (Nunthara 2004). The chiefs were the custodians of the village land (Zatluanga 1968), and along with the elders selected the jhum sites for distribution to different households. Jhum lands were changed yearly. Fertile virgin jungle was abundant, so the jhum cycle ranged between 10 and 15 years. Once the fertility of the nearby land diminished, the land was left fallow. The jungle was cleared from early January to the middle of March; this was usually men's work but women also took part. Then, the cut trees were left to dry in the sun. The *chap* (felled trees) was burnt in March or early April. The next step in the process, *mangkhawh* (clearing unburned tree branches), involved moving the scorched unburned tree trunks and branches to the corner of the jhum field before the field was prepared for sowing.

Rice and millet were sown separately. Sometimes cucumber, pumpkin, melon and sweet potato were grown. The jhum plot required at least three or more weedings. In the first round, called *hnuhlak* or *hnuhpui*, young and tender weeds were removed. The second round, *hnuhhram,* was a very strenuous job. Partnerships were popular, with young men working with unmarried girls in pairs; the girl had to carry all the agricultural tools of her male co-worker to and from the field, and care for him, washing and mending his clothes. Parents and other members of the family and elders also took part in *hnuhhram* work. The third round was the *thual*. The fourth and fifth rounds, *thial* and *thet thet*, were performed only when absolutely necessary (Lalthangliana 1992). The rice harvest was gathered in late October, November and December by both women and men; mainly women did post-harvesting work. Women also did the hard work of carrying harvested rice over the hilly terrain from the jhum lands to the village. When the rice crops failed they largely depended on maize (*vaimim*) and the tubers, yam (*ba*) and sweet potato (*kawl-bahra*), sometimes subsisting only on wild fruits, roots and shoots. Hunting and trapping, rearing and domesticating animals, fishing and catching other aquatic animals, collecting wild fruits and plants provided them with other sources of food besides the agricultural products (Rengsi 1999).

Agriculture and Women

Agricultural work had to be carried out in sun and rain; men used *khumbeu* (hat) and women, old clothes as a means of protection. Their main implements were the iron *dao*, axe, hoe and sickle, together with the *ipte* (bag) and *em* (basket), which were light and easy to handle. But weeding demanded long hours of continuous bending. As British ethnographer Shakespear (1912: 16) has pointed out, it was hard and backbreaking work, often resulting in fever. Women did the major work of weeding though men helped (ibid.). There was also the risk of snakebites (McCall 1977). While working in the field, the women smoked to keep away the mosquitoes, which would certainly have had an ill effect on their health. Most writings of Mizo history speak of the high rate of infant mortality and miscarriages. One reason for this could have been the kind of work that women performed in the field and home endlessly, even during pregnancy and soon after delivery. Besides the main jhum land, some big families with a large labour force cleared the nearby jungle where they grew vegetables and cereals. This is the *leipui*, usually referred to as *nu leipui*, 'mother's garden'. Unmarried girls also had their own leipui. They cultivated mustard, onions, leeks, brinjals, etc. for subsistence. The population being small, this was by and large sufficient to support their subsistence lifestyle.

Traditional Mizo Household Economy and Women

Traditionally, Mizo women worked from dawn to dusk. Processing of rice for domestic consumption involved a series of activities like pounding, husking (*deng*) and de-husking (*buh thlei*) of rice. Women had to perform these tasks with the utmost speed to allow them time to manage other household tasks like cooking, looking after the children and feeding domestic animals. They had to collect water from the village water points which were always far in the outskirts and often had to climb steep terrain with their heavy loads. Women also collected firewood. They had to grow, collect and process cotton for weaving and provide clothing for the family. Feasting, rituals, celebrations of any kind were not done without *zu* (rice beer); brewing and preparing *zu* was single-handedly done by women. Traditionally the Mizo women practically worked from dawn to dusk (see McCall 1977; Nunthara 2004; Shakespear 1912).

Land System and Gender Relations in Traditional Mizo Society

In the absence of a monetary economy, prosperity depended largely on agricultural produce. Those who could produce more could easily earn the status of an elder. But irrespective of their economic position, members of the Sailo clans were accorded a higher status and a higher bride price could be demanded for their daughters (Nunthara 2004). Apart from this, their position was similar to that of women from other clans. Women had a very low status, no claim on family property except her personal belongings that she brought at the time of her marriage. Among all the clans, the youngest son was the heir although other male children had a share in the family property. Even in the absence of a male child, the daughter had no rights, as the family property went to the nearest male relative (ibid.). The only condition under which women enjoyed proprietorship was when they were bereft of all male relations and did not intend to adopt a male. The house and the property belonged to the father, who was also the 'proprietor' of the children (Sangkhuma 1995). The product of a woman's labour in her husband's house also belonged to the husband (McCall 1977).

After the clearing of the jungle men were relatively free. During such times they often carried out raids in other villages and into Manipur and Cachar, which continued even after the British annexed Cachar. The region ultimately came under the control of the British after the expedition of 1889 (ibid.).

Rice Economy and Women

In the colonial and post-colonial periods the traditional method of cultivation and women's roles in this process continued without much change. The British introduced wet rice cultivation along with ploughing; cows and bulls were brought into the region. However, due to dearth of lowland/plains areas, this system of cultivation, though more productive and easier, could not be practised on a large scale. The British also introduced cash crops like potato, bean, cabbage, tomato, etc. and opened market places. But the market economy remained very weak till independence (Lalrindiki 1998).

The British also introduced administrative changes in the region and brought to a halt the constant raids, inter-village war and constant movement. The region was brought under administrative rule, which was completely alien to the tribes. It brought far-reaching changes in the social, economic, political and religious life of the people. Land passed into the hands of the British who then assigned the land to the chiefs (McCall 1977). The British government passed the Inner Line Regulation in 1873 by which outsiders were prohibited to hold land within the boundary of the Lushai Hills. The Land Settlement Act was passed in 1898, demarcating land as decided by the British administrators (Sangkima 1992). They collected a house tax of ₹1 and 10 baskets of rice at the rate of about ₹2 per maund from every household. Each family was also required to render free labour to the government at least for six days in a year (Lalrindiki 1998).

Soon after the British administrators, missionaries entered Mizoram. They were largely responsible for the introduction of formal education that paved the way to salaried jobs. Such jobs provided relief from the hard work of cultivating the field and were a new status symbol. Those who were free from daily toil in the field were regarded as the well-to-do. Initially, most families gave priority to boys' education rather than that of girls but later, with missionary initiatives, girls' education was started. Educated women were in a position to hold an independent status in contrast to their traditional position in society. The material base of the customs and traditions, evolving out of the agrarian economy, began to take a new shape and the traditional value system was replaced by a modern value system. With the creeping in of modernisation there was a tendency to look down upon traditional occupations; most parents wished that their children would not need to toil as hard as themselves. So by means of education, at the secular level, women's position did improve. However, in the ecclesiastical sphere, the position of women in the church seems no better than their position in traditional religious life.

When Aizawl became the seat of British administration, people started moving to Aizawl in large numbers with the hope of getting government jobs and escaping hard agricultural labour. Agriculture was widely neglected and considered the work of the less advanced people who did not have access to formal education and government. With the coming of a cash economy, some people took to petty trade. In the long run this trend towards salaried jobs rather than farming caused a serious threat to food security as jhum cultivation with its low yield could not meet all the requirements and rice had to be imported from the plains.

Certain developments were seen like the introduction of the hulling machine that brought changes in the economy of rice and the condition of women. It eased the women's labour of pounding rice. The introduction of rice mills in this region also lifted the burden of grinding the much favoured *buhban* (sticky rice), which always had an important place in festive occasions, especially after conversion to Christianity. However, the machines were owned and controlled by a few men, who benefited from the income, although women carried the rice from their homes to the mills.

Land System: Changes and Continuity

The colonisation of the area led to certain changes in the land system which though not intentional, altered the womens' right to property with regard to land. The establishment of the Mizo District Council in April, 1952 and the abolition of chieftainship by the Abolition of Chief's Right Act marked the transfer of all rights on land customarily owned by the chief into the hands of the government. The Mizo District (Land Revenue) Act, 1956 introduced the concept of private property and created two types of landholders: a pass-holder and a settlement-holder. A pass-holder had rights over the land only for the specified period and had no right of transfer or subletting. A settlement-holder had the heritable, transferable and subletting right. The owner was also liable to pay land revenue and taxes. The Mizo District (Agriculture Land) Act, 1963 required that occupation of land be regularised by obtaining fresh 'patta', without which the pass or permit could be cancelled. The size of land holding depended on the size of the family (Lianzela 1994).

The Mizo District (Agriculture Land) Rules introduced in 1971 brought in a new kind of patta called 'periodic patta'. The regulations of 1956, 1963 and 1971 are still operative in Mizoram. New Acts enacted in 2000 and 2003 are yet to be enforced.

These changes in the land system opened a way for the women to inherit land if it was the will of the rightful owner, whereas in the traditional system a married woman had no property right except some personal moveable property which she brought to her husband's house at the time of marriage. However, the patriarchal norms and standards which were followed, characterised the customary law and in actual practice the question of a woman inheriting property came up only in the absence of a male heir. Widowhood and remarriage further limited the securing of property rights by women. In a situation like the sudden death of a husband and absence of a legal will, coupled with the absence of male children, presumably the wife has the right to the property; however, the customary law is applicable when the husband's family claims the property. There also remains some societal discouragement for a widow to inherit property if she has no male child and remarries, even if she continues to shoulder the responsibility of the children of her late husband. Thus, it becomes very evident that the new laws have been far from women-friendly and the patriarchal values of the Mizo society restrict the rights of the women even where some laws may have at least made land available to the women.

Government Policies and Measures for Food Security

In the post-1947 period, the government undertook various steps to develop agriculture but self-sufficiency in food was not achieved, and the schemes and new technology introduced do not seem to have benefited the women much.

During the first two Five Year Plans (1951–61), various schemes like minor irrigation, establishment of seed farm, popularisation of fertilisers, green manuring, soil conservation, etc. were launched. In 1957–58, the government took steps under the Grow More Food programme to develop the agricultural sector. The third Five Year Plan (1961–66) emphasised development of means of communication, agriculture and marketing of agricultural products (Thanga 1979). The region faced a severe famine called *mautam* in 1959, which led to the setting up of a relief organisation *Tam Do Pawl*, popularly known as the Mizo Famine Front. This eventually led to the formation of the Mizo National Front, which led an armed uprising against the government in 1966 on account of the inadequate famine relief measures. The insurgency led to a massive regrouping of villages. This process together with the imposition of long hours of curfew and regular inspection by the security forces as part of the counter-insurgency measures disrupted government undertakings. In the midst of the insurgency, the mobility of men was restricted because they feared attacks both from the Indian army and insurgents; hence, women were compelled to move around as they were more free from army and insurgent threat. Thus, women started taking on the task of sustaining the family by selling vegetables. For instance, as pointed out by Lalrindiki (1998), women from the villages surrounding Aizawl began selling vegetables at the Aizawl market. Interestingly, before 1966, mostly men were engaged in vegetable vending. Traditionally, men who helped women collect vegetables were considered lazy (Thanga 1979), but when it came to commercial transactions of vegetables, however small they may be, men seem to have taken control. The insurgency also greatly disturbed the normal process of jhuming, causing large-scale migration to the urban areas and dependence on food grain supplies from outside (Lalrindiki 1998: 84).

The fifth Plan (1974–79) gave priority to agricultural development. Terraced cultivation was introduced to minimise shifting cultivation. But the *thingtam* famine occurred in 1977, which greatly thwarted these plans. During the sixth Plan (1980–85) the government tried to achieve self-sufficiency in food grain production. Under the New Land Use Policy (NLUP) of 1984, the village council temporarily allotted 2 ha of land to selected families. They were to be issued land settlement certificates (LSCs) on the basis of their temporary utilisation of the land. This programme gave importance to the development of plantation crops like teak, rubber and orange.

In 1987, with the change in government, the Jhum Control Project replaced the NLUP. Attention was given to develop horticulture, piggery, poultry, carpentry, tailoring, etc. The project made an effort to introduce wet rice cultivation, bench terracing and contour bunding wherever it was suitable. However, the NLUP was revived in 1990–91 to put an end to the unproductive method of cultivation by providing alternative land for permanent occupation.

The central government–funded Mizoram Intodelh Project (MIP) or Project for Self-Sufficiency in Mizoram for the year 2002––03 aimed to uplift the rural poor, especially shifting cultivators. The main purpose was attainment of self-sufficiency, food security and better livelihood for the cultivators. The MIP project had undertaken land development in lowland areas and terraces in the upland areas and development of piggery. To help the poor farmers the government is selling improved seeds, fertilisers and agricultural machinery and implements at 50 per cent subsidy. It appears that all these schemes basically aim at ending shifting cultivation because of its destructive and low-yielding nature and introducing alternative and more productive rice farming systems and alternative means of livelihood to improve the living conditions of the manual workers and rural poor and for food security in general. These schemes have not been very successful due to many reasons including lack of specific guidelines, weak technical supervision, follow-up action both from the government and the beneficiaries, short-sighted vision, etc. However, the total area under jhum cultivation has decreased from 55,265 ha in 1980–81 to 35,798 ha in 2000–01. The total area under wet rice cultivation increased from 6,804 ha in 1980–81 to 12,953 ha in 2000–01. The total area under the introduced High Yielding Variety seeds increased from 119 ha in 1980–81 to 3,088 in 2000–01 (Government of Mizoram 2004: 22, 28).

Though the area under jhum cultivation has come down and more area have been brought under a more productive system of wet rice cultivation, looking at the total production of rice, the achievement of Mizoram is not very remarkable. Calculating the average requirement of rice per person per day as 450gm., the average requirement of rice per person per year is 164 quintals. So the total requirement of rice for the whole population of Mizoram which stands at 891,058 according to the 2001 Census is 14,61,335 qtls. The miscellaneous consumption of rice by pigs, chicken, dogs, cattle and the floating population is calculated to be around 410,625 qtls. The total requirement of rice for Mizoram is thus calculated to be 18,71,960 quintals. But the total production of rice in Mizoram during 2002–2003 was only 764,430 quintals. If we compare the annual requirement of rice with the actual production of Mizoram we find that there is a deficiency of 1,107,530 quintals, i.e. 59.20%. Mizoram actually produced only 40.80% of required rice (ibid.: 73).

Of the 84,308 cultivator families, 70 per cent were marginal farmers holding only 0.5 ha of land and 20 per cent were small farmers with an average land holding of 1.5 ha. Only 6 per cent were medium farmers with 7 ha and 4 per cent large farmers with 14 ha of land (ibid.: 67). The average productivity of rice per hectare is only 1.3 quintals. So, 90 per cent of the farmers could not even produce enough rice for themselves and had to depend on other sources.

Summary and Conclusions

An examination of the present situation of the rice economy and gender relations leads us to the conclusion that the traditional agricultural system and practices, especially jhuming, have not undergone much change including in the division of labour between the sexes. In jhum cultivation the role of women at present is essentially the same as in the traditional society. In wet rice cultivation the introduction of new technology like tractors, power tillers and irrigation have considerably helped to lighten the burden of physical labour but this does not seem to help the women much as many of them do not have access to the new technology.

Even those who have access do not handle these machines themselves and these are operated by the men in the family.

During and after British rule, the main traditional occupations of men — hunting and felling trees — became less important. British rule prevented inter-tribal warfare; British administrative policy also necessitated voluntary or forced labour of men. Gradually, the men's labour input in agricultural operations decreased. In such a situation with the frequent absence of men, women's participation in work traditionally assigned to men, like tree felling, would have increased. With men leaving their traditional occupations for white-collar jobs, the women's burden doubled; a woman could not neglect her responsibility either in the domestic sphere or in the field while men were relatively free from household work and from much of their responsibility in the field.

Our study found that younger women respondents from Thingsulthliah and Champhai and also from some other villages seem no longer to conform strictly to traditional ideas in the context of reproductive health. Now, younger women do not work much in the field during pregnancy and are aware of the risk of working immediately after delivery as the older village women did in their youth. The traditional belief that the speedy resumption of normal activity after delivery is a measure of a woman's efficiency and the fear of dying as *raicheh* does not seem to hold.[5] Most older rural women interviewed complained about the pain of going to the jhum field to work just one or two days after delivery.

In Champhai, many of the families doing wet rice cultivation were not the actual owners of the land. The cultivator's share is usually two-thirds of the total produce, while the expenditure incurred in the entire operation of cultivation is met by the owner. Hence, the position of the landless cultivator seems to be comparatively better than in other parts of the country. The existing land system also paves the way for the large-scale selling of village plantation land to the urban well-to-do. These lands are largely distributed to the beneficiaries of the various developmental schemes. This is so especially in Thingsulthliah village. The sample that was taken, though small, reflects the new trend of land tenancy. The position of women amongst the landless cultivator families is presumably no better but needs further research.

The findings of this study suggest that the division of labour based on gender, land system and the customary laws which are culturally created, needs to be questioned. The complete absence of women in the decision-making bodies because of the patriarchal norms also simultaneously seems to reflect in the developmental schemes of government. Hence, the introduction of new technology in the agriculture sector appears to benefit men, reducing their labour but not that of women. The justice of categorising household work performers, mostly women, as non-working women in the census data and other government statistics needs to be re-examined. The institutions of society, which predominantly exhibit patriarchal values and traditional organisations that may have gender biases, also need to be questioned. As ownership of material wealth/property including land was mainly confined to men, it further contributed to the overall subordination of women because women are socialised and trained not to own but to be supportive of those who control the material wealth, politically and economically. Hence, for women the social ladder of success and recognition depends on the level of adjustment to and acceptance of patriarchal norms and values.

At present the main bulk of Mizoram's requirement of rice is procured from other states by the government. How will Mizoram meet its requirement for food security and will it ever be self-sufficient again like in the olden days, are key questions today. The answer, however, does not seem to lie in what looks like promising political party propaganda nor in the flowery writings that glorify the past. Perhaps gender sensitive developmental policy and schemes may make a difference. If women must continue to contribute the major part of agricultural labour it is important that steps be taken to introduce women-friendly technology, educate and help women farmers and eliminate the discrimination against women in terms of wage labour in the agricultural sector.

Notes

* This is a slightly edited version of a paper published in *North East India Studies* issue on 'Gender, Agriculture, Development', January 2006, 1(2): 107–29. It incorporates some data collected by the authors for their Ph.Ds submitted to the North Eastern Hill University, Shillong.

1. For a detailed discussion of the migration of the Mizos see, amongst others, Lalthangliana (1975); Verghese and Thanzawma (1997); Thanga (1979: 3); Nunthara (1995).
2. For more on the *zawlbuk* see Verghese and Thanzawma, and McCall (1977).
3. The period when they started using these sayings cannot be ascertained. That these sayings were prevalent during Sailo rule can be established from the writings of the British ethnographers like A. G. McCall and J. Shakespear (1912).
4. For a discussion on this aspect of gender relations in Mizo society after the intervention of the missionaries in Mizo socio-religious life, see Lalrinchani (1998).
5. *Raicheh* is the term given to the death of women during or after childbirth. In traditional belief, there is a taboo attached to it and this kind of death is much feared. So, to evade being labelled as dying as *raicheh*, women used to fetch water or firewood even on the day of delivery.

References

Government of Mizoram. 2004. *Statistical Abstract of the Department of Agriculture and Minor Irrigation 2002–2003*. Aizawl: Directorate of Agriculture and Minor Irrigation, GoMi, Mizoram.

Lalrinchani, B. 1998. 'Christianity and Women in Mizoram: A Study of the Impact of Christianity on Women in Lunglei District', unpublished M.Phil. dissertation, NEHU.

Lalrindiki, 1998. 'Analysis of the Socio-Economic Situation of Mizo Women Vegetable Vendors and their Contribution to the Subsistence Economy', thesis submitted to the Senate of Serampore College for the degree of Master of Theology (Social Analysis), Arasaradi, March, Madurai: Tamil Nadu Theological Seminary.

Lalthangliana, B. 1975. *History of the Mizos in Burma*. Aizawl: Zawlbuk Agencies.

———. 1992. *Hmasang Mizo Nun*. Aizawl: RTM Press.

———. 2001. *Mizo Chanchin*. Aizawl: Remkungi.

Lehman, F. K. 1963. *The Structure of Chin Society*. Champaign, Il.: University of Illinois Press.

Liangkhaia (rev.). 1951. *History of Lushai*. Aizawl: Hmingliana and Sons.

Lianzela. 1994. *Economic Development of Mizoram*. Guwahati: Spectrum Publications

McCall, A. G. 1977. *Lushai Chrysalis*. Calcutta: Firma KLM Pvt. Ltd.

Nunthara, C. 1995. *Mizoram; Society and Polity*. New Delhi: Indus Publishing Company.

Nunthara, C. 2004. 'Land Control, Land Use and Kinship Structure in "Lushai" Hills', in Mignonette Momin and Cecile A. Mawlong (eds), *Society and Economy in North East India*, Vol I. New Delhi: Regency Publications, pp. 74–75.

Rengsi, Vanlalruata. 1999. 'Reconstruction of Traditional Mizo Society: A Technological Perspective', unpublished Ph.D. thesis submitted to the Department of History, NEHU.

Sangkhuma, Rev. Z. T. 1995. *Missionary te Hnuhma.* Aizawl: M. C. Lalrinthanga.

Sangkima. 1992. *Mizo: Society and Social Change.* Guwahati: Spectrum Publications.

Shakespear, J. 1912. *Lushai-Kuki Clan.* London: Macmillan.

Thanga, Selet. 1979. *Pi Pu Leniai.* Aizawl: Lianchhungi Book Store.

Verghese, Brigdaier C.G. and R. L. Thanzawma. 1997. *A History of the Mizos, Vol. I.* New Delhi: Vikas Publishing House.

Zatluanga. 1968. *Mizo Chanchin.* Aizawl: Khuma Printing Press.

10

Gender Ideologies and the 'Price' of Rice in Northeastern India*

Sumi Krishna

The cultural and ecological diversity of the northeastern region is apparent in the heterogeneity of its rice-farming systems. Paddy occupies a primary position in a composite and varied mix of crops (including other cereals, millets, tubers, bananas, squashes, beans, and leafy vegetables), animal foods (pigs, poultry and fish), and non-food crops like palms, bamboos and canes. Uncultivated land (forests and seasonal or temporary fallows) and water courses are integral to the system. Rice is the major cereal. There is an extraordinary range of rice diversity in the region including wild varieties (Hore 2005; Nagachan et al. 2011). Maize is cultivated in Sikkim and parts of Arunachal Pradesh, Meghalaya and Mizoram. Some wheat is grown in Arunachal's Tawang district. The centrality of rice is reflected in various ceremonies. The Wanchos of Tirap believe that rituals to protect paddy in the granary will also protect other grains (Srivastava 1973: 91). Rice is not only a significant part of the diet. Rice stores are important in ascribing men's status; this must be rice grown in the family's paddy fields, not bought in the market. Rice is also used for different celebrations, and not least, for the nutritious rice-based liquor called *apong, zu,* etc.

Mainly indigenous varieties of paddy are cultivated either in *jhum kheti* (swidden or slash-and-burn fields) or *pani kheti* (wet rice fields). There is some 'dry' (i.e., rain-fed) rice cultivation on terraced hill slopes. 'Wet' rice, irrigated by gravity channels from the perennial hill streams, is grown on the flatter lands in the valleys and near riverbanks. In the hills, tilling is entirely by hand. In Arunachal, only the Sherdukpen and the Khampti use the plough on level lands. Shallow tube wells have been introduced in the Assam plains that earlier were entirely dependent on monsoon rain. Tractors are also being used in some plain areas. Government policy has consistently discouraged jhum and supported the technological transformation of agricultural production. However, there is a growing public movement for rethinking agricultural policy in the region. The external policy environment and internal processes of social transformation are both underpinned by gender ideologies that systematically subordinate women.

This essay examines the practices of gender ideology among the rice-farming groups of the region. It first explores the linkages between gendered knowledge and skills, gender roles and labour, and customary norms and power structures. Then, I attempt a comparative analysis of the states in the region using selected gender disparity indicators, which suggest that there is a gendered price to pay for food sustainability. The essay argues that food and livelihood security cannot be 'engendered' by the current development and agricultural policies.

Gender and Rice Farming

GENDERED KNOWLEDGE AND SKILLS

Whether or not women first domesticated rice, its cultivation has traditionally been in the women's domain of knowledge. The wide variety of rice in the region reflects the women's extensive knowledge of seeds and plant breeding. Indeed, in the proportionately small geographical area of northeastern India there is as much diversity of rice as in all of Asia; yet the germplasm collection from the region, running into thousands, is still 'far from exhaustive' (Pathak 2001: 54). Assam and the surrounding hills are recognised as a centre of origin of rice, but this genetic base may have diminished since the introduction of modern high-yielding varieties in the 1960s (Richaria and Govindaswami 1990). Of the Garo in Meghalaya at the turn of the century, Agarwal (1994: 104, citing Burling 1963) notes that 'some women knew of over 300 indigenous varieties of rice'.

When women are displaced from their original villages and migrate to new settlements, they take their knowledge with them. Assam's Dhemaji district, on the north bank of the Brahmaputra, has several migrant settlements. In 2004, floods ravaged the area, burying fields under sand and rendering cultivation impossible. Many men left to seek work in the tea- and oil-producing areas south of the Brahmaputra or even in western India. In Harinathpur Hajong village women responded swiftly to a question about the paddy varieties grown. They first mentioned the main 'classes' of rice (as they perceived these): *dumahi*, 'two months' short-duration monsoon harvest; *ahu*, monsoon harvest; *hali* or *sali*, winter harvest; *boro*, summer harvest; and *bao*, deep-water 'floating' rice sown in summer and harvested in winter. They then named some 20 local and improved varieties; those that required more work or were prone to pest infection were not favoured. Of the winter rices, some women cultivated the scented fine-grained *joha* for special occasions or for sale, but all preferred the glutinous, sticky *bora* for their own consumption because it gave a feeling of fullness.

Arunachal is yet to be fully explored but 105 land races of paddy have been identified and, together with the local cultivars, this represents an extraordinarily rich heritage of germplasm (Sharma 2002: 4). This diversity has evolved under different farming practices, at high, middle and low altitudes, in varied upland and wetland conditions. The food-gathering Idu of the Mathun and Dri valleys in eastern Arunachal collect leafy greens, edible mushrooms, berries, fruits and nuts from the forests, and supplement this with jhum cultivation, growing two early-maturing varieties of paddy, *apu* and *entro* (*ng*) and six late-maturing varieties: *keochi, ketara, kejari, kebora, kememora,* and *kembomar* (Bhattacharjee 1983: 59). Many local varieties are deliberately selected for specific locations, soil conditions, growing durations, and other characteristics. The glutinous rice varieties grown by the Khamptis at low altitudes in Lohit and Tirap are well known for their softness. The Apatani valley, over 1,500 m high, in Lower Subansiri district, is world-famous for its unique irrigated wet rice and fish cultivation. An Apatani woman farmer told me (Krishna 1998b) that she planted five local varieties for different reasons: *pyapi* 'with a black husk', *allang amo* 'which retains its red colour even after it is cooked', *aino ari* 'which can be harvested quickly', *amo hasso* and *rarre amo*, which are suited for different kinds of soil. Of these, she preferred the quick growing aino ari. Whether in the wet rice fields of the Apatani, the jhum fields of other groups, in terraced fields or plains cultivation, the combination of particular crops varies from one family to the next in keeping with the ecological conditions of the family's land and its other livelihood activities (like weaving, basketry or service occupations). This variegated mosaic reflects the collective wisdom that has evolved over several decades.

Both in the hills and the plains, women prefer staggered growing seasons to ease the work of harvesting, which is done by hand by women alone or together with men. Only the panicle, the grain-bearing inflorescence, is cut. Sharma (2002: 6) says, 'The logic for panicle selection among local cultivars which together show a long range of discontinuous variation for maturity has been that the farm women can do the manual harvesting operations more comfortably and effectively over the entire crop maturity span in the valley. The widely adapted, high yielding IRRI rice cultures such as IR-8 and IR-26 have been little accepted . . . due to their short stature and, thereby unsuitability for panicle harvesting using the existing manual practices'.

Generally, women select the seed for sowing but their methods may vary from place to place. Years of observation and practice have given them a seemingly intuitive understanding of paddy seeds and the ability to select viable pure strains. Some women say they take care to select only sheaves that do not have different 'mixed' strains. They 'feel the weight' of the seed by holding it up from the cut end. Some examine the seeds minutely for size, shape and colour. Formerly, the Adi in Arunachal's West Siang district used a *hushak*, a basket of closely woven bamboo dedicated for paddy seed storage, but now they use tins. Many groups do not store paddy seed separately from other harvested grain. Mizo women in Aizawl district use wood ash to preserve paddy seeds in bamboo baskets and tin drums, and keep small quantities of other seeds like maize in dry gourds (Krishna 1998c). Women's rich farming heritage and experience is inadequately recognised by their own communities.

Gender Roles and Labour

In Nagaland, the landscape and natural resources are gendered in common speech: fields for women, forests for men; domestic animals for women, wild animals for men. Broadly, across the region, a particular domestic or farming task (like collecting firewood and water, or sowing and winnowing) may be undertaken by women in certain locations or by men in others (see Tables 10.1–10.5). In the Mizo hills, all tasks in the jhum cycle, apart from felling trees,

Table 10.1: Gender Roles: Herma Village, West Tripura

Women	Men	Women and/or men
Husking rice	Jhum cutting	Sowing seeds
Pressing oil seeds	Setting fire to jhum	Weeding
Collecting firewood	Fire protection	Watching over jhum
Banana leaves	Basket-weaving	Harvesting crops
Fetching water	House-building	Threshing paddy
Feeding pigs	Hunting	Shelling sesame
Feeding poultry		Ginning cotton
Carding cotton		Cutting and separating jute
Spinning yarn		from stalk
Weaving cloth		Transporting jhum to market
Cooking food		Selling jhum products
Brewing rice beer		Purchasing goods from market
Cleaning house		Fishing

Source: Collated from Ganguly, J. B. 1993. 'Development of Peasant Farming in the North-Eastern Tribal Region', in Mrinal Miri (ed.), *Continuity and Change in Tribal Society*. Shimla: Indian Institute of Advanced Study.

Table 10.2: Gender Roles: Aizawl District, Central Mizoram

Women	Men	Women and/or men
Jhum weeding	Cutting large trees	Clearing forest
Small storage	Protecting jhum (youth)	Burning
Vegetable marketing	Large storage	Sowing
Animal husbandry	Marketing	Harvesting
Home-gardening	Collecting fuel (youth)	Celebration
Cooking		Collecting water (youth)
Child care		

Source: Krishna, Sumi. 1998c. 'Mizoram' in M. S. Swaminathan (ed.), *Gender Dimensions in Biodiversity Management*. New Delhi: Konark Publishers.

Table 10.3: Gender Roles: Nishi, Arunachal Pradesh

Women	Men
Clearing undergrowth	Slashing and burning the forest cover
Sowing	Removing unburnt logs
Weeding	Building and fencing field
Harvesting	Skeeping watch over crops
Storing grain in baskets or granaries	Searching for new plots
Preparing old plots for next season	Hunting
Spinning	Fishing
Weaving	Tending mithuns
Making earthen pots	

Source: Collated from Mishra, Kiran. 1991. *Women in a Tribal Community*. New Delhi: Vikas Publishing House.

Table10.4: Gender Roles: Japhuphiki (Southern Angami), Nagaland

Women	Men	Women and men
Work in the field	Demarcate plots	Harvest
Scarry agricultural implements	Cut trees for jhum;	
and food to the fields	burn branches	
Clear paths	Till soil	
Sow	Cut trees for	
Weed	firewood/other uses	
Collect firewood in the forest		
Carry firewood from the forest		
to their village		

Source: Collated mainly from D'Souza, Alphonsus. 2001. 'The Traditional Angami Naga Forest and Water Management: Implications for Climate Change and Sustainable Tribal Living,' in Walter Fernandes and Nafisa Goga D'Souza (eds), *Climate Change and Tribal Sustainable Living: Responses from the Northeast.* Guwahati: North Eastern Social Research Centre and Indian Network of Ethics and Climate Change; Mehrotra, Nikita. 1992. 'Angami Naga Women: Some Reflections on their Status', cited in D'Souza, Alphonsus, 2001, pp. 147–80.

Table 10.5: Gender Roles: Tanghul Naga, Manipur

Women	Men
Tending saplings	Clearing forest for cultivation
Transplanting	Ploughing
Weeding	Building dykes
Harvesting	Preparing land
Husking and pounding	Hunting and trapping
Storage of food crops	Constructing, repairing fence, shed and house
Lighting the hearth	Collection of materials for house-
Cooking	building and agricultural implements
Taking care of children	Construction and quarrying
Taking care of sick, elderly	Collection of honey
Tending kitchen garden	Cane and bamboo work
Cleaning and washing	
Knitting and weaving	

Source: Adapted from Shimray, U. A. 2004. 'Women's Work in Naga Society: Household Work, Workforce Participation and Division of Labour', *Economic and Political Weekly,* 24–30 April, 39(17), p. 1706.

are done jointly or by women alone. Women participate in clearing the slashed and burned debris and prepare the land for sowing. Broadcasting or dibbling is usually done by women; weeding is always the woman's task. Harvesting and seed selection may be done jointly. Saikia's study (2000: Table 10.6) of three villages near Jorhat (Assam) shows that women undertake sowing, transplanting, irrigating, hand-weeding, harvest, and post-harvest activities. They perform 80 per cent of transplanting and harvesting but do not spray insecticides and other pesticides, use tractors and power tillers, or purchase inputs. For other tasks women provide 10–30 per cent of the total labour. She notes that this specificity cuts across all farm sizes and has not changed in 15 years since 1980–81. The variability of gender-specific work in the hills and plains indicates that socio-cultural factors rather than just women's physical and physiological attributes determine the assignment of tasks to women or men (Krishna 1998a, 2004a).

Northeastern women traditionally work harder than men and now they also undertake tasks that were in the men's domain. As young men and women are getting educated and moving away from farm work, the burden of farming is shifting to older women, with young girls helping with domestic tasks. Young Apatani girls collect water and carry loads of husked rice, tasks that used to be done by boys. I have also observed Nishi women chopping wood, although women are not supposed to use the axe. Among the Apatani, it is said that land preparation is men's work and that only men may handle the spade, but women do use spades in the fields. Yet, as elsewhere in India, there is a widespread perception that the gendering of tasks is 'natural' (biologically determined) and that men 'naturally' do the heavier, riskier tasks while women (presumed to be weaker in body and mind) do the light, easy work. Researchers often reinforce these local stereotypes by carrying their own perceptions into the field. It is exceptional to come across an account that does not simply reproduce the stereotype about 'hard, masculine work'.

In a village near Basar, the sub-divisional headquarters of West Siang district, I met middle-aged Nyayo Bam in her house as dusk was falling. She had returned from the fields and was grinding bamboo shoots. Interrupting her work to talk with us about women's work in paddy cultivation, she said her family has both jhum and pani kheti. Work on the jhum is seasonal. 'When

Table 10.6: Gender-specific Roles in Cultivation, Jorhat District, Assam

	Average person days (8 hours) per worker									
	Marginal		Small		Medium		Large		All Sizes	
	Male	Female	Male	Female	Male	Female	Male	Female	Male	Female
Land preparation, ploughing, etc.	25.6		31.0		38.5		42.6		34.4	
Irrigation	9.4	2.4	11.3	2.9	14.5	3.4	16.8	3.6	13.0	3.1
Fertiliser application	8.6	1.6	10.6	2.3	12.9	3.5	15.9	4.8	12.0	3.1
Sowing	8.8	2.5	12.8	3.4	15.9	3.5	17.2	4.2	13.7	3.4
Transplanting	4.7	24.5	5.8	29.6	6.4	32.8	8.9	35.5	6.4	30.6
Use of insecticides, pesticides	4.2		5.3		7.4		8.5		6.3	
Hand weeding	8.3	2.8	10.7	3.4	14.3	3.6	16.3	4.2	12.4	3.5
Use of weeder/herbicide	4.2		5.3		6.8		8.5		6.2	
Harvesting	6.0	26.5	7.0	30.4	8.1	32.0	10.2	36.4	7.8	31.3
Post-harvest operations	38.7	9.0	40.5	8.7	51.0	8.5	53.5	11.7	45.9	9.5
All operations	118.2	69.3	140.0	80.6	175.6	87.3	198.5	100.4	158.1	84.4
Total working days	187.5		220.6		262.9		298.9		242.5	

Source: Saikia, Anuva. 2000. 'Employment Patterns of Rural Women and Their Involvement in Decision-Making: A Study in Jorhat District of Assam', in *Women in Agriculture and Rural Development*. Proceedings of the Workshop, 9–10 November. New Delhi: Indian Society of Agricultural Economics, p. 47.

the jhum rests we also rest', she said. Wet rice gives better yields but has increased women's labour. So, 'a woman's work is never finished.' Wet rice requires transplantation and more weedings than jhum rice. Women say that men do not have the patience for weeding. The only circumstances in which weed formation is limited are where wet rice fields stand in continuously flowing water from perennial hill streams. Women and men feel that alien weed species have been introduced into the area along with the fodder that is being brought in for the animals of the Indian army.

Even when women's labour contribution is recognised it is not perceived as a cost. In a comparative study of the labour input of two groups in Arunachal, Gangwar and Ramakrishnan (1992: 126) note that the traditional systems 'respond both to human needs and ecological imperatives'. They point out that the Sulung at Tabumah village are mainly gatherers and hunters while the Nishi at Yazali are engaged in jhum cultivation and animal husbandry. The Sulung get more foods from the forest than the Nishi do, and grow a lesser variety of crops, but in both cases the system ensures a balanced diet. Among the Nishi, animal husbandry supplements farming and cycles the agricultural wastes, increasing the food available for humans with minimal effect on the environment. The study concludes: 'If labour costs are computed, then the financial investment in slash and burn agriculture is high. However, their labour output is geared to the maximum utilising family labour. As such, it does not have actual financial costs.' The study does not disaggregate the labour input by gender, but ethnographic accounts (Mishra 1991) and my own observations in the Yazali area confirm that Nishi 'family labour' on the jhum fields is almost entirely female.

Some groups share jhuming activities, but the post-harvest and processing tasks are done by women (if not by machines). Time-use studies of post-harvest drying of paddy and seed, husking and pounding show the predominance of women's labour among the Tanghul Naga of Manipur (Table 10.7; Shimray 2004). De-husking and hand-pounding grain in a mortar and pestle is laborious and time-consuming; women no longer do this in peri-urban and relatively better-off areas in the hill states and the Assam plains. In Ahom villages in upper Assam, families may possess the *dheki* (grinding stone) but do not use it. Some families own mechanical grinders but most take their grain to local shops to be de-husked and ground for a small service charge. This has

Table 10.7: Weekly Average Time Spent* in Selected Post-harvest Activities, Tanghul Naga, Manipur

Feeding domestic animals		Home garden		Drying paddy and seed		De-husking and pounding	
Female	Male	Female	Male	Female	Male	Female	Male
2.00	1.42	2.25	1.12	6.00	5.00	8.19	0.30
2.10		2.00		6.15		4.60	

Source: Extrapolated from Shimray, U. A. 2004. 'Women's Work in Naga Society: Household Work, Workforce Participation and Division of Labour', *Economic and Political Weekly*, 24–30 April, 39(17), pp. 1708–9.

Note: * Weekly average time disposition = Total hours spent by total number of persons.

greatly eased women's labour. Pounding small quantities to make the flattened rice required for special preparations is still done by hand. In rural Arunachal there are several thousand traditional bamboo and stone *ghattas* that use the energy of flowing streams to grind grain into flour.

Because of the composite nature of agriculture, women also undertake multifarious activities, livestock care being among the most time- and labour-intensive. Women look after poultry and ducks; women and children also fish with their bare hands in the water channels beside the fields, or collectively in deep-water paddy fields. Indeed, in some areas, women are spending as much time on hunting animals, birds and fish as in crop cultivation, but this is rarely recognised as work. Saikia (2000: 50) notes of Assam that the 'share of women in livestock and poultry related activities are greater among small and marginal farms than among larger farms. Further, despite the considerable hours spent in caring for animals, since such work is frequently dubbed as household chores, no attention is paid to increasing efficiency or encouraging better management practices in these activities.' In Mizoram women speak of the hard daily work involved in rearing pigs, which is exclusively women's work although the buying and selling of pigs is mainly done by men. Women are able to retain control over the cash earnings from livestock and poultry and this is an incentive to labour.

Traditionally, women have managed the petty trade and men the larger markets. The only major exception is the women's rice market in Imphal, Manipur. In Basar town, in the mid-hills of West Siang (Arunachal), the small, traditional daily market is entirely occupied by elderly women who sell miniscule quantities of produce (fish, leafy vegetables, tubers, bananas, etc.) and retain the cash earnings for their own needs. Women run all the small local market stalls in Mizoram. In most parts of upper Assam the little rice that is traded in local markets is entirely in the hands of men. In the large, crowded weekly market in Borbaruah village in Dibrugarh district, enormous quantities of meat are sold (by men), as also fish and vegetables (mainly by women), some salt and spices (by women), baskets and clothes (by men and women).

Customary Norms and Power Structures

Compared to many other parts of rural India, adolescent boys and girls converse with easy familiarity and mix freely (except among some Muslim and upper-caste Hindu groups in the plains). The relatively greater freedom in the choice of marriage partners, the right to divorce, and a widow's right to remarry give the impression of equality among the sexes. Yet, the lack of gender seclusion only masks underlying power structures (Krishna 2004b). Women's lives are circumscribed by *niyam* (laws/rules/norms/ customary practices) that govern social relations in the community. Srivastava (1973: 87 and 183) says the Hindi (also Assamese) word 'niyam' is used indiscriminately by the Wancho in Tirap to signify many things: 'Whatever a Wancho would be doing he says he is doing his *niyam*. Whatever he cannot explain, he puts it aside by saying it is Wancho *niyam*.' This was also what one observed in the Adi villages of West Siang where 'niyam' operates at many levels of everyday life. Niyam prescribes the gendered spaces within a house and modes of behaviour: men and women must enter through different staircases; women do not appear on the men's veranda or speak in public, especially if outsiders (males) are present; within the house, the seating places around the hearth are marked out by niyam, and so on. Although the niyam is clearly stated, the rules are not always observed in practice. This seems to reflect a tension between the prescribed ideal way of life and changes now taking place as younger women overcome their socialisation and are more casual about observing customary norms (Krishna 2009).

Northeastern women have a visible role in the economic life of their communities because they are responsible for producing and processing food for their families. Physical mobility, the freedom to work and to take certain kinds of decisions gives women a sense of self-worth and identity. Yet, throughout the region, women have no substantial property rights (Table 10.8). The Khasi, Garo and Jaintia in Meghalaya are matrilineal, tracing inheritance and descent through the female line but authority is vested in the mother's brother. The matrilineal Tiwa (formerly called Lulungs) in Assam are in the process of transformation to patriliny. Among the Dimasa-Kachari in Assam, daughters trace lineage through the mother and sons through the father. All the other communities in the region are patrilineal and patrilocal. Most are monogamous, but polygyny is also practised, especially among the wealthy. Very few are polyandrous. Family structures vary from extended families to nuclear, or may be unique as in the case of the Nishi 'long house'. A Nishi's many wives and their children live together in a literally long house, each wife having her own hearth and access to independent jhum fields where she grows food for her own children. All the wives are subordinate to their common husband who pays bride price for each and claims full control over her and the produce of her labour. Bride price is embedded in wifehood; in fact, the Taraon-Mishmi word for marriage, *miyabraiya*, means 'buying a woman' (Baruah 1976: 111). Yet, bride price does not protect women from exploitation within the family. Apatani women, known to be most hardworking, have a high bride price that is compensated by their labouring in their husbands' fields; so married women are afraid to be seen at leisure. Mizo women are liberated to work but their earnings belong to the men; a widow's place in society is precarious because she is herself considered the property of her son (Krishna 1998b, 1998c).

The rich spectrum of cultures in the region encompasses considerable variation with regard to kinship, class and gender relations among the different socio-cultural groups. Inter- and intra-group relations are affected both by traditional hierarchies (ruler-commoner, patron-client) and the social stratifications that have emerged in modern times (see Chowdhury 1976; Fernandes and Barbora 2002; Krishna 1998b, 1998c, 2004b; Sinha 1998; Zehol 2003). Yet, gender discrimination is common to all, regardless of the belief system or religion a community follows: animist, Doini-polo, Christian, Buddhist, Hindu or Muslim. Women's low

Table 10.8: Aspects of Patriarchy among Selected Groups

	Descent and family structure	Property inheritance	Women's participation in religious and public decision-making
MIZORAM			
Mizo	Patrilineal, patrilocal; extended family	Youngest son inherits; women have no property rights	None
MEGHALAYA			
Garo	Matrilineal, matrilocal, may be virilocal	Men cannot inherit but land may be gifted to sons; Youngest daughter inherits	None
Khasi	Matrilineal, matrilocal	Youngest daughter inherits	None. Women's participation in public affairs is ridiculed by the saying 'a hen has crowed'
ARUNACHAL			
Monpa	Buddhist, patrilineal, patrilocal; extended and nuclear family	All sons inherit; daughters inherit mother's ornaments; in the absence of sons, daughters can claim property which reverts to the male line in the next generation	None
Sherdukpen	Buddhist, patrilineal, patrilocal	Women have no rights of inheritance but can independently rear livestock and poultry, and keep money earned from the activity.	None
Sulung	Patrilineal, patrilocal	Women have no rights but under certain circumstances widow may have a share in husband's property	No role but sometimes allowed to attend village meetings as onlookers.

Group	Family/Marriage	Inheritance	Public role
Nishi (also Bangni Hill Miri)	Patrilineal, patrilocal; polygynous; 'long house' (many wives in one house) family; bride price	Eldest son inherits; women have no rights except to ornaments and utensils (brought as dowry)	None
Apatani	Patrilineal, patrilocal; monogamous, polygyny permitted to wealthy; bride price	Eldest son inherits; mother may be consulted on property matters; women inherit clothes and ornaments	None
Adi-Gallo	Patrilineal, patrilocal; formerly, elder brother's wife could be 'shared' by younger brothers; polygyny also permitted to wealthy; bride price	Sons inherit; rarely daughters may receive land in dowry; unmarried daughters can retain their own earnings; women inherit beads and ornaments	Participate in religious ceremonies; no role in public decision-making; (Adi women recently appointed to the traditional council, kebang, make tea for members but are not allowed to speak.)
Idu-Mishmi	Patrilineal, patrilocal; polygyny permitted to wealthy; extended and nuclear family; bride price	Sons inherit; daughters inherit ornaments	Participate in religious activities; no role in public decision-making
Khampti	Hindu, patrilineal, patrilocal; monogamous but polygyny also permitted to wealthynuclear and extended family		None
Tangsa	Patrilineal, patrilocal; monogamous	Women have no rights to property but have free access	None
Nocte	Patrilineal, patrilocal; monogamous but polygyny permitted to wealthy; extended and nuclear family		None
Wancho	Patrilineal, patrilocal; monogamy and polygyny practised	Women have no rights	None

Source: Krishna, Sumi. 2009. *Genderscapes: Revisioning Natural Resource Management*. New Delhi: Zubaan. Collated from various authors and field interactions with some tribal groups.

status is maintained by traditional practices governing descent, property and inheritance, and by systematic exclusion from participation in religious ceremonies and community decisions. This has the sanction of customary law, which is safeguarded in certain cases by the constitutional arrangements between the Government of India and some of the states (see Krishna 2004b for more detailed analysis). Critiquing the 'ethnographer's romanticised model', Nongbri (1998: 223) says that the tribal women's 'greater economic independence and freedom of movement' compared to 'their counterparts in non-tribal societies cannot be disputed,' but it is 'naïve to equate this with superior social status'. Further, 'a closer look would show that gender inequality is not alien to tribal societies but it is obscured by their poor economic conditions which forces men and women to co-operate and share in joint economic activities'.

Cultivable land is the most productive asset and the basis for livelihood and food security. Naga women are generally not allowed to inherit property (Kelhou 1998) but D'souza (2001: 89) says that among the Japfuphiki (southern Angami Naga), while 'landed property' is inherited through the male line, 'movable property may be inherited by females', so a woman can buy land on her own and receive land bought (i.e., not inherited) by her parents. It is not clear whether this actually happens in practice. Moreover, even among the matrilineal Garo and Khasi, Agarwal (1994: 150–51) notes that 'property rights did not alter the overall gender division of labour' or 'guarantee women the same sexual freedom as men'. Husbands, brothers, and maternal uncles had the 'formal managerial authority over land' and customary institutions and jural power were a male monopoly; even the Khasi women heiresses did not have the kind of local influence that the chiefs commanded.

Some Arunachali women admit privately that they do take decisions about which crops to plant and where — 'What do the men know?' — but they hesitate to say this in men's presence. In earlier times, communities owned natural resources; as markets in land and forest resources have developed, women's customary lack of property rights reinforces their subordinate position and exclusion from public decision-making. These are not minor social restrictions but are fundamental to the power hierarchy that structures the rice-farming groups.

The Meitei of the Manipur valley are among the few communities in the region who do not socialise women into subordinate status. The women's sphere of work has been enlarged since the early 19th century, when the wars with Burma (now Mynamar) led to a severe decline in the male population. Vaishnavite Hinduism (which had begun to spread in the area before the Burmese wars) was intensely promoted by the ruling elite. But it did not succeed in overthrowing the traditional gender-egalitarian practices. Hindu customs — child marriage, the prohibition of divorce and widow-remarriage — were rejected. So too Pangan (Muslim Meitei) women rejected purdah. As I have written elsewhere (Krishna 2004b: 385), 'Caste Hinduism was not able to curtail the customary male-female cooperation in the religious sphere or change women's socio-economic role, which centres on the market for rice. Meitei women's control of the rice trade gives them a powerful public voice. So although the Meitei are a patriarchal society and men have the position of authority as fathers and husbands, the women's socio-economic power and collective strength counteracts male domination.' Writing two decades ago about 'the traditional political power of the market network', Chaki-Sircar (1984: 223) commented that 'the women can paralyse the political and administrative system when the need arises'. This power has been demonstrated on more than one occasion, and most recently in the summer of 2004 as the market women led sustained protests against the presence and actions of the paramilitary force, the Assam Rifles, in Manipur. Yet, as elsewhere in the region, women's participation in public movements has not ensured a place for them in public decision-making bodies, traditional or modern.

So, we need to recognise that the rich diversity of rice in the northeastern region, which has been nurtured by women's knowledge and skills, is the result of a gendered division of labour, of roles learnt and practised over generations. These roles are reflective of the patriarchal ideology that determines gender relations and the value that is ascribed to different spheres of work.

Gender Disparities

The ethnographic picture can be substantiated by data on gender disparities in the region. Rustagi (2003) has collated a wide range of gender indicators using state-wise and gender-disaggregated data across Indian states. These indicators cover demographic factors, women's health, education, economic participation, decision-making, and security. Based on her analysis and supplemented by that of Kishor and Gupta (2004), I have selected 11 significant gender indicators (choosing between one and three from each of the six sectors identified by Rustagi) and extracted the data for eight northeastern states (Table 10.9).

Substantial positive and negative divergences (based on absolute numbers or trends) from the average for all-India are noted for each indicator. According to Planning Commission data for the percentage of population below the poverty level, in 2001 Mizoram was the only northeastern state that fared better than the national average; in 2004–05 (by different criteria) all the eight states were better placed (see Appendix). Without going into the controversy over methodologies for measuring poverty, the Planning Commission data for 1999–2001 have been used (column A). The child sex ratio (column B) is a critical indicator of levels of female discrimination because it is less affected by migration than the overall sex ratio (column C). Although all the states in the region score better than the all-India average, between 1991 and 2001, the child sex ratio improved only in Sikkim, Tripura and Mizoram.

The accuracy of the National Family Health Survey (NFHS-2, conducted in 1998–99) in certain northeastern states is in some doubt; it has been suggested that in Arunachal Pradesh and Manipur the survey does not effectively capture the rural situation. In the absence of other data we have to use this bearing in mind its limitations. The survey shows that one out of two women in India suffers from severe, moderate or mild anaemia, reflecting an aspect of women's under-nourishment. Assam, Meghalaya and Sikkim show high levels of severe and moderate anaemia (column D); Arunachal, Assam and Tripura have high levels of mild anaemia (column E).

Instead of looking at school enrolment or literacy rates, I have taken the gender gap in literacy rates (column F) as more indicative of women's status vis-à-vis the men of their own communities. Mizo and Ao Naga women are well known for their high literacy, on par with Kerala, and indeed all the northeastern states are better than the all-India average. Manipur shows a decline in

Table 10.9: Selected Gender Disparity Indicators, Northeastern States

States	Demographic, survival factors			Health: anaemia		Education	Rural female work participation		Private decision-making %			Crimes against women	
	(A) Below poverty level % 2001	(B) Child sex ratio 2001	(C) Sex ratio above 6 years 2001	(D) Severe & moderate anaemia % 1998–99	(E) Mild anaemia % 1998–99	(F) Gender gap in literacy rate 2001	(G) RVFP rate 1993–94	(H) RVFP rate 1999–2000	(I) Involved in decisions on own health 1998–99	(J) Freedom to go to the market 1998–99	(K) Freedom to decide about own earnings 1998–99	(L) Recorded cases per million population 1999	(M) Composite gender rank (B to L)
(Listed in order of poverty levels)													
MIZORAM	19.5	971	932	12.8	35.2	4.6	31.7	44.0	73.2	64.2	26.4	176	1
MANIPUR	28.5	961	981	7.1	21.7	18.2	30.8	25.3	43.3	28.6	59.0	29	3
NAGALAND	32.7	975	899	9.7	27.8	9.9	21.6	44.1	69.4	17.3	17.8	11	5
ARUNACHAL	33.5	961	888	11.9	50.6	19.8	40.9	31.0	70.0	46.8	46.4	148	7
MEGHALAYA	33.9	975	974	29.9	33.4	5.7	49.3	41.8	78.9	46.5	40.7	25	2

(Table 10.9 continued)

(Table 10.9 continued)

States	Demographic, survival factors			Health: anaemia		Education	Rural female work participation		Private decision-making %			Crimes against women	
	(A) Below poverty level % 2001	(B) Child sex ratio 2001	(C) Sex ratio above 6 years 2001	(D) Severe & moderate anaemia % 1998–99	(E) Mild anaemia % 1998–99	(F) Gender gap in literacy rate 2001	(G) RWFP rate 1993–94	(H) RWFP rate 1999–2000	(I) Involved in decisions on own health 1998–99	(J) Freedom to go to the market 1998–99	(K) Freedom to decide about own earnings 1998–99	(L) Recorded cases per million population 1999	(M) Composite gender rank (B to L)
(Listed in order of poverty levels)													
TRIPURA	**34.4**	_975_	947	16.3	**43.0**	16.1	**12.8**	**7.3**	51.2	27.4	37.7	98	6
ASSAM	**36.1**	**964**	926	**26.5**	**43.2**	15.9	**15.9**	**15.1**	65.1	**13.2**	40.0	138	8
SIKKIM	**36.5**	**986**	**858**	**23.8**	37.3	15.3	**19.8**	_24.1_	60.2	38.2	_69.8_	56	4
All-India	26.1	927	934	16.7	35.0	24.5	32.8	29.9	51.6	31.6	41.1	127	

Source: Derived from Rustagi, Preet. 2003. _Gender Biases and Discrimination against Women: What Do Different Indicators Say?_ New Delhi: CWDS and UNIFEM; Kishor, Sunita and Kamla Gupta. 2004. 'Women's Empowerment in India and Its States: Evidence from the NFHS', _Economic and Political Weekly_, 14–20 February, 39(7): 694–712.

Notes: Bold font indicates negative divergence, underscore indicates positive divergence from national average, except where indicated.
A. % of population Below Poverty Level, Planning Commission, Central Statistical Organisation, 2001.
B. Child sex ratio (number of females per 1,000 males in population below 6 years), calculated from

Census of India. 2001. *Provisional Population Totals*. New Delhi: Registrar General of India, Government of India.
(Bold font: most unfavourable ratio among northeastern states, underscore: improved ratios over the previous decade.)

C. Sex ratio in population above six years (number of females per 1,000 males),
Census of India. 2001. *Provisional Population Totals*. New Delhi: Registrar General of India, Government of India.

D. and E. % of women with Severe and Moderate Anaemia (taken together); and Mild Anaemia, NFHS-2. 2000. *National Family Health Survey-2, 1998–99, India*. Mumbai: International Institute for Population Services.

F. Gender Gap in Literacy, difference in % of literacy of females and males, Census of India, 2000.
Bold font: most unfavourable position among northeastern states, underscore: among the five lowest gender gaps in literacy (all-India).

G. and H. Rural Female Workforce Participation Rate (proportion of total workers among population above 6 years), calculated from NSS. 1995. *Employment and Unemployment Situation in India – 1993–94*, NSS 50th Round, National Sample Survey Organisation, Ministry of Statistics and Programme Implementation. New Delhi: Government of India; NSS. 2001. *Employment and Unemployment Situation in India – 1999–2000*, NSS 55th Round, National Sample Survey Organisation, Ministry of Statistics and Programme Implementation. New Delhi: Government of India.

H. bold font indicates decline, underscore indicates increase in RFWP rate over the previous decade.

I., J. and K. % of ever-married women (aged 15–49) involved (with husbands/family) in decisions about their own health; who do not require permission to go to the market; who are free to take independent decisions on their own earnings, NFHS-2. 2000. *National Family Health Survey -2, 1998–99, India*. Mumbai: International Institute for Population Services.

L. Crimes against Women, number of cases per million population, National Crime Research Bureau, 1999.

M. Estimated on basis of B to L.

the female–male literacy gap during 1991–2001. Despite improvement in female literacy, Arunachal continues to hover near the low national average.

Women's economic participation is known to be related to improved social status but women's productive work continues to be under-estimated despite efforts to improve enumeration. For farming communities the proportion of workers in relation to the total population, that is, the Rural Female Workforce Participation (RFWP) rate, is of great significance (columns G and H). According to the National Sample Survey, between 1993–94 and 1999–2000, the all-India average RFWP rate declined, but it increased in five states: Nagaland, Mizoram and Sikkim in northeastern India, and Punjab and Gujarat. The RFWP rate in Meghalaya and Arunachal, although still above the national average, showed a decline. In the major paddy-growing states, Manipur, Tripura and Assam, the RFWP rate was already below the all-India average and declined further.

Measures of women's autonomy and their power to take decisions about their own lives are relatively recent. Traditionally, women have been free to take decisions about the domestic sphere. This is borne out by NFHS data, which show that an average 85 per cent of women in India take decisions about what to cook. In Arunachal this is 94 per cent. About one in two adult married women in India is involved (with husbands/families) in decisions about their own health; women in Meghalaya, Mizoram, Arunachal, and Nagaland are especially well placed in this regard (column I). Women's mobility, or its lack, is generally seen as a key indicator of their position in society. One in three women in India needs permission to go to the market. Among those who do not need such permission (column J), Mizoram ranks high, on par with Goa but still far behind Tamil Nadu. Both Assam and Nagaland lag behind the national average. Taking independent decisions on one's own earnings is yet another indicator of women's autonomous position (column K). Here, Sikkim and Manipur rank much higher than the national average but Mizoram and Nagaland fare badly (which is reflective of a Naga saying that women are free to work but not to earn).

Women's lack of safety and security within the home and in public spaces is a significant indicator of gender disparity, which is rarely measured in large surveys. The National Crimes Record

Bureau of the Ministry of Home Affairs records registered crimes against women, including cognisable offences under the Indian Penal Code and other laws, such as those relating to dowry, sati, child marriage, etc. Even this inadequate data reveals a picture of the nature of crimes against women and reflects the rising trend. In 1999, the all-India figures showed that cruelty at home accounted for 36 per cent of all crimes; followed by molestation, rape, kidnapping and abduction of girls, sexual harassment, and dowry death. The 1999 figures for different states are extremely variable, ranging from 246 cases per million in Rajasthan to zero cases in Lakshadweep. In northeastern India, Mizoram has the highest record of crimes against women with 176 cases comprising rape and molestation (column L). Arunachal Pradesh with 148 cases also has a high, and rising, level of crime, comprising mainly molestation, rape, kidnapping and abduction, and cruelty at home. Nagaland, Meghalaya and Manipur show low levels of crime against women.

As with Rustagi's all-India analysis, the data for northeastern India shows that all states have both positive and negative indicators of gender disparity. This is sometimes counter-intuitive, as in Mizoram's high level of crimes against women, but is comparable to the trends in certain other high female literacy states, such as Kerala and the Union Territory of Chandigarh, although the linkage between high literacy and crimes against women is unproven. The data reinforce the qualitative findings in certain respects. They show that broadly, women in the northeastern region, like women in other hill areas and rice-growing states, have higher work participation rates, mobility and power to take certain kinds of decisions. This is offset by the fall in the rural female work participation rates in rice-growing Assam, Tripura and Manipur. As in other parts of the country, greater levels of poverty, particularly in Sikkim, Assam and Tripura, may be contributing to women's lower levels of literacy and health. This is again offset by the gender gap in the female–male literacy rate in the northeastern states, which is high in Manipur despite its relatively lower level of poverty.

Based upon both the positive and negative indicators of gender disparity, I have suggested a composite gender rank (column M). The composite ranking shows that in the northeastern region, gender disparity is least in Mizoram and less in Meghalaya and that it is greatest in Assam. Despite greater autonomy for women in certain respects, Arunachal Pradesh also ranks low. While Meghalaya's position may reflect the relative gender balance in the past among matrilineal groups in the state, that of Mizoram is clearly related to all-round development, which is perhaps helping to counter gender bias in customary practices. The low position of Arunachal undermines any attempt to generalise about gender equity in 'tribal' communities. The similar position of Assam and Arunachal at the lower end of the scale reflects similarities in the child sex ratio, levels of anaemia among women, gender gap in literacy and surprisingly comparable rates of crime against women. Overall, Arunachal ranks somewhat higher than Assam on account of women's greater work participation and mobility.

In the more specific context of gender and rice farming, it may be useful to relate the gender rank of the northeastern states postulated in this essay with the position of these states in the *Atlas of the Sustainability of Food Security in India* (MSSRF 2004). The *Atlas* uses 17 selected indicators (driven by the secondary data available across states) such as the weighted net sown area, the per capita forest cover, the future availability of surface and ground water, percentage of degraded area, percentage of non-agricultural workers, infant mortality, and percentage of households with access to safe drinking water. Based on the indicators, index values have been calculated and the states classified in five groups, ranging from the extremely unsustainable to the sustainable. According to this mapping, Nagaland is the most unsustainable, and the only such state in the country (mainly because of land degradation), while Arunachal is sustainable because it has more forests and fewer people.

Given the ground situation of the food production system in northeastern India, as in the rest of India, any assessment of food sustainability would be incomplete if gender indicators are not taken into account. In Table 10.10, I have juxtaposed the composite gender rank (taken from column M of Table 10.9) and the sustainability of food security index (taken from the *Atlas*). This comparison reveals that Arunachal, which has high gender disparity, is sustainable in terms of food security, while Mizoram with the least gender disparity is moderately sustainable in terms of food. Nagaland, which is the most unsustainable state for food security

Table 10.10: Comparison of Gender Disparity and Food Sustainability

States by gender rank	Gender disparity level	Food sustainability
1. MIZORAM	Least disparity	Moderately sustainable
2. MEGHALYA	Some disparity	Unsustainable
3. MANIPUR	Moderately high disparity	Unsustainable
4. SIKKIM	Moderately high disparity	Unsustainable
5. NAGALAND	Moderately high disparity	**Extremely unsustainable**
6. TRIPURA	High disparity	Moderately unsustainable
7. ARUNACHAL	High disparity	Sustainable
8. ASSAM	**Extremely high disparity**	Moderately unsustainable

Source: Gender Disparity Level: Estimated on basis of Composite Gender Rank
(Column M of Table 10.9)
Food Sustainability: Derived from 'Sustainability of Food Security Index
Values' (MSSRF. 2004. *Atlas of the Sustainability of Food Security*. Chennai:
M. S. Swaminathan Research Foundation).

Notes: Extremely unsustainable: Below 0.300
Unsustainable: 0.301–0.350
Moderately unsustainable: 0.351–0.400
Moderately sustainable: 0.401–0.460
Sustainable: Above 0.460

in the entire country, has a moderately high level of gender disparity. There are, of course, limitations to this exercise because the gender indicators do not capture critical areas of women's lack of autonomy and subordination within the family and community. However, if such information were available, it is likely to reinforce one inference that can be drawn even on the basis of the available qualitative and quantitative data. This inference is that Arunachal is paying an extremely high gendered price for the sustainability of its food security, with Assam and Tripura not far behind. Indeed, in all of the states of the northeastern region, agricultural production has an in-built gendered price.

So, What Does It All Mean for Women?

Changes in farming have arisen because of the growing density of population around cultivated areas (Burman 2002), and government policies limiting the area available for jhuming in order to promote settled wet-rice cultivation. The outcome of this process for the matrilineal Garo in Meghalaya is well documented. Agarwal (1994: 132) says 'Variations in the extent of shift out of jhum into diversified production led to two forms of economic differentiation in the Garo Hills: inter-village, and inter-household within villages. Inter-village variations stem essentially from differential availability of irrigable flat land for settled rice cultivation.' Villages that shifted entirely to wet rice, with some jhum, are self-sufficient in food production. But those that depended entirely on jhum are impoverished. When such differences occurred within a village, inter-household inequality increased. She notes (1994: 158) that wet rice cultivation has reduced the need for labour cooperation between villages, which was essential for clearing jhum forests, and that women have become 'helpers' to men. 'This includes harvesting, an operation in which, under jhum, men were women's helpers.' Wet rice cultivation has affected the traditional land ownership pattern of the Garo. Privatisation has resulted in *pattas* for land ownership being granted in men's names and this in turn has eroded the customary matrilineal inheritance and marriage patterns. As Agarwal points out, the pressure of increasing population might have led eventually to the decline of jhum, but the erosion of women's rights in land is directly attributable to the male bias of state agencies.

Government interventions in agricultural development may have helped people in some areas to improve productivity and perhaps to reduce intra-village inequalities. Far from recognising the gendered price of rice in the region, however, agricultural extension continues to be geared to men (as in the 1960s Green Revolution interventions). A watered-down version of the early 1950s middle-class American Home Economics model and the 'welfare' approach of Indian development planning (see Krishna 1995) continues to provide skilled farming women with lessons in home-based activities like juice-making and embroidery, even as DONER prides itself on its new generation projects for women: fashion 'technology' and toy-making! Food and livelihood security cannot be 'engendered' without addressing the structural aspects of development. In an era of globalisation, the 'Green Revolution' approach cannot just be grafted onto existing farming systems without sensitivity to the known social and ecological problems of intensive agriculture (see Krishna 1996, 2000). This could have disastrous consequences for the region.

Positive indicators of women's status, such as higher rates of literacy, work participation and greater autonomy in the north-eastern states, do not seem to be sufficient safeguards against the erosion of women's traditional knowledge and skills, increase in their labour, and regressive changes in gender relations. The significant correlation between high levels of gender disparity and even moderate levels of food sustainability in some states is a clear pointer to the increasingly gendered price of rice. One can speculate about the reasons for this correlation but it seems to be linked to the emphasis on increasing agricultural productivity at any cost. Gender disparities in customary practices are reinforced by conventional development and agricultural policies, which together advance new forms of patriarchy. The clearest reflection of this is in greater control over women's sexuality, increasing violence against women and the declining trend in the sex ratio in some states. The adverse gender outcome of conventional development in northeastern India is, thus, similar to trends in the rest of the country. These are major social changes forming the substratum, the power structure, upon which the rice-farming system rests.

Appendix

Percentage of Population Below Poverty Line (Combined rural and urban)

	1999–2000	2004–05 *Uniform reference period*	2004–05 *Mixed reference period*
MIZORAM	19.5	12.6	9.5
MANIPUR	28.5	17.3	13.2
NAGALAND	32.7	19.0	14.5
ARUNACHAL	33.5	17.6	13.4
MEGHALAYA	33.9	18.5	14.1
TRIPURA	34.4	18.9	14.4
ASSAM	36.1	19.7	15.0
SIKKIM	36.5	20.1	15.2
All-India	26.1	27.5	21.8

Source: Derived from Databook for DCH. 1 November 2011, p. 40 of 189; Planning Commission and NSSO Data 61st Round. See http://planningcommission. nic.in/data/datatable/0211/data%2040.pdf (accessed 31 January 2012).

Note

* An earlier version of this essay first appeared in 2005 as 'Gendered Price of Rice in North-Eastern India', in *Economic and Political Weekly*, 40(25): 2555–562. A more detailed version forms a chapter in the author's 2009 book *Genderscapes: Revisioning Natural Resource Management* (New Delhi: Zubaan).

References

Agarwal, Bina. 1994. *A Field of One's Own: Gender and Land Rights in South Asia.* New Delhi: Cambridge University Press.

Baruah, T. K. 1976. 'The Effect of Bride-price on a Mishmi' *Resarun 1975.* Shillong: Department of Information and Public Relations, Government of Arunachal Pradesh, pp. 110–13.

Bhattacharjee, Tarun Kumar. 1983. *The Idus of Mithun and Dri Valley.* Itanagar: Directorate of Research, Government of Arunachal Pradesh.

Burling, Robbins. 1963. *Rengsanggri: Family and Kinship in a Garo Village.* Philadelphia: University of Pennsylvania Press.

Burman, B. K. Roy 2002. 'Demographic Profile of the Hill Areas of North East India', in Sarthak Sengupta (ed.), *Tribal Studies in North East India.* New Delhi: Mittal Publications, pp. 1–19.

Census of India. 2001. *Provisional Population Totals.* New Delhi: Registrar General of India, Government of India.

Chaki-Sircar, Manjusri. 1984. *Feminism in a Traditional Society: Women of the Manipur Valley.* New Delhi: Shakti Books.

Chowdhury, J. N. 1976. 'Evidence of Some Caste-like Features in Some Arunachal Tribes', *Resarun 1975.* Itanagar: Department of Information and Public Relations, Government of Arunachal Pradesh, pp. 43–56.

D'Souza, Alphonsus. 2001. 'The Traditional Angami Naga Forest and Water Management: Implications for Climate Change and Sustainable Tribal Living', in Walter Fernandes and Nafisa Goga D'Souza (eds), *Climate Change and Tribal Sustainable Living: Responses from the Northeast.* Guwahati: North Eastern Social Research Centre and Indian Network of Ethics and Climate Change, pp. 88–113.

Fernandes, Walter and Sanjay Barbora. 2002. *Modernisation and Women's Status in North-Eastern India.* Guwahati: North Eastern Social Research Centre.

Ganguly, J. B. 1993. 'Development of Peasant Farming in the North-Eastern Tribal Region', in Mrinal Miri (ed.), *Continuity and Change in Tribal Society.* Shimla: Indian Institute of Advanced Study, pp. 298–313.

Gangwar, A. K. and P. S. Ramakrishnan. 1992. 'Agriculture and Animal Husbandry among the Sulungs and Nishis of Arunachal Pradesh', in Walter Fernandez (ed.), *National Development and Tribal Deprivation.* New Delhi: Indian Social Institute, pp. 100–28.

Hore, D. K. 2005. 'Rice Diversity Collection, Conservation and Management in Northeastern India', *Genetic Resources and Crop Evolution,* 52(8): 1129–140.

Kelhou. 1998. 'Women in Angami Society,' in Lucy Zehol (ed.), *Women in Naga Society*. New Delhi: Regency Publishers, pp. 55–61.

Kishor, Sunita and Kamla Gupta. 2004. 'Women's Empowerment in India and Its States: Evidence from the NFHS', *Economic and Political Weekly*, 14–20 February, 39(7): 694–712.

Krishna, Sumi. 1995. 'It's Time to Clear the Cobwebs: The Gender Impact of Environmentalism', *The Administrator*, August, 40(3): 93–104.

———. 1996. *Environmental Politics: People's Lives and Development Choices*. New Delhi: Sage.

———. 1998a. 'Gender and Biodiversity Management,' in M. S. Swaminathan (ed.), *Gender Dimensions in Biodiversity Management*. New Delhi: Konark Publishers, pp. 23–61.

———. 1998b. 'Arunachal Pradesh', in M. S. Swaminathan (ed.), *Gender Dimensions in Biodiversity Management*. New Delhi: Konark Publishers, pp. 148–81.

———. 1998c. 'Mizoram' in M. S. Swaminathan (ed.), *Gender Dimensions in Biodiversity Management*. New Delhi: Konark Publ., pp. 182–210.

———. 2000. 'The Impact of the Structural Adjustment Programme on Gender and Environment in India', in CWDS (ed.), *Shifting Sands: Women's Lives and Globalization*. Kolkata: Stree, pp. 173–234.

———. 2004a. 'A "Genderscape" of Community Rights in Natural Resource Management', Overview in Sumi Krishna (ed.), *Livelihood and Gender: Equity in Community Resource Management*. New Delhi: Sage, pp. 17–63.

———. 2004b. 'Gender, Tribe and Political Participation: Control of Natural Resources in North-eastern India', in Sumi Krishna (ed.), *Livelihood and Gender: Equity in Community Resource Management*. New Delhi: Sage, pp. 375–96.

———. 2009. *Genderscapes: Revisioning Natural Resource Management*. New Delhi: Zubaan.

M. S. Swaminathan Research Foundation. (MSSRF). 2004. *Atlas of the Sustainability of Food Security*. Chennai: M. S. Swaminathan Research Foundation.

Mishra, Kiran. 1991. *Women in a Tribal Community*. New Delhi: Vikas Publishing House.

National Family Health Survey (NFHS-2). 2000. *National Family Health Survey-2, 1998–99, India*. Mumbai: International Institute for Population Services.

National Sample Survey (NSS). 1995. *Employment and Unemployment Situation in India – 1993–94*, NSS 50th Round, National Sample Survey Organisation, Ministry of Statistics and Programme Implementation. New Delhi: Government of India.

National Sample Survey (NSS). 2001. *Employment and Unemployment Situation in India – 1999–2000*, NSS 55th Round, National Sample Survey Organisation, Ministry of Statistics and Programme Implementation. New Delhi: Government of India.

Nagachan, S. V., A. K. Mohanty and A. Pattanayak. 2011. *Status Paper on Rice in Northeast India*. New Delhi: Indian Agricultural Research Institute, available at http://rkmp.co.in/research-domain/rice-statewise/north-east/status-paper-on-rice-in-north-east-india (accessed 28 September 2011).

Nongbri, Tiplut. 1994. 'Gender Relations in Matrilineal Societies', *Lokayan Bulletin*, 10(5/6): 79–90.

———. 1998. 'Gender Issues and Tribal Development', in Bhupinder Singh (ed.), *Antiquity to Modernity in Tribal India*. (Vol. II, Tribal Self Management in North Eastern India.) New Delhi: Inter-India Publications.

Pathak, P. K. 2001. 'Major Cereal Crops of Assam', in A. C. Thakur, Ashok Bhattacharyya and D. K. Sarma (eds), *Agriculture in Assam*. Jorhat: Assam Agriculture University, Directorate of Extension Education.

Richaria, R.H. and S. Govindaswami. 1990. *Rices of India*. Kashell, Maharashtra: Academy of Development Science. (First edition 1966.)

Rustagi, Preet. 2003. *Gender Biases and Discrimination against Women: What Do Different Indicators Say?* New Delhi: Centre for Women's Development Studies and United Nations Development for Women.

Saikia, Anuva. 2000. 'Employment Patterns of Rural Women and Their Involvement in Decision-Making: A Study in Jorhat District of Assam', in *Women in Agriculture and Rural Development*. Proceedings of the Workshop, 9–10 November. New Delhi: Indian Society of Agricultural Economics.

Sharma, B. D. 2002. 'Crop Genetic Resources of Arunachal Pradesh', in K. A. Singh (ed.), *Resource Management Perspective of Arunachal Pradesh*. Basar: ICAR Research Complex for NEH Region, Arunachal Pradesh Centre.

Shimray, U. A. 2004. 'Women's Work in Naga Society: Household Work, Workforce Participation and Division of Labour', *Economic and Political Weekly*, 24–30 April, 39(17): 1698–710.

Sinha, A. C. 1998. 'Social Stratification among the Tribes of North-East India', in Bhupinder Singh (ed.), *Antiquity to Modernity in Tribal India: Vol. II – Tribal Self Management in North Eastern India*. New Delhi: Inter-India Publications.

Srivastava, L. R. N. 1973. *Among the Wanchos*. Shillong: Directorate of Information and Public Relations, Arunachal Pradesh.

Zehol, Lucy V. 2003. 'Status of Tribal Women', in T. R. Subba and G. C. Ghosh (eds), *The Anthropology of North East India*. Hyderabad: Orient Longman.

PART III

SEARCH FOR ALTERNATIVES

11

Integrated Rubber Farming
and Livelihood Systems
in Northeastern India*

P. K. Viswanathan

Growing empirical evidence demonstrates that globalisation causes tremendous transformation even in the most traditional agrarian and mountainous societies that practise shifting cultivation. Recently, such societies in the South Asian and South East Asian region have been undergoing significant socio-economic transformation as they adapt to the changing environments and the crisis in livelihoods ensuing from the global trade regime (Abiziad and Koomes 2004; Dendi et al. 2005; Kuniyasu 2002; Lee 2004; Malik 2003; Midmore and Jansen 2003; Sikor 2004). The emerging agrarian systems are more dynamic in terms of diversified land-use and farming. Various development interventions by the state in country-specific contexts aimed at sedentarisation of the pastoralists and shifting cultivators, have also stimulated the process of agrarian transformation in many of these regions (Baxter 1994; Dyer 2001; Fratkin 1997; Hansen 1995; Hung 1995; Melnyk 1993; Zahir 2000). However, despite dynamic agrarian transformation, the livelihoods of the mountainous communities are highly vulnerable in the absence or failure of effective institutional mechanisms covering the broad spectrum of farm production systems. The policies and programmes aimed at sedentarisation of the pastoral communities, and the sustainable development of the mountainous regions, do not seem to have been designed in conformity with the needs and aspirations of the local communities. The result is that the hill communities remain alienated and physically detached from the mainstream development process.

By and large, researchers have studied the process of development of rubber-farming systems in mainland as well as mountainous regions in terms of rubber agroforestry perspectives and accordingly characterised the prominent typologies based on the type, extent and integration of different cropping livelihood systems. Empirical information from the major rubber-producing countries of Indonesia and Malaysia indicates the growing prominence of rubber-integrated farm livelihood and agroforestry systems. This shows that the traditional shifting agriculture-dominant societies in Indonesia have gained economic dynamism from their rubber-based agroforestry systems. Dove (1993) suggests that rubber was well integrated into the Bornean systems of swidden agriculture in Indonesia. While rubber occupied a distinct niche in the farm economy and catered to the need for market goods, the swidden agriculture fulfilled the subsistence requirements. The 'jungle rubber' widely prevalent in Indonesia (Angelsen 1995; Gouyon et al. 1993; Joshi et al. 2002; Penot and Wibawa 1997) is yet another example of the rubber agroforestry integration. Rubber agroforestry systems in Malaysia have included fruit trees, bamboo, poultry, vegetables and other short-term crops as well as animal rearing (Arshad 2000). Studies also indicate that by planting rubber in a swidden system, the tribal communities have been able to secure property rights and tenurial security over land (Barlow and Muharminto 1982; Cramb 1988; Shepherd 1991; Suyanto et al. 2001) as well as overcome the economic consequences arising from harvest failure or harvest shortfalls in the swidden system (Chin 1982; King 1988; Ward and Ward 1974). Studies from Bangladesh also report that the adoption of diversified cropping systems along with innovative elements of modern rubber-farming systems have been beneficial and rewarding as the previously shifting cultivator farmers have tended to be less dependent on forests and other common property resources (CPRs) for eking out their livelihood (Dendi et al. 2005; Nath et al. 2005). From Thailand, Somboonsuke et al. (2001) reported the emergence of four main rubber-integrated farming systems as farmer adjustment strategies to overcome the adverse effects of the financial crisis in 1997. The important rubber-integrated farming systems identified are: (*a*) rubber intercrop farming system; (*b*) rubber–rice farming system; (*c*) rubber–fruit tree farming system; and (*d*) rubber–livestock farming system.

Objectives and Data

The literature is replete in terms of identification and characterisation of rubber-integrated farming systems, but there is a lack of empirical understanding of the likely impact on the livelihoods of the smallholder communities in the mountainous regions in particular, and from the perspective of a livelihood systems analytical framework. This essay seeks to understand the dynamics of the smallholder rubber-integrated farming systems in the three hill states of Assam, Meghalaya and Tripura in northeast India by (*a*) examining the socio-economic and institutional contexts within which rubber-farming systems become relevant in the NE region; (*b*) understanding the sustainable livelihood outcomes of the rubber and rubber-integrated farming systems in the three NE states; and (*c*) bringing out the institutional responses towards scaling up and promotion of sustainable rubber-integrated farm livelihood systems in the region.

The analysis is based on a farm household survey undertaken between April and June 2005 in the rubber-growing villages in Assam, Meghalaya and Tripura covering 309 rubber growers. The key informant survey was administered through a structured schedule, and Participatory Rural Appraisal (PRA) methods were used for interactions and discussions with the other stakeholders and development and extension agents. In Assam, the growers were selected from Goalpara and Kamrup districts which account for more than 70 per cent of the area with rubber plantations in the state. In Meghalaya, the sample was drawn from the East Garo Hills and Ri Bhoi districts which have a relatively higher concentration of mature rubber holdings. In Tripura, the growers were from West Tripura and South Tripura districts that together make up 87 per cent of the rubber-tapped area.

The essay is organised into four sections. Section 1 briefly discusses the conceptual framework of the study. Section 2 elaborates the socio-economic contexts and institutional processes underlying the development and expansion of the rubber smallholder system in the northeastern states. Section 3 makes a comparative economic assessment of the rubber monoculture vs rubber-integrated farm livelihood systems and its impact on the livelihoods of the tribal smallholder communities. Section 4 concludes the essay by reflecting upon the imperative of strengthening the institutional contexts for scaling up of rubber-integrated sustainable farm livelihood systems in the region along with its agro-ecological integrity and diversity.

Sustainable Farm Livelihood Systems: Conceptual Framework

The dynamic interface between household economic diversification and sustainable livelihood systems has received greater academic attention after the path-breaking study by Chambers and Conway (1992: 6) who argued that 'a livelihood comprises the capabilities, assets (including both material and social resources) and activities required for a means of living. A livelihood is sustainable when it can cope with and recover from stress and shocks, maintain or enhance its capabilities and assets, while not undermining the natural resource base'. Following this, there has been a surge of interdisciplinary research, both theoretical and empirical, across countries and regions. Of particular relevance are the studies by Carney (1998, 1999), Scoones (1998) and Ashley and Carney (1999), which have been instrumental in developing the DFID framework for sustainable livelihoods analysis (SLA) developed by the British government's Department of International Development. The DFID framework has since then been widely replicated by researchers to analyse the household strategies in diversification of sustainable livelihood systems in heterogeneous socio-economic and agro-ecological contexts both in the rural and urban environments (Singh and Gilman 1999; Tacoli 1998). Ellis (1998, 2000) argues that livelihood diversification and a portfolio of activities have become imperative as farming on its own rarely provides a sufficient asset and resource base for the rural farm households. Extending the DFID framework to the analysis of peasant viability, Bebbington (1999) considers that rural livelihoods need to be understood in terms of peoples' access to five types of capital assets: (*a*) natural capital; (*b*) human capital; (*c*) physical capital; (*d*) economic or financial capital; and (*e*) social capital (for more discussion on this, see Perz 2005; Scoones 1998).

There is, however, a perceptible gap in theoretical and empirical research on measurement of diversity in household assets and its impact on sustainable livelihoods. In this regard, some of the empirical analyses by Zhen and Routray (2003), Shrestha and Shivakoti (2003), Perz (2005), Shivakoti and Shrestha (2005a and b), VanLoon et al. (2005), and Choudhury et al. (2006) have tried to develop and use various indicators/scales to measure the degree(s) of sustainability of the parameters representing various livelihood assets. Particularly, the studies by Shivakoti and Shrestha (2005a, 2005b) and Choudhury et al. (2006) provide a comprehensive analytical framework for assessing the livelihood systems in terms of access to the five capital assets. Using the livelihood asset 'pentagon' approach, Shivakoti and Shrestha (2005a and 2005b) have analysed the livelihood effects relating to the performance of Farmer Managed Irrigation Systems (FMIS) in Nepal. The conceptual framework used in the present study is presented in Figure 11.1.

Sustainability of the livelihood systems may be assessed based on a hypothetical ranking of sustainability into four value scores on a scale of 0 to 1, that is, (a) highly sustainable (0.8–1.00); (b) moderately sustainable (0.6–0.79); (c) less sustainable (0.40–0.59); and (d) unsustainable (<0.40) as discussed in Choudhury et al. (2006).

The human capital signifies the active labour stock (both male and female) available for wage work with qualitative dimensions denoted by literacy, better health, etc. Natural capital refers to the tribal smallholders' access to land, particularly for growing rubber and other subsistence/food crops, as also access to land for undertaking jhum cultivation. Natural capital also relates to access to water, particularly drinking water, and availability of fish ponds for growing fishery as a source of supplementing the household income. Physical capital is represented in terms of access to infrastructure facilities, like roads, rubber and other agriculture markets, rubber processing facilities, access to post-harvest technology in the case of crops other than rubber, etc. Financial capital relates to income from rubber cultivation, off-farm activities like fishery, livestock, poultry, wage work, salary, sales of minor forest produce, etc. Social capital is made up of the smallholders' access to institutional support provided by the governmental agencies for growing rubber, the technology, research and development (R&D) facilities, training in tapping, skill formation in crop processing, extension services, help from self-help groups (SHGs), rubber grower co-operatives, social relations, networking, gender equality, access to information, collective processes, etc.

Figure 11.1: Linkages between Livelihood Assets of Rubber Smallholders

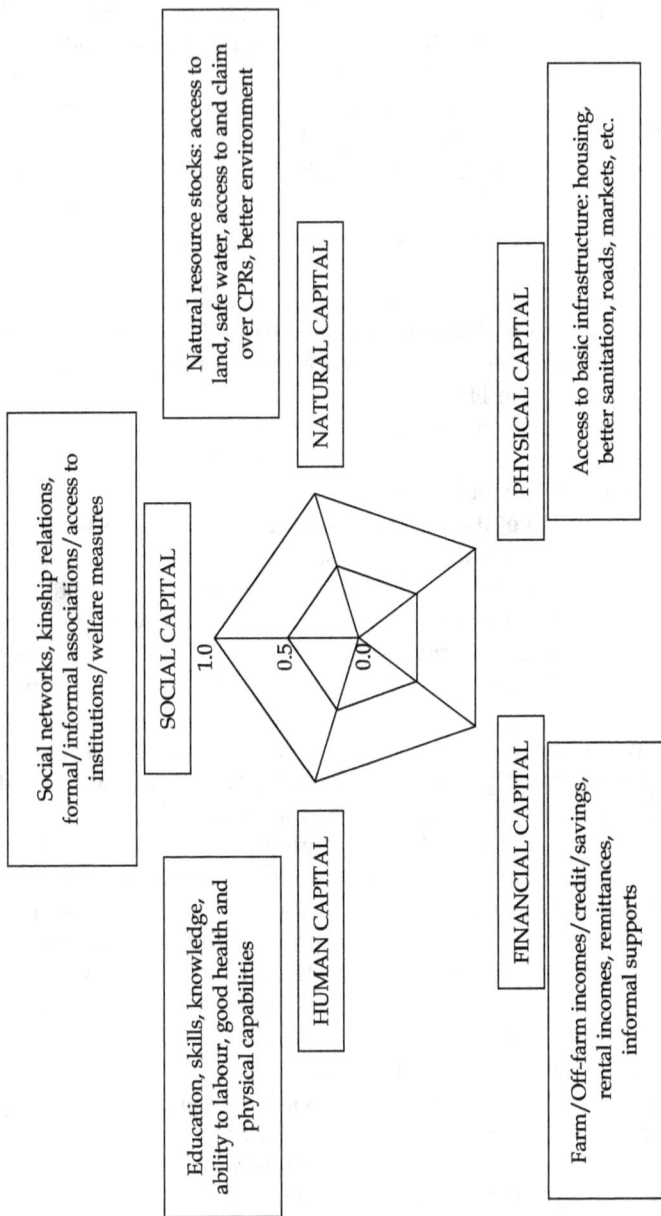

Social networks, kinship relations, formal/informal associations/access to institutions/welfare measures

SOCIAL CAPITAL

Natural resource stocks: access to land, safe water, access to and claim over CPRs, better environment

NATURAL CAPITAL

Education, skills, knowledge, ability to labour, good health and physical capabilities

HUMAN CAPITAL

Access to basic infrastructure: housing, better sanitation, roads, markets, etc.

PHYSICAL CAPITAL

Farm/Off-farm incomes/credit/savings, rental incomes, remittances, informal supports

FINANCIAL CAPITAL

1.0   0.5   0.0

Source: Modified from Shivakoti, G. P. and S. G. Shrestha. 2005a. 'Analysis of Livelihood Asset Pentagon to Assess Performance of Irrigation Systems, Part 1 – Analytical Framework', *Water International*, 30(3): 356–62.

Rubber Development and the Institutional Processes

In India, though rubber was first introduced by the colonial powers in the southern states of Kerala, Tamil Nadu and Karnataka as early as 1902, the expansion of rubber towards the northeastern region (NER) was initiated only in the late 1980s by the central government mediated through the institutional interventions of the Rubber Board. Two important considerations justify the expansion of rubber cultivation in the NER. First, the industrial demand for natural rubber is ever growing even as the traditional rubber-growing regions have already reached the limits of expansion. Second, the promotion of rubber cultivation in the NER is seen as an effective measure to wean the tribal communities away from shifting cultivation (Krishnakumar and Meenattoor 1999; Mohanan et al. 2003).

The exploratory surveys by the Rubber Board in the early 1960s identified a vast potential of about 450,000 ha in the NER for rubber cultivation (Krishnakumar et al. 1990). At the national level, the NER accounts for the second largest area under rubber (51,500 ha) with a relative share of 9 per cent and 3 per cent of the rubber production during 2003–04. Tripura accounts for the highest share in area (56 per cent), followed by Assam (26 per cent), Meghalaya (9 per cent), and then the remaining (9 per cent) four states, Nagaland, Manipur, Mizoram, and Arunachal Pradesh. Since the three states of Tripura, Assam and Meghalaya account for 91 per cent of the total rubber planted area and 96 per cent of the rubber production in the NE region, the present study was confined to these states. Altogether there are about 25,000 rubber smallholders spread over the three states, with Tripura accounting for 61 per cent, Assam 24 per cent and Meghalaya 15 per cent. The average rubber holding size as per the historical trends in rubber planted area shows a relatively higher size of farm holdings in Tripura (1.18 ha), followed by Assam (0.85 ha) and Meghalaya (0.56 ha).

PROFILE OF THE RUBBER SMALLHOLDERS

The study covered cross-sectional data from 309 rubber smallholders (predominantly tribal) from the states of Tripura (127), Assam (94) and Meghalaya (88). Of these, tribals comprised

54 per cent in Tripura, 62 per cent in Assam and 74 per cent in Meghalaya. The majority of the tribal growers in Assam were Rabha and Boro; in Meghalaya the growers were Marak, Sangma and Momin (Table 11.1).

Table 11.1: Profile of Rubber Smallholders in Northeastern India

Farm household characteristics	Tripura (n = 127)	Assam (n = 94)	Meghalaya (n = 88)
1. Male headed households (%)	93.00	91.00	92.00
2. Average age of the smallholder (years)	46.08	40.37	41.15
3. Experience in rubber farming (years)	12.95	10.68	10.20
4. Average family size (no.)	5.92	6.28	6.09
5. Male family members (%)	53.00	47.00	54.00
6. Children studying (%)	25.00	36.00	34.00
7. Economically active population (%)	63.00	57.00	59.00
8. Farmers growing rice (no.)	71.00	77.00	77.00
9. Farmers practising jhum cultivation (no.)	23.00	28.00	44.00
10. Farmers growing other crops (no.)	82.00	89.00	86.00
11. Average holding size (ha)	2.67	2.29	2.35
12. Average rubber area (ha)	1.81	1.52	1.49
13. Average rice area (ha)	0.34	0.46	0.37
14. Households growing fishery (%)	48.00	46.00	57.00
15. Households growing piggery (%)	26.00	54.00	64.00
16. Households growing poultry (%)	59.00	69.00	66.00
17. Households growing livestock (%)	65.00	64.00	70.00

Source: Viswanathan, P. K. 2006. *A Comparative Study of Smallholder Rubber and Rubber Integrated Farm Livelihood Systems in India and Thailand*, Report of the postdoctoral research study submitted to the Asian Institute of Technology, Bangkok, January 2006, p. 33.

An overwhelming majority of the households are headed by men aged 40 to 46 years. Given that rubber development on a commercial scale has been introduced in the region since the late 1980s, the rubber farming experience hovers in the range of 10–13 years. The importance attached to educating children is almost similar between Assam and Meghalaya with more than 30 per cent of the children attending school compared to only 25 per cent in Tripura. The proportion of economically active population is reported at higher levels in Tripura (63 per cent) than in Meghalaya (59 per cent) and Assam (57 per cent). The average family size is the highest in Assam (6.28 members per family), followed by Meghalaya (6.09) and Tripura (5.92). The pursuit of farming-related activities other than rubber cultivation mainly includes rice cultivation either in the plains or hills, growing cash crops and vegetables, and jhuming with different degrees of intensity. While rice cultivation is the predominant activity across the three states (71–77 per cent), the practice of jhuming differed, with the highest intensity reported from Meghalaya (44 per cent), followed by Assam (28 per cent) and Tripura (23 per cent). The average size of holdings, including possession of rubber area, is over 2 ha in all the states and this signifies the strength of the smallholders in terms of access to and control over natural capital, which is the mainstay of their livelihoods. An overwhelming majority of the households hold more than one rubber plot, the proportion of which was the highest in Meghalaya (64 per cent), followed by Tripura (56 per cent) and Assam (45 per cent).

The extent of household diversification into activities other than rubber and other farming practices is an important indicator determining the sustainability of livelihoods of the smallholders. In this regard, all the three states have a diversified farm livelihood system. The multiple household activities include fishery, livestock, piggery, and poultry. However, it is important to note that the tribal communities have been pursuing such diverse combinations of activities since historic times.

INSTITUTIONAL PROCESSES IN RUBBER DEVELOPMENT

The entire life cycle of a rubber plantation spans over about 30–32 years, comprising five–seven years of an unproductive period, followed by an economic life of 23–25 years. This long spell of the plantation life also involves huge initial investments for development as well as the management and upkeep of plantations. Since almost 90 per cent of the rubber plantations in India are owned and operated by smallholders with an average holding size of 0.5 ha, the Government of India has been highly proactive in supporting this segment by providing various institutional support measures through the Rubber Board. Accordingly, the expansion of rubber cultivation in NE states has also been underway through the institutional support provided by the Rubber Board comprising an array of R&D, extension and financial support, which includes: (a) newplanting and replanting grant of ₹20,000 per ha for holdings up to 5 ha and ₹16,000 per ha above 5 ha up to 20 ha; (b) integrated village-level rubber development; (c) supply of farm inputs: fertilisers, high-yielding planting materials, rubber rollers for processing rubber, smoke house, etc.; (*d*) demonstration of agro-management practices; (*e*) human resources development through educational campaigns, farmers' training in tapping and processing, formation of rubber growers' societies, women's SHGs etc.; and (*f*) quality upgradation activities including scientific post-harvest processing of latex into marketable forms of rubber (Rubber Board 2005). The rubber development programmes in the NE states are designed under three major schemes: (*a*) block planting scheme (BPS); (*b*) group planting scheme (GPS); and (*c*) individual planting scheme (IPS). It is envisaged that the tribal communities taking up rubber cultivation are initially wage workers in the holdings and earn their livelihood till the plantations start yielding (say five–eight years). Once the plantations mature, the farms are transferred to the tribal farmers for permanent cultivation and reaping the benefits thereon.

The institutional support also covers R&D, extension and marketing facilities. The rubber marketing system is institutionalised through the licensing system regulated by the Rubber Board. There are about 119 licensed rubber dealers in Tripura, followed by 24 dealers in Assam and 15 dealers in Meghalaya (Rubber Board 2004). There are also numerous unlicensed private rubber dealers at the village level who act as middlemen between the rubber growers and the dealers/traders at the sub-district or district levels. Being the sole promotional agency for the expansion of rubber cultivation, the Rubber Board itself is also very active in the market through numerous rubber producers'/growers' societies (RPS/RGS) and rubber-marketing societies at the village level. Under such institutional arrangements, rubber smallholders sell their produce (mostly in sheet form) to any of the above three buyers depending on their proximity and the price. Field officers stationed at various locations provide rubber growers extension services and advice on farm management practices. Supply of inputs such as planting materials, fertilisers, etc. is also carried out through such field offices.

The institutional arrangements facilitating access to land for growing rubber are still in the formative stages with the absence of a formal mechanism. Although the land-based property rights systems in NER vary across tribes and regions, these are primarily characterised by communal property rights over village commons, especially in Meghalaya and Assam. The village commons remain under the ownership of the *nokma* (*gaon bura*), the village head, who distributes the land for rubber cultivation to individuals based on the number of working hands in each tribal household (Viswanathan and Shivakoti 2006).

Rubber Monoculture *vs* Rubber-integrated Farming Systems

A comparative assessment of the rubber monoculture vs rubber-integrated farm livelihood systems in the study regions was done to evolve perspectives on the socio-economic viability and sustainability of the existing rubber farming system along with the co-existing farm livelihood practices. The analysis, based on the data on crop output, costs and returns from rubber farming and other farm livelihood systems, household expenditure, asset base, etc. also provides an overview of the synergies and contrasts of the socio-economic and environmental conditions prevalent in the study areas.

RUBBER FARMING ENVIRONMENT IN THE STUDY AREAS

The existing land-use pattern indicates that rubber occupies the dominant position in terms of area in Tripura (67 per cent), Assam (66 per cent) and Meghalaya (63 per cent). Rice occupies the second position as a single crop with a relative share of 20 per cent in Assam, 16 per cent in Meghalaya and 13 per cent in Tripura. The involvement of family labour is an important aspect of rubber-farming systems. The labour-use pattern reveals the higher extent of family labour use for rubber and other farming operations in all three areas with the highest ratio reported in Meghalaya (76 per cent), followed by Assam (74 per cent) and Tripura (67 per cent). By and large, family labour engages in routine agro-management practices, like annual weeding, fertiliser/manure application and rubber tapping. The use of hired labour for tapping is highest in Tripura (26 per cent), followed by Assam (23 per cent) and Meghalaya (18 per cent). The tapping wages, paid on a monthly basis, range between ₹1,200 and ₹1,800. Women family members engage in rubber farming including tapping, with the percentage ranging from 38 per cent in Meghalaya to 29 per cent in Assam and 25 per cent in Tripura. Women's roles are mostly confined to rubber tapping, collecting and carrying the rubber latex and assisting the men tappers to complete tapping tasks.

The topography of rubber holdings differs in the study regions, with most of the holdings located on a hill–plain interface (30–36 per cent), followed by holdings in undulating terrains (16–32 per cent) and gentle slopes (15–22 per cent). The study areas also differ in terms of access and rights to land. While the majority of the rubber smallholders have secure land titles in Tripura, in Assam and Meghalaya land is allotted by the nokma for undertaking rubber cultivation. The proportion of rubber holdings operated on such an insecure property rights regime is as high as 68 per cent in Meghalaya and 60 per cent in Assam.

The three areas show a similar pattern with respect to the adoption of high-yielding rubber clones, as the majority of the holdings are planted with a mix of these clones (varieties) of RRIM 600, GT1 and PB 235. Particularly in Tripura, around 90 per cent of the holdings are RRIM 600 and GT1 mixed plantings. Application of farm inputs is an important factor for augmenting yield as high-yielding rubber clones are extremely sensitive to chemical fertilisers. However, considerable differences were observed with respect to the application of inorganic fertilisers as the majority of the smallholders in the NE states have not adopted modern farm management practices as applicable to rubber including the use of fertiliser. The percentage of smallholders applying inorganic fertilisers is 35 per cent in Meghalaya compared to 44 per cent in Assam and 52 per cent in Tripura.

PARAMETERS OF PERFORMANCE

Given the synergies and contrasts in resource-use and management practices in rubber farming systems in the three study areas, the performance of monoculture rubber farming systems vs the rubber integrated farm livelihood systems was analysed. Table 11.2 provides a summary of the important parameters of performance of monoculture rubber farming system in the study areas. It shows that the proportion of smallholdings under tapping is the highest at 84 per cent in Tripura, followed by Assam (77 per cent) and Meghalaya (73 per cent).

The average stand of rubber trees available for tapping is 394 trees per ha in Meghalaya, compared to Assam (388 trees per ha) and Tripura (367 trees per ha). The number of tapping days (harvesting of latex from rubber tree) reported for the previous year

Table 11.2: Comparative Economic Assessment of Rubber Monoculture

Descriptives	Tripura	Assam	Meghalaya
1. Rubber tapped area (ha)	177.10	119.36	95.72
2. Tapped area (% of total rubber area)	77.00	84.00	73.00
3. Rubber trees tapped per ha	367.00	388.00	394.00
4. No. of tapping days per plot	145.00	147.00	138.00
5. Fertiliser use per ha (kg)	178.00	146.00	135.00
Cost components (₹)[a]			
1. Cost of fertiliser per ha	926 (8)	672 (4)	685 (6)
2. Organic manure cost per ha	795 (7)	1020 (6)	854 (8)
3. Cost of plant protection per ha	463 (4)	712 (4)	286 (3)
4. Tapping cost per ha	6,305 (57)	10,794 (67)	6,912 (63)
5. Other labour costs per ha	1,405 (13)	1,548 (10)	1,027 (9)
6. Material costs per ha	1,131 (10)	1,336 (8)	1,248 (11)
Total costs per ha	11,025	16,082	11,012
Output, prices and profit (₹)			
1. Dry rubber (per ha)[b]	1,238.00	1,153.00	1,043.00
2. Average rubber price (per kg)	52.76	52.48	54.20
3. Value of output per ha	65,317.00	60,509.00	56,531.00
Net profit per ha	54,292.00	44,427.00	45,519.00
Net profit per ha (US$)	1,206.00	987.00	1012.00

Source: Viswanathan, P. K. 2006. *A Comparative Study of Smallholder Rubber and Rubber Integrated Farm Livelihood Systems in India and Thailand,* Report of the postdoctoral research study submitted to the Asian Institute of Technology, Bangkok, January 2006, p. 19.

Note: 1 US$ = ₹45; [a] Labour costs also include imputed value of family labour; [b] Represents the weighted average yield; Figures in parentheses are respective shares in total cost of production.

was almost similar for Tripura and Assam (145–47 days) compared to Meghalaya (138 days). These parameters, that is, proportion of tapped area, number of trees per ha available for tapping and the average number of tapping days, are the three important factors that determine rubber yield in a well-managed rubber plantation.

The average quantity of fertiliser applied was the highest in Tripura (178 kg/ha) and the lowest in Meghalaya (135 kg/ha). In fact, the reported levels of fertiliser application (on a per tree basis) ranging from 340 grams in Meghalaya to 380 grams in Assam and 490 grams in Tripura is far lower than the recommended dosage of 500 grams per plant for the entire NE region (Rubber Board 2004: 20). However, an overwhelming majority of the smallholders apply organic manures, mainly dung generated from their own livestock, which are integral to livelihood systems in the region. An earlier study by Joseph and Rajasekharan (1991) also reported the limited application of chemical fertilisers by the rubber smallholders in Tripura.

Based on the reported yield levels, rubber productivity is highest in Tripura (1,238 kg/ha), followed by Assam (1,153 kg/ha) and Meghalaya (1,043 kg/ha). The rubber prices varied with the highest price realised by rubber growers in Meghalaya (₹54.2/kg), followed by Tripura (₹52.76/kg) and Assam (₹52.48/kg). Evidently, the reported net profit was the highest at ₹54,292 per ha in Tripura, followed by Meghalaya (₹45,519 per ha) and Assam (₹44,427 per ha).

MONOCULTURE RUBBER FARMING SYSTEM: A CASH FLOW ANALYSIS

While static analysis for a given year/period is more appropriate for seasonal and annual crops, perennial crops like rubber require inter-temporal analysis (Rae 1977). Hence, to account for the value of time and include the concept of time preference, a cash flow analysis of the monoculture rubber farming system is attempted here based on the discounted cash flow approach (DCFA) as suggested in Predo (2003) and Brian et al. (2004). Since collection of time series data pertaining to single farm holdings is difficult, the analysis used the life cycle data generated based on the cross-sectional information from rubber holdings of different ages to approximate the entire plantation life cycle. All cost items were considered including the initial plantation development costs as well as the routine agro-management costs, like the costs for weeding, inorganic fertiliser application, tapping, etc. for each region.

The analysis considers two discount rates: 7.5 per cent and 12 per cent, which justify the market rate of interest in the former case and standard commercial rate in the latter case, as also observed in the analysis of agroforestry projects (for instance, Nadkarni 2001) in India. The internal rate of return (IRR) is used here to evaluate the overall feasibility of monoculture rubber-farming systems across the study regions. This is the discount rate that would be required to make the net present value of the costs of farming operations equal to the present value of benefits accrued from rubber farming. The results of the cash flow analysis are summarised in Table 11.3 which reveals that the survival period of the rubber holdings differed from 26 years in Tripura to 18 years in Meghalaya, which is inclusive of the unproductive period of seven–nine years.

Table 11.3: Cash Flow Analysis of Monoculture Rubber Farming System

Descriptives	Tripura	Assam	Meghalaya
1. Average life of the holding (years)	26.00	19.00	18.00
2. Cumulative costs (undiscounted) per ha (US$)	4,801.00	5,156.00	4,325.00
3. Cumulative benefits (undiscounted) per ha (US$)	25,019.00	10,167.00	8,027.00
4. NPV (undiscounted) per ha (US$)	20,219.00	5,011.00	3,703.00
5. Benefit cost ratio (BCR)	4.17	1.59	1.25
6. Discounted costs (US$/ha–@ DF-7.5%)	2,304.00	2,848.00	2,308.00
7. Discounted benefits (US$/ ha–@ DF-7.5%)	11,162.00	5,233.00	4,081.00
8. NPV (US$/ha–@ 7.5%)	8,858.00	2,385.00	1,773.00
9. IRR at 7.5% DF	9.63	24.90	22.54
10. Discounted costs (US$/ha–@ DF 12%)	1,786.00	2,231.00	1,828.00
11. Discounted benefits (US$/ ha–@ DF–12%)	8,449.00	3,982.00	3,162.00
12. NPV (US$/ha–@ 12%)	6,663.00	1,751.00	1,334.00
13. IRR at 12% DF	37.42	22.48	20.44

Source: Viswanathan, P. K. 2006. *A Comparative Study of Smallholder Rubber and Rubber Integrated Farm Livelihood Systems in India and Thailand,* Report of the postdoctoral research study submitted to the Asian Institute of Technology, Bangkok, January 2006, p. 21.

As a major share of the tapped rubber holdings in Assam and Meghalaya falls in the initial productive period, the important measures of economic performance, that is, benefit cost ratio (BCR), net present value (NPV) and internal rate of return are reportedly low for these regions compared to Tripura. The highest performance indicators have been reported for smallholdings in Tripura, followed by Assam and Meghalaya. Overall, the analysis indicates that rubber monoculture is a viable system by itself, provided the rubber prices remain remunerative throughout the entire life cycle and the marketing practices remain efficient.

Rubber-integrated Farm Livelihood Systems: Comparative Perspectives

The analysis of the rubber monoculture farming system shows that rubber as a single crop is a resilient system provided the prices are remunerative and marketing practices remain transparent and effective. However, the above scenario is not a realistic one in view of the uncertainties that persist especially in the case of commercial crops like rubber, which is highly vulnerable to price fluctuations in the free trade regime. Moreover, by tradition, the smallholder communities have a diversified and integrated farm livelihood system. Rubber is new to the system, imposed into the NE ecosystems by the Rubber Board (an external agent). Given this, it is important to examine how both the systems could co-exist and help the smallholders to make a sustainable and resilient livelihood system in the long run. Table 11.4 gives a summary of the relative profitability of the rubber-integrated farm livelihood systems in the study regions.

While rubber and livestock combinations fetch the maximum household income in Tripura and Assam, in Meghalaya, rubber and fishery provide the highest income. However, it is important to note that income from rubber cultivation occupies the dominant share in most of the combinations in view of the relative profitability and stability in cash flow of rubber *vis-à-vis* other crops and livelihood options.

Table 11.4: Rubber Monoculture *vs* Rubber-integrated Farm Livelihood Systems

	Tripura		*Assam*		*Meghalaya*	
Type of farming system	*Income (₹)*	*Rank*	*Income (₹)*	*Rank*	*Income (₹)*	*Rank*
1. Rubber monoculture	54,292	7	44,427	7	45,519	7
2. Rubber + fruit + agriculture	57,057	5	47,672	5	49,837	4
3. Rubber and poultry	55,715	6	45,807	6	46,764	6
4. Rubber and livestock	60,325	1	50,288	1	51,316	2
5. Rubber and rice	58,080	4	49,412	3	49,595	5
6. Rubber and fishery	58,466	3	47,733	4	51,502	1
7. Rubber and piggery	59,398	2	50,193	2	51,030	3

Source: Viswanathan, P. K. 2006. *A Comparative Study of Smallholder Rubber and Rubber Integrated Farm Livelihood Systems in India and Thailand*, Report of the postdoctoral research study submitted to the Asian Institute of Technology, Bangkok, January 2006, p. 22.

The combined farming systems amply provide for resilience and ensure the subsistence needs of the smallholder households. More importantly, the impact of integrated systems on livelihoods needs to be assessed in terms of the extent to which these help the smallholders to avoid purchasing these items from the market. Tribal households report that one of the most explicit positive impacts of such integrated commercial crop-livelihood systems integration is that the income from the sale of rubber helped stop the 'distress sale of paddy', which they could not avoid when producing only traditional crops. As a result, the rice saved from distress sales is now kept as a buffer for their own future consumption. Similarly, since a regular income is assured through rubber cultivation, the livestock-related activities such as piggery, poultry and fishery are now pursued both for their own needs and for sale.

RUBBER FARMING SYSTEMS AND SUSTAINABLE LIVELIHOOD OUTCOMES

It is apparent that various farm livelihood options which combine traditional farming with rubber cultivation can form an integral aspect of sustainable farm livelihoods in the mountainous regions. The process of rubber development in the NER needs further scaling up, more in favour of an integrated farm livelihood system that does not obstruct or compromise on the agroecological diversity as well as the (pre-rubber) existing land-use systems of the region.

In this regard, it is all the more important to determine the sustainability of the livelihood outcomes of the rubber-integrated smallholder systems. In order to do this, the various components of the five types of the capital and livelihoods assets of the rubber smallholders were measured based on procedures discussed in Shivakoti and Shrestha (2005a and b), VanLoon et al. (2005), and Choudhury et al. (2006). The various components used for measuring the index of human capital assets included: (a) experience in rubber farming; (b) educational status of the household head; (c) availability of family labour; (d) women's participation in rubber farming activities; (e) children's education; and (f) annual household expenditure on healthcare. For determining natural capital assets, the indices considered are: (a) rubber area owned by smallholder; (b) quality of land; and (c) household access to safe drinking water. Physical capital assets have been measured using index of market access and the access to a rubber processing facility, which represents the overall availability of and access to infrastructure and technological facilities in the rubber-growing regions. Financial capital assets have been measured as indices of: (a) income of the household from sources other than rubber, like wages, salaries, farm and off-farm income, etc.; (b) savings; and (c) value of household assets (both essential and semi-luxury items). Social capital assets of the households have been measured using indices such as: (a) access to R&D and institutional support (planting grant for new planting or replanting, subsidy for inputs, plant protection, etc.); (b) access to training in rubber tapping and processing; (c) access to extension activities; and (d) access to local development institutions, co-operatives/SHGs, etc.

The indices so derived range from 0 to 1 with highest values indicating the greater strength of the livelihood assets possessed by the smallholder households. To relate the values of assets with respect to sustainable livelihood outcomes, three scores have been used representing indices on a 0–1 scale. Thus the assets index values falling between 0 to 0.33 have been considered as unsustainable; 0.34 to 0.66 as moderately sustainable; and 0.67 to 1 as highly sustainable. The values of the indices representing the five livelihood capital assets of the rubber smallholders across the study regions are shown in Table 11.5.

Table 11.5: Values of the Livelihood Capital Assets of the Rubber Smallholders

Capital assets	Tripura	Assam	Meghalaya
1. Human capital	0.38 (2)	0.27 (3)	0.35 (2)
2. Natural capital	0.73 (1)	0.78 (1)	0.83 (1)
3. Physical capital	0.57 (2)	0.46 (2)	0.48 (2)
4. Financial capital	0.33 (3)	0.28 (3)	0.26 (3)
5. Social capital	0.56 (2)	0.54 (3)	0.63 (2)
Overall livelihood score	0.514	0.466	0.510

Source: Viswanathan, P. K. 2006. *A Comparative Study of Smallholder Rubber and Rubber Integrated Farm Livelihood Systems in India and Thailand*, Report of the postdoctoral research study submitted to the Asian Institute of Technology, Bangkok, January 2006, p. 60.

Note: Figures in parentheses indicate the hypothetical scores of sustainability of the assets.

Ranking 1 = (0.67–1): highly sustainable; 2 = (0.34–0.66) moderately sustainable; 3 = (0–0.33) unsustainable.

Access to and control over natural capital assets enable the livelihoods of the rubber smallholder households to be highly sustainable when compared to the rest of the capital assets. The financial capital assets base of the households appears to be rather weak and unsustainable for all the areas, which suggests that the income realised from rubber farming and other integrated activities is inadequate or not effectively utilised for building up or strengthening the economic or financial asset base of the smallholders. Human capital asset values are moderately sustainable for Tripura and Meghalaya. Physical capital assets also appear to be moderately sustainable for the three areas. Social capital assets are at moderately sustainable levels with the highest score reported for Meghalaya (0.63), followed by Tripura (0.56) and Assam (0.54).

The relatively higher values of social capital as reported from Meghalaya may be attributed to the social development outcomes in the state following the introduction of rubber cultivation. The study site, Mendipathar village in Meghalaya, has witnessed the emergence of local initiatives leading to the development of a rubber growers' co-operative, the Mendipathar Multi-purpose Co-operative Society (MMCS). Notably, the MMCS plays a significant role in terms of mobilising the local people in matters of scaling up of rubber-integrated farm livelihood systems with greater impacts on the local communities leading to better collective action outcomes compared to other rubber-growing areas within the NER (Viswanathan 2006). The values of the capital assets as shown in Table 11.5 are plotted in a radar diagram, representing the livelihood assets pentagon (Figure 11.2).

It is important to note, however, that though the rubber smallholders are relatively better off in terms of access to natural capital assets like possession of rubber area and quality lands, the sustainability of this is subject to constraints. Particularly, as discussed earlier, the access to rubber area is constrained by agro-climatic suitability factors as well as the prevailing property rights regime in the NER which does not ensure secure property rights to the tribal rubber growers. Given this, an increase in population coupled with increasing demand for land for expanding the rubber area, stimulated by its profitability, may adversely affect the sustainability of the natural capital assets base.

Figure: 11.2: Livelihood Asset Pentagon of Rubber Smallholders

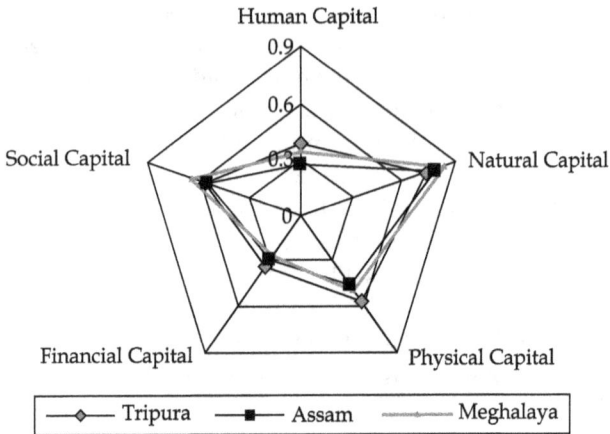

Human Capital

Social Capital

Natural Capital

Financial Capital

Physical Capital

| ◆ Tripura | ■ Assam | Meghalaya |

Source: Based on field data gathered by the author.

Conclusions and Policy Implications

This essay has explored the significance of evolving cash crop integrated farming systems, for the mountainous regions in particular, as a sustainable livelihood strategy to counter the crisis in livelihoods in the era of globalisation. At the same time, the judicious choice of a cash crop would enable the communities to integrate with the global economic process with definite impacts on their socio-economic well-being and sustainable livelihoods. Though the analysis of rubber-integrated farm livelihood systems indicates the value of income from rubber cultivation in the gross household income, the socio-economic significance of rubber-integrated farm livelihood systems is such that various combinations of rubber integration amply provide for resilience and ensure subsistence of the smallholder households. Their impact on livelihoods is mostly in terms of avoiding the market dependence of the households for the purchase of essential food items including pulses and vegetables.

Viewed from this perspective, there is a strong case for further promotion and scaling up of rubber-integrated farm livelihood systems in India and other smallholder-dominated rubber-growing countries. Rubber is a crucial industrial raw material for the development of the automotive industry, and in view of its future potential, there has been tremendous economic activism towards further expansion of rubber even in the marginal and sub-marginal climatic zones of India and the countries of South East Asia, Thailand, Indonesia, China, Vietnam, Laos PDR, Myanmar, Cambodia, and the Philippines. However, the plantation mode of the rubber production process being followed in these countries needs a thorough restructuring as an integrated system favouring the smallholder producers. This is because the prevailing rubber production structure in most of these countries is characterised by the predominance of small and marginal holdings with a vast base of population still pursuing diversified farm livelihood systems, including shifting cultivation. Despite this empirical reality, most of these countries (barring India, Malaysia and Thailand) are distinctly lacking in terms of institutional interventions, financial support mechanisms, R&D and extension activities to facilitate scaling up rubber farming as an integrated farm livelihood system. The rubber development experience in NE India shows that the sustainability of the rubber smallholders largely depends on their access to secure property rights, and efficient and transparent rubber marketing systems. This necessarily calls for policy and institutional interventions covering a broad array of activities, that is, (*a*) secure property rights regime; (*b*) financial support for rubber planting and development of integrated systems; (*c*) R&D support for quality rubber planting materials, plant protection, yield enhancement, crop processing, and product development; (*d*) efficient marketing and price control; (*e*) value addition with due share of the smallholders in the value chain; (*f*) development of ancillary and by-product segments, etc. These activities also simultaneously call for crafting and/or strengthening of the institutional linkages so as to empower and build capacity among the local communities and thereby achieve better outcomes of mobilisation and collective action and the sustenance of livelihoods of the rubber smallholders.

Note

* This essay draws upon a report (Viswanathan 2006) which was based on the postdoctoral research undertaken by the author at the Asian Institute of Technology (AIT), Thailand during January–December 2005. The author thanks the AIT for offering the fellowship and research grant for undertaking the study and Prof. Ganesh P. Shivakoti

for his intellectual support. Thanks are also due to Dr K. Tharian George (Joint Director, Economics) and Dr N. M. Mathew (former Director, Research) of the Rubber Research Institute of India (RRII) for their encouragement and support in various capacities. The help rendered by Dr S. K. Dey (Deputy Director, Regional Research Station, Rubber Board, Agartala), Dr D. Chaudhuri (Regional Research Station, Rubber Board, Guwahati) and Dr A. P. Thapliyal (Regional Research Station, Rubber Board, Tura, Meghalaya) is also gratefully acknowledged. Discussions with Prof. Amalendu Guha were highly useful in the formative stages of the study. The usual disclaimers apply.

References

Abiziad, C. and O. T. Koomes. 2004. 'Land Use and Forest Fallowing Dynamics in Seasonally Dry Tropical Forests of the Southern Yucatan Peninsula, Mexico', *Land Use Policy*, 21(1): 71–84.

Angelsen, Arild. 1995. 'Shifting Cultivation and Deforestation: A Study from Indonesia', *World Development*, 23(10): 1713–729.

Arshad, Najib Lotfy. 2000. 'Excellent Example of Agroforestry . . . Growing Pineapples and Banana in a Rubber Plantation', *New Straits Time*, 25 July 2000.

Ashley, C. and D. Carney. 1999. *Sustainable Livelihoods: Lessons from Early Experience*. London: Department for International Development (DFID).

Barlow, Colin and Muharminto. 1982. 'The Rubber Smallholder Economy', *Bulletin of Indonesian Economic Studies*, 27(3): 29–54.

Baxter, P. T. W. 1994. 'Pastoralists are People: Why Development for Pastoralists, Not the Development of Pastoralism?', *Rural Extension Bulletin*, University of Sussex, 4, pp. 3–8.

Bebbington, Anthony. 1999. 'Capitals and Capabilities: A Framework for Analyzing Peasant Viability, Rural Livelihoods and Poverty', *World Development*, 27(12): 2021–44.

Brian B., N. Rujehan Imang and S. Achdawan. 2004. 'Rattan, Rubber or Oil Palm: Cultural and Financial Considerations for Farmers in Kalimantan', *Economic Botany*, 58 (Suppl.): S77–87.

Carney, D. (ed.). 1998. *Sustainable Rural Livelihoods: What Contribution Can We Make?* London: Department for International Development (DFID).

———. 1999. *Holistic Approaches to Poverty Reduction: Where Does Agricultural Research Fit In?* London: Department for International Development (DFID) (unpublished).

Chambers, R. and G. Conway. 1992. 'Sustainable Rural Livelihoods: Practical Concepts for the 21st Century', *IDS Discussion Paper 296*, Brighton, IDS.

Chin, S. C. 1982. '"The Significance of Rubber as a Cash Crop in Kenyah Village in Sarawak', *Federation Museum Journal*, 27: 23-28.

Choudhury, Md Arif, Ganesh P. Shivakoti and Md Salequzzaman. 2006. 'A Conceptual Framework for the Sustainability Assessment Procedures of the Shrimp Aquaculture Industry in Coastal Bangladesh', *International Journal of Resources, Governance and Ecology*, 5(2 & 3): 162-84.

Cramb, R. A. 1988. 'The Commercialisation of Iban Agriculture', in R. A. Cramb and R. H. W. Reece (eds), *Development in Sarawak: Historical and Contemporary Perspectives*, Monash Paper on Southeast Asia No. 17, Centre of Southeast Asian Studies, Monash University, pp. 105-34.

Dendi, A., G. P. Shivakoti, R. Dale, and Ranamukhaarachi. 2005. 'Evolution of the Minangkabau's Shifting Cultivation in the West Sumatra Highland of Indonesia and Strategic Implications toward Dynamic Farming Systems', *Land Degradation and Development*, 16(1): 13-26.

Dove, Michael R. 1993. 'Smallholder Rubber and Swidden Agriculture in Borneo: A Sustainable Adaptation to the Ecology and Economy of the Tropical Forest', *Economic Botany*, 47(2): 136-47.

Dyer, Caroline. 2001. 'Nomads and Education for All: Education for Development or Domestication?', *Comparative Education*, 37(3): 315-27.

Ellis, F. 1998. 'Household Strategies and Rural Household Diversification', *Journal of Development Studies*, 35(1): 1-38.

——. 2000. *Rural Livelihoods and Diversity in Developing Countries*. Oxford: Oxford University Press.

Fratkin, E. 1997. 'Pastoralism, Governance and Development Issues', *Annual Review of Anthropology*, 26: 235-61.

Gouyon A., H. de Foresta and P. Levang. 1993. 'Does Jungle Rubber Trees Deserve its Name? An Analysis of Rubber Agro-forestry', *Agroforestry Systems*, 22(3): 181-206.

Haan, Leo de and Annelies Zoomers. 2005. 'Exploring the Frontier of Livelihoods Research', *Development and Change*, 36(1): 27-47.

Hansen, Peter Kurt. 1995. 'Shifting Cultivation Adaptation and Environment in a Mountainous Watershed in Northern Thailand', Ph.D. Dissertation Submitted to the Institute of Agricultural Sciences, Royal Veterinary and Agricultural University, Copenhagen.

Hung, Le Duy. 1995. 'Some Issues of Fixed Cultivation and Sedentarisation of Ethnic Minority People in Mountainous Areas of Vietnam', in A. T. Rambo, R. Reed, Le Trong Cue and M. R. Di Gregorio (eds), *The Challenges of Highland Development in Vietnam*. Honolulu: East West Centre, pp. 63-67.

Joseph, Toms and P. Rajasekharan. 1991. 'Status Report on the Rubber Smallholdings of Tripura', *Rubber Board Bulletin*, 26(4): 16-24.

Joshi, Laxman, Gide Wibawa, G. Vincent, D. Boutin, R. Akiefnawati, G. Manurung, M. V. Noordwijk and S. Williams. 2002. *Jungle Rubber: A Traditional Agroforestry System under Pressure.* Indonesia: ICARF-World Agroforestry Centre.

King, V. T. 1988. 'Social Rank and Social Change Among the Milo', in M. R. Dove (ed.), *The Real and Imagined Role of Culture in Development.* Honolulu: University of Hawaii Press, pp. 219–53.

Krishnakumar, A. K. and Meenattoor. 1999. 'Cultivation in Non-traditional Areas', in P. J. George and C. Kuruvilla Jacob (eds), *Natural Rubber: Agromanagement and Crop Processing.* Kottayam: Rubber Research Institute of India, pp. 487–500.

Krishnakumar, A. K., T. Eappen, D. V. K. N. Rao, S. N. Potty and M. R. Sethuraj. 1990. 'Ecological Impact of Rubber (*Hevea brasiliensis*) Plantations in North East India: Influence on Soil Physical Properties with Special Reference to Moisture Retention', *Indian Journal of Natural Rubber Research*, 3(1): 53–63.

Kuniyasu, Momose. 2002. 'Ecological Factors of the Recently Expanding Style of Shifting Cultivation in Sotheast Asian Subtropical Areas: Why Could Fallow Periods Be Shortened?', *Southeast Asian Studies*, 40(2): 190–99.

Lee, Hua Seng. 2004. '"Introducing the Cultivation of Medicinal Plants and Wild Fruits in Forest Rehabilitation Operations on Former Shifting Cultivation Sites in Sarawak Malaysia: Issues and Challenges', *Southeast Asian Studies*, 42(1): 60–73.

Malik, Bela. 2003. 'The Problem of Shifting Cultivation in the Garo Hills of North East India, 1860–1970', *Conservation and Society*, 1(2): 87–115.

Melnyk, M. 1993. 'The Effects of Sedentarisation on Agriculture and Forest Resources in Southern Venezuela', Network Paper 16b, *Rural Development Forestry Network* (London), Overseas Development Institute.

Midmore, D. J. and H. G. P. Jansen. 2003. 'Supplying Vegetables to Asian Cities: Is There a Case for Peri-urban Production?', *Food Policy*, 28(1): 13–27.

Mohanan, K. G., A. K. Krishnakumar and E. Lalithakumari. 2003. 'An Overview of Rubber Plantation Development in North-East India', in C. Kuruvilla Jacob (ed.), *Global Competitiveness of Indian Rubber Plantation Industry, Rubber Planters Conference, India 2002*, Full Text of Papers, Kottayam: Rubber Research Institute of India, pp. 359–68.

Nadkarni, M. V. 2001. 'Economic Potential of Waste Lands', in Wastelands: A Symposium on 'Regenerating Our Degraded Land Resources', *Seminar #499*, March 2001.

Nath, K. Tapan, M. Inoue and Myant Hla. 2005. 'Small-scale Agroforestry for Upland Community Development: A Case Study from Chittagong Hill Tracts, Bangladesh', *Journal of Forest Research*, 10(6): 443–52.

Penot, E. and Gide Wibawa. 1997. 'Complex Rubber Agroforestry Systems in Indonesia: An Alternative to Low Productivity of Jungle Rubber Conserving Agroforestry Practices and Benefits', in *Proceedings of Symposium on Farming System Aspects of the Cultivation of Natural Rubber (Hevea Brasiliensis)*, Beruwala, Sri Lanka, 5–8 November 1996, International Rubber Research and Development Board (IRRDB), London, UK, pp. 56–80.

Perz, Stephen G. L. 2005. 'The Importance of Household Asset Diversity for Livelihood Diversity and Welfare among Small Farm Colonists in the Amazon', *The Journal of Development Studies*, 41(7): 1193–220.

Predo, Canesio D. 2003. 'What Motivates Farmers? Tree Growing and Land Use Decisions in the Grasslands of Claveria, Philippines', Economy and Environment Program for Southeast Asia (EEPSEA), Singapore, Research Report No. 2003-RR7, available at http://irnr.files. wordpress.com/2009/10/canesiorreport1.pdf (accessed 22 February 2012).

Rae, A. N. 1977. *Crop Management Economics*, London: Granada Publishing Ltd.

Rubber Board. 2004. *Indian Rubber Statistics*, Vol. 27. Kottayam, India: Rubber Board, Government of India..

——. 2005. *Rubber Growers Companion*. Kottayam, India: Rubber Board, Government of India.

Scoones, I. 1998. 'Sustainable Rural Livelihoods: A Framework for Analysis', *IDS Working Paper*, Brighton: Institute of Development Studies.

Shepherd, G. 1991. 'The Communal Management of Forests in the Semi-arid and Sub-humid Regions of Africa', *Development Policy Review*, 9(2): 151–76.

Shivakoti, G. P. and S. G. Shrestha. 2005a. 'Analysis of Livelihood Asset Pentagon to Assess Performance of Irrigation Systems, Part 1 – Analytical Framework', *Water International*, 30(3): 356–62.

——. 2005b. 'Analysis of Livelihood Asset Pentagon to Assess Performance of Irrigation Systems, Part 2 – Application of Analytical Framework', *Water International*, 30(3): 363–71.

Shrestha, S. G. and Ganesh P. Shivakoti. 2003. 'Prominent Livelihood Asset Pentagon within the Analytical Framework of Irrigation System Performance Assessment', *Asia Pacific Journal of Rural Development*, 13(1): 60–88.

Sikor, Thomas. 2004. 'The Commons in Transition: Agrarian and Environmental Change in Central and Eastern Europe', *Environmental Management*, 34(2): 270–80.

Singh, N. and J. Gilman. 1999. 'Making Livelihoods More Sustainable', *International Social Science Journal*, 51(4): 539–45.

Somboonsuke, Buncha, Ganesh P. Shivakoti and H. Demaine. 2001. 'Agricultural Sustainability Through the Empowerment of Rubber

Smallholders in Thailand' *Asia-Pacific Journal of Rural Development,* 11(1): 65–89.

Suyanto, S., T. P. Tomich and K. Otsuka. 2001. 'Land Tenure and Farm Management Efficiency: The Case of Smallholder Rubber Production in Customary Land Areas of Sumatra', *Agroforestry Systems,* 52(2): 145–60.

Tacoli, C. 1998. 'Rural-Urban linkages and Sustainable Rural Livelihood', Papers presented at the Department for International Development's Natural Resources Advisers' Conference, DFID, London.

VanLoon, G. W., S. G. Patil, L. B. Hugar. 2005. *Agricultural Sustainability: Strategies for Assessment.* New Delhi/Thousand Oaks/London: Sage.

Viswanathan, P. K. 2006. *A Comparative Study of Smallholder Rubber and Rubber Integrated Farm Livelihood Systems in India and Thailand,* Report of the postdoctoral research study submitted to the Asian Institute of Technology, Bangkok, January 2006.

Viswanathan, P. K. and Ganesh P. Shivakoti. 2006. 'Economic Integration of Tribal Societies in the Post-reforms Era: Perspectives on Rubber Based Farming Systems in North East India', *North East India Studies,* 1(2): 80–106.

Ward, M. W. and R. G. Ward. 1974. 'An Economic Survey of West Kalimantan', *Bulletin of Indonesian Economic Studies,* 10(3): 26–53.

Zahir, Syed Sadeque. 2000. 'Shifting Cultivation in Eastern Himalayas: Regulatory Regime and Erosion of Common Pool Resources', Paper presented at 'Constituting the Commons: Crafting Sustainable Commons in the New Millennium', the Eighth Conference of the International Association for the Study of Common Property, 31 May–4 June 2000, (Bloomington).

Zhen, L. and J. K. Routray. 2003. 'Operational Indicators for Measuring Agricultural Sustainability in Developing Countries', *Environmental Management,* 32(1): 34–46.

12

Organic Farming in the Northeastern Hill Regions

NILABJA GHOSH

The use of chemical fertilisers in agriculture enhances yields but also contaminates soil, water and air and results in residues in the produce, thus undermining the quality of food and the environment. Fertiliser use in the hills can also affect the plains. An analysis of the data on cultivation practices collected by the National Sample Survey Organisation (NSSO 1999a), shows that the northeastern hill states have retained traditional practices, and that they reflect an inclination towards organic agriculture, which can be harnessed for the development of the region with ecological benefits. This essay investigates whether organic farming is focused on any particular groups of crops, or sections of farmers, and whether organic farming is exclusively practised without other chemical inputs.[1] Identifying the factors that can be associated with farming using only manures, the essay reflects on whether the technology of organic farming in the hill states could be a suitable strategy for enhancing the well-being of the people of the hills and the plains.

The fertiliser-based technology of the Green Revolution and the much promoted growth-oriented strategy pursued in agriculture has so far proved to be inappropriate for several agricultural systems in the developing world. In many of these systems, based on the ground realities of the agro-ecology, farmers have opted to retain traditional practices, emphasising their objectives of stability, resilience and long-term sustainability rather than emulating other neighbouring systems that are geared to high productivity.

The centralised process which guides agricultural growth strategy in India is now giving way to a more sustainable road-map to development backed by indigenous knowledge and participation through regional planning (Alagh 1991). The key directions to such a plan may be provided by the regional strengths, weaknesses and the emerging market potentials. Such a strategy could draw upon the ways in which the concerned agro-ecosystems respond to the incentives and limitations imposed by the mainstream development process. Hill ecosystems are generally fragile systems that also have interactions with other regions; so far these systems have not been adequately addressed by agricultural policy and deserve more attention. A regionally differentiated approach can aid the national effort to bring down dependence on fossil fuel–based and environmentally damaging chemicals. Increasingly, this reduction will help the country to face the challenges of globalisation, liberalisation and global warming. With changes taking place in the domestic and international economies, India's agricultural strategy could learn from the 'failure' of the northeastern hill economies to respond to the Green Revolution and focus on an acceptable path of development for the region.

Analysing the household-level NSSO data, this essay seeks to understand how the practices in the northeastern hill states stand apart from other states in India, even after decades of a subsidy-backed policy, and what factors drive the decisions pertaining to these practices.[2] The unit of investigation is the crop enterprise, as each enterprise is itself a decision centre with relevance regardless of the area it covers. The essay is structured as follows: The next section provides the background to the study and profiles the socio-agro-economic features of the concerned states. The following sections then deal with the practices in the region by cross-tabulation and econometric analysis of data. The conclusions are in the final section.

The Northeastern Hills: A Socio-economic Profile

Seven states of the northeastern hill region in India are included in this study.[3] These are Arunachal Pradesh, Manipur, Meghalaya, Mizoram, Nagaland, Sikkim, and Tripura. Constituting more than 5 per cent of India's geographical expanse and a little more than 1 per cent of the population these are some of the most underdeveloped states in the country. Because of their remoteness and relative inaccessibility the socio-economic fabric has retained the traditional character to a large degree. Even compared to other hill regions including Jammu and Kashmir which has its own problems, and Himachal Pradesh which is greatly advanced on a conventional scale, the northeastern states stand out. Their proximity along the borders to foreign nations and within India to the eastern states, that themselves call for developmental attention, their great physical distances from the national capital and the centres of policy-making and the distinctive economic and strategic policies they are subjected to define their locus within the country.

In most hill ecosystems, the specific features that constitute their limitations and strengths have an important bearing on the adjoining plains (Chand 1997). Flood control, silting and fertiliser run-offs are attributes that tie the hills and plains together. These ecological implications tend to drastically limit the choices available to the hill systems in terms of technology and products and this abstinence may, therefore, be seen essentially as a form of service rendered or a cost borne by the hill people. On the one hand, the northeastern region has remarkable advantages of being endowed with fertile and organically rich soils, ample rainfall and water resources, river valleys, swamps and streams, and great climatic diversity supporting diverse cropping possibilities. On the other hand, the slopes and heavy rain make soil unstable and acidic, even as conditions favourable to rapid vegetative proliferation make agriculture and land management a tedious and highly labour-intensive process. A large part of the region is forested, contributing significantly to the national average of 22 per cent forest cover and its importance in effecting forest conservation to the country at large cannot be underestimated. The forest cover, combined with the constraint of labour scarcity leaves a meagre share of land resources for cultivation (Table 12.1).

Despite the remoteness, that the states deserve special attention has been acknowledged by the development programmes of the country and is borne out by the official recognition of the area as a special category. The formation of the North Eastern Council (NEC) in 1971, for the social and economic development of the region, the North Eastern Development Finance Corporation Ltd. (NEDFi) in 1995 and finally the creation of the separate Ministry of Development of North Eastern Region (DONER) in 2001, further

Table 12.1: Some Agro-economic Indicators of Northeastern States

States	Average farm size (ha)	Crop area irrigated (%)	Fertiliser intensity NPK (kg/ha)	Population density per sq km	Forest/repo. area (%)	NSA/geog. area (%)	Cropping pattern percentage of gross cropped area (%)				
							Rice	Maize	Pulse/oilseeds	Fruits	Vegetables
Arunachal Pradesh	3.7	14.4	2.9	13.0	93.9	2.2	48.0	13.6	12.4	7.2	9.6
Manipur	2.2	34.7	105.0	107.0	27.2	6.3	76.3	1.4	4.3	3.9	14.0
Meghalaya	1.8	20.8	17.2	103.0	41.8	9.2	41.8	6.8	4.8	8.8	27.9
Mizoram	1.4	9.0	13.7	42.0	75.8	5.2	60.2	7.1	10.6	9.7	10.6
Nagaland	6.8	25.5	2.2	120.0	55.3	15.1	55.8	11.5	17.3	3.5	6.5
Sikkim	2.1	12.6	9.5	76.0	36.2	13.4	11.3	28.2	12.0	4.2	25.3
Tripura	0.9	13.5	34.0	304.0	57.8	26.4	56.6	0.4	6.1	13.4	10.9
India	1.5	39.2	90.1	324.0	22.8	43.2	22.8	3.4	24.6	1.7	3.9

Source: FAI. 2003. *Fertilizer Statistics.* New Delhi: The Fertilizer Association of India. Available at http://www.faidelhi.org.; Government of India. 1996-97. *Land Use Statistics at a Glance.* New Delhi: Ministry of Agriculture, Directorate of Economics and Statistics; Government of India. 2002. *Agricultural Statistics at a Glance.* New Delhi: Ministry of Agriculture, Directorate of Economics and Statistics.

Note: Farm size is for 1900–91, land-use for 1997–98.

lend credence to the significance attached by the country to the development of the northeastern states. From the Sixth Five Year Plan (1980–85) onwards, extra resources have been consistently allocated for the development of the region, with special emphasis on agriculture and small rural industries. The Seventh Plan (1985–89) provided for Special Central Assistance and a large component as grants with a thrust on hill area development programmes. Scientific land-use, the conservation of forest resources, and high-value and less resource-demanding cash crops were emphasised. The Ninth (1997–2002) and Tenth Plans (2002–07) in general emphasised a regionally differentiated strategy based on agro-climatic conditions and natural resources for sustainable development. Despite the intentions, progress has been slow. Population pressure is not a problem in this region, the population density being far less in all states than the national average. A large part of the population in Mizoram, Nagaland and Meghalaya is tribal. Shifting cultivation or jhuming covers about 90 per cent of agricultural land (Saleh 1989; Borah 1999) in Mizoram and Nagaland. This traditional practice of 'slash and burn' agriculture, which evolved from primitive times through the pressure to generate food under difficult circumstances has been associated by many scientists with several deleterious effects on ecology and soil fertility as a result of which it has been discouraged greatly by the government. However, the lack of infrastructural development, and the failure of the government to meet the basic needs of the people by other means like public distribution and the failure of the Green Revolution in settled farming have been responsible for the continuation of the old methods in agriculture.

The literacy rate is reasonably high (Saleh 1989) in the region. Female labour participation is high in Meghalaya and Nagaland and in general women enjoy a relatively elevated position in society. Industrialisation has been very limited with handicrafts being a traditional strength. Industries based on forest products like paper and small enterprises catering to the service sector are common non-agricultural occupations, though agriculture remains the mainstay of the population. The tribal people depend on animal products to a large extent for nutrition and women have a major role in rearing and caring for animals. Poverty remains widespread despite the development plans and the income level is low by national standards.

Agricultural indicators show the differences and similarities of the hill states compared to the rest of India. Small farm size is not as much a problem as it is at the national level, as the average farm is of medium size in four of the states, Arunachal Pradesh, Nagaland, Manipur, and Sikkim and small in two, Meghalaya and Mizoram. It is only in Tripura that the average holding is below the national average of 1.56 ha. Figure 12.1 indicates that while the largest number of farm enterprises is in the smallest size class classified as Marginal, it is the third and medium size class that holds the major share of area. Land is not a serious constraining factor in agriculture because of the customary communal land holding system of most tribal groups, the lack of clear-cut ownership laws and relatively free access to land for cultivation. Given the extent of the geographical area relative to the population, the forested and sloping terrains and the system of land rights, the farm size itself could even incorporate an element of choice. Irrigation intensity is low as the mountain terrain makes it difficult to exploit the ample water potential and rain-fed agriculture is common. In most states the harvesting of rainwater rather than canals and wells supplies almost all the irrigation water.[4] The minimal use of chemical fertiliser reflects the low penetration of modern technology in the region as compared to the

Figure 12.1: Percentage Distribution of Number and Area of Crop Enterprises into Farm Size Classes

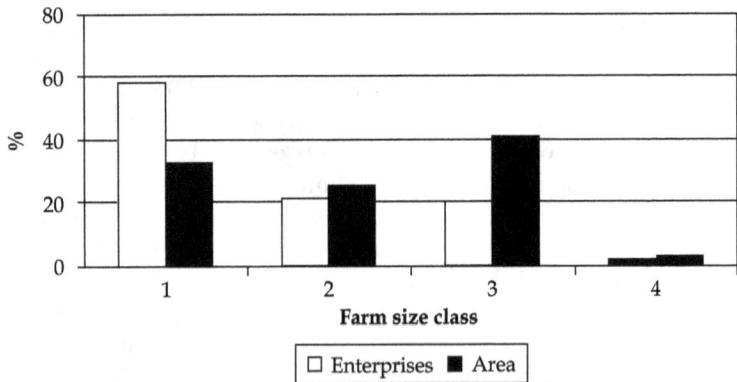

Source: Based on data from NSSO's 54th Round Survey.
Note: Farm size classes: 1 = Marginal, 2 = Small, 3 = Medium, 4 = Large.

nation as a whole. The cropping pattern, however, suggests the known tendency to concentrate on food grains, rice in this case, mainly driven by the need for subsistence. Wheat and sugarcane are grown where conditions are suitable but the region stands out in its emphasis on fruits and vegetables. These aspects are seen in Table 12.1.

Diversity of Fertiliser-use Practices

The NSSO's data clearly shows the diversity of fertiliser-use practices and the prevalence of organic methods. The practices are categorised, for analytical convenience, into three regimens: use of fertiliser (F); use of manure with no use of fertiliser (M), and use of neither fertiliser nor manure (N). Both N and M regimens constitute techniques that eschew use of chemical fertilisers where N represents the purely traditional natural practice with no external input for restoring soil fertility. While the choice of the traditional technique is partly associated with the practice of jhuming and reflects the lack of resources and amenities, it is the organic richness of the forest soils that also makes applications redundant. Regimen M stands for organic farming as denoted in this study. The term organic, however, is used in reference to the non-use of chemicals as fertiliser only since pesticide is not considered in this definition. Further, use of biofertilisers is also not included in this definition. It may be admitted that biofertilisers, promoted in Indian agriculture for their ecological benefits (Ghosh 2004) also constitute organic means of fertilising soils but their use is concentrated in the southern and western parts of India. However, admittedly, there is some notable progress in their use in certain northeastern states like Nagaland and Mizoram. Regime F is the most modern method that involves either exclusive fertiliser use or its conjunctive use with manure. The histograms in Figure 12.2 based on sample data show that fertiliser use has become widespread in India spanning 70 per cent of the enterprises but the pattern of practices is quite different in the northeast where farming with no external fertilising input still dominates and fertiliser use is the least adopted of the practices (see also Table 12.2).

In all the regions combined and for each region separately, the largest section of enterprises use fertiliser, but the northeastern region is the lone exception. Indeed, regimen N that constitutes

Figure 12.2: Frequency Distribution of Sample Crop Enterprises into Fertiliser-use Categories

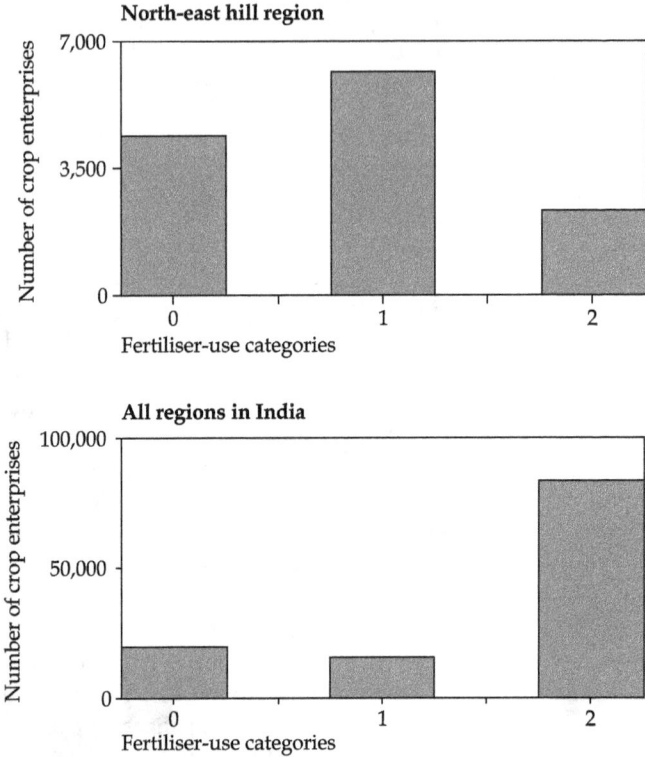

Source: Computed based on data from NSSO's 54th Round Survey.
Note: Fertiliser-use categories are 0 = Use of manure with no use of fertiliser, 1 = Use of neither fertiliser nor manure, 2 = Use of fertiliser (F).

the smallest part of the total number of enterprises for all regions combined at the national level is the largest for the northeast covering nearly half of all the enterprises. The view is no different when the area share is considered though the figures differ. Interestingly, the other hill region in the northern Himalaya shares practices with the plains regions and indicates the acceptance of external inputs and fertiliser-based technology. The northeastern region, however, retains its traditional character to a large degree but this persistence of the organic practices also draws attention to the possibilities inherent in the region.

Table 12.2: Distribution of Crop Enterprises and Area into Fertiliser-use Categories by Regions in India

	% of crop enterprises			% of area		
Category	M	N	F	M	N	F
Total	15.4	9.5	75.1	11.8	7.2	81.0
South	13.2	8.5	78.3	8.6	4.8	86.5
Northeast hills	27.5	45.4	27.1	26.7	45.5	27.7
East	15.0	11.8	73.2	11.9	9.1	79.0
North	13.6	5.7	80.7	4.2	3.0	92.8
West-central	18.40	11.4	70.2	17.2	9.2	73.6
Northern-hill	17.0	1.6	81.5	15.5	0.8	83.7

Source: Computed based on data from NSSO's 54th Round Survey.
Note: (i) Farm size classes are 1 = Marginal, 2 = Small, 3 = Medium, 4 = Large.
(ii) Fertiliser-use categories are M= Use of manure with no use of fertiliser, N = use of neither fertiliser nor manure, F = Use of fertiliser.

Cross-sectional View of the Practices

The farm holding size found in Table 12.1 and Figure 12.1 and the major land holding patterns of the region do not particularly indicate any land constraint, although labour constraint may be more important. The data in Table 12.3 suggest that traditional and organic practices are not exclusive to any farm size defined by the land operated, though fertiliser use is found more extensively among smaller farmers and is quite low among the large-sized farms. The share of area allocated by small farms to fertiliser-based agriculture exceeds their share in total crop enterprises, meaning that relatively larger plots of land are devoted

Table 12.3: Distrbution of Crop Enterprises and Area by Farm Size Classes into Fertiliser-use Categories in the Northeastern Hill Region

	% of crop enterprises				% of area			
Class	M	N	F	All	M	N	F	All
1	26.5	40.8	32.7	100.0	21.5	36.5	42.0	100.0
2	26.9	50.2	22.9	100.0	22.6	46.9	30.5	100.0
3	30.4	53.8	15.8	100.0	32.8	51.6	15.6	100.0
4	49.0	44.1	6.9	100.0	54.6	40.4	4.0	100.0
Total	27.5	45.4	27.1	100.0	26.8	45.3	27.9	100.0

Source: Computed based on data from NSSO's 54th Round Survey.
Note: See notes in Table 12.2.

to such use by small farms. The largest size farms also have the largest share of enterprises and area under organic manure-based agriculture with no use of chemical fertilisers. However, even among the small farms, nearly 27 per cent of the enterprises and 22 per cent of the area are subjected to purely manure-based soil fertilisation techniques, though the largest share is claimed by the purely traditional practice. The hill region emerges as a typically low external input system by this measurement.

The size of land holding is a standard measure of the economic class of the farmers in India but it is by no means the only yard-stick. Ownership of, or access to, other kinds of assets also deter-mine a farmer's productive potential and investment capacity. Taking account of other indicators, one can look for a relation-ship between the use of fertiliser and wealth. Land ownership, as opposed to operational holding (that includes leased land), is an important wealth indicator. The term 'landed' is defined to comprise those who own land above 2 ha. Common property is a significant source of access to necessary inputs in hill and tribal economies. Here, only the common properties used for fod-der and manure collection are considered (CPR-livestock, CPR-manure) as these may be relevant for the choice of the fertiliser practice. Table 12.4 indicates that small and marginal farmers owning less than 2 ha of land comprise a relatively large por-tion of fertiliser-based enterprises, as the landed group constitute only 12.5 per cent of the category. However, a significantly larger portion than in other categories is found to be under irrigation. The machinery-owning group (farm asset) is very small for all

Table 12.4: Percentage of Different Fertiliser-use Categories Owning Assets

	% of crop enterprises		
Assets	*M*	*N*	*F*
Landed	24.3	25	12.5
Irrigated	12.6	7.9	43.3
Livestock	71.6	63.3	54.6
CPR-livestock	6.7	13.7	6.4
CPR-manure	0.7	0.7	0.3
Farm assets	1.5	1.4	4.3

Source: Computed based on data from NSSO's 54th Round Survey.
Note: As in Table 12.2. Farm assets are tractors/harvesting machine.

categories but is largest at 4.3 per cent for the fertiliser-using category. Organic enterprises are the largest possessors of livestock, as may be expected, but these are mostly enterprises characterised by lack of irrigation and farm assets. The share of enterprises using the commons for fodder is larger in the traditional category than the others. Curiously, both the manure-using category (M) and the traditional category (N) have low shares of enterprises using the commons for collecting manure (0.7 per cent and 0.7 per cent respectively). Their shares of enterprises owning farm assets are also low (1.5 per cent and 1.4 per cent respectively). In the case of the traditional category the manure may be actually collected for sale to other households, which is not uncommon (Chopra and Dasgupta 2003).

Fertiliser Practices and Other Improved Methods

How far the hill agriculture has retained its 'traditionality' and even remained 'primitive' can be assessed by the available information on the use of external inputs other than chemical fertilisers. The view of the cultivation practices as presented in Table 12.5 supports the notion that larger proportions of fertiliser users go for improved seed, mechanisation and insecticides than the purely traditional and manure-using categories who do not use chemical fertilisers. However, traditionality is a multi-dimensional aspect and these improved practices also accompany the traditional

Table 12.5: Percentage of Different Fertiliser-use Categories also Using Specific Modern Technology

Technology	% of crop enterprises			% of area		
	M	N	F	M	N	F
Improved seeds	25.4	35.2	63.6	20.4	32.6	71.43
Machines	6.5	3.2	33.4	9.3	3.7	42.86
Insecticide	17.0	11.7	66.4	32.7	19.8	75.00
Soil test	3.6	3.9	4.9	4.4	4.8	5.7

Source: Computed based on data from NSSO's 54th Round Survey.
Note: Insecticide includes weedicides, etc. Machines include mechanised sowing, harvesting, irrigation. See note in Table 12.2.

and organic soil fertilising practices to an extent. Even non-users of chemical and organic soil nutritioners apply improved seeds and chemical pesticides and use machines. Cultivation based on organic manure is accompanied to a significant extent by the use of improved seeds (25.4 per cent) and also by insecticides (17.0 per cent). The practice of soil testing has a generally low share and is relatively more common in the fertiliser-using category.

Table 12.6 further breaks down the farm size categories by their tendencies to use the different fertilising practices along with chemical insecticides. Among all the enterprises, over 40 per cent use no fertiliser, no manure, and no insecticide, nearly 23 per cent use manure but no insecticide and 18 per cent use both chemical fertiliser and insecticide. No definite direction is evidenced in the tendency to use organic manure with no accompanying use of insecticide with regard to farm size. In fact, all sizes show similar proclivity to use the organic with no insecticide method except that the smallest and the largest farms have a slightly higher share under this practice than the two intermediate-size categories. The tendency to use insecticide along with the organic manure definitely rises with farm size but the tendency of using insecticide in a purely traditional fertilising practice increases as farm size increases only up to the medium size, but the share is extremely low (1.4 per cent) in the largest class. Interestingly, the use of fertiliser both with and without the use of insecticide comes down in share as farm size increases and the share of conjunctive users of chemicals as fertiliser and as pesticide declines from 21.1 per cent in the smallest holding to 2.7 per cent in the largest.

Table 12.6: Distribution of Crop Enterprises Under Each Farm Class into Organic and Non-organic Practices (%)

Class	M-no insecticide	M-insecticide	F-no insectcide	F-insecticide	N-no insecticide	N-insecticide
1	23.8	2.7	11.6	21.1	37.1	3.7
2	22.1	4.8	7.0	15.9	45.7	4.5
3	20.6	9.8	4.4	11.4	42.8	11.0
4	23.7	25.3	4.2	2.7	42.7	1.4
All	22.8	4.7	9.1	18.0	40.1	5.3

Source: Computed based on data from NSSO's 54th Round Survey.
Note: See note in Table 12.2.

Crops and Fertiliser Practices

To find out which crops lend themselves to the practices of not using chemical fertiliser, six crop groups are considered. The cereal crop paddy is important in the uplands for subsistence and for the local market in general and this is considered by itself as 'crop 1'.[5] Fodder and coarse cereals that are known to demand less water than other crops in India are taken as a group in 'crop 2'. Pulses, oilseeds and mixed crops constituting a minor group of crops are denoted as 'crop 3'. Vegetables and fruits are considered as 'crops 4 and 5' respectively. Wheat and sugarcane are commercial crops grown only to a limited extent where conditions permit and are, therefore, combined with other cash crops as 'crop 6'. Table 12.7 shows that the largest share in each crop group, excepting vegetables, falls in the purely traditional practice category (N). Paddy among all the crops has the largest share of enterprises, 40.3 per cent, under fertiliser-based cultivation. The share in terms of area is somewhat less, at 33.8 per cent, indicating that these are small-sized land holdings. Coarse cereal and fodder, denoted as crop 2, and vegetables denoted as crop 4 have relatively large shares of enterprises (40.2 per cent and 38.5 per cent respectively) and area under the organic practice category compared to the other crops. Vegetables account for the largest share of organic

Table 12.7: Distribution of Crop-wise Enterprises and Area into Fertiliser-use Categories (%)

Crop	% of crop enterprises				% of area			
	M	N	F	T	M	N	F	T
1	18.6	41.1	40.3	100	20.6	45.6	33.6	100
2	40.2	45.9	13.9	100	40.5	41.9	17.6	100
3	19.5	68.9	11.6	100	19.0	70.2	10.8	100
4	38.5	36.1	25.4	100	48.8	29	22.2	100
5	10.8	80.6	8.6	100	16.4	73.7	9.9	100
6	30.1	44.3	25.6	100	32.7	41.5	25.8	100
Total	**27.5**	**45.4**	**27.1**	**100**	**26.8**	**45.3**	**27.9**	**100**

Source: Computed based on data from NSSO's 54th Round Survey.
Note: Crops are 1 = paddy, 2 = other cereals and fodder, 3 = pulses, oilseeds, mixed crops, 4 = vegetables, 5 = fruits and nuts, 6 = wheat sugarcane cash crops. See note in Table 12.4.

Figure 12.3: Crop-wise Distribution of Organic Farms

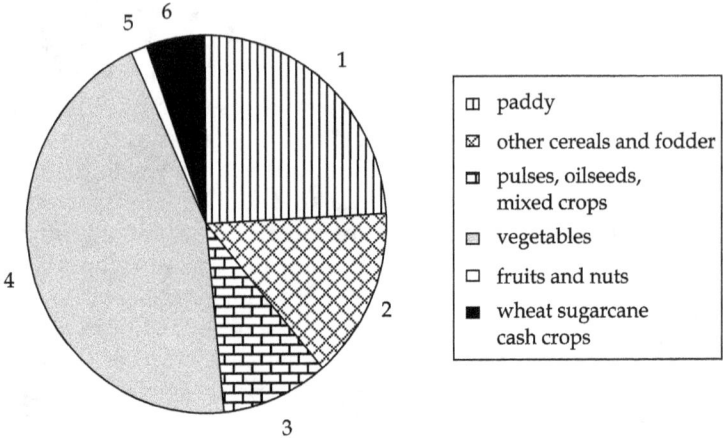

practices, followed by rice and coarse cereals and fodder combined (Figure 12.3).

Pesticides too constitute chemical use in agriculture, and when organic agriculture is broadly defined to take into account the use of pesticide also, vegetables fall behind the coarse cereal group (Table 12.8). Each of these two crop groups however has a high share (exceeding 30 per cent) of enterprises falling in the category using organic manure with no use of chemical pesticide compared to others. It is interesting to note that both these groups benefit from wastes turned into manure and themselves also serve the waste generation process through animal feed and vegetal wastes. In each crop group, a relatively small share of enterprises uses organic manures along with chemical pesticides. The share ranges from 1.3 per cent for the coarse cereal and fodder group to 6.3 per cent for vegetables. Users of the traditional method (N) along with pesticide account for 8 per cent of total enterprises for rice growers, 6.4 per cent for pulses and oilseeds (crop 3) and less for others. Paddy has the largest share (31.1 per cent) in the category using chemicals as both fertiliser and insecticide but the generally low shares of enterprises under the crops using fertiliser but no insecticide possibly suggest that the two practices of using fertiliser and pesticides may be associated.

Table 12.8: Distribution of Crop-wise Enterprises into Organic and Non-organic Practices Taking Account of Fertiliser and Insecticide Use (%)

Crop group	M-no insecticide	M- insecticide	F-no insecticide	F- insecticide	N-no insecticide	N- insecticide
1	13.9	4.7	9.3	31.1	8.0	33.0
2	38.8	1.3	9.8	4.2	5.4	40.5
3	16.6	2.9	3.1	8.5	6.4	62.5
4	32.2	6.3	12.0	13.5	2.5	33.5
5	6.6	4.1	6.0	2.7	3.2	77.4
6	24.0	6.1	6.8	18.8	3.2	41.1
Total	22.8	4.7	9.1	18.0	5.3	40.1

Source: Computed based on data from NSSO's 54th Round Survey.
Note: See notes in Tables 12.5 and 12.6.

Explaining the Fertiliser-use Practices

The likelihood of choosing any fertilising practice is expected to depend on the nature of the crop raised and the agro-climatic conditions (including soil) of the region. The season of the enterprise, kharif (summer/monsoon) or rabi (winter), carries its own implications of weather-related risk. In particular, the competing use of the same raw materials as fuel instead of manure in the drier season provides a seasonal dimension to the choice of this practice. In view of the peculiarities of the region with respect to the access to land, farm size could be an indicator of scale and labour adequacy (though household sizes are unknown) for farming. Ownership of farm assets and livestock, access to the commons and availability of irrigation are other relevant indicators that shape the choice of practice.

Based on a framework provided by McFadden's random utility function (1974) the factors that determine the fertilising practice are identified. The farmers are assumed to choose from three possible options of fertiliser practices, namely use of chemical fertiliser with or without organic supplement (F), use of only organic manure (M) and the practice involving no external supplement (N), the base category of choice being the fertiliser-based practice (F). The results of the regression suggest that smaller farms are more inclined towards the fertiliser-based practice (F) than the organic (M) or purely traditional regimes (N). If irrigation is available, the fertiliser-based practice becomes the most preferred. The likelihood of choosing organic farming (M) practice is enhanced in the kharif season and more so when the household owns livestock. The possibility of fertiliser leaching out due to rainfall and the difficulty of producing fuel with the same material in the rainy season may have some role in the avoidance of chemical fertilisers in the monsoon season. The use of the commons for manure collection is associated with the organic practice over other practices, while the ownership of farm assets is associated more with the fertiliser-based practice. The responses also differ depending on the crops. Coarse cereal/fodder and vegetables are more likely to be farmed with an organic method. Both groups, that is, pulses/oilseeds/mixed crops (group 3) and fruits (group 5) are the most likely to be cultivated by the purely traditional method (N), with fertiliser-use being the last choice. For paddy, however, the fertiliser-based practice is the first preference and organic (M) the last.

Concluding Remarks

The northeastern hill states in India, characterised by predominantly rural and agriculture-based economies, have remained relatively backward in economic development. The fertiliser-based technology associated with the Green Revolution in agriculture has not penetrated this threshold due to inherent constraints. The agro-ecology and the social customs of this region differ from the rest of the country and land scarcity does not appear to be a binding constraint for agriculture in the region as much as the ability to make gainful use of the land that is available. There is a need for careful planning of alternative and suitable strategies for the development of the region that takes full view of the strengths and limitations of agro-ecology, and the market potentials of the emerging era. Cutting across farm sizes, the largest share of crop enterprises and that of the crop area too is devoted to purely traditional methods that make minimum use of external inputs, especially chemical fertilisers. The use of chemical fertilisers is common among small farms but is associated with the ownership of farm assets and access to irrigation, which is itself a scarce resource in hill agriculture. The use of chemical fertiliser is also found to be associated closely with the use of chemical pesticides.

Organic farming is positively associated with the ownership of livestock. Coarse cereals and fodder, and vegetable are preferred crops for organic practices, while oilseeds, pulses, mixed crops, and fruits are preferred for the purely traditional method. Fertiliser is more likely to be used for wheat, rice and sugarcane.

In the northeastern hill region, given the abundance of difficult yet fertile tracts of land, its tribal customs of land tenure, economic strength in terms of livestock ownership and limitations of terrain and irrigation, organic farming seems a promising avenue to development. The positive association of organic farming practices with land possession enhances the scope of the practice in view of the large share of land in the medium-size category and the higher average farm size of the region. Empirical analysis also reveals the relative potentials of vegetables and fodder in this regard. The advantages that these crops also have in recycling wastes directly into crop bio-mass or indirectly through animals suggest a synergic relation that can be tapped. At the same time livestock and vegetable products promote value addition through processing activities. The promotion of systematic organic farming and food processing may also help in drawing investment to the region. All this will enable meaningful participation of the labour force, especially the women who are observed to be more closely associated with livestock rearing in India.

Notes

1. An earlier version of this essay was submitted to the 3rd Biennial Conference held by the Indian Society for Ecological Economics (INSEE) at the Indian Institute of Management, Kolkata in December 2003 on 'Biodiversity and Quality of Life' and was published in *Biodiversity and Quality of Life* edited by Nirmal Sengupta and Jayanta Bandyopadhyay (2005: 188–204).

2. The analysis here is based on the National Sample Survey Organisation's (NSSO) 54th Round Survey on cultivation practices conducted in over 78,990 households with agricultural year 1997–98 as the reference period. The unit of observation is a single crop enterprise adding up to a total of 12,829 cases in the selected states, each of which belongs to a set of the five most important field crops (FFC) raised by an individual household from among the following 12 crop groups: paddy, wheat, other cereals (including coarse cereals), pulses, oil seeds (excluding plantation crops), mixed crops, sugar cane, vegetables, fodder, fruits

and nuts, other cash crops (like cotton, jute and mesta) and other crops (all other field and seasonal crops). The survey provides categorical information on input use by responses to queries such as whether the units applied fertiliser and manure (partly, entirely or not). Fertiliser refers to factory-made chemical fertiliser nutrients and manure is constituted of farmyard manure, compost and biogas slurry. The survey also provides information on access to common property resources (CPRs), defined as 'resources accessible to and collectively owned/held/managed by an identifiable community and on which no individual has exclusive property rights'. In this study CPR is considered in a *de facto* sense where the property has been actually used. NSSO reports on various uses of CPR but there are two ways CPR use can be meaningful for fertiliser-use practice; (*a*) use of CPR for livestock feeding, i.e., either by grazing or collection of fodder and (*b*) use of CPR directly for collecting manure.

3. The seven states considered for the study are different from the so-called Seven Sister states, a sobriquet coined in the year 1972; the group of states excludes Assam but includes Sikkim which became a full state only in 1975. Partly due to the coverage of the survey and partly our choice there are some notable exclusions. For Nagaland, only the villages located within 5 km of a bus route constituted the sampling frame for the survey. The hill areas of Assam and the northern part of West Bengal that principally are part of the northeastern hill region of India, are not covered in this study. About half of Tripura and 10 per cent of the area in Manipur are flood plains but the data make no distinction between plains and hills.

4. Traditionally rice terraces were irrigated with bamboo pipes which tapped stream and spring water. A more scientifically and intricately designed system for flooding rice fields is the Apatami that consists of contour bunds, bamboo frames and conduits connecting inlets to and outlets from the plots. Bamboo drip irrigation is practised in Meghalaya.

5. No distinction is made between upland and plains rice.

References

Alagh, Yoginder K. 1991. *Indian Development Planning and Policy*. New Delhi: Vikas.

Borah, K. C. 1999. 'Land Utilisation and Cropping Pattern in Mizoram', in Gursharan Singh Kainth (ed.), *Developing Hill Agriculture*. New Delhi: Regency Publications, pp. 168–77.

Chand, Ramesh. 1997. *Agricultural Diversification and Development of Mountain Regions*. New Delhi: M. D. Publications Pvt. Ltd.

Chopra, Kanchan and Purnamita Dasgupta. 2003. *The Nature of Household Dependence on Common Pool Resources: An Econometric Study of India,* Working paper No. 232, Institute of Economic Growth, Delhi, India.

The Fertiliser Association of India (FAI). 2003. *Fertilizer Statistics.* New Delhi: The Fertilizer Association of India. Available at http://www.faidelhi.org.

Ghosh, Nilabja. 2004. 'Promoting Biofertilizers in Indian Agriculture', *Economic and Political Weekly,* 25 December, 39(52): 5617–625.

———. 2005. 'Organic Farming in North-East Hill Region in India', in Nirmal Sengupta and Jayanta Bandyopadhyay (ed.), *Biodiversity and Quality of Life.* New Delhi: Macmillan, pp. 188–204.

Government of India. 1996–97. *Land Use Statistics at a Glance.* New Delhi: Ministry of Agriculture, Directorate of Economics and Statistics.

———. 2002. *Agricultural Statistics at a Glance.* New Delhi: Ministry of Agriculture, Directorate of Economics and Statistics.

McFadden, Daniel. 1974. 'Conditional Logit Analysis of Qualitative Choice Behaviour', in Paul Zarembka (ed.), *Frontiers in Econometrics.* New York: Academic Press, pp. 105–42.

National Sample Survey Organisation (NSSO). 1999a. 'Cultivation Practices in India', in January to June 1998, Report No. 451 (54/31/3), Department of Statistics and Programme Implementation, Government of India.

———. 1999b. 'Common Property Resources and Village Facilities', Unit-level NSS Data on CDs, Schedule No. 3.3.

Saleh, Swabera Islam. 1989. *Nagaland's Economy in Transition since 1964.* New Delhi: Omson Publications.

Sengupta, Nirmal and Jayanta Bandyopadhyay. 2005. *Biodiversity and Quality of Life.* New Delhi: Macmillan.

13A

The Potential of Horticultural Intervention for Livelihood Enhancement and Biodiversity Conservation in Tripura, Mizoram and Arunachal Pradesh

SUMI KRISHNA

Horticulture has been recognised as eminently suitable for the northeastern region because of the richness and variety of its topography, soil and agro-climate. The cultivation of vegetables, fruits, flowers, spices and medicinal plants — primarily on lands not suitable for seasonal crops — is being vigorously promoted, often in conjunction with organic farming. Horticultural plantations are intended to reduce shifting cultivation, control soil erosion, enhance livelihoods and prevent out-migration. A Technology Mission for Integrated Development of Horticulture in the NER was initiated in the ninth Five Year Plan (1997–02) with four mini-missions to address all aspects of horticulture: research; production and productivity; post-harvest management, marketing and export; and processing. A Central Institute for Horticulture has been set up in Medziphema, Nagaland, and a horticultural marketing centre in Tripura. Central and state-level interventions have helped to increase the area under various horticultural crops (NEDFi 2006).[1] But despite the efforts, the extent, production and productivity are still limited. One challenge is developing the technology for domestication on a large scale; an even greater challenge is marketing. There are also issues related to land tenure, labour relations and gender concerns.

This essay briefly describes the horticultural diversity and potential, followed by case studies of pineapple, squash (the gourd, *Sechium edule,* known as chow-chow in India), and orchid cultivation.

Wild Foods and Home Gardens

The eastern Himalaya has a rich diversity and genetic variability of taro (*Colocasia*), yam (*Dioscorea*), citrus and banana, besides spices, ornamental, medicinal and aromatic plants (Arora and Pandey 1996; Asati and Yadav 2004; Goswami, Haridasan and Basar 2002). Horticultural interventions focus mainly on the wild relatives of food crops (Tables 13A.1 and 13A.2): 17 citrus species, 52 of their cultivars and a few naturally occurring hybrids have been identified; 32 strains of lemon alone are available (Bhatacharya and Dutta 1956). Meghalaya leads in the cultivation of mandarin oranges. The maximum genetic variability of banana (cultivated and wild) and mango occur in the region. The hills and valleys harbour a wide diversity of fruits. Arunachal is especially rich in wild cherries, plums, pears, and gooseberries (Asati and Yadav 2004).

Several vegetables, fruits, spices, medicinal herbs, flowers and even fodder are traditionally cultivated in home gardens, usually in conjunction with livestock activities. Located near homesteads, these small, low-input but intensively farmed home gardens are an important buffer against scarcity and provide nutritional balance. Over time, home gardens have become extremely diversified — for example, 128 plant species have been recorded in home gardens in Nagaland — and have been used as an entry point to enhance the productivity of the farming system (Aier and Changkija 2003).

Notable among cultivated vegetables is a wide range of *Solanum* (brinjal–tomato family). The tomato was introduced in the 18th century but a wild tomato is also known. The chilli has been widely domesticated. Fifteen different cucurbitous vegetables are found in home gardens — indigenous cucumber and gourds, and 'exotics' like pumpkin and squash or chow-chow.

> Pumpkin varieties abound in number with variation in fruit size, fruit skin, flesh colour thickness, sweetness, etc. The wild species *Cucumis hardwickii,* the likely progenitor of cultivated cucumber, is found growing in natural habitats in the Himalayan and NE region particularly in Meghalaya. *C. sativus* var. *sativus* is cultivated [all over] the North Eastern region in tropical and subtropical conditions.

Table 13A.1: Major Fruit Diversities in Northeastern India

Common name	Species	No. of cultivars in the region	No. of wild relatives (approx.)	Distribution
Tropical				
Mango	*Mangifera indica* L.	25	2	Tropical areas of Assam, Meghalaya, Mizoram, Tripura
Ber	*Ziziphus mauritiana* Lamk	8	3	Plains and hills up to 500 m
Pineapple	*Ananas comosus* L.	7	–	Introduced and naturalised in the region. Jaldhup and Lakhat type pineapple found in Assam
Aonla	*Emblica officinalis* Gaertn	5	2	Star aonla found in Mizoram and round aonla found in all states of northeast
Guava	*Psidium guajava* L.	7	1	Tropical and subtropical (up to 1,000 m) zone of India
Banana	*Musa acuminata* Colla. *Musa balbisiana* Colla.	501	143	Throughout the tropical and subtropical zones of the country
Subtropical				
Lime, lemon and oranges	*Citrus spp.*	17 plus their 52 vars.	–	Lime and lemon in both tropical and subtropical while oranges in subtropical zone
Peach	*Prunus persica* Benth & Hook.f.	7	3	Meghalaya, Nagland and Arunachal Pradesh
Plum	*Prunus domestica* L. spp. institia (L)	11		Meghalaya, Mizoram
Strawberry	*Fragaria vesca* l.	3		Hills of NE region
Apple	*Malas sylvestris* (L)	4	1	Arunachal Pradesh and introduced in Nagaland

Source: Asati, B. S. and D. S. Yadav. 2004. 'Diversity of Horticultural Crops in North Eastern Region', *Envis Bulletin Himalayan Ecology,* 12(1), pp. 5–6.

Table 13A.2: Major Vegetable Diversities in Northeastern India

Indigenous	Eggplant [brinjal or aubergine], *lablab* (Indian) bean, cucumber, smooth gourd, ridge gourd, snake gourd, sweet gourd
Introduced: Ancient	Garden pea, onion, bottle gourd, cowpea, *okra* (ladies finger), etc.
Introduced: Recent	Tomato, chilli, cauliflower, cabbage, French bean, etc.

Source: Asati, B. S. and D. S. Yadav. 2004. 'Diversity of Horticultural Crops in North Eastern Region', *Envis Bulletin Himalayan Ecology*, 12(1), p. 6.

Among gourds, in [the] North Eastern region maximum variability has been recorded for bottle gourd in fruit shape and size. The NE region has rich diversity in genetic resources of ridge gourd (*Luffa acutangula*) and sponge gourd (*L. cylindrica*). Small as well as large sized forms of bitter gourd are also available (Asati and Yadav 2004: 5).

In the 14th and 15th centuries, European traders introduced the cruciferous vegetables cauliflower, cabbage and kohlrabi/knolkhol (Seshadri and Srivastava 2002). Many leafy vegetables and legumes are also cultivated. The climbing French bean is grown together with maize, the maize stem supporting the bean stalk. There are also several tubers and rhizomatous crops. The tribals of Tripura cultivate the tuberous legume *Vigna vexillata* (Arora and Pandey 1996). The greatest number of 'lesser known' vegetables occur in Arunachal; the multipurpose tree bean (*Parkia*) is grown in Manipur and Mizoram; the perennial shrub that produces the vegetable *tamarillo* (tree tomato) is a backyard crop in Meghalaya. The drumstick is popular at lower altitudes.

There is considerable variability in ginger and turmeric; wild relatives of large cardamom (*Amomum subulatum*) and cinnamon grow in the forests. Black pepper, cumin, large cardamom, and saffron have been recently introduced as commercial crops. The large cardamom is being cultivated in Sikkim and parts of Arunachal. Chilli, ginger and turmeric are the main marketable crops in the hill states. Assam also produces green ginger (Asati and Yadav 2004).

Of hundreds of species of ornamental flowers, including rhododendron, magnolia, bahunia, cassia, erythrina (coral), etc., the most spectacular are the 600 and more orchid species. As vast tracts are yet unexplored, new species are often found (Krishna 1998b). Epiphytic orchids in particular are much in demand. For decades orchids like the lady's slipper have been smuggled out in a flourishing illegal trade (Chauhan 1981; Krishna 1998b). Significant orchid species include the *Dendrobiums (paciflorum* and *nobile), Diplomeris hirsute* and *Paphiopedilum*. Some orchids are also used as medicine.

Information on medicinal plants (Haridasan et al. undated) is still limited. All kinds of animal parts are also used medicinally often inter-twined with ritual/superstitious uses (Borang 1996). The rhizome of *Coptis teeta* is well-known in Chinese medicine for its anti-inflammatory and anti-microbial properties. The shrub is said to be the umbilical cord of the sky, Dote-Abu, who is hurt when the plant is picked, so the root must be taken secretly, unseen by people or the sky and the plant left in the soil (Krishna 1998b). The *Coptis teeta* and other medicinal plants (like *Rauvolfia serpentine*), once widely available in the wild, have been severely depleted. The Mishmi now cultivate *Coptis teeta* and sell it in the markets of upper Assam. Of medicinal and aromatic plants, agar wood (which produces agar oil) and the insecticidal *Java citronella* have been cultivated commercially. The common yew *Taxus batata* (used to make the anti-cancer drug taxol) occurs throughout the temperate forests of Arunachal. The pipli (*Piper longum*) is one of 20 species of long pepper cultivated in Arunachal. Tribals collect *amla*/wild Indian gooseberry (*Embilica officinalis*) and sell it to ayurveda companies. There are also three varieties of ginseng (ibid.).

Plantation crops include mainly coconut and arecanut besides tea, coffee and rubber. Some cashew-nut and walnut are also grown.

According to Asati and Yadav (2004: 10), national research institutes such as the National Bureau of Plant Genetic Resources of the Indian Council of Agricultural Research (ICAR), the Botanical Survey of India, and various universities in northeastern India have made 'tremendous impacts in collection, evaluation, conservation and utilization of regional germplasm for development of horticultural varieties in this region'. Given the regional demand for horticultural crops 'more germplasm needs to be identified for collection particularly for high yield, quality, resistance to diseases and pests, tolerance to frost and acidity'. They recognise, however, that problems relating to the conservation and development of horticultural diversity also relate to cultivation practices, land-tenure issues, smuggling and insurgency, besides interdepartmental coordination.

Commercial Cultivation

Specific fruits, vegetables, spices and plantation crops have been identified as suitable for large-scale cultivation and marketing in each state (Table 13A.3); state-level horticultural zones have also been demarcated, as for Arunachal (Table 13A.4). Yet, both technical and social issues related to production and marketing remain challenging as the following cases of pineapple (Tripura), chow-chow (Mizoram) and orchids (Arunachal) reveal.

Pineapple Production in Tripura

The case of pineapple production reflects some of the challenges faced by horticulture in the region. Pineapple was a traditional home garden crop till the union government's Technology Mission for Integrated Development of Horticulture provided the impetus to increase cultivation to enhance local incomes and meet a growing export market, particularly in Europe. The area under pineapple cultivation and productivity increased significantly but the lack of infrastructure, processing and marketing has led to huge wastage of this perishable crop.

Ratna Bharali Talkudar (2008) reports that the Darlongs of north Tripura (who have an improvised tradition of pineapple cultivation) harvest bumper crops from the hill slopes. Multicropping with jackfruit and other firewood trees is also practised instead of jhuming. The traditional pineapple growers used to have a regular market in Bangladesh. But the trade dried up after the international border was fenced with barbed wire. The trade with Assam has been affected by insurgency. Without adequate processing facilities in the area, Tripura's pineapple trade is in jeopardy. Talukdar (2008) says that government procurement is not matching the massive harvests. So, although pineapple is easy to cultivate, farmers feel rubber will be the more profitable option in the future (see also Viswanathan in this volume).

Table 13A.3: Major Horticultural Crops Identified for Different States

States	Fruits	Vegetables	Spices	Plantation crops
Arunachal Pradesh	Citrus, apple, walnut, banana, pear, plum, kiwi	Pea, beans, colocassia	Ginger, large cardamom, turmeric	
Assam	Banana, citrus, pineapple, jackfruit, guava, papaya	Potato, cabbage, sweet potato, brinjal, onion, cauliflower	Chilli, ginger, turmeric, black pepper	Arecanut, cashew nut, coconut
Manipur	Pineapple, citrus, banana, passion fruit	Tomato, cabbage, cauliflower	Chilli, ginger, turmeric	
Meghalaya	Pineapple, citrus, banana	Potato, cabbage, cauliflower, radish, french bean, tomato, capsicum	Ginger, turmeric	Arecanut
Mizoram	Citrus, banana, passion fruit	Chow-chow, cabbage, pumpkin, brinjal, beans	Ginger, turmeric, chilli	Arecanut
Nagaland	Pineapple, banana, citrus, passion fruit	Colocasia, chow-chow, tapioca, potato, pea	Garlic, chilli, ginger	
Sikkim	Citrus, kiwi fruit	Cabbage, french bean, chow-chow	Large cardamom, chilli	
Tripura	Citrus, pineapple, banana, jackfruit, mango, litchi	Potato, brinjal, sweet potato, beans, tomato	Chilli, ginger, black pepper	Arecanut, coconut, cashew nut

Source: Yadav, R. K., D. S. Yadav, N. Rai, and K. K. Patel. 2003. 'Prospects of Horticulture in North Eastern Region', *ENVIS Bulletin, Himalayan Ecology,* 11(2), p. 28.

Table 13A.4: Fruit and Vegetable Crops Suitable for Cultivation in Arunachal Pradesh

Horticultural zone (altitude/rainfall)	Fruit crops
Foothills and valley (170–915 m)	Mandarin, acid lime, assam lemon, amla (indian gooseberry), pineapple, jackfruit, papaya, beans, cucurbits, potato
Mid-hills (915–1,803 m)	Peach, plum, apricot, pear, pomegranate, grapes, low-chilling apple, persimmon, kiwi, off-season vegetables, potato
High-hills (above 1,803 m)	Apple, cherry, walnut, chestnut, kiwi, off-season vegetables
Rain-shadow areas	Apple, pear, plum, peach, almond, walnut, etc.

Source: Mishra, S. S., K. A. Singh and T. K. Bag. 2002. 'Present Status and Prospects of Diversified Fruit and Plantation Crops Production in Arunachal Pradesh', in K.A. Singh (ed.), *Resource Management Perspective of Arunachal Agriculture.* Basar, Arunachal Pradesh: ICAR Research Complex for NEH Region, p. 13.

She writes:

> To provide growers more market linkage, the North Eastern Regional Agriculture Marketing Corporation (NERAMC) had set up a fruit juice concentration plant, way back in 1988, in Nalkata with an initial capital investment of ₹36 million. The aim was to purchase surplus marketable pineapple and other fruits. The plant has an installed capacity of 48 metric tonnes per day. In 2007–08 NERAMC procured 750 metric tonnes of pineapple from the growers, much below the average production of the state.
>
> The officials of the department of horticulture revealed that in 2008–09, NERAMC is likely to enhance its procurement to 1500 metric tonnes. Meanwhile, the state government has already initiated a plan for reconstructing and modernisation of the plant in Nalkata, which is under consideration for the approval of Ministry of Development of North East Region (DONER).
>
> Dabur Food Pvt. Ltd. of West Bengal has procured 1000 metric tonnes of pineapples from identified blocks of Agri-Export Zone in 2007–08. Their procurement is likely to be increased in 2008–09 by 4,000 metric tonnes.
>
> Taking all these projected procurement figures into account, barely 6000 metric tonnes of more than one lakh metric tonnes of pineapples estimated to be produced this year [2008–09] is going to be procured for processing and subsequent supply to the domestic and international markets.[2]

Chow-chow Production in Mizoram

The fast-growing cucurbit chow-chow (*Sechium edule*), was introduced into the Mizo hills by the Welsh missionaries over a century ago.[3] Easily available bamboo was used to provide shade and support the vine. It soon became a 'traditional' Mizo vegetable, grown in home gardens. All parts of the plant are used: the fruit for human food; stems and leaves for garnishing; what's left is used as pig feed. Official policy in Mizoram promotes agricultural self-sufficiency, encouraging farmers to cultivate and market vegetables as an alternative to shifting cultivation. So, in the late 1980s, extensive chow-chow cultivation was started in the large village of Sihphir, ideally located in an area with a moderate climate, good soil and on the main highway south from Aizawl town. It soon became the staple cash crop and a means of livelihood for farmers in Sihphir. However, as Chawii (2007: 45) comments, 'the hilly terrain necessitates huge investments for large-scale cultivation — poles and wires for the climber, water tanks for irrigation, transportation facilities along the three to four kilometers length of the steep farms, cold storage facilities, and labour'.

The Iskut (Mizo for chow-chow) Growers Association was established in 1986 with 80 members and began exporting to Assam. Within two decades, the membership was 800 and was expected to reach 1,200. The Mizo's traditional sense of community service, *tlawmngaihna*, may have also enabled the community to work together. The Sihphir association now has four branches in neighbouring villages, which together earned ₹10 million in 2000–01. Sihphir alone earned ₹8.5 million, according to a Horticulture Department report cited by Chawii (2007: 48–49):

During the initial years, from 1992–1993, the state Agriculture Department provided a price support subsidy of about Re. 0.50 per kilogram to the growers. But the assistance discontinued due to the increasing number of families involved in squash cultivation. Once market channels were established the association received assistance from the North Eastern Council in the form of two trucks to facilitate transportation, and ₹500,000 for the construction of a storage depot. On a monthly rotation basis, one member of the association is assigned the responsibility of maintenance of these trucks. However, some association members believe that pool trucks are often misused, shoddily maintained, and carelessly handled, which reduces them to a semi-permanent state of disrepair, making them more of a liability than a support and incurring extra cost that eats into the coffers of the association. Recently the Horticulture Department, through the Technology Mission Scheme of the central government, has provided ₹5 million worth of GI wires and about 150 community water tanks.

Chawii (2007: 47) has reported the case of chow-chow farmer Zahmingliana who − as 'the result of 20 years of hard work cultivating iskut, from which he earns over ₹100,000 annually' − owns 5.6 ha of farmland and an 8-by-10 m double-storied house:

> He also rears seven cows, which fetch approximately ₹15,000 per month from the milk and dung sales. During the dry season following the harvest, he grows cabbages for the market in Aizawl. Despite having to feed a family of 15, Zahmingliana sets aside ₹60–70,000 annually as savings from his squash earnings alone.
>
> Zahmingliana's case is not unique. After investing in large-scale cultivation the improvement in the quality of life is evident in Sihphir. Many families now afford better education for their children; some even send them to reputed boarding schools outside the state.
>
> In 1982, as a migrant from another village, Zahmingliana toiled long and difficult hours to provide two square meals a day to his family of 13. Back then, as a carpenter he considered himself fortunate when he got work for two days of the week. Subsequently, his earning as a teacher in a local primary school barely met the daily needs of his growing family. After wading through various jobs with limited or no success, the turning point came when he decided to invest in a 5.6 square meters plot for the purpose of squash cultivation. Since then there has been no looking back. The first harvest from the small plot yielded a generous 10 quintals of squash that was completely sold out, despite the lack of a proper marketing channel. Over the years, Zahmingliana bought land from different parts of Sihphir with savings from squash sales. At present, he owns a total of 5.6 hectares of land.
>
> Not surprisingly, the story of this successful initiative caught on and it was not long before other households in Sihphir village started similar undertakings, which led to a revolution of sorts.

Chawii further says that in 1992, Sihphir village alone earned ₹5.2 million from sales. In 2004, Zahmingliana earned ₹120,000.

The record belonged to Sangkhuma of Sihphir, who earned ₹400,000 the same year. However, not all farmers could make the large investment required and some abandoned the effort. Considering the labour and resources required, Sihphir has had remarkable success in cultivating and marketing chow-chow in an organised manner. Not only has this influenced nearby villages and the marketing of other vegetables, it has also led to visits by farmers from other northeastern states, and interactions with students of agricultural universities in the region. Yet, some fear that the inflow of new settlers is upsetting the cohesive fabric of the village. Hill-side agriculture is mainly rain-fed and chow-chow is a water-intensive crop. Water shortage is a big problem. Setting up irrigation channels is time-consuming but community water tanks and private water harvesting structures are being installed. In 2000, Mizoram switched to organic farming and stopped the state supply of chemical fertilisers (although some farmers continued to buy fertilisers in the unofficial market). Yields had earlier begun to decline and with the switch to organic manure, often in short supply, yields declined further, reports Chawii (2007).

Moreover, as Elizabeth Saipari, deputy director, Horticulture Department, Aizawl told Chawii (ibid.: 50), squash production had not reached its optimum because many growers could not afford the infrastructural facilities, the support poles and wires required. Transportation from the interior to the highway becomes especially difficult in the monsoon. There is no cold storage; if the chow-chow deteriorates the price falls. There is no formal marketing agency; the trade depends entirely on private intermediaries. Chow-chow has proved to be a viable alternative to jhuming but some farmers favour multi-cropping for long-term sustainability.

Orchid Cultivation in Arunachal

Habitat destruction and rampant collection from the wild of both plants and cut flowers (for export) have swiftly depleted the wonderful orchid wealth of the northeastern region, especially Sikkim and Arunachal. Despite favourable agro-climates, commercial floriculture in northeastern India is minimal (Hegde 2002), with the very few nurseries clustered around Kalimpong (in the West Bengal hills), Gangtok (Sikkim), Shillong (Meghalaya), Guwahati, and Tezpur (Assam). With funding support from

WWF, the Arunachal State Forest Research Institute has attempted to promote orchid farming as a supplementary crop and a 'cottage industry' through micro-propagation, farming on wasted lands, and developing a market for orchids (Hegde 1984; Krishna 1998b). At its tissue culture laboratory at Tipi in West Kameng, 10 selected clones of *Cymbidium* species ('boat' orchids) were micro-propagated to be multiplied and transplanted. Farmers' training introduced local farmers to orchid cultivation. The most successful entrepreneurs are Tilling Doley (a botany graduate) and his wife Tilling Muniya. Interactions with the orchid farmers in Sikkim helped them set up their own orchid nursery and farm in a small, marshy plot near their home in Hapoli. Initially, it was very hard work for Muniya, who nurtured the plants while her husband managed the business. Starting with 5,000 plants of six hybrid *Cymbidium* species, within three years they had 20,000 plants and good profits. This encouraged them to cultivate mushrooms (an even more profitable crop) and to start a tourism business. The Tillings' enterprise is now a private limited agro company. But their example is not typical. Another farmer in the same area who also took up orchid cultivation soon lost interest.

Impact on Women's Labour

The introduction of new crops into traditional agricultural systems impacts upon the existing agro-biodiversity and on human labour. Information on women's labour may be gleaned from more general research. For instance, Ramakrishnan's (1993) data from a khasi village in Meghalaya shows that of the two traditional cash crops, ginger and pineapple, the labour input required for ginger was much higher. When tea and coffee were introduced experimentally it was observed that tea required more labour than coffee. As I have written elsewhere (Krishna 1998a: 28), 'From a gender perspective, what is significant is that the male and female labour input is almost the same for the low-labour cash crops, i.e. the traditional mixed pineapple cropping and the experimental coffee. But in the case of the high-labour crops (both traditional and experimental), women's labour is much more than that of men.' This indicates that changes in the pattern of crops grown have to be assessed from many different perspectives to factor in multiple dimensions.

Constraints on Commercial Horticulture

Bhattacharya (2001: 108) had earlier suggested that the lag in productivity 'shows that either the technology is not available (which
is not correct), or it has not been reaching the farmers, despite
an extensive technology transfer system, or the farmers do not
have enough returns' to invest in improved technologies. Some of
these concerns were addressed in subsequent years through the
Technology Mission but although the area under fruit and vegetable crops and the total production has increased, productivity
has not kept pace (NEDFi 2006). At least a part of the problem
may be due to the inability to plan for the varied micro-contexts in
which horticultural interventions take place in the region (see also
Jayahari and Sen in this volume). The strategy for new interventions needs to incorporate local traditions of mixed home garden
farming and help people strengthen the linkages in the complex
chain from lab-to-farm-to-market.

Notes

1. Yadav et al. (2003) estimate — based on ICAR's 2002 figures — a total
   production of 6,818.4 thousand tonnes from 822.5 thousand hectares
   (3.14 per cent of the region). See also Sycom (2001), World Bank (2007)
   and NEDFi (2006).
2. See http://www.india together.org/2008/may/agr-pineapple.htm,
   accessed 24 April 2011. The Agri-export Zone Scheme of the Ministry
   of Commerce is located at Tripura and caters to the entire northeastern
   region. Farmers are to be provided international market access, infrastructure, credit, transport assistance and other facilities for promoting pineapple exports. New government policies have also removed
   certain export restrictions (see Sema et al. 2010).
3. This case study is based on the detailed study by Chawii (2007). I have
   also drawn on my own visit to Sihphir (Krishna 1998c).

References

Aier, Anungla and Sapu Changkija. 2003. 'Indigenous Knowledge and
    Management of Natural Resources', in T. B. Subba and G. C. Ghosh
    (eds), *The Anthropology of North-East India*. Hyderabad: Orient
    Longman, pp. 333–78.

Arora, R. K. and Anjula Pandey. 1996. *Wild Edible Plants of India – Diversity, Conservation and Use.* New Delhi: Indian Council of Agricultural Research, National Bureau of Plant Genetic Resources.

Asati, B. S. and D. S. Yadav. 2004. 'Diversity of Horticultural Crops in North Eastern Region', *Envis Bulletin Himalayan Ecology*, 12(1): 1–11.

Bhattacharya, S. C. 2001. 'Horticultural Crops — Fruits and Vegetables', in ASU (ed.), *Agriculture in Assam.* Jorhat: Assam Agriculture University, pp. 104–13.

Bhatacharya, S. C. and S. Dutta. 1956. *Classification of Citrus Fruits of Assam.* ICAR Monograph No. 20.

Borang, Asham. 1996. 'Ecological Status of Capped Langur in Arunachal Pradesh', *Arunachal Forest News*, 13(1&2): 26–28.

Chauhan, Sumi Krishna. 1981. 'India's Orchid Smugglers', *Earthscan Features*. London: Institute for Environment and Development.

Chawii, Liam. 2007. 'Exploring the Commercial Prospects of *Squash* in Siphir, Mizoram', Appendix D of Background Paper 14 'Natural Resource Based Initiatives and Livelihood Improvement Initiatives in Northeast India'. Commissioned as input to the 2007 World Bank study, *Development and Growth in Northeast India: The Natural Resources, Water, and Environment Nexus.* World Bank Report No. 36397-IN. Washington DC: The International Bank for Reconstruction and Development/The World Bank.

Goswami, M., K. Haridasan and J. Basar. 2002. 'Biodiversity of Medicinal Plants and Rattans in Arunachal Pradesh — Prospects for Commercial Cultivation', in K. A. Singh (ed.), *Resource Management Perspective of Arunachal Agriculture.* Basar, Arunachal Pradesh: ICAR Research Complex for NEH Region, pp. 31–45.

Haridasan, K., G. P. Shukla and B. S. Beniwal. n.d. *Medicinal Plants of Arunachal Pradesh.* Itanagar: State Forest Research Institute, Dir-ectorate of Environment and Forests, Government of Arunachal Pradesh.

Hegde, S. N. 1984. *Orchids of Arunachal Pradesh.* Itanagar: Government of Arunachal Pradesh.

———. 2002. 'Prospects of Floriculture Industry in Arunachal Pradesh and Other Parts of North-East India with Special Reference to Orchids,' in K. A. Singh (ed.), *Resource Management Perspective of Arunachal Agriculture.* Basar, Arunachal Pradesh: ICAR Research Complex for NEH Region, pp. 17–30.

Krishna, Sumi. 1998a. 'Gender and Biodiversity Management', in M. S. Swaminathan (ed.), *Gender Dimensions in Biodiversity Management.* New Delhi: Konark, pp. 23–61.

———. 1998b. 'Arunachal Pradesh,' Case Study in M. S. Swaminathan (ed.), *Gender Dimensions in Biodiversity Management.* New Delhi: Konark, pp. 148–81.

———. 1998c. 'Mizoram,' Case Study in M. S. Swaminathan (ed.),

Gender Dimensions in Biodiversity Management. New Delhi: Konark, pp. 182–210.

Mishra, S. S., K. A. Singh and T. K. Bag. 2002. 'Present Status and Prospects of Diversified Fruit and Plantation Crops Production in Arunachal Pradesh', in K.A. Singh (ed.), *Resource Management Perspective of Arunachal Agriculture.* Basar, Arunachal Pradesh: ICAR Research Complex for NEH Region, pp. 9–16.

NEDFi. 2006. *Databank Quarterly* (Horticulture), 5(1).

Ramakrishnan, P. S. 1993. *Shifting Agriculture and Sustainable Development: An Inter-disciplinary Study from North-eastern India.* New Delhi: Oxford University Press and Paris: UNESCO.

Sema, Akali, C. S. Maitie and Diethiolo. 2010. 'Pineapple Cultivation in North-east India — A Perspective Venture', available at http://www.cihner.org.in/paper-presentation/134-pineapple-cultivation-in-north-east-india-a-prespective-venture (accessed 24 April 2011).

Seshadri, V. and Umesh Srivastava. 2002. 'Evaluation of Vegetable Genetic Resources with Special Reference to Value Addition', International Conference on Vegetables, Bangalore, 11–14 November, *Proceedings* (CD Rom). Vegetable Science International Network, pp. 41–62.

Singh, K. A. (ed.). 2002. *Resource Management Perspective of Arunachal Agriculture.* Basar, Arunachal Pradesh: ICAR Research Complex for NEH Region.

Sycom Projects Consultants Pvt Ltd. New Delhi. 2001. 'Pre-Investment Feasibility Report on Commercial Floriculture in Northeastern Region', Submitted to North Eastern Development Finance Corporation Ltd. Guwahati.

Talukdar, Ratna Bharali. 2008. 'Tripura: Troubled Pineapple Growers: Too Much Fruit, Too Little Bounty', *India Together*, available at http://www.indiatogether.org/2008/may/agr-pineapple.htm (accessed 24 April 2011).

Yadav, R. K., D. S. Yadav, N. Rai, and K. K. Patel. 2003. 'Prospects of Horticulture in North Eastern Region', *ENVIS Bulletin, Himalayan Ecology*, 11(2): 13–28.

World Bank. 2007. 'Development and Growth in North East India: The Natural Resources, Water and Environment Nexus'. Draft. Strategy Report. No. 36397-IN. Joint Study of DONER, Ministry of Development of North Eastern India, Govt of India and World Bank. Washington DC: World Bank.

13B

Rhododendron Conservation and Squash Production: A Case Study from Arunachal Pradesh*

K. M. JAYAHARI AND MONALISA SEN

Northeastern India is a global biodiversity hotspot. The region's unique biodiversity requires global conservation efforts. The major portion of its forest ecosystems categorised as 'Unclassed State Forests (USF)' is under the control of the local communities, where community decision making plays a critical role in forest management, land-use conversion and resource utilisation. The ecological and local economic scenarios are intertwined; as a result, despite conservation efforts, the biodiversity of the region is under threat. Over time, the communities of the region have developed economically and the traditional system of community ownership has been replaced by individual or family ownership of land and resources. However, the system of collective decision making through traditional community institutions still exists, even though it has seen some remarkable changes.

Different state and central schemes are being implemented in Arunachal Pradesh for the economic upliftment of the communities. The promotion of horticulture plantations is one such major livelihood enhancement scheme. The state is witnessing a wide expansion of horticulture areas, mainly on abandoned jhum lands. Unless there is a trade-off to give up jhum cultivation to expand the area for horticultural plantations, this trend will have a negative impact on the forest cover and biodiversity of the region. As per the present assessment, only 5.2 per cent of the land area of the state falls under cultivable land for horticulture. However, over-exploitation of new forest areas for jhum cultivation, in lieu of the earlier jhum land being converted to horticulture plantation, will result in an increase in cultivable areas. This increase will definitely be at the cost of biodiversity and the forest cover of the state, as more and more forest area will be cleared for cultivation by the jhum farmers.

With the mission to develop and implement solutions which balance the need for food, income and environmental quality, Winrock International India (WII, a not-for-profit organisation registered in India in 1998) has been working on three broad thematic areas, namely — energy and environment, climate change and natural resources management. For the last 13 years, WII has worked on strengthening local forest institutions through capacity building; with civil society organisations to develop effective community-based enterprises; informing policy through evidence-based research; action research projects to pilot innovative concepts; developing outcome-oriented monitoring systems; knowledge management and communication services; addressing issues related to biodiversity conservation and sustainable utilisation of natural resources. In Arunachal Pradesh, the focus has been on biodiversity conservation and forest enrichment through establishing a 'conservation landscape' (Box 13B.1) in the western part of the state. Initial analysis revealed insufficient livelihood opportunities as a major threat, resulting in over-dependence of the communities on forest resources. Though the state has high horticultural productivity, the wastage (due to remoteness of the villages, poor post-harvest infrastructure facilities and road blocks) is also high. Wastage to the tune of 30–40 per cent occurs every year which leads to huge economic losses for the farmers. Due to this enormous wastage, horticulture is unsustainable, especially for the small and marginal farmers of the state. In this situation, simply extending the area under horticulture would not enhance livelihoods nor protect the biodiversity and natural resources. Rather, this would have tremendous adverse impacts on the forest cover and biodiversity of Arunachal.

This essay discusses WII's initiatives to conserve degrading rhododendron forests over three years. Rhododendron is one of the dominant genera in the temperate and timberline ecosystems in the eastern Himalaya. The aim was to convert an indigenous tree species, facing extinction due to over-extraction, to a horticulture species ensuring livelihood enhancement along with conservation in the natural habitat. This study highlights the need for

Box 13B.1: Conservation Landscape

This is a demarcated geographic area with an existing set of conservation issues. Its size would depend upon the conservation objectives. The overall objective is to ensure that the environmental services function efficiently and aesthetically for the well-being of both nature and human beings including the native plants and animals which are to be conserved. With the broad objective of conserving rhododendrons in western Arunachal Pradesh, the areas falling under the altitude and habitat ranges of different rhododendron species were aggregated to form the landscape. Accessibility was also considered as a criterion and so the accessible areas on the Bhalukpaung–Tawang road were included.

Source: Field notes.

undertaking case-specific participatory planning instead of uniformly increasing the horticulture areas. The study may thus provide a new dimension to the present thinking on improving horticultural activities in the state.

Study Area

The conservation landscape in western Arunachal Pradesh encompasses most of the areas of Tawang district and a considerable portion of the West Kameng district, demarcated on the basis of bio-geographic factors. Longitudinally, the landscape extends between the international border with China in the north and Rupa village in the south.

The land-use and land cover map was prepared from the Landsat image of the area using a Geographic Information System software — ERDAS Imagine 8.4 (supervised classification). Consultations were carried out with experts with regard to the vegetation classes to be prioritised and included in the landscape (Figure 13B.1). The major portion of the landscape is covered by temperate conifers and evergreen forest. The landscape has 18.5 per cent of agricultural land, far higher than the percentage for the entire state (Table 13B.1).

Objectives

Of more than 90 recorded species of rhododendrons in India, Arunachal harbours 61 species, 17 subspecies and 12 varieties.[1] The state also has a high number of endemic rhododendrons

Table 13B.1: Extent of Land Cover (by Classes) in the Conservation Landscape, Western Arunachal Pradesh

S. No.	Land class	Percentage	Area (ha)
1	Grass land	9.50	864,978.00
2	Water	1.50	136,262.00
3	Snow	8.00	728,983.00
4	Temperate broad leaf	7.79	709,480.00
6	Temperate conifer	33.39	3,040,579.00
7	Open area/agriculture land/grassland	18.57	1,691,309.00
8	Evergreen	21.25	1,935,646.00
		100.00	9,107,237.00

Source: Landsat satellite image processing carried out by Winrock International India.

(nine species and one subspecies). Much of the state still remains unexplored with respect to inventorisation; 43 of the known species have been categorised as rare, threatened and endangered by the Botanical Survey of India. Most of the rhododendron habitats near roads are in a degraded condition due to easy accessibility to local communities who use rhododendron wood for fuel. Besides, extension of grazing areas, agricultural land and shifting cultivation, human settlement and uncoordinated developmental activities like construction work have also resulted in habitat degradation. Natural calamities and forest fires have also affected the rhododendron habitats.

Constraints Faced and Way Out

There were several constraints to initiating a programme on conservation of rhododendrons, including the lack of detailed scientific information regarding the species and limited awareness among the local communities regarding the wider potential usefulness of rhododendrons. A landscape with a forest cover solely owned by the local communities cannot be conserved if the communities do not derive the tangible economic returns of protecting their forests. The activities of NGOs like WWF India in western Arunachal Pradesh showed the willingness of the local communities to set aside forests for protection, however, only as a trade-off once their livelihood was ensured. In this scenario the programme was designed in such a manner that a rhododendron-based enterprise for realising tangible benefits for the communities would be established, and for its part, the community would establish a rhododendron arboretum in the community forest area.

In Uttarakhand state in the central Himalayan region, rhododendron squash processing has been known since the 1970s and today is an established small-scale business. But rhododendron squash is not known to the people of northeastern India, even though the raw material is available in plenty. The standards for rhododendron squashes prescribed by the Department of Food Processing, Government of Uttarakhand and Central Food Technological Research Institute (CFTRI), Mysore, were proposed to be followed and the community trained to produce the rhododendron squash on a commercial scale and to market the product.

Methods

Selection of villages for the implementation of the programme was carried out through community consultation. Then, a SWOT (Strengths/Weaknesses/Opportunities/Threats) analysis was carried out in the possible villages by community meetings and semi-structured interviews. Based on the outcome of the SWOT analysis village Sakpret in Tawang district was selected for implementation of the project.

Any community initiative based on natural resources requires investigating and ensuring the availability of the natural resource in and around the area. As part of the rhododendron squash preparation initiative in Sakpret, a field survey was conducted in the community land to assess the availability of rhododendron flowers during the season. Eight hectares of thick rhododendron forest were delineated using GPS for the establishment of the arboretum and about 22 ha of the community forest area was surveyed. Quadrate studies using 10 × 10m quadrates recorded an average density of 20 rhododendron trees per 0.001 ha. It was thus found that the area has the potential of sustainable extraction of 120,000 kg of rhododendron flowers from the community forest area (30 per cent extraction).

Next, a village-level committee with the following responsibilities was constituted for the administration of the rhododendron squash processing unit: (*a*) Ensuring a benefit sharing process so that the profit from the processing centre is distributed equitably among all the participating families; (*b*) Ensuring a constant supply of the required chemicals in the processing centre; (*c*) Identifying a local person who will be responsible for the maintenance of the machines; (*d*) Ensuring smooth functioning of the processing centre; and (*e*) Collecting a defined percentage from the profits generated and using it for other village development activities.

A community food processing centre was constructed in the village; the construction work was carried out by the villagers for a wage of ₹200 per day. The building has an area of 54 sq m, with a ceiling height of 2.5 m. The walls are made of bamboo mats, locally fabricated by the villagers and the flooring has a tiled finishing. The roof is covered with tin sheets with wooden support. In all, 262 person days of labour were required for the construction of the processing centre, through which the villagers received a direct benefit of ₹52,400.

In keeping with WII's gender-equitable policy, the 140 men and 122 women involved in the work were all paid the same agreed wage of ₹200 per day. However, according to the conventional local system, women are only entitled to ₹150 a day. Therefore, the women's 'additional' amount of ₹50 per day totalling ₹6,100 was set aside as a corpus fund to be used for village development activities.

The basic equipment for rhododendron squash production was installed in the processing centre at Sakpret by November 2009 (Table 13B.2).

In March 2010, the villagers underwent a three-day training on rhododendron squash preparation in the processing centre. These trainings were attended by 42 persons of whom 31 were women. Training was provided for all steps — sustainable extraction of flowers, cleaning the flowers, petal separation, boiling, pulping, adding preservative, bottling and packaging of the final product.

Large stretches of rhododendron forests in western Arunachal Pradesh have become degraded primarily due to over extraction for firewood. The seedlings of *Rhododendron arboreum* were collected from the grazing lands. The pastures are subject to controlled fire every year to ensure growth of fresh and luxurious grass cover for the cattle, sheep and yak to graze. The seedlings were removed before the annual burning for maintenance. The saplings were potted in plastic bags and maintained in the nursery.

Table 13B.2: Equipment Installed in the Initial Phase

S. No.	Equipment/item details	Quantity	Cost (₹)	Purpose & usage
1	BSB Super Refractometer	1	1,350	For checking the sugar concentration of the squash
2	BSB stainless steel tray	1	900	For collection of squash
3	BSB fruit-cutting knives	4	200	Cutting raw material into smaller pieces
4	BSB mushroom grading sieve with wooden frame	1	740	To sieve the squash before bottling it.
5	BSB bottle washing machine	1	15,800	To wash bottles before packaging the squash
6	Steam jacketted kettle	1	44,800	To boil the flower petals
7	BSB crown-corking machine	1	5,600	To cork the bottles after filling them with squash
8	BSB fruit mill	1	124,000	To pulp the boiled flowers and extract the juice
9	Goldtech electronic weighing balance	1	5,063	To weigh the chemicals and preservatives
10	Distillation unitInnotech Engineering Devices Pvt Ltd	1	70,000	To distill water
11	Bottling unit S.S. Pharma Tech	1	36,414	To bottle the squash

Source: List of equipment installed in the processing centre compiled by the authors.

The potted saplings were planted in the degraded forest areas during the favourable spring season. But initial efforts to raise the seedlings from the *Rhododendron arboreum* seeds have not met with success.

Results

Village Sakpret has 44 families with a total population of 115 men and 118 women. Half of the families depend upon labour work for their livelihood. The average monthly income per family from labour was calculated to be only ₹1,364 (Table 13B.3).

During 21 days in March and April 2010, 3,448 litres of rhododendron squash was produced in the processing centre. Of a total 605 person days of labour, more than half (361) was contributed by women. The details of person-days employed in squash production are provided in Figure 13B.1.

No wages were initially paid for this work. The village-level committee for the administration of the project maintained a detailed account of the labour involved, and the wages were distributed after the squash was sold. Part of the expenditure towards the purchase of sugar, citric acid and the preservatives, sodium benzoate and sodium hydroxide, was borne by WII; the balance was taken from the corpus fund of the village (i.e., the amount contributed by the women).

Table 13B.3: Income Status of Families in Village Sakpret

Source of income	Number of families	Income per family per month (₹)
Labour	22	1,364
Contract	1	2,917
Government service	5	3,233
Agriculture	8	1,896
Cattle rearing	1	1,250
Carpentry	1	2,500
Service pension	1	3,500
Priesthood	3	667
Petty shop	1	833
No income	1	0

Source: Based on socio-economic survey carried out in the village by Winrock International India.

Figure 13B.1: Details of Labour Employed in Rhododendron Squash Production

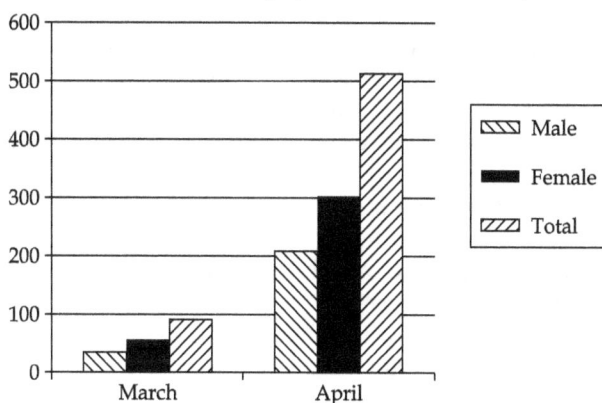

Source: Based on data collected during the project period by Winrock International India.

Marketing of Rhododendron Squash

Before the initiation of marketing, the squash was tested in the Research and Analysis Centre of the Federation of Indian Chambers of Commerce and Industries (FICCI) for food product organisation (FPO) certification which confirms that the product conforms to prescribed standards.

The villagers were provided training for marketing the squash in the local market. Sales counters were established in different places — in Tawang and Lumla during Independence Day celebrations, in the Tawang Market and in different other local fairs. A total of 420 litres of squash was sold in the 'brisk sales programmes'. The villagers involved in the programme received an encouragement commission of ₹15 per bottle sold.

Many villagers were also involved in carrying out direct marketing of rhododendron squash within Tawang district. This was done through sales in local *melas*. The villagers also motivated some of the shopkeepers in Tawang to keep these bottles in their shops and promote the sale of this new product.

Earlier, rhododendron squash was not available in the markets of eastern India. The market response to the new product from the dealers and distributors was not as positive as expected. Since the unit is producing only a single product using a new brand name, and the product and brand were quite new to the region, there was a little hesitation from the retailers to provide shelf space. Door-to-door marketing agencies were approached to resolve the issue of lack of sufficient shelf space. However, this strategy also was not able to resolve the problem because door-to-door marketing people preferred low volume units of the product to reduce the weight they had to carry and needed higher margins than that fixed for the product. For making the product familiar in the market and the region too, catering agencies and even management units were approached to introduce the squash as a special drink in parties and other events.

Overall, 3,448 litres of the rhododendron squash were marketed by the collective efforts of the villagers.

Livelihood Impact

The overall business profit details are listed in Table 13B.4.

Table 13B.4: Overall Business Financials (Quarterly)

Item	Rate (₹)	Total	Grand Total
1. Sale return (3,448 lts squash)	65.00	224,120.00	224,120.00
2. Variable cost			−191,916.00
2.1 Bottle cost*	4.00	−13,798.00	
2.2 Bottle transport cost*	5.00	−20,688.00	
2.3 Firewood (210 kg)	60.00	−12,600.00	
2.4 Wages for production#	200/150.00	−102,950.00	
2.5 Sugar (1,068 kg)*	35.00	−37,380.00	
2.6 Chemicals*			−4,500.00
3. Overall profit (1–2)			32,204.00
4. Total benefit for the community (profit + wages)	135,154.00		
5. Average per family (total 38)	3,556.00		

Source: Calculations based on the actual figures obtained in Winrock International India's initiative of the processing centre in village Sakpret.

Notes: *Provided by a grant from Sir Ratan Tata Trust in the initial phase
*Partially supported by Department of Science and Technology
#The wages distributed within the community

The community has received an overall labour benefit of ₹102,950 from the programme which has provided an additional monetary benefit of ₹3,557 per family in three months (without disturbing their normal labour opportunities). The additional benefit from the programme was, thus, 2.5 times of the annual family income. A profit of ₹32,204 has been generated for usage in community benefit activities, which the villagers have deposited in the bank; this will be used to upscale the process. The community has also set aside 8 ha of rhododendron forest as community-conserved area where no anthropogenic disturbances are permitted. They also raised 3,000 saplings of *Rhododendron arboreum* in the nursery and planted these in the degraded community forest area. About 1 ha of additional rhododendron forest area has been created through the plantation activity.

Discussion

The biodiversity in Arunachal Pradesh is depleting because of many reasons, including over-extraction of resources and other land-use changes. Horticulture is being popularised in the area as a measure to improve the livelihood of the poor communities. But the expansion of horticulture areas is at the cost of increasing degradation of the forest cover of the state, as the horticulture plantations are raised in the community areas, which are either forest areas (even degraded) or abandoned jhum areas where secondary forests are emerging.

This case study highlights an example of additional livelihood generation for the communities through value addition of natural and wild resources without disturbing the ecosystem. The project has also demonstrated the need for awareness generation and capacity building of the local communities for protecting their natural resources and regulating forest dependency. The case study reveals the need for detailed participatory planning, which is critical for the expansion of horticulture activities in Arunachal Pradesh, while balancing other options for the improved conservation of available natural resources.

The success in plantation of *Rhododendron arboreum* trees in the degraded forest areas shows its scope as a horticultural species. Many species of rhododendrons after hybridisation are already being used globally as ornamental plants. This species is, however, not used in India as a horticultural species. In order to ensure sustainable livelihood systems, we have to explore some out-of-the-box ideas, which need to be blended with the conventional horticultural practices, especially in biodiversity hotspots like the eastern Himalayas.

Notes

* The authors would like to thank the Science and Society Division of the Department of Science and Technology, Government of India and Sir Ratan Tata Trust for extending financial support to the project.

1. A *species* is defined as a group of organisms capable of interbreeding and producing fertile offspring.

   A *subspecies* is a taxonomic category denoting a fairly permanent geographically isolated race. Organisms that belong to different subspecies of the same species are capable of interbreeding and producing fertile offspring, but they often do not interbreed in nature due to geographic isolation or other factors.

   A *variety* is a taxonomic rank below subspecies. Varieties are usually the result of selective breeding and diverge from the parent species or subspecies in relatively minor ways.

14

Community-based Approaches to Local Natural Resource Management*

VINCENT DARLONG AND S. K. BARIK

Seven states of northeastern India (NE India), Arunachal Pradesh, Assam, Manipur, Meghalaya, Mizoram, Nagaland, and Tripura account for nearly one-fourth of India's forest cover. The region is rich in biodiversity with two of the 34 biodiversity hot spots of the world. It is estimated that at least half of the forests have been under jhum (shifting cultivation). The total forest cover is 170,423 sq km, which is 66.81 per cent of the geographical area and three times greater than the national average of 21.02 per cent. Very dense, moderately dense and open forests constitute 14.64 per cent, 43.42 per cent and 41.94 per cent of the area respectively (FSI 2009). Nearly 34 per cent is 'reserved' forest, 13 per cent 'protected', and 53 per cent 'unclassed'. The unclassed forests are generally under the traditional control or ownership of the tribal communities who have distinct customary practices and unique governance structures for managing their forests and other natural resources.

Since independence, national and state governments have attempted to enforce a set of national development policies, especially relating to the administration of public forest land. The states in NE India continue to present unique situations and challenges. Unlike much of the Indian subcontinent, where forest departments have functioned as state forest managers for over a century, in NE India most state forest departments came into existence only after 1960. While about two-thirds of the region's forests are under the legal authority of local communities, close to 90 per cent of the forests are physically controlled by the rural communities through Indigenous Cultural Institutions (ICIs) or Traditional Village Institutions (TVIs) such as village councils, chieftainships and councils of elders (Palit and Poffenberger 2005).

In general, the objective of traditional management is to protect the forest resources that support collective needs and interests through the involvement of small but homogenous village-level institutions. Community forest management systems have existed in diverse forms throughout NE India for centuries and continue to be the primary mode of forest conservation and protection in the region. This system has also been a key mechanism in guarding the region's immense biodiversity. However, in recent years, many of these systems are under growing external pressure from various forces including industries and the private sector. Besides, cultural change, commercialisation of resources, dominance of market forces, weakening of traditional institutional authority are some of the other factors leading to the deterioration of community forest management systems in the region. As a result, many community-managed resources are increasingly over-exploited, fragmented and degraded leading to major land-use changes in the region. Concurrently, there has been increasing privatisation of communally held forests leading to deforestation, conversion into sedentary agricultural land, mines, commercial species farms and monoculture plantations (Barik and Poffenberger 2005).

There has also been a resurgence of community initiatives in forest conservation and management among various communities in recent years, both through government programmes such as Joint Forest Management (JFM), and the efforts of environmental NGOs such as Nature's Beckon and Aranyak in Assam, Peoples' Group in Nagaland and Young Mizo Association (YMA) in Mizoram. A few externally funded projects such as the Nagaland Environment Protection and Economic Development (NEPED), the Indo-German Development Cooperation participatory natural resource management project in Tripura, and the North Eastern Region Community Resource Management Project for Upland Areas (NERCORMP) funded by the International Fund for Agricultural Development (IFAD) in Meghalaya, Manipur and Assam, have also contributed significantly in this direction. Elsewhere, communities have taken initiatives to rejuvenate and revitalise their own community forests without any external interventions but based on their adverse local experiences of deforestation. The initiation of 'Asha Van' by the Jamatias of Killa in Tripura is an example of such an initiative (Darlong and Barik 2007).

This essay describes some of these diverse community initiatives in forest conservation and management in NE India with particular reference to the experiences and lessons learned from the interventions of the IFAD-supported NERCORMP project in rejuvenating the community initiatives in forest conservation and management. Various management challenges encountered by the communities in achieving economic and livelihood benefits from such conservation practices are also discussed.

Forest Administration

Unlike other regions of the country, the administration of forests in NE India is distributed among the state governments, autonomous district councils (under the Sixth Schedule of the Constitution of India) and the communities. In the absence of a cadastral survey in most hill areas of NE India, the exact areas under various administrative regimes are difficult to ascertain; however, based on available forest data, nearly 45 per cent of the forests of the region are under the government while the remaining 55 per cent, the unclassed forests (Table 14.1), are under the control of various tribal communities.

The extent of community-controlled forests varies greatly among the states; from 91 per cent of state forests in Nagaland, to 33 per cent in Mizoram and Assam (Table 14.2). In Tripura, about 41 per cent of forest is shown as community-controlled, most of which is under JFM; traditional community control is minimal.

The management of both government- and community-controlled forest has suffered in the recent past due to pressure on land, exploitation for timber, decreasing cycle of jhum and lack of scientific management practices. Shifting cultivation in community forests has been an important cause of land degradation in recent years. About 443,336 families in NE India annually cultivate about 3,869 sq km of forests, whereas the minimum total area affected by jhum is believed to be 14,660 sq km (NEC 2002). Other estimates claim about 450,000 families in the region annually cultivate 10,000 sq km of forests and jhum is practised in more than 44,000 sq km of 76,303 sq km of community-controlled forests (Palit and

Table 14.1: Administrative Classification of Forest Areas (in Sq Km) of Northeast India Based on Legal Status

State	Total geographical area	Reserved forest	Protected forest	Unclassed forest	Total recorded forest
Arunachal Pradesh	83,743	15,300	4,200	32,000	51,500
Assam	78,438	18,000	......	8,900	27,000
Manipur	22,327	1,400	4,100	11,800	17,400
Meghalaya	22,429	700	300	8,500	9,500
Mizoram	21,081	7,100	3,600	5,200	15,900
Nagaland	16,579	300	500	7,800	8,600
Tripura	10,486	3,600	500	2,900	7,000
Total	**255,083**	**46,600**	**13,200**	**77,100**	**136,900**
		(34.04%)	(9.64%)	(56.32%)	

Source: Adapted from Poffenberger, M. 2007. *Indigenous Forest Stewards of Northeast India*. California: Community Forestry International, p. 6.

Note: (Figures in Parentheses Represent the Percentage of Total)

Table 14.2: Proportion of Forest Lands under Community Control

State	% of forest to total geographical area (after FSI 2009)	% of forest under community control (after Poffenberger 2007)
Arunachal Pradesh	80.43	62
Assam	35.30	33
Manipur	77.40	68
Meghalaya	77.23	90
Mizoram	91.27	33
Nagaland	81.21	91
Tripura	76.95	41*

Source: FSI. 2009. *State of Forest Report 2009*. Forest Survey of India, MoEF, Dehradun, p. 18; and Poffenberger, M. 2007. *Indigenous Forest Stewards of Northeast India*. California: Community Forestry International, p. 13.

Note: *Includes certain areas under Joint Forest Management (JFM).

Poffenberger 2005). Degraded secondary forests, bamboo thickets and weeds or simply poorly vegetated near-barren land dominate today's 'jhumscapes' in many parts of NE India.

Although much remains to be achieved through the JFM approach in NE India, community conservation efforts have received a significant boost under the Forest Development Agency (FDA) in recent years. The persistent efforts of various environmental NGOs, civil society organisations, and externally funded projects have resulted in renewed interest among the communities in terms of forest and biodiversity conservation. Meanwhile, the importance of community involvement in forest management has gained widespread acceptance in the forest sector globally. It is critical to support and strengthen community initiatives in NE India where the vast majority of upland forests are legally owned by rural communities through the stewardships of their traditional village institutions. While many of these forest and biodiversity conservation and management systems are time-tested, several other community initiatives in forest conservation and management are fairly recent in origin and are evolving.

Community Initiatives in Forest and Biodiversity Conservation

The tribal communities of NE India traditionally lived in and around forests which were extremely biodiversity rich. Their live-lihoods were greatly dependant on forests and local biodiversity for food, fodder and various social, economic and religious needs. Forests were also protected and enriched around the villages for defence from enemies, besides securing environmental services like water, edible plants, honey, construction materials, medicinal and dye plants. These processes led to the development of dif-ferent categories of community-conserved areas across the tribes and regions. Some of the significant historical and contemporary community initiatives in forest and biodiversity conservation and management practices in NE India are summarised in Table 14.3.

Most of these conservation initiatives reflect the success of cooperation between the people, government and NGOs. All the traditional forest conservation practices were the initiatives of communities themselves. Only the recent conservation practices were introduced through the government, NGOs or specific projects like NERCORMP-IFAD, NEPED and IGDC.

A remarkable feature of the Khasi Hills are the sacred forests, like the Mawphlang Sacred Forest in the East Khasi Hills, about 25 km from Shillong. The Mawphlang sacred grove is considered to be at least 600 years old though the forest itself could be much older. Although many community leaders no longer practise traditional religion, yet the community's collective wisdom protects the sacred grove for its cultural values. The grove has amazing plants, flowering trees, ferns, orchids and varieties of butterflies and

Table 14.3: Categories of Traditional and Recent Initiatives in Community-conserved Areas

A. TRADITIONAL PRACTICES

1. Conservation based on religious beliefs: Sacred groves (Meghalaya, Assam, Manipur, Arunachal Pradesh); Sacred landscape (Tripura, e.g., Longtrai Hill Range)

2. Conservation based on village needs: Village safety and supply forest reserves (Mizoram); *Asha Van* (Forest of Hope, of the Jamatias, Tripura)

3. Conservation based on agro-ecosystem/agro-forestry practices: Alder-based jhum (Nagaland); Apatani agro-forestry practices (Arunachal Pradesh); Home gardens agro-forestry (various tribes)

B. RECENT INITIATIVES

4. Conservation based on government-people partnership: 'Anchal' Forest Reserves (Arunachal Pradesh); 'Apna Van' (Arunachal Pradesh); JFM community forest reserves (all NE states)

5. Conservation based on NGO initiatives: Kharsati Wildlife Reseve (Meghalaya); Chakrasila Wildlife Sanctuary (Assam); YMA Forest Reserves (Mizoram); Nature Conservation and Tragopan Sanctuary (Khonoma village, Nagaland)

6. Conservation based on externally funded and government initiatives for biodiversity and livelihoods: NEPED's Tree Farmings/Village Reserves/agro-forests (Nagaland); NERCOMP-IFAD's community forest/community biodiversity conservation initiatives (Assam, Manipur and Meghalaya); IGDC Community Biodiversity Conservation Areas (North Tripura and Dhalai)

Source: Compiled from the presentation by V. T. Darlong on 'Community's initiatives in forest conservation and management in Northeast India' in the national seminar on Community Forestry Management in India, ICFRE, Dehradun, 2007.

insects; it is virtually nature's own museum, dominated by *Quercus* (oak) and *Castonopsis* trees, heavy with epiphytic aroids, pipers, ferns, fern-allies, and orchids. The ground is covered with thick humus accumulated over decades harbouring a myriad specimens of plant life, which may not be found elsewhere. Life scientists and students consider it a place of botanical pilgrimage and it has been studied in detail (Barik 2010; Tiwari et al. 1999).

Another successful community initiative is the Asha Van. A case study of Toirupha village near Killa in south Tripura showed how the Jamatias (a dominant tribal group in Tripura) have regenerated the Daikong Bolong (traditional community forest). Since the early 1970s, the women began to protect and manage over 300 ha of forest which they now call Asha Van, Forest of Hope (Darlong and Barik 2007).

Recent documentation (Pathak et al. 2008) showed that large areas have been conserved as forest and wildlife reserves in Nagaland by various tribes, with over 100 villages (such as Khonoma, Luzuphuhu, Chizami, and Sendenyu) managing several hundred square kilometres of forests as community forests, community-conserved areas or community wildlife sanctuaries. These efforts often involve the integration of customary and official law, sometimes even the granting of full legal ownership over a community-conserved area. In Tokpa Kabui village in Churachandpur District, Manipur, 600 ha of regenerated village forest have been preserved in the Loktak Lake catchment by the Rongmei tribe. These unofficial protected areas provide a critical refuge for many endangered birds, including Blyth's tragopan, Grey sibia, Beautiful sibia, Grey peacock pheasant, Rufous-necked hornbill, and White-naped yuhina. Villagers also report sighting other rare species in their village forest, including the Spotted linsang, Tiger, Leopard, Wild dog, Stump-tailed macaque, and Asiatic black bear.

The Project: Forest and Biodiversity Conservation

The North Eastern Region Community Resource Management Project for Upland Areas (NERCORMP) was a joint initiative of the Government of India and International Fund for Agricultural Development (IFAD), a specialised agency of the United Nations, based in Rome, for agricultural development. The North Eastern Council (NEC) under the Ministry of the Development of North Eastern Region (DoNER) represents the Government of India; the United Nations Office for Project Services (UNOPS) based in Bangkok acted as the cooperating institution for this project. NERCORMP-IFAD was initiated in 1999 and ended in 2008. The project also cooperated with various technical, research and knowledge-generating institutions or organisations such as International Centre for Integrated Mountain Development (ICIMOD), Kathmandu, for technical support; International Development Research Centre (IDRC), New Delhi, for knowledge sharing; and Centre for International Forestry Research (CIFOR), Bogor, Indonesia, for research input in development, particularly in the areas of forests and livelihoods. The North Eastern Hill University, Shillong, also participated in its baseline and endline surveys and environmental impact assessments.

The overall objective of the project was 'to improve the livelihood of vulnerable groups in a sustainable manner through improved management of their resource base in a way that contributes to protecting and restoring the environment'. The project adopted a holistic approach with two broad focus areas: (*a*) Social mobilisation, organisation and capacity building to tap and realise the inherent latent potential of the communities employing time-tested traditional value systems; and (*b*) Economic and social interventions and village infrastructure; predominantly income-generating activities (IGAs).

The project operated in six districts: Karbi Anglong and North Cachar Hills (Assam); Senapati and Ukhrul (Manipur); and West Garo Hills and West Khasi Hills (Meghalaya). The project included 860 villages with 39,196 households covering 19 major tribes. The project management functioned through a Regional Society with a Professional Support Unit (PSU) in the Project HQ in Shillong and District Societies with a Development Support Team (DST) in the respective district HQ. Partner NGOs in each district assisted the DST for project deliveries to the communities.

The project is now being jointly re-financed by IFAD and Government of India (North Eastern Council) as NERCORMP-II to cover 400 more villages in the same six districts, and 20,000 more households. The project will run until 2015 (NERCORMP 2009).

Project Initiatives

Among the many objectives of the project was 'to promote biodiversity preservation and conservation ' through social mobilisation, awareness education and serious dialogue between the traditional village institutions and the project-induced community institutions, that is, Natural Resource Management Groups (NaRMGs). Effective linkages with various line departments, particularly the state forest departments, helped to achieve the objectives.

NERCORMP initiated a wide range of integrated natural resource management promoting community-based forest and biodiversity conservation, rejuvenation and restoration of existing village-reserved forests. Although the communities had traditionally protected local forests, these were in severe stages of degradation, fragmentation and mismanagement. Through the project interventions, many of the pristine forest patches, degraded forest areas located in critical water catchments areas, jhum fallow re-growths dominated by bamboo, thatch, broom, and other Non-timber Forest Product (NTFP) resources, etc. have been brought under community-based forest conservation and management. By 2008, 1,837 sq km (Table 14.4) of forest area was under community forest and biodiversity conservation. The NaRMGs, in collaboration with the village authorities or traditional village councils, took the necessary initiatives in rejuvenating and enhancing the community forest and biodiversity conservation and management. In many villages, the women's SHGs also played direct and indirect roles in such initiatives.

The district-wise various categories of community forest and biodiversity conservation areas collectively termed 'community conserved areas' (CCAs) continue to be judiciously exploited by the communities with rules and regulations, particularly for the collection of NTFPs (Table 14.5).

The notable CCAs are given in Table 14.6. Most are traditional village-reserved forests that were either formalised (i.e., entrusted to the NaRMGs) or rejuvenated. In some cases, the rules and regulations for the protection and management of CCAs were

Table 14.4: Total Area of Community-conserved Forests

State	Districts	No. of participating villages	Community forest conservation area (in sq km)
Meghalaya	West Garo Hills	192	600
	West Khasi Hills	162	253
Manipur	Senapati	106	331
	Ukhrul	103	436
Assam	Karbi Anglong	166	140
	N.C. Hills	131	77
	Total	**860**	**1837**

Source: Compiled from the *Annual Status Report of NERCORMP*, 2007–08, Shillong.

Table 14.5: Categories of Community Forest Conservation Initiatives in the Project

Districts	Categories of community forest conservation initiatives
West Garo Hills	Village Forest Reserves
	Water Catchments Reserves
	Village Bamboo Reserves
	Village Broom Grass Reserves
	Village Thatch Grass Reserves
	Wildlife and Elephant Corridor Reserves
	Stream Bank Cum Riverine Fish Pool Reserves
West Khasi Hills	Village Forest Reserves
	Community Pine Forest Reserves
Senapati	Village Community Reserved Forest
	Community Fuel and Timber Reserves
	Village Sacred Groves
	Community Germplasm Forest Reserves
Ukhrul	Village Reserved Forest
	Water Catchments Reserves
	Wildlife Reserves
	Bamboo Reserves
	Green Belt Reserves
	Wild Goose berry reserves
Karbi Anglong	Community Forest Reserves
	Water Catchments Reserves
	Village NTFP Reserves
	Community Bamboo Reserves
	Community Broom Reserves
	Streamline Protection Reserves
	Village Sacred Groves
N.C. Hills	Community Mixed Forest Reserves
	Community Bamboo Reserves
	Community Water Catchments Reserves

Source: Adapted from the *Annual Status Report of NERCORMP*, 2007–08, Shillong.

Table 14.6: Successful Community-conserved Areas under the Project

State	District	Village/Tribe	Area (sq km)	Year
Manipur	Senapati	Upper Ngatan (Maram)	4.00	2004
	Ukhrul	Ngainga (Tangkhul)	23.00	2002
Assam	N.C. Hills	New Kubing (Zeme)	6.00	2002
	Karbi Anglong	Kawrakrai (Karbi)	7.00	2003
Meghalaya	West Garo Hills	Rombagre (Garo)	8.00	2002
	West Garo Hills	Marakhapara (Garo)	6.00	2001
	West Khasi Hills	Nongpdeng (Khasi)	0.48	2004

Source: Unpublished internal Study Report of NERCORMP on Community Based Biodiversity Conservation, Shillong, 2008.

refined. For example, the New Kubing village in North Cachar Hills had a village-reserved forest since the 1950s but this was severely degraded. The project facilitated rejuvenation and protection; today, it has been restored and the community has made rules regulating the collection of NTFPs. Similarly, the traditional village-reserved forest in Ngainga in Ukhrul district was entrusted to the NaRMG with the concurrence of the village authorities for protection, management and restoration.

In the West Garo Hills district, Meghalaya, notably in the buffer zone areas of the Nokrek Biosphere Reserve, the project has been able to create a network of community-conserved areas in 33 villages. This network of forests represents about 5,567.28 ha of community-conserved areas. These estimates are based on sample surveys done with the Forest Department of the Garo Hills Autonomous District Council and the project team based at Tura, Meghalaya. The communities have started appreciating the benefits of these CCAs in improving the local environment and the availability of NTFPs, particularly edible vegetables, mushrooms, small timbers, bamboo shoots, leaves for packaging, and honey. In many villages the communities have reported significant reduction in the frequency of elephant depredation in their jhum fields and home gardens due to better forest cover surrounding the villages, which indicates improved availability of food plants for the elephants. Further, a number of communities have reported increased additional income through the sales of various forest products. The communities have also reported overall reduction in jhum areas under their respective villages due to increased awareness and benefits of forest conservation. The neighbouring non-project villages have also started restoring or rejuvenating their community or village-reserved forests.

Process of Community Mobilisation

The process of community mobilisation taken up by NERCORMP-IFAD was either for demarcation of new community-conserved areas or the restoration/revitalisation of existing ones.

Community forest management practices or management of village-reserved forests were not new to the communities that NERCORMP was working with. The novelty was in the process: the constitution of NaRMGs and their involvement in the village development planning, implementation and monitoring, including activities to protect and improve their natural resources, local forests and biodiversity, with the collaboration of village authorities or traditional village institutions.

The NaRMGs together with traditional village institutions managed the village-reserve forests and water catchments areas; the primary motivation for conservation was livelihood as the communities expected to benefit from the continuous availability of forest products to meet their needs. They framed rules and regulations for forest management; characteristics of typical rules and regulations were preventive, prohibitive, punitive, facilitative, and regulatory in nature; among many communities this was simple codification of customary practices on forest and natural resource management. NaRMGs, with support from traditional village institutions, implemented the rules and regulations. In some cases, sub-committees or sub-groups were formed exclusively to look after the conservation, protection and management of community/village-reserved forests. The NaRMGs conducted meetings every month to discuss various aspects of project interventions and activities being taken up by the members, including conservation and management of village forest reserves or community biodiversity conservation areas. The project provided direct funding for raising bamboo nurseries, broom grass plantations, wild arum plantations in the jhum and fallow land to meet the demand or requirements of forest produce so that the villagers create less pressure on village-protected forests. The project adopted a participatory bottom-up planning approach for these activities. The project extensively promoted home gardens for growing seasonal vegetables and developed agro-forestry models to create less pressure on their community-conserved forests. In some districts, notably in the N.C. Hills, the project was successful in linking the communities with existing JFM programmes of the government; this has strengthened the process of community forest conservation and management systems. The small amount of funds made available from the forest department through the JFM was used for various entry point activities by the communities.

Challenges and Opportunities

Community initiatives for forest and biodiversity conservation and management faced several challenges as well as opportunities. Sustainable management required a continuous process of social mobilisation for awareness, education, motivation, and conviction. While this was undertaken by partner NGOs, the tasks were gradually transferred to the respective NaRMGs in the concerned villages. The process involved: PRA exercise for resource mapping and land capability assessment with the communities; studies of traditional institutions, particularly land-use patterns and systems together with continuous interactions and dialogue with the traditional village institutions/authorities; and Natural Resource Management (NRM) sensitisation for the NaRMGs and SHGs. The NaRMGs were federated into an association and the SHGs were grouped as federations; the tasks of sensitisation were taken up by these bodies. Comprehensive forest management and/or biodiversity conservation trainings were organised by the project in collaboration with the state forest department, local NGOs and educational institutions. Community education and training on the decision-making process on NRM were undertaken through participatory land-use planning using 3-dimensional models in some villages. Farmer to farmer exchange/community exchange programmes/exposure tours within the district or outside were also organised to learn the forest management practices. Special focus was given to women in all the training programmes on forest and biodiversity conservation and management.

Forest conservation was linked to overall livelihoods such as availability of foods and feeds, as well as ecological services such as availability of water. This approach triggered greater interest in the conservation of forest and biodiversity, and also helped in the sustainable harvesting of forest products.

Community Forest Management
with Participatory Rules and Regulations

Sustainable management of community forests and biodiversity reserves was a serious challenge, which the communities addressed through various means:

- Framing and enforcing rules and regulations by the NaRMGs in consultation with the village authorities. In some villages, the youth were part of the protection force.
- Focusing on biodiversity conservation and forest management issues in the monthly meetings of the NaRMGs and their federations.
- Conducting special half-yearly meetings of the NaRMGs, as in the N.C. Hills, or assigning a day in a year as 'NRM Awakening Day' as in Ukhrul district, to deliberate on various developmental activities taken up by the groups, including management of community forests, protected areas and other NRM issues.
- Identifying key forest-user groups or forest-dependent groups within the NaRMG members and sharing responsibilities to protect forests.
- Prohibiting and strictly enforcing rules and regulations for non-forestry activities like jhum, and illegal felling of trees in the community-reserved forest areas.
- Building linkages with the forest department for technical support and financial assistance.

As mentioned earlier, in some districts, notably in N.C. Hills and West Garo Hills, the project funded bamboo nurseries, broom plantations, and wild arum plantations in jhum areas and homestead gardens in order to enhance the availability of these resources outside the common protected areas and thereby reducing collection pressures on the community conservation areas; in other districts, such as West Khasi Hills, planting materials were obtained from the State Forest Department. It also strengthened the existing village institutions by registering these as Joint Forest Management Committees (JFMC), as in the N.C. Hills district in Assam. In order to secure legal and customary rights, the community forests were registered under the District Council Forest Acts/Rules and Regulations (in Garo Hills). Such efforts also helped linkages with the officials of the Autonomous District Council.

The community-based forest and biodiversity conservation and management rules and regulations were far-sighted and practical. Although many were simple 'do's and don'ts', they included features that were preventive, prohibitive, punitive, appreciative (giving recognition and rewards), extractive (sustainable harvesting), regenerative (emphasis on forest regeneration), facilitative (of harvesting by the poorer sections of the village) and explorative (seeking convergence and assistance from government programmes). Most of these regulations were in local dialects: No villager would jhum in the demarcated community forest or biodiversity conservation areas. Extraction, harvesting or cutting of any plant/tree in the protected areas and catchment areas was prohibited. Persons violating these rules were fined up to ₹1,000 (or more). If unable to pay, a domestic animal (pig or buffalo or cattle) was confiscated for auctioning. Proper fire lines during burning and slashing of jhum were mandatory for every household. Anyone deliberately causing a forest fire was fined ₹1,000 or more.

The period of jhum burning was to be discussed and decided during the NaRMG meeting. Every household would burn jhum only during the specified period. Protecting community forest areas from deliberate or accidental fires was the duty and responsibility of every member or household in the village. Planting economic timber species and plants in fallow land and homestead gardens by every household was encouraged. Protection and conservation of flora and fauna within the village boundary, particularly in the demarcated village-reserved forests, was ensured; any person violating the rules and regulations would be fined heavily (at least ₹1,000) and repeat violators would be expelled from the village. The practices of protecting and conserving abandoned jhum land for at least 10 years for regeneration were adopted by certain villages in the N.C. Hills and Ukhrul district.

NTFPs, particularly wild vegetables and medicinal plants, were collected primarily for self-consumption and not for large-scale trade without disturbing the other components of vegetation. Of late, it has been observed that a number of communities have relaxed the rules for collection of wild vegetables, particularly wild banana flowers, as these are abundantly available. The conservation initiatives helped many poorer families collect and trade in these vegetables in the local weekly markets.

Cutting of timber for house construction was allowed only from un-protected areas with the permission of the NaRMG and the traditional village institution; harvesting of timber from community forest areas was done with proper preparation of a management and harvesting plan in consultation with the State Forest Department. Firewood was collected from outside the conservation/protected areas. Only naturally dead wood or dead branches were to be collected as firewood from protected areas with the supervision of appropriate authorities in the village.

Periodic review meetings were held to discuss the forest management and biodiversity conservation activities, including effectiveness of the rules and regulations. No one from outside the village/community was permitted to enter into the village-protected or -reserved forest. For proper management of the common properties, Forest Protection Committees were constituted in many villages with the *Gaobura* (village headman) as president. This was enforced in N.C. Hills and Karbi Anglong villages. Youth (and Church elders) were involved as much as possible in these processes. Women, particularly members of SHGs, were actively engaged in many villages in the protection and regulation of harvesting of forest products from community forest reserves. Rewards were given to the persons who reported illegal acts committed in the community forest and biodiversity conservation areas.

ACCESS AND BENEFITS SHARING

The NRM sensitisation programmes for the communities also included the issues of equitable access, rights and benefit sharing mechanisms for all the members/stakeholders of the communities, particularly the poorest and marginalised. The communities were also made aware of the tangible benefits and intangible benefits from such conservation practices and encouraged to evaluate these benefits collectively in their meetings, which in turn could trigger more serious conservation and sustainable management practices.

Direct or tangible benefits recognised by the communities include:

- Collection of NTFPs (e.g., bamboo, broom, bamboo shoot, mushroom, wild edibles fruit, vegetables, honey, roots, and tubers) for consumption and selling in the local market for additional income.
- Collection of firewood and small timber (for house construction and for use as agricultural implements).
- Collection of feeds and fodder for domestic animals.
- Availability of water throughout the year for agricultural and households requirements.
- Additional income generation from forest resources.
- Employment livelihood generation.
- Sources of raw materials for handicrafts (bamboo), and woodcrafts (wood/timber).

The importance of forest conservation was also discussed and intangible benefits recognised, such as:

- Increase in water retention capacity of the land and hence better plant growth.
- Prevention of soil erosion thereby increased soil fertility.
- Increase in vegetative cover in barren and degraded lands.
- Change in local climatic conditions.
- Forests close to paddy fields and terraced fields acted as nutrient sinks, and also harboured beneficial insects and pollinators for the crops. Such forests also harboured predators for insect pests. This included birds and other predator insects.

Additional benefits as perceived and experienced by the communities in project villages due to the promotion of community-reserved forests and biodiversity management include: greater awareness of the need and benefit of forest and biodiversity conservation with increasing efforts to promote such conservation practices. The communities realised the importance of improved agro-forestry practices and land-use practices to enhance both their livelihood and daily needs from the forests. There was a

greater effort towards adopting soil and water conservation practices and a visible change in mindset among the communities
towards permanent settled cultivation as shifting cultivation was
no longer remunerative in most situations. However, the changes
from communally held land for jhum to privatisation of land with
settled agriculture or horticulture had different challenges in terms
of social justice and equity in land access. Economic improvement
and greater food security were achieved through various land-
based and off-farm activities. There was a visible improvement of
local environment, land and water resources, and greater social
cohesiveness to address these issues.

Besides providing better livelihood, conservation efforts and
collective decision-making processes helped the villagers in
bringing greater peace, unity and harmony. Conflicts over natural
resources (both inter-village and intra-village) were remarkably
reduced; communities were more often able to appreciate the
values of common property resources and sustainable applications
of integrated NRM practices. People's experiences of climate
variability and consequences (e.g., less or irregular rain, more
severe water scarcity in winter and dry seasons, increased incidence
of pests and diseases both for crops and livestock) were compelling
the communities to think and act together more often than earlier.
They also appreciated the need for expert advice as and when
required.

COOPERATION BETWEEN PROJECT AND NON-PROJECT VILLAGES

There were several examples where there was increased cooperation between project and non-project villages through community
initiatives in forest conservation. One such example is from West
Garo Hills where eight project villages and 10 surrounding non-
project villages came together. The Simsang river passes through
all these villages. The NaRMGs from the project villages and the
traditional institutions from non-project villages (under the aegis
of the Chinabat Cluster Association) decided to protect selected
stretches of the river and river-bank forests as community-conserved areas.

Similarly, the project promoted community forests or community-
conserved areas in 33 villages within the Nokrek Biosphere Reserve

in Garo Hills. These villages subsequently influenced the other non-project villages in creating similar community-conserved forests in neighbouring areas to improve the habitat for the migrating elephant population and thereby reduce the human–animal conflicts in many of these villages.

GENDER BALANCE

The project made special efforts to address the concerns of the women in the community forests and biodiversity conservation initiative. Local ecosystem-specific wild vegetables, grains, animal, fish, and other biological products and resources contributed to local food and nutritional security. In their traditional roles, women have been especially mindful about the contribution of biodiversity to household food and nutrition. They were also concerned about the dwindling availability of firewood in their immediate surroundings, besides the drying up of natural springs that provide drinking water. Prior to the project intervention, women's participation in NRM was lacking. The project identified the following constraints: As social values, attitudes and strategies were still traditional, women concentrated more on domestic activities – securing household food and water, fodder for domestic animals, firewood – and on their children's health and education, besides non-land-based income-generating activities. Because of illiteracy, superstitions and taboos based on cultural and traditional beliefs, overall backwardness and low economic status, women were unable to work their way out of poverty. Women's aptitude was generally oriented towards better and sustainable biodiversity conservation, yet they lacked space and voice within the communities. Male domination in the forestry sector and biodiversity conservation processes had kept women away from effective participation and decision making.

To overcome the constraints on women's participation, the project involved women in all the forestry and biodiversity awareness training programmes. Forest-based livelihoods and the need to protect and conserve natural resources were a key agenda of SHG meetings. In all the institutions 50 per cent membership was for women and at least 33 per cent of the executive committee of the NaRMGs were women. Most NaRMG meetings frequently discussed issues relating to women's concerns such as firewood, wild edible plants, mushroom, bamboo shoots, and drinking water. In many villages, women were members of the forest protection committees.

Women also decided the kinds of species to be planted in their homestead gardens and jhum areas and they were the active preservers of seeds. Women were the main collectors, processors and sellers of NTFPs, particularly edible plants and mushrooms from the community-conserved areas.

PERSPECTIVE PLANNING

The project mobilised and motivated the communities to pre-pare community perspective plans on forest and biodiversity conservation and management. The reflections on the synthesis of various perspective plans and subsequent plan outputs may be summarised as follows: Most villages planned to bring more degraded areas or jhum under forest cover and community-con-served areas. There was an attempt to rationalise and optimise land-use clearing only minimum land. Good community-based fire management strategies were practised so that jhum fires do not escape and burn nearby forest areas. Fruit-bearing and nitro-gen-fixing trees were planted along with the traditional crops in the jhum. Economically valuable NTFP species (bamboo, Indian gooseberry, tree bean, drumstick, bay leaf) were planted along with the jhum crop and in abandoned jhum land. Terracing and bunding across the slope, and in horticultural farms, were done to conserve soil and water. Various off-farm activities such as bee-keeping, petty businesses, weaving, etc. were promoted to reduce pressure on forests and local biodiversity. Conservation and management of local wilderness and wildscapes were planned to ensure the availability of flowering plants throughout the year for improved bee-farming. Attempts were made to conserve common village land with good forest cover and/or to restore the degraded lands with the assistance of the local forest depart-ment; the villagers did not promote any non-forestry activities in such areas. The rules and regulations were framed for regulative or sustainable harvesting of forest resources, particularly NTFPs from their protected or conservation areas; focus was on regen-eration of degraded forests under community control. The com-munities established linkages with line departments and financial institutions to improve conservation. Terrace fields and home gardens were promoted.

In order to realise these perspective plans, the communities expected sustained financial, technical, institutional, and other support from project authorities and the government (even after project closure): Financial assistance for conservation and reforestation; technical support and knowledge in forestry management (particularly for training-cum-exposure visits to successful conservation sites within and outside the region); training in value additions and skill development along with marketing support on biodiversity/forestry-based livelihood activities; formal recognition of community efforts on forest and biodiversity conservation; support for preparing forest working schemes, specially for harvesting timber from community or village forest reserves, besides new and modern farming practices that are suitable to upland areas and that could replace jhum, augment jhum productivity, produce more crops in a given area, and introduce high-value low-volume crops that could be more remunerative, etc.

EMERGING ROLE OF NGOS AND MEDIA IN COMMUNITY EDUCATION AND DEVELOPMENT

The project sponsored young local journalists and media professionals to visit project villages, become more sensitive to the local issues, strategies and development interventions vis-à-vis environmental management, learn about impacts of project interventions and community initiatives in forest and biodiversity conservation and management. They were to report on their experiences in the local newspapers and local media to communicate about the project to society at large. When people read their own stories in local newspapers or heard them on the local Doordarshan channel (TV), they were further encouraged and motivated to do better in their efforts for forest and biodiversity conservation and management.

The partner NGOs who had worked with NERCORMP for project implementations are today champions of environmental education, community forest management, and community biodiversity conservation. Quite a number continue to work with the communities.

Success Indicators of Community Initiatives

Several indicators of success and sustainability of community forest conservation initiatives and management have emerged in many project villages. NaRMGs were advised to use these indicators to evaluate the success of their own respective conservation efforts. Ecological success indicators included visible regeneration and improved quality of community-conserved forest areas, thereby ensuring returns of many of the native wildlife, birds and fish in the local streams and rivers; significant improvement in water retention, discharge and availability for drinking and irrigation; increasing areas under the control of the village authorities and community-based institutions; improved availability of native NTFPs including firewood, fodder, roots, tubers, honey, edible, medicinal and aromatic plants, dyes, etc. in the project villages; and improved vegetation along the protected river banks.

Economic success indicators included easy access and improved availability of construction materials, firewood, NTFPs, wild edible plants, etc.; higher household incomes from sales of NTFPs (bamboo, thatch, broom, mushroom, honey, etc.) and from the sale of wild edible plants and other produce in the local weekly markets; more road-side *haats* (temporary markets) for local forest and home garden produce; increased fish resources in the protected stretches and higher fish catches down-stream. Overall food and nutritional security of the households improved.

Social success depends on community forests and biodiversity conservation becoming a community 'movement' rather than a compulsory government intervention, with communities outside the project area too being influenced to create such conservation areas in their villages. Indicators included reduced incidence of human–animal conflicts in some pockets of Garo Hills (where elephant corridors and reserves have been created); fewer intra- and inter-village conflicts over natural resources; less drudgery for women in collecting firewood, drinking water and wild edible plants as testified by the women themselves; reduction in children's malnutrition and women's anaemia, enhancing household well-being. Increased community appreciation of the tangible and intangible benefits of forest reserves and good social agreement between traditional institutions and NaRMGs, and improved forest and biodiversity management regulations facilitated addressing equity in access and benefit-sharing of the poorest households and women.

Lessons Learnt

The experiences of NERCORMP-IFAD in promoting community-based forest and biodiversity conservation and management have begun to show signs of transformation and integrated development processes among the communities, particularly livelihoods improvement through improved forest and biodiversity conservation and management.

Apart from the professional experiences of the project team to mobilise the communities through a series of trainings, the project's financial investment has been minimal in promoting the community forest and biodiversity conservation and management. Creation or development of a network of community-conserved areas across 1,800 sq km in six districts in three states is a big gain.

Community mobilisation and motivation process has to be a continuous endeavour if community conservation and management is to be sustained. Building community institutions and capacity require constant attention. Though community institutions are not new, project interventions were most effective when various community-based institutions like NaRMG (which also acts as a village development agency in close consultation with the self-help groups) emerged. Some of the visible changes that have taken place are as follows:

- Through the NaRMGs and SHGs, the project impacted the development thought processes among the communities. Unity among the villagers has become stronger; they now think and act together for common goods and benefits.
- Decision making is no longer confined to the village headman or elite members of the traditional village institutions but the whole village participates in the process.
- These institutions are bestowed with the responsibility of planning and implementation of various developmental activities as well as judicious management of available resources.

- Operating bank accounts and handling cash/finance has given them a new experience, particularly with the values of thrift and savings for their own prosperity.
- Accountability and transparency have been strengthened through proper management of records and regular meetings, and also auditing processes.
- The participation of women in decision-making processes has increased but needs to be encouraged further among many sections of the communities.
- Forest and biodiversity conservation are becoming increasing areas of focus by many of the community institutions, as well as traditional village authorities.
- Appropriate facilitation is needed in order to create space for voices of the women.
- To achieve all these, appropriate nurturing, mentoring and hand holding is essential by the project team and partner NGOs.

INCREASED COMMUNITY APPRECIATION AND AWARENESS OF CONSERVATION

Although village- or community-reserved forests is not a new idea among many communities in NE India, many communities of the region traditionally or primarily perceived this practice for the purpose of shifting cultivation or jhum or hunting. When the project brought in new ideas and orientation to forest conservation particularly linking with biodiversity, water availability and other environmental services, the communities' enthusiasm in the processes became much more proactive. By then, many of the communities were already experiencing the problems of water scarcity, firewood availability, problems of non-availability of construction materials, wild edible plants, small animals for food, and so on.

When these new approaches and orientations were discussed with the indigenous community institutions and the NaRMGs, the communities in many villages were more than willing to rejuvenate or revive their traditional practices of village-reserved forests. As a result, the communities are now more aware of the importance and values of conserving natural resources in the villages. Though often the communities are not able to state how much area is to be conserved, they are now more than convinced that more forests mean more opportunities for their livelihoods.

Prior to the project intervention, the villagers had never heard of biodiversity conservation. Now they are thrilled to hear the word 'biodiversity', as it conveys to them everything (plants and animals in the forests, fish in the river, crops in the jhum fields, terraces and home gardens) that they need for their sustenance, including for the future of their children and grandchildren. Materials required for the construction of their houses and shelter for their domestic animals also come from conservation of biodiversity. So also the fodder needs for their domestic animals or plants required for the cure of certain ailments. Many communities are also well aware that materials needed for their religious rituals that they have to collect from their forests are all the gift of their local biodiversity.

However, the practice of jhum cultivation still remains one of the main sources of livelihood in many villages, though the scenario is changing gradually with the effective interventions of NERCORMP. Alternatives provided through the project interventions are yielding the desired results, that is, reduction in jhum and increased forest cover in many villages. These forest reserves are being maintained as per customary practices or have been registered or are in the process of registration under the District Council Forest Acts as in West Garo Hills, which give them both customary and legal rights.

Positive Impact on Reducing Jhum

Livelihood activities are now collectively addressed by the NaRMGs, SHGs and individual households much more vigorously and sustainably. Revolving funds and grants for various income-generating activities and social benefits (drinking water supply, low-cost latrines, inter-village road improvement, orchard development, etc.) have given them wider choices for improved livelihood activities.

Jhum cultivation remains the main source of livelihood. However, the jhum area has greatly reduced by about 40–60 per cent in most villages. As a result, the jhum cycle of four–five years has become at least seven–nine years in many villages. The cultivation system of minimum tillage with no irrigation facilities still remains unchanged with few options for technical intervention and other soil and water conservation measures. Comparative analysis of the input–output ratio of jhum and terrace crops needs to be undertaken to convince villagers about the benefits of optimising jhum practices. Interventions in jhum practices have extended the cropping phase from the traditional one year to two years or more by introducing nitrogen-fixing cover crops in the second or third year. Extensive promotion of traditional agri-horticulture crops, mainly vegetables, with appropriate interventions for marketing and transport, has significantly improved the cash income from jhum. There is a continuous expansion of terrace fields in the villages. Paddy is the main crop, sown only once with the land being rested for the remaining period of the year. The farmers have experienced better paddy yield in terraces as compared to jhum. Terrace production systems are being linked with minor irrigation systems and short-gestation high-yielding varieties to enable cultivation twice a year, off-season vegetable cultivation in terraces, etc. But the attempt to introduce two-season paddy cultivation has not picked up as the practice involved too much labour in the midst of labour-shortages among many communities. The introduction of perennial horticultural crops in jhum areas is transforming the household economies, resulting in increased annual income and savings of the households. The promotion of fishery, apiculture, sericulture, coupled with non-farm-based activities has improved livelihood opportunities. Home gardens have also yielded significantly higher cash incomes for many households in most of the project villages, besides improving their nutrition from the vegetables grown.

WOMEN'S EMPOWERMENT AND PARTICIPATION

The project interventions, particularly through forest and bio-diversity conservation initiatives, have facilitated women's participation in development processes in general. The women have become more aware of the linkages between improved health, nutrition and sanitation and conservation and management of forests, biodiversity and other natural resources. It has meant direct and easy access to firewood, wild food and fodder plants, etc., besides improved availability of quality drinking water for the communities. The voices of women are also becoming louder in decision-making processes in the communities. In general, they have developed better communication skills and become more confident in public speaking. Moving beyond traditional activities related to the kitchen, family and jhum fields, many women have now started taking up responsible positions in community-based organisations like the NaRMGs. The training for women on various livelihood opportunities including kitchen gardens, food processing, accounts management, etc. has transformed them into more empowered and confident individuals.

Particularly the mobilisation and organisation of women as SHGs has given them new vistas in society. Their ability to discuss freely among themselves about women's issues and development needs has been altogether a new experience for them. They are also transferring their knowledge and experience to their children/daughters and daughters-in-law as junior or second-generation SHGs. They feel that each household is now a new transformed unit with better cleanliness, hygiene, childcare, improved nutritional level, etc. Interventions such as low cost latrines in the villages which require water, generally provided by the women, has made the women more proactive in forest conservation initiatives as forest protection improves water availability in the villages. The availability of revolving funds and credit opportunities has given the women new responsibilities, besides improving their livelihoods, income, savings, and above all, the total family resource capital. There is significant decrease in domestic violence against women in the households. Disparity between the women in terms of their income is also reducing, as they are able to help each other through the SHGs.

IMPROVED LIVELIHOOD OPPORTUNITIES

Forest and biodiversity conservation and management can only be practical and acceptable if it also results in improved income and livelihoods for the communities. The first priority of all villages is water and catchment reserves to secure constant and good water supply for drinking and minor irrigation, which in turn increases crop production and food security. Besides these, community forests or village-reserved forests linked with bamboo, cane and timber reserves are also becoming increasingly popular because of the direct benefits for livelihoods and improved income. It is important that any conservation efforts should be directly linked to livelihoods.

Effective Networking through
Conservation Initiatives

Since the initiation of the project in these villages, the community mobilisation and capacity-building activities have been directed towards securing greater linkages with various line departments and development agencies (agriculture, horticulture, soil conservation, DRDA, etc.). Constant efforts of the DST, partner NGOs and the community leaders have resulted in increased participation of the line departments in community development activities. Collaboration with the Forest Department in the N.C. Hills through the promotion of Joint Forest Management and biodiversity conservation initiatives impacted in the improved knowledge sharing mechanism among the members of the cluster associations of NaRMGs and SHG federations There has also been improved networking between the project and non-project villages, particularly for replication of forest and biodiversity conservation initiatives.

Increased Promotion of Local
Trade and Eco-tourism

Improved biodiversity through community conservation initiatives has had a remarkable impact in many villages. For example, the fresh water fish pool reserves created in West Garo Hills are attracting local people and local tourists to observe and appreciate the varieties of fish available in their river systems. The fish sanctuary at Rombagre and nearby waterfall at Rongbangre are linked with popular road-side stalls for vegetables produced/gathered from the wild and sold by members of local NaRMGs and SHGs. In Ukhrul district, Manipur, the project has promoted a resource centre for the promotion of local eco-tourism linked with conserving of the Siroy lily, an endangered endemic plant of Siroy Hills in the district. The local people are also benefiting by engaging in different occupations related to the popular tourist destination Siroy Peak.

Strengthening Community Participatory
Management Processes

A very clear message emerging from the project is that community conservation efforts can be effective only if the whole village participates. This is because the rules and regulations are built upon voluntary agreement. The sanctity of these agreements also rests on a similar commitment and social agreement from the neighbouring villages to sustain the practice. The process of declaring forest reserves and river sanctuaries can only happen by ensuring absolute voluntary participation from all the partners and stakeholders concerned. The project has been able to demonstrate this success as in the Chinabat Cluster in West Garo Hills where 18 villages, both project and non-project villages, came together to preserve four Riverine Fish Sanctuaries.

Strengthening Community Advocacy

As many of the rules and regulations framed by the communities are to be respected, practised or followed by the communities voluntarily, they have become proactive in advocacy about the conservation initiatives, rules and regulations. Advocacy and regulations coming from the highest village/community authorities are always binding for the communities. Thus, forest conservation initiatives have strengthened the advocacy tasks of the community leaders and at the same time, through advocacy, the cause of forest and biodiversity conservation has been strengthened.

Factors Contributing to Sustainability of Community Conservation Initiatives

It is important to identify and appropriately address the factors that could contribute to the sustainability of community conservation initiatives. While NERCORMP deliberated and identified some of these issues, experiences were also drawn from other sources, particularly from the works of Pathak (2008) on community-conserved areas in India.

For a community to effectively conserve and sustainably manage its natural resources, it must have a sense of responsibility and custodianship towards these resources. This develops through economic or cultural interaction and association with these resources. The most successful community conservation initiatives are often those where the communities enjoy full legal ownership or control over an area, such as among the Naga communities in Ukhrul and Senapati, and among the Khasis and Garos in Meghalaya. On the other hand, some of the Kukis from a number of villages in Manipur and N.C. Hills and the Karbis in Karbi Anglong in some villages did have some reservations about full participation, perhaps due to the system of land tenure through the chiefs among the Kukis and the district council authorities among the Karbis.

Conservation is often considered a part of livelihood insurance but its success also depends on existing social dynamics. While community conservation initiatives may lead to greater equity or empowerment, these could also promote the conservation of natural resources. However, successful initiatives in conservation cannot be isolated from other social, economic and political processes in the community. Sustainability of community-conserved areas also requires sensitivity towards the poorest households

Free, prior informed, transparent and impartial processes of decision making with the involvement of as many community stakeholders as possible from the village men, women and youth are essential features of successful, sustained community conservation initiatives. Misuse of power with questionable integrity, abuse of community funds, or other forms of social and power inequities often threaten or undermine conservation efforts. Successful community initiatives share an open, just system of decision making and accounting, where records are regularly disclosed at NaRMG and village council meetings. Through such open, transparent and trusted processes, conservation initiatives have resolved troubling issues and stumbling barriers such as encroachments, illegal grazing, forest fires, poaching, and timber smuggling. Such processes have also avoided potential conflicts over natural resources and resolved existing ones.

Openness to partnership with the government and NGOs that could contribute technical and financial resources goes a long way in successful community conservation initiatives. The presence of second and third parties could contribute to resolving or avoiding potential conflicts, as also withstanding possible political and commercial pressures. External partners could also contribute significantly to raising awareness and introducing information and perspectives from the outside world. In most successful community conservation initiatives, local leaders play a crucial driving role. Such leaders are typically inclined towards the larger social good and common benefits. They may not be traditional or political leaders, but those who touch the soul and heart of the community by their dedication and commitment, and thereby motivate the communities towards positive change, often at tremendous personal cost and sacrifice. When such leaders move on, many communities find it difficult to identify a second generation of leadership with similar dynamism and charisma. Thus, it is important for supporting communities to identify strong and committed local leaders and facilitate their work (without changing or co-opting effective local institutions and relationships), and for the community to continuously foster a new, younger corps of leaders, both men and women.

Community conservation efforts are best sustained where communities have been able to effectively balance and secure the involvement of women and youth alongside the existing traditional leaderships. Shared responsibilities and envisioning from women and youth go a long way in making the conservation initiatives pro-people, pro-nature, pro-poor, and pro-equity.

Legal Aspects

Projects and organisations that promote community conservation initiatives should also be able to provide guidance to the communities on existing legal and policy issues as well as support linkages with such policies. Some national legal and policy provisions that could support current community conservation initiatives are outlined in the Appendix. In addition, each state in NE India, including those governed under Autonomous District Councils also has policy provisions that could strengthen community conservation .

Four project districts, the West Garo Hills and West Khasi Hills in Meghalaya, and the Karbi Anglong and N.C. Hills in Assam are under the Autonomous District Councils (ADCs) constituted under the Sixth Schedule of the Constitution. The ADCs have legislative and executive power over a wide range of subjects such as managing non-reserved forests and regulating shifting cultivation. The ADCs have their own forest laws and regulations under which community forests and/or village forests can be constituted. For example, the United Khasi-Jaintia Autonomous District (Management and Control of Forests) Act, 1958, provides legal space for constitution of village forests as well as protection of sacred groves. Similarly, the Garo Hills District (Forest) Act of 1958 provides for constitution of council-reserved forests and village forests.

Concluding Remarks

In typical tribal, upland communities of northeastern India, maintenance of village or community reserve forests is part of the traditional/customary practices and indigenous knowledge systems. As indicated earlier, many of these traditionally protected community forests continue to provide glimpses of the rich biodiversity in the region. However, in recent years, many of these practices have been influenced by overriding development initiatives and challenges. As the population is increasing, there is more competition for space for human habitation, agricultural expansion, industrial and other infrastructure development. The greatest impact has been on the forest cover and traditional forest conservation practices. Although traditional practices continue to survive in several isolated pockets, interventions by the government, NGOs and externally funded development projects were needed to restore, rejuvenate or start new initiatives. Achievements are possible in spite of various challenges (like the separatist and extremist movement) if appropriate strategies and intervention models are adopted with communities being equal partners in planning and implementation. Most importantly, such efforts must be strongly linked to livelihoods or economic benefits and not just ecological benefits.

From the legal perspective, there remain a few challenges. For example, village reserves need to be registered with the competent district authority and JFM areas need further legal support and professional input. This would also facilitate preparation and approval of 'Forest Working Schemes' for harvesting and legal trade of timber from such community-conserved areas in the future, if the communities so wish. By establishing and building linkages with the State Biodiversity Boards in the northeastern states, sustainable livelihoods through biodiversity conservation and community forest management could get an impetus.

In a natural resource rich area like northeastern India, a project aiming to combat rural hunger and poverty requires a strategy that caters to the development needs of the communities and ensures conservation of local forests and biodiversity. The NERCORMP was able to do this while addressing the poorest and the vulnerable communities. A key to this success was through promoting a symbiotic relationship between livelihoods and community-based forests and biodiversity conservation and NRM. The project has also successfully demonstrated that the the central and state governments, international development agencies, local partner NGOs, communities and development professionals can foster new and sustainable development models suited to upland areas like northeastern India.

In a region where over 50 per cent of the forest is under community control, community forest conservation initiatives are complementary to on-going efforts of the central and state government to establish a network of protected areas, as also promote JFM. The central government/Supreme Court requirement for Autonomous District Councils and Forest Departments to prepare Working Plans/Working Schemes for all forests in the region has made little headway, however, particularly under the community-controlled forest areas. A major constraint to these initiatives has been limited interface with local communities that are engaged in forest protection and management.

These issues should be addressed at the earliest. According to the *Conservation Atlas of Tropical Forests: Asia and the Pacific* (Collins et al. 1991), 'Northeast India is one of the most crucial areas in the sub-continent for attempts to develop a comprehensive conservation network' due to its rich diversity of habitats, and significant levels of endemism in a wide variety of flora and fauna. Even if community-controlled forests cannot be covered under forest working schemes, attempts should be made to link community-conserved areas with payment for environmental service (PES) for their stewardships, even through appropriate government funding. At a time of global warming and future water shortages, there should be centrally funded incentives for practices and groups which protect the forests and environment, especially in areas where forest and water resources are not government-owned or -controlled but under the jurisdiction of traditional institutions or communities, clans or even individuals, as in northeastern India.

As observed by Poffenberger (2007), there is the need for new innovative, participatory and remunerative programmes that seek to address the failure of past conservation initiatives in northeast India by creating management partnerships that respect the legal authority of communities and work through indigenous institutions drawing on centrally funded schemes. By empowering and enabling traditional insttutions and building modern management capacities within them, the forest departments will have viable partners to craft new landscape management systems that rely on networks of villages and community-conserved areas. In return, communities will be able to develop new resource management plans that address forest conservation and livelihood issues, and gain formal tenure security for their ancestral domain. Retaining ancestral domain under communal tenure is one of the most effective strategies to maintain forest cover and protect biodiversity. In this philosophy and strategy perhaps lies the future of the forest, biodiversity and the people of northeastern India.

To make community forest and biodiversity conservation initiatives meaningful and rewarding, there is a need for massive social programmes. Awareness and training are needed for the communities and the leaders of the traditional village institutions on the importance of biodiversity conservation in the local, national and global context. Other important areas for capacity building also include issues relating to gender and social equity, local forest and biodiversity governance, and rights with respect to resources and protected areas. Support for youth (leadership) programmes, and other local groups and initiatives would also go a long way in promoting community conservation. Promoting, cataloguing and reinforcing local knowledge and management systems would also have to be part of the overall initiatives for CCAs. Identification and facilitating the involvement of marginalised groups, both within and outside of CCA communities, as well as social recognition and awards to exemplary CCA initiatives could be part of larger efforts for promoting and sustaining community forest and biodiversity conservation and management in NE India.

Appendix
Key national and local laws and regulations relevant to community conservation

Indian Forest Act, 1927 and the Assam Forest Regulation, 1891

Both the Acts provide for the declaration of village forests that can be handed over to local communities for use and management while ownership remains with the government. This provision has not been used much and there appears to be a general reluctance by state governments to implement it. These acts are enforced by the states of NE India either after adoption or directly.

The Wildlife (Protection) Act, 1972 and Amendments

The amended act incorporates two new categories of protected areas (in addition to national parks and sanctuaries, which are not compatible with CCAs) for which community participation in conservation is envisaged: Conservation Reserves and Community Reserves (CRs). However, these categories remain quite restrictive. Community Reserves are applicable only to community and private lands, and benefits to be accrued to the communities by creating CRs are not very clear. There are also CCAs that have been created on government-owned lands, particularly those induced by JFM. Another constraint is that the Act specifies a uniform institutional structure for managing CRs, which may stifle the diverse range of institutional and customary structures/rules that communities have created based on traditional and customary practices.

Environment Protection Act, 1986

Under this Act sites can be declared ecologically sensitive areas (ESAs), helping to restrict environmentally destructive activities. However, this provision has not been used by local communities, presumably out of ignorance of such a legal provision.

National Forest Policy (NFP) 1988 and JFM Guidelines

The NFP specifies that meeting the livelihood needs of local people should be placed above national industrial and commercial interests. It also emphasises the need for participatory conservation mechanisms (including participation by women) to meet this objective. This policy was translated into action in 1990 through the Joint Forest Management programme. Although millions of hectares of forest have been brought under JFM, many remain critical of the policy which is considered as top-down rather than promoting existing community efforts and devolution of authority. Many of the current JFM resolutions of the states in NE India also do not seem to provide encouraging policy environment for the communities to offer forests or CCAs under their control to be brought within the ambit of JFM.

Panchayati Raj (Extension to Scheduled Areas) Act, 1996

Though not relevant to the current NERCORMP project areas, nevertheless it is important to be aware about the PESA Act. The Act emphasises a more decentralised system of governance to rural bodies like *panchayats* (village councils) and *gram sabhas* (village assemblies) in predominantly tribal ('scheduled') areas in Schedule Fifth Areas. PESA confers the ownership and decision-making rights over non-timber forest products to local institutions. The Act also mandates consultation with local communities regarding many developmental and other issues. Unfortunately, government forests and protected areas have been excluded from the jurisdiction of the Act, and most states (where it is applicable) have been somewhat reluctant to push for its effective implementation.

Biological Diversity Act, 2002

Formulated as a response to the Convention on Biological Diversity, this Act emphasises the participation of local communities in the conservation and use of biodiversity. It provides for the declaration of Biodiversity Heritage Sites (BHSs), which could in theory be used by communities involved in biodiversity conservation. However, to date there is no clear definition or guideline for this category, though there could be many such sites in NE India that could come under BHS, such as the sacred groves.

The Wildlife Action Plan, 2002–16

The Wildlife Action Plan emphasises the role of people in conservation. The Plan incorporates time-bound targets to achieve involvement of local people in protected area management, and encouragement of CCAs. However, efforts made so far for implementation of the action plan remain visibly minimal, particularly in NE India.

National Biodiversity Strategy and Action Plan Draft, 2004

An ambitious action plan, though still in draft form, the Plan sets out detailed strategies for conservation, sustainable use and equitable sharing of biodiversity, linking to the Biological Diversity Act and the UN Convention on Biological Diversity. It was produced through a country-wide participatory process, and advocates a major role for CCAs.

Note

* The contribution of the project managers and Development Support Team (DST) of West Garo Hills and West Khasi Hills districts in Meghalaya, Senapati and Ukhrul districts in Manipur, and Karbi Anglong and N.C. Hills districts in Assam is gratefully acknowledged. Special thanks to Mr Daniel Ingty, the then Project Manager of West Garo Hills in Meghalaya and now the Project Director of another IFAD-supported Meghalaya Livelihoods Improvement Project and his team, particularly Mr Senti Jamir, the then PTO and presently the Project Manager, West Garo Hills, and Mr Sitaram Prasad, Institution Development Officer who took extra efforts to verify the CCAs within the buffer zone of Nokrek Biosphere Reserve. The encouragement received from Mr Mattia Prayer Galletti, CPM for India, IFAD, Rome and the colleagues at the India Country Office is also gratefully acknowledged.

References

Barik, S. K. 2010. 'Saving Sacred Forests of Meghalaya', *Heritage Amruth*, 6(1): 37–39.

Barik, S. K. and M. Poffenberger. 2005. 'Community Forests in North-east India in Transition', in Mark Poffengerber (ed.), *Community Forestry in Northeast India*. California: Community Forestry International, pp. 1–9.

Collins, M. N., J. A. Sayer and T. C. Whitmore. 1991. *Conservation Atlas of Tropical Forests: Asia and the Pacific.* New York: IUCN and Simon & Schuster.

Darlong, V. T. and S. K. Barik. 2007. 'Forest of Hope: Case Study from the Jamatia Village of Toirupha, Tripura', in Mark Poffenberger (ed.), *Indigenous Forest Stewards of Northeast India.* California: Community Forestry International, pp. 38–44.

Forest Survey of India (FSI). 2009. *State of Forest Report 2009.* Dehradun: FSI, MoEF.

North Eastern Council (NEC). 2002. *Basic Statistics of NER 2002.* Shillong: NEC, Government of India

North Eastern Region Community Resource Management Project (NERCORMP). 2009. *Project Design Report: Proposal for Expansion of the North Eastern Region Community Resource Management Project for Upland Areas (NERCORMP-II) through Supplementary Funding from IFAD & GOI Funding.* Shillong: NERCORMP.

Palit, S. and M. Poffenberger. 2005. 'Introduction to Community Forestry in Northeast India', in Mark Poffengerber (ed.), *Community Forestry in Northeast India.* California: Community Forestry International, pp. 1–9.

Pathak, N. 2008. *Community Conserved Areas in India: An Overview.* Pune: Kalpavriksh.

Pathak, N., T. Balasinorwala, A. Kothari and B. R. Bushley. 2008. *People in Conservation: Community Conserved Areas in India.* Pune: Kalpavriksh.

Poffenberger, M. 2007. (ed.). *Indigenous Forest Stewards of Northeast India.* California: Community Forestry International.

Tiwari, B. K., S. K. Barik and R. S. Tripathi. 1999. *Sacred Forests of Meghalaya: Biological and Cultural Diversity.* Shillong: Regional Centre, National Afforestation and Eco-development Board, North-Eastern Hill University.

Appendix

Changing Land Relations in Northeastern India: A Comparative Study of Six Tribes and a Non-tribal Group*

WALTER FERNANDES AND MELVIL PEREIRA

The rest of India often views the ethnic conflicts in the northeast as secessionist or terrorist, thus oversimplifying a complex phenomenon. Basing our effort to understand the issue on our past studies we began with the assumption that among the causes are changing land relations conditioned by immigration, encroachment and the adverse impact of the changes that the modern legal system introduces in the tribal tradition. These do not begin the conflicts but exacerbate those already existing. We tested this hypothesis through a study of six tribes and a non-tribal group. Through 60 group discussion sessions and interviews with 662 families, we studied the Aka of Arunachal Pradesh, the Adivasi, Boro, Dimasa, and the non-tribal Assamese of Assam, the Garo of Meghalaya, and the Rongmei of Manipur.

Among them the Aka are close to their traditional values but their customary law is not recognised, nor do they come under the Sixth Schedule. The Dimasa, though exposed to the outside world for long, have retained their customary law but are changing. They and the Garo come under the Sixth Schedule while the Adivasi are not even recognised as a Scheduled Tribe. The Rongmei who are a tribe not included under the Sixth Schedule, have lost much land to ethnic conflicts and to development projects. The Boro, a plains tribe again not included under the Sixth Schedule, have won a territorial council after a struggle. The Assamese were a control group (see Table 1A).

Table 1A: The Villages and the Sample of the Study

Tribe/Village	Adivasi M	Adivasi F	Aka M	Aka F	Assamese M	Assamese F	Boro M	Boro F	Dimasa M	Dimasa F	Garo M	Garo F	Rongmei M	Rongmei F	Total M	Total F	Total
Arunachal																	
West Kameng District (Aka)																	
Palitari	–	–	12	2	–	–	–	–	–	–	–	–	–	–	12	2	**14**
Palizi	–	–	12	1	–	–	–	–	–	–	–	–	–	–	12	1	**13**
Balipho	–	–	5	6	–	–	–	–	–	–	–	–	–	–	5	6	**11**
Subbu	–	–	2	3	–	–	–	–	–	–	–	–	–	–	2	3	**5**
Assam																	
Nagaon District (Non-tribal Assamese)																	
Medhchuk	–	–	–	–	12	8	–	–	–	–	–	–	–	–	12	8	**20**
Srimala	–	–	–	–	9	11	–	–	–	–	–	–	–	–	9	11	**20**
Jagiyal	–	–	–	–	9	11	–	–	–	–	–	–	–	–	9	11	**20**
Bhotarigaon	–	–	–	–	9	11	–	–	–	–	–	–	–	–	9	11	**20**
Assam																	
Kokrajhar District (80 Boro and 20 Adivasi)																	
Lokhipm	4	1	–	–	–	–	7	8	–	–	–	–	–	–	11	9	**20**
Owabari	–	–	–	–	–	–	10	10	–	–	–	–	–	–	10	10	**20**
Bhatarmari	–	–	–	–	–	–	10	10	–	–	–	–	–	–	10	10	**20**
Bedlaobari	10	5	–	–	–	–	4	1	–	–	–	–	–	–	14	6	**20**
Besargami	–	–	–	–	–	–	9	11	–	–	–	–	–	–	9	11	**20**
Assam																	
N. C. Hills District (Dimasa)																	
Wari	–	–	–	–	–	–	–	–	10	10	–	–	–	–	10	10	**20**
Naidingpur	–	–	–	–	–	–	–	–	10	10	–	–	–	–	10	10	**20**
Gurubari	–	–	–	–	–	–	–	–	10	10	–	–	–	–	10	10	**20**
Hojai	–	–	–	–	–	–	–	–	10	10	–	–	–	–	10	10	**20**
Anlongbra	–	–	–	–	–	–	–	–	10	10	–	–	–	–	10	10	**20**

Region / Place				Total
Assam	*Lakhimpur District (Adivasi)*			
Puthimari	10	10	–	20
Borbil	11	9	–	20
Rangajan	10	9	–	19
Assam	*Tinsukia District (Adivasi)*			
Dibrujan	10	10	–	20
Kathalguri No. 3	11	9	–	20
Kanapathar No. 2 & 3	9	11	–	20
Manipur	*Bishnupur District (Rongmei)*			
Chalungkhou	12	12	8	20
New Canan	8	8	12	20
Majuron	6	6	14	20
Chinikon	11	11	9	20
Zeikulong	10	10	10	20
Meghalaya	*West Garo Hills (Garo)*			
Chigjianggri	12	12	8	20
Meghalaya	*East Garo Hills (Garo)*			
Chisim	20	20	10	30
Matchokgri	–	–	–	–
Dalbingri	19	19	21	40
Mendal	15	15	15	30
Total	75 64 31 12 39 41 40 50 50 40	66 54	47 53	348 314 662

The tribes were chosen according to their relationship with the land. Our past studies show that the Aka, being close to their customary law, depend mostly on common property resources (CPRs). They use as much land as they need in the jhum (shifting or slash and burn) cultivation season. It reverts to the community after the season. The Dimasa too are close to their traditional values but have absorbed many new ones. Their elite are demanding individual land documents but their tradition remains strong. The Adivasi were forced out of Jharkhand in eastern India by the colonial policy of Permanent Settlement (1793). Once they lost their land they had no choice but to migrate away from their homeland in search of sustenance. They and other land losers were taken as indentured labour to the plantations and mines in the British colonies the world over, from the West Indies and Papua New Guinea to Malaysia, Singapore, Sri Lanka, South and East Africa. A large number of them were brought to North Bengal and Assam as tea garden workers. The tea garden workers number five to six million in Assam or 20 per cent of the state's population. Between 50 and 60 per cent of them are tribals who have almost lost their tribal identity. Though the Rongmei have lost their land to ethnic conflicts as well as to the Loktak project (in Manipur), they are not counted among the land losers because their community ownership is not recognised by formal law. The Garo are a matrilineal tribe that is undergoing changes. These changes are visible in their land relations which is the centre of the identity of all the tribes. That is the reason for choosing this theme as the testing ground. Besides, almost all the conflicts in northeastern India are around land.

Our hypothesis is that changing land relations, especially land alienation, cannot be attributed to any one cause but takes many forms. So the solution too cannot be simple. Action has to be taken on several fronts simultaneously. Among the causes are: the individual orientation of the administration, modernisation of the customary laws often supported by elite aspirations, and displacement by development projects.

Some Major Findings

In an effort to understand the conflicts emanating from land alienation we studied the demographic data which is linked to land relations. Among five of the six tribes studied, the male inherits land. So the division of family members by age group and sex showed us the future implications for land ownership. Education takes the child away from the land. So their educational and occupational status gave us another view of land relations. We then studied the nature and extent of control over land and of changes in it during the last three decades, its causes, the alterations caused by modern crops and other inputs such as fertilisers.

Table 2A: Family Members (by Tribe/State, Age Group and Sex)

Tribe sex	Age (years)							Total
	0–4	5–9	10–14	15–19	20–29	30–54	55+	
Adivasi								
Male	45	33	25	28	53	71	31	**286**
Female	24	43	28	27	70	51	19	**262**
Total	**69**	**76**	**53**	**55**	**123**	**122**	**50**	**548**
Aka								
Male	24	26	15	6	15	31	5	**122**
Female	20	22	20	11	29	35	7	**144**
Total	**44**	**48**	**35**	**17**	**44**	**66**	**12**	**266**
Assamese								
Male	13	19	16	16	49	76	27	**216**
Female	12	12	15	30	51	63	37	**220**
Total	**25**	**31**	**31**	**46**	**100**	**139**	**64**	**436**
Boro								
Male	14	24	12	25	47	77	22	**221**
Female	18	23	25	23	47	70	18	**224**
Total	**32**	**47**	**37**	**48**	**94**	**147**	**40**	**445**
Dimasa								
Male	51	35	42	33	49	65	24	**299**
Female	32	28	37	37	58	61	10	**263**
Total	**83**	**63**	**79**	**70**	**107**	**126**	**34**	**562**
Garo								
Male	45	53	48	48	57	86	30	**367**
Female	52	49	46	39	71	75	22	**354**
Total	**97**	**102**	**94**	**87**	**128**	**161**	**52**	**721**
Rongmei								
Male	3	35	71	76	76	94	40	**395**
Female	1	25	63	62	55	90	32	**328**
Total	**4**	**60**	**134**	**138**	**131**	**184**	**72**	**723**
Grand Total								
Male	195	225	229	232	346	500	179	**1,906**
Female	159	202	234	229	381	445	145	**1,795**
Total	**354**	**427**	**463**	**461**	**727**	**945**	**324**	**3,701**

POPULATION GROWTH AND COMPETITION FOR LAND

The demographic data showed a bigger than average family size. This is in consonance with the land-based economy to which most of the tribes in the study belong, but it also indicates a high population growth; one cause of this is immigration which leads to competition for land and jobs. Linked to this is a contradiction: land has become scarce so they need non-land alternatives, which is possible because the educational status in most states is higher than the national average, but jobs are scarce since the secondary sector has been neglected. Seven states (Assam, Arunachal, Manipur, Meghalaya, Mizoram, Nagaland, and Tripura) together have only 166 industries, many of them sick. The tertiary sector, mainly jobs in the administration to which the educated flock in the absence of other alternatives, is saturated. That lays the foundation of ethnic conflicts such as the recent anti-foreigner movement 1979–85 and the anti-Bihari riots of 2003 in Assam (see Table 3A).

GROWING AMBIGUITY AROUND LAND

We also noticed a growing ambiguity around land among the communities studied. Most of them want to retain control over land and simultaneously move away from it as their sustenance. Most Aka and Dimasa families sustain themselves on land and very few of them have salaried jobs away from their village. It is different in the case of the Rongmei, Adivasi and to some extent Boro who have lost much of their land to development projects or to ethnic conflicts. The Adivasi own very little land. Most of the Rongmei had land before the ethnic conflicts or before the Loktak project alienated it from them. Today, they try to find an alternative that uses land as the basis but their sustenance is elsewhere. Some of them have sold or mortgaged their land in order to bribe officials and get a job in the administration or to pay for their children's education. Their tradition is of a symbiotic relationship with land and forests but they have lost hope in it as their sustenance. They are, thus, ready to part with it for an alternative, particularly children's education. The Adivasi would like to own some land, mainly as a mode of re-acquiring their tribal identity, but are unable to do it. Many of them have a job in the tea gardens but would like alternatives away from their present exploited status.

Table 3A: Occupation of the Family Members (by Tribe, Sex and Age Group)

Tribe/Occupation	Age (years)								Total		
	10–14		15–19		20–29		30+				
	M	F	M	F	M	F	M	F	M	F	Total
Adivasi											
Cultivators	–	–	–	–	24	33	80	51	104	84	188
Landless labourers	–	–	–	–	–	–	3	1	3	1	4
Home-based workers	–	1	–	–	2	1	1	2	3	4	7
Daily wage earners	–	–	9	8	25	23	19	10	53	41	94
Domestic workers	–	1	2	–	1	2	–	1	3	4	7
Businessmen	–	–	–	–	2	–	2	1	4	1	5
Plantation labourers	4	2	2	4	7	14	13	20	26	40	66
Unskilled (monthly)	–	–	–	–	2	–	2	–	4	–	4
Semi-skilled (monthly)	–	–	–	–	3	–	2	–	5	–	5
Other (monthly)	–	–	–	1	2	–	5	–	7	1	8
Housewives	–	–	–	4	–	11	–	14	–	29	29
Students	38	37	15	14	6	8	1	1	60	60	120
Unemployed	–	–	3	1	–	1	6	3	9	5	14
Total	42	41	31	32	74	93	134	104	281	270	551

(Table 3A continued)

(Table 3A continued)

Tribe/Occupation	Age (years)										Total	
	10–14		15–19		20–29		30+		Total			
	M	F	M	F	M	F	M	F	M	F	M	F	Total
Aka												
Cultivators	–	–	–	–	9	18	33	28	42	46	88
Landless labourers	–	–	–	–	1	–	–	1	1	1	2
Home-based workers	–	–	–	–	–	–	–	–	–	–	–
Daily wage earners	–	–	–	–	–	–	–	–	–	–	–
Domestic workers	–	–	–	–	–	–	–	–	–	–	–
Businessmen	–	–	–	–	–	–	3	–	3	–	3
Plantation labourers	–	–	–	–	–	–	–	–	–	–	–
Unskilled (monthly)	–	–	–	–	–	–	–	–	–	–	–
Semi-skilled (monthly)	–	–	–	–	–	–	–	–	–	–	–
Other (monthly)	–	–	–	–	1	1	–	1	1	2	3
Housewives	–	–	–	–	–	4	–	12	–	16	16
Students	12	11	5	5	3	6	1	–	21	22	43
Unemployed	–	–	–	–	1	–	1	–	2	–	2
Total	**12**	**11**	**5**	**5**	**15**	**29**	**38**	**42**	**70**	**87**	**157**
Assamese												
Cultivators	–	–	–	–	33	25	65	35	98	60	158
Landless labourers	–	–	–	–	–	–	–	–	–	–	–
Home-based workers	–	–	–	–	–	–	–	–	–	–	–
Daily wage earners	–	–	2	–	3	–	9	1	14	1	15
Domestic workers	–	–	–	–	–	2	–	4	–	6	6
Businessmen	–	–	–	–	3	–	10	1	13	1	14

Plantation labourers	–	–	–	–	–	–	–	–	–	–	–
Unskilled (monthly)	–	–	–	–	2	–	1	–	3	–	3
Semi-skilled (monthly)	–	–	–	–	–	–	–	–	–	–	–
Other (monthly)	–	–	–	–	3	2	14	3	17	5	22
Housewives	–	–	–	–	–	7	–	54	–	61	61
Students	18	12	10	26	4	6	–	–	32	44	76
Unemployed	–	–	–	–	3	8	2	1	5	9	14
Total	**18**	**12**	**12**	**26**	**51**	**50**	**101**	**99**	**182**	**187**	**369**
Boro											
Cultivators	–	–	–	–	11	2	36	7	47	9	56
Landless labourers	–	–	–	–	–	–	3	–	3	–	3
Home-based workers	–	–	–	1	1	3	3	8	4	12	16
Daily wage earners	–	–	–	–	–	–	6	2	6	2	8
Domestic workers	–	–	–	1	2	4	–	1	2	6	8
Businessmen	–	–	–	–	7	1	13	1	20	2	22
Plantation labourers	–	–	–	–	–	–	–	–	–	–	–
Housewives	–	–	–	–	–	17	–	48	–	65	65
Unskilled (monthly)	–	–	–	–	1	–	1	–	2	–	2
Semi-skilled (monthly)	–	–	–	–	1	–	3	2	4	2	6
Other (monthly)	–	–	–	–	7	2	21	2	28	4	32
Students	14	21	24	18	12	9	4	–	54	48	102
Unemployed	–	–	–	–	10	8	7	16	17	24	41
Total	**14**	**21**	**24**	**20**	**52**	**46**	**97**	**87**	**187**	**174**	**361**

(Table 3A continued)

(Table 3A continued)

Tribe/Occupation	Age (years)								Total		
	10–14		15–19		20–29		30+				
	M	F	M	F	M	F	M	F	M	F	Total
Dimasa											
Cultivators	–	–	7	11	29	54	81	64	117	129	246
Landless labourers	–	–	–	–	–	–	–	–	–	–	–
Home-based workers	–	–	–	3	–	2	–	–	–	5	5
Daily wage earners	–	–	–	–	–	–	–	–	–	–	–
Domestic workers	–	–	–	–	–	–	–	–	–	–	–
Businessmen	–	–	–	–	3	–	1	–	4	–	4
Plantation labourers	–	–	–	–	–	–	–	–	–	–	–
Unskilled (monthly)	–	–	–	–	1	–	1	–	2	–	2
Semi-skilled (monthly)	–	–	–	–	–	–	–	–	–	–	–
Other (monthly)	–	–	2	1	7	–	4	1	13	2	15
Housewives	–	–	–	–	–	–	–	–	–	–	–
Students	37	31	21	21	4	4	–	–	62	56	118
Unemployed	–	–	–	–	–	–	–	–	–	–	–
Total	37	31	30	36	44	60	87	65	198	192	390
Garo											
Cultivators	–	–	3	2	16	21	35	33	54	56	110
Landless labourers	–	–	–	–	–	–	–	1	–	1	1
Home-based workers	1	–	1	–	–	1	–	2	2	3	5
Daily wage earners	–	–	4	3	17	12	40	27	61	42	103
Domestic workers	–	–	–	–	–	–	1	3	1	3	4
Businessmen	–	–	–	–	5	–	11	3	16	4	20
Plantation labourers	–	–	–	–	–	–	–	–	–	–	–
Unskilled (monthly)	–	–	–	–	–	1	6	–	7	1	–
Semi-skilled (monthly)	–	–	–	–	1	1	–	–	7	1	8

											Total
Other (monthly)	–	–	1	–	4	5	13	3	18	8	26
Housewives	–	–	–	3	–	12	–	18	–	33	33
Students	43	37	38	30	13	14	4	3	98	84	182
Unemployed	1	–	2	2	1	3	10	11	13	16	29
Total	**44**	**37**	**49**	**41**	**57**	**69**	**120**	**104**	**270**	**251**	**521**
Rongmei											
Cultivators	–	–	–	–	2	4	63	83	65	87	152
Landless labourers	–	–	1	–	–	–	3	3	4	3	7
Home-based workers	–	–	–	–	–	–	–	1	–	1	1
Daily wage earners	–	–	–	–	–	–	–	1	–	1	1
Domestic workers	–	–	–	–	–	–	–	–	–	–	–
Businessmen	–	–	–	–	–	–	4	2	4	2	6
Plantation labourers	–	–	–	–	–	–	–	–	–	–	–
Unskilled (monthly)	–	–	–	–	–	–	27	2	27	2	29
Semi-skilled (monthly)	–	–	–	–	–	–	15	3	15	3	18
Other (monthly)	–	–	–	–	4	–	–	–	4	–	4
Housewives	–	–	–	–	–	–	–	16	–	16	16
Students	65	59	69	53	62	37	4	2	200	151	351
Unemployed	–	–	–	–	–	1	11	–	11	1	12
Total	**65**	**59**	**70**	**53**	**68**	**42**	**127**	**113**	**330**	**267**	**597**

(Table 3A continued)

(Table 3A continued)

Tribe/Occupation	Age (years)								Total		
	10–14		15–19		20–29		30+				
	M	F	M	F	M	F	M	F	M	F	Total
Grand Total											
Cultivators	–	–	10	13	124	157	393	301	527	471	998
Landless labourers	–	–	1	–	1	–	9	6	11	6	17
Home-based workers	1	1	1	4	3	7	4	13	9	25	34
Daily wage earners	–	–	15	11	45	35	74	41	134	87	221
Domestic workers	–	1	2	1	3	8	1	9	6	19	25
Businessmen	–	–	–	1	20	1	44	8	64	10	74
Plantation labourers	4	2	2	4	7	14	13	20	26	40	66
Unskilled (monthly)	–	–	–	–	9	–	29	2	38	2	40
Semi-skilled (monthly)	–	–	–	–	5	2	26	4	31	6	37
Other (monthly)	–	–	3	2	24	10	61	10	88	22	110
Housewives	–	–	–	7	–	51	–	162	–	220	220
Students	227	208	182	167	104	84	14	6	527	465	992
Unemployed	–	–	5	3	16	20	36	32	57	55	112
Total	232	212	221	213	361	389	704	614	1,518	1,428	2,946

Such changes are a result of modern inputs without any preparation. The first of these is the individual *patta* (ownership document)-based land laws that are alien to their CPR culture. The individual-oriented administration recognises the CPRs only in the Sixth Schedule areas and in Nagaland and Mizoram where it recognises the customary law. However, in the Sixth Schedule areas inputs without protective measures, such as subsidies for commercial crops to patta owners alone, encourage the transition of land from a livelihood resource and centre of their culture and identity to a commodity to be sold or leased to the highest bidder. They lose the sacredness attached to land and a new worldview emerges that they are not familiar with. Indeed, much of the mortgaging and sale of land are within the community. That results in class formation in egalitarian societies. These processes also strengthen patriarchy and reduce the little power that women enjoy.

LAND RELATIONS AND CONFLICTS

These processes also lay the foundation of ethnic and other conflicts. Land alienation is not the only cause but is a crucial one. The legal system too is not the only cause of conflicts around land but is basic to them. Land encroachment by immigrants is a major issue. In other words, the main problem is not immigration in itself but land encroachment by the immigrants that becomes an attack on the natives' livelihood in the predominantly agrarian economy with jhum as its main form in the hills. The legal system facilitates encroachment because the individual-based law does not recognise community rights over it. As a result, when the immigrants encroach on the land, the communities are unable to defend themselves except through violence.

Thus, conflicts arise because different groups vie for limited land. Given their symbiotic relationship with it, they also perceive conflicts as defence of their culture, identity and livelihood. Moreover, most immigrants are landless agricultural labourers who are paid low wages in the feudal areas of Bihar, Uttar Pradesh, Nepal, and Bangladesh where land reform legislation has either not been passed or has not been implemented. Thus, their poverty is the push factor while the legal system of the CPRs not being recognised functions as a major pull factor, especially because land in much of the northeast is fertile.

On this fertile land many immigrants use the agricultural techniques they bring from their place of origin and prosper by cultivating three crops. So the local people feel a threat both from encroachment and from the fact that those who occupy it prosper while they themselves remain behind. Most of them have lived in a single crop culture or jhum or within the sharecropper system that developed in the colonial age. Between 50 and 60 per cent of what they grew had to be given to the landlord. That discouraged any cultivation beyond subsistence. So recent changes have both intensified traditional rivalries and created new ones with outsiders. To these rivalries they have added competition for the remaining land within the region.

Table 4A refers to land controlled by the respondents, not necessarily owned by them in the legal sense of the term but land which they are occupying although not recognised by the present law. In some cases they are referring to community land that has been allotted by the village to the individual family. Some others have taken land in mortgage or have encroached on what is called state property according to the present eminent domain–based land laws that recognise only individual ownership documents. Table 5A shows that the Aka who are close to their tradition do not have a concept of individual ownership and depend only on the CPRs. The 37 respondents who gave no information (Table 4A), however, report (Table 5A) that they depend on the CPRs. Also, some Boro respondents live on community land but after a century of the colonial law they have internalised the individual ownership ideology to such an extent that they call themselves encroachers and not CPR dependants.

Most Adivasi respondents live on patta land but they have very little of it. So many of them rent land or take it in mortgage. In fact, 'rented in' is often a euphemism for land taken on mortgage. The Rongmei who are victims of ethnic conflicts and development-induced displacement have the biggest number of persons depending on the category 'others'. In most cases it is land belonging to another tribe that they have occupied after a conflict. In some cases members of their own tribe abandoned the land and they occupied it when they felt that some security had returned to their area. It is true also of the Boro who have had a land-centred conflict with the Santhals. Many of them have occupied land during the conflict.

Table 4A: Extent of Land Controlled by the Respondents (in Acres)

Tribes	Landless	-.01–1.00	1.01–2.50	2.51–5.00	5.01–10.00	10.01 +	Not Avai	Total
Adivasi	2	30	40	42	22	3	–	139
Aka	–	–	–	4	1	1	37	43
Assamese	1	11	20	36	13	–	–	80
Boro	1	15	6	73	23	12	1	80
Dimasa	–	8	73	16	3	–	–	100
Garo	13	30	36	27	7	6	1	120
Rongmei	–	5	57	33	5	–	–	100
Total	**16**	**99**	**232**	**180**	**74**	**22**	**39**	**662**

Table 5A: The Type of Land Controlled by the Respondent Families (by Ethnic Group)

	Adivasi	Aka	Assamese	Boro	Dimasa	Garo	Rongmei	Total
Landless	2	–	–	1	–	13	–	16
Only Patta	78	2	51	46	–	80	14	271
Only Community Land	–	37	–	–	96	17	4	154
Rented in from Others	3	1	–	–	–	–	–	4
Taken in Mortgage	1	–	–	–	–	–	–	1
Encroached	16	–	–	12	–	–	–	28
Patta+Community Land	–	–	–	–	4	–	52	56
Patta+Rented in	23	–	28	5	–	10	3	69
Patta+Taken in Mortgage	13	–	1	–	–	–	1	15
Patta+Encroached Upon	1	–	–	1	–	–	–	2
Others	1	3	–	15	–	–	26	45
Not Available	1	–	–	–	–	–	–	1
Total	139	43	80	80	100	120	100	662

SUBSISTENCE TO COMMERCIALISATION

A crucial issue is the transition from subsistence to a commercial economy or of the changing concept of land from livelihood to commodity. Linked to this is the changeover from an egalitarian to a class society. For example, the matrilineal Garo tribe took to commercial crops without taking into account its in-built hazards. Only individuals and heads of families, understood as men, were offered subsidies and loans. This strengthened class formation and patriarchy in their society. Among other tribes too an important consequence of this process is weakening of the traditional culture that gave some decision-making power to women in the family. Men who earlier shared power with women have slowly taken over all decision-making.

Table 6A confirms the transition to the individual ownership system. The Garo were a CPR-based tribe till less than three decades ago. Today very little community land remains with them. That explains why around 30 per cent of them are landless today, a phenomenon that was unheard of in a CPR culture. The Boro and the Adivasi have much encroached land falling under the category 'others' in Table 5A. In most cases it is land that belonged to a tribe they were in conflict with or to members of their own tribe who abandoned it during a conflict. They occupied it later and they speak of it as encroachment. Much of what is presented as 'rented in' is in reality mortgaged in. That explains why land has become a source of conflict.

Search For Solutions

Keeping the above information in mind one can suggest certain remedies to avoid the existing tensions and the upcoming conflicts. Though tentative they show a direction.

REVIVING THE SECONDARY SECTOR

The first point is the neglect of the secondary sector combined with the high level of education. The economic data indicate that the region has been treated as a supplier of raw material such as tea, coal and petroleum. Its net result is massive unemployment that, together with land, has been the major but not the only cause

Table 6A: Total Land Owned According to Type of Land and Ethnic Group (in Acres)

	Adivasi	Aka	Assamese	Boro	Dimasa	Garo	Rongmei
Only house site	3.06	–	4.67	8.03	-.17	3.34	6.80
Patta	352.04	8.33	175.93	367.38	2.00	269.69	141.37
Community land	–	7.30	–	–	173.40	51.33	67.12
Rented in / from others	54.47	15.00	60.33	59.67	–	1.60	29.66
Taken in mortgage	25.33	–	2.00	1.67	–	–	9.89
Encroached	40.00	–	–	123.90	–	–	–
Got in rehabilitation	–	–	–	-.33	–	–	–
Others	5.00	–	-.00	–	–	–	–
Not available	–	-.00	–	-.00	–	-.00	–
Not applicable	–	–	–	7.20	–	-.00	–
Total	479.91	30.63	242.93	568.18	175.57	325.96	254.85

of unrest that the dominant sections call terrorism or secessionism. With its rich raw material base of natural and mineral resources, the secondary sector should have generated many job opportunities. In practice its raw materials are exported to other parts of the country. Thus, a challenge that the region faces is to generate ongoing stable income and massive employment.

In late August 2001, Mr Tarun Gogoi, chief minister of Assam, said, while inaugurating a seminar on peace in Assam, that the state has an unemployed backlog of 2 million persons. This is probably an underestimate. The Annual Economic Reviews of Assam show that since 2003, around 1.6 million persons are on the live registers of the Employment Exchange. It is well known that only the urban youth register in these exchanges and that most of the rural unemployment and underemployment as well as that in the urban slums goes unreported. Thus, unemployment probably exceeds 3 million. In the northeast as a whole it probably exceeds 4 million or 25 per cent of the active workforce.

With the hope of creating jobs several governments of the region are inviting the private sector to invest in major industries. This sector depends on high land acquisition, mechanisation and low job creation. For example, the proposed Assam Gas Cracker Project is expected to cost around ₹40 billion and create some 30,000 direct and indirect jobs at a massive ₹1.33 million per job. Each direct job alone would probably cost around ₹3 million. Thus, even if we were to accept the figure of 2 million unemployed in Assam and another 1 million in the rest of the region, at the rate of ₹1.33 million per job it will require ₹400 billion to deal with the backlog. That amount is not available. Besides, the growing population and high literacy will add to the demand.

OPTIMISING PRODUCTION

Thus, the problem of massive unemployment cannot be solved by high investment mechanised industries but through creative use of the abundant bio-resources of the region. The low investment–based industries would be in keeping with the need to optimise the use of land, make it productive without destroying the equitable culture of the CPR-based northeastern communities. Many communities thus have to be helped to renew their link with land as their livelihood and to create a new relationship with the economy based on it.

In other words, the first issue around land is creation of low cost jobs by increasing the output in the agricultural sector. Far from taking a stand against commercial crops, we feel that some of them are required but not necessarily those that the state wants to encourage. They should be chosen carefully by looking at possible changes in land relations and the consequent class formation. For example, some Dimasa villages have started growing oranges without changing land relations. It shows that some commercial crops can be introduced without damaging their culture. The Dimasa land-use has changed but not its ownership pattern. By growing fruits they have added a commercial angle to their thinking on land while retaining its role as sustenance and identity.

That is where the state and civil society need to evolve creative programmes that can yield good results. While introducing new programmes and initiatives the facilitators can build on the tribal ethos. A significant finding was the need to increase agricultural output and land productivity by using new inputs including fertilisers. These inputs are required to meet new needs such as children's education and other emergencies like illness, marriage and death in the family. Both the state and the civil society have failed in this area with the solitary exception of the Dimasa who show the possibility of growing commercial crops with communal ownership. An example of failure of this policy are the Garo with their unequal landholdings, high proportion of daily wage earners and the big number of women declaring themselves as only housewives. In their tradition, the woman enjoyed a relatively high social status because of her active participation in the productive processes around land and forests. Today, in many families her control over the resource has all but disappeared and she is not an active participant in its decision-making processes.

COMBINING CULTURE WITH LAND

Ways have to be found of rebuilding their community and culture around land by combining higher productivity to meet new needs with protection of their value system. The present administrative approach to land has led to the break up of their communities, hardened ethnic identities and conflicts. A crucial issue in this process is control, not merely over land but also over the rest of the economy, including production and marketing. Much of the economy is in the hands of outsiders. The local communities will not be able to wrest complete control over it overnight. Processes have to be put in place that can strengthen the community by training them to go beyond agricultural production to processing the produce and marketing the product. Today, they experience the debilitating effect of the middleman grabbing the lion's share of the income from their produce. This indicates both the poor marketing facilities in the northeast and that the focus has been on the individual and production, not on the community and marketing. While marketing is the main source of exploitation, the focus has been on production alone.

The community has to be strengthened in order to facilitate a new marketing system that they can cope with. A possible way is to help them to form cooperatives based on their tradition, not on what the administration thinks these should be. Most tribes of the region have a community culture that can be modernised instead of imposing cooperatives based on another history on them. It can strengthen their customary laws because as our past and present studies show, official inputs have failed to achieve a viable integration of the modern with the traditional. The state recognises their laws through various measures but has not integrated official inputs with their community tradition.

Dealing with the market by using their community ethos is a mode of strengthening it. That is what we have seen happening at Mendipathar in East Garo Hills. Individual ownership appeared because of processes such as introduction of rubber plantation for which the Rubber Board gave subsidies and loans to individuals. However, they only grew rubber but had no control over its price. They used to be paid as low as ₹20 per kilo of rubber. It was less than 40 per cent of the market price. That is when they formed the rubber cooperative. Today, it has grown into a multipurpose cooperative that sells different products at a lower price and gets a higher price for the produce than do the other merchants.

The rubber cooperative certainly faces some problems. For example, it was unable to change the individual ownership system because the community leaders had accepted it. The cooperative tried to solve this problem through a community approach to marketing. In that sense it can provide an answer to the Dimasa who have produced commercial crops but do not get a good price for the oranges they grow. Another group at Langting in the

Dimasa area is searching for a solution by combining self-help groups with cooperative marketing.

COMBINING THE MODERN WITH THE TRADITIONAL

The effort should not merely be to sell the produce but also to let the community grow together with it, that is, combining the traditional with the modern. While their past cannot be kept intact, what is modern is not all for their good. Some of them hold the romantic notion of the past as perfect and prevent its renewal while others have sold their rich cultural heritage and embraced what is called modernisation with no reservations. Either option goes against them. Opting for the modern without preparation can destroy their community while opting for the past without changes can stunt their growth. That is a challenge to the state and the civil society.

When their culture, economy and identity are under attack, those involved in development and education have to strengthen their community ethos. This requires much investment in a new type of education. While literacy is high, the priority in higher education has been for the humanities and social sciences, which are needed, but to build a good secondary sector and create productive jobs, they also need technically trained persons. Besides, the present education takes the student away from land to an administrative post. Instead, it has to help them to develop confidence in their capacity to take the risk of growing new varieties, producing more than one crop and processing the produce. In other words, they have to be helped to return to their land with a new identity.

Education can also help them to acquire the self-confidence required to take control of their economy and deal as equals with the outsiders who by trying to impose their culture can confirm them in their inferior status. Such self-confidence has to be combined with the value of peace based on equality, autonomy and social liberation. Though at times expressed through violence, what the people of the region are demanding is their right to a life with dignity. In their tradition their land gave them that value. The official and civil society inputs should be instrumental in strengthening their right to a life with dignity enshrined in Article 21 of the Constitution by strengthening their community and renewing its link with land in a new form.

THE INPUTS REQUIRED

The study also shows that the whole community has to internalise the self-confidence and risk element required to take control of their economy without destroying their value system. The Rongmei and Dimasa experience shows that when some individuals grow new crops, others accept them if they see their success. They internalise the need for change to such an extent that they refer to themselves as facilitators of change (Table 7A). In their case the new crops were not imposed from above but were based on the community's needs. The reasons given for acceptance of new methods show that they want to grow more than one crop but that the species introduced has to be what the community can grow without destroying its culture and which they can process locally. The community too changes through a cooperative approach that can go together with different forms of individual ownership. More important than its external form is the community ethos adapted to new needs. They need training to process the produce and to sell the finished goods as a group.

That brings us to what the Government of India calls Integrated Tribal Development Plans (ITDP). Subsidies and loans are given to individuals though theirs is a community-based system. Instead of building on the community, the IRDP approach breaks it up. We believe that the state can entrust the same projects to a clan or a village or a community, not to individuals, thus making a contribution to rebuilding their community and identity. One sees it happening through several self-help groups but the state seems to see them as one more project and does not encourage the whole community to come together in a culture of self-help. For ITDP to play this role creatively, the government officials have to encourage the community to make its own choices as the Dimasa have done. The state and the civil society can take steps such as training the community to produce the crops, process the produce as communities and form themselves into legally recognised cooperatives to take control of their local economy. They need training particularly in community-based marketing.

THE ROLE OF EDUCATION

Civil society, especially those involved in education, can assist the communities to build on their past. The school is probably the best place for this effort. It can become a place where the children are

Table 7A: Source of Encouragement to Grow New Crops and Use Fertilisers

Agency	Adivasi	Aka	Assamese	Boro	Dimasa	Garo	Rongmei	Total
Some NGO	–	–	–	–	44	–	–	44
Agriculture dept	–	–	–	2	–	–	–	2
Other farmers	27	–	6	–	23	10	2	68
Local organisation	–	–	–	3	–	–	–	3
Rubber board	–	–	–	–	–	2	–	2
Self	37	–	28	22	–	–	73	160
Soil conservation dept	–	–	–	6	–	1	–	7
Not available	–	–	1	–	–	79	–	80
Not applicable	75	43	45	47	33	28	25	296
Total	**139**	**43**	**80**	**80**	**100**	**120**	**100**	**662**

encouraged to work as a community and also take new initiatives such as growing new crops that can improve their nutritional status. It can help the children to absorb the value of using their land to rebuild their community and economy and also rebuild the value of community work, growing new crops and of tilling land as livelihood. They, thus, become 'lead farmers' who motivate their community to accept new practices that can rebuild their community and give them income for new needs and not transfer the fruit of their work to a middleman.

Obviously, that has to go hand in hand with processing and marketing. Education can also play a role in this field. The level of education is high in the region but most are arts graduates, with relatively little importance given to technical education. Focus on developing technology required to update their traditional techniques to suit present needs can be a contribution that education can make to their communities.

Note

* This Appendix is the summary of a report completed in 2004, *Land Relations and Ethnic Conflicts: The Case of North Eastern India* by Walter Fernandes and Melvil Pereira (Guwahati: North Eastern Social Research Centre, 2005).

About the Editor

Sumi Krishna, an independent scholar and writer based in Bangalore, has 40 years of experience in gender, environment and development at field, programme and policy levels. Previously president of the Indian Association for Women's Studies, she has been guest faculty/adviser at various universities and institutions, and earlier worked for many years in development communication. She serves on the boards of ANTHRA (livestock development and sustainable natural resource use) and the South Asian Consortium for Interdisciplinary Water Resources Studies. Her publications include *Genderscapes: Revisioning Natural Resource Management* (2009), several other books, edited volumes, and essays mainly relating to gender, natural resource management and livelihoods. She was founder-moderator of 'jivika', an e-group for gender and equity.

Notes on Contributors

S. K. Barik is Professor of Ecology, Centre for Advanced Studies in Botany, North Eastern Hill University (NEHU), Shillong, and currently also the Chief National Technical Advisor for the Indo-German Development Project in Tripura. He has coordinated several all-India research projects of the Indian government's Department of Science and Technology and has served on the Environmental Impact Assessment Committee of the Meghalaya state government. As a member of the National Afforestation and Ecodevelopment Board he contributed significantly to the Joint Forest Management programme in northeastern India. He is involved in activities related to sustainable rural development, poverty eradication and taking science to communities, and has published widely.

S. Deb Barma is currently Associate Professor and Head, Department of History, Tripura University, Agartala. He graduated with distinction from NEHU, Shillong, and has received various research scholarships for his work in the fields of history, social development and human rights. He specialises in the socio-economic history of north-eastern India, and modern US history, particularly capitalism. He has authored several research articles. An active social worker, he is keenly interested in the culture and rights of indigenous communities.

Dhrupad Choudhury is currently Programme Coordinator with the International Centre for Integrated Mountain Development (ICIMOD), Kathmandu. He has worked for many years among ethnic communities in northeastern India on issues of livelihood security, traditional natural resource management practices, access and control regimes, and livelihoods. Formerly chief natural resource management adviser, based in Shillong, for a joint project of the International Fund for Agricultural Development (IFAD) and the Government of India, he pioneered an innovative approach (in collaboration with ICIMOD) to land-use planning and managing shifting cultivation in the West Garo Hills, Meghalaya. He has also served with the GB Pant Institute of Himalayan Environment Development in charge of northeastern India. His D.Phil. in Ecology is from the University of Oxford, UK.

Vincent Darlong has extensive experience in natural resource management in northeastern India, and particularly community resource management, both with the Government of India (Ministry of Environment and Forests) and international organisations. He is presently with the International Fund for Agriculture and Development (IFAD) as country programme officer of the India Country Office, New Delhi and the officer in charge of IFAD for Bhutan. IFAD is a specialised agency of the United Nations, working towards eradicating rural poverty in developing countries. He has authored several essays and reports.

Walter Fernandes, founder and till very recently Director of the North Eastern Social Research Centre (NESRC), Guwahati, is now senior faculty at the Centre. Formerly he was director of the Indian Social Institute, New Delhi. He has been a pioneering researcher on tribal and gender issues, displacement and livelihoods in central and northeastern India for many decades. He has published numerous books and essays and served as editor of the journal *Social Action*. The NESRC combines intellectual pursuits and engagement with activist groups and people working for social change in the region; it aspires to be a platform and a node where groups in conflict situations can meet and find solutions.

Nilabja Ghosh, currently faculty at the Institute of Economic Growth, Delhi, has taught economics for several years and served in reputed institutes as a researcher in agricultural economics and rural development. As a consultant with the United Nations University, she has participated in international and national collaborative research projects and contributes regularly to government policy-making processes. Her research interests are econometric modelling, and issues related to agricultural supply, food markets, gender, environment, and climate change. She has written several articles for national and international journals and conferences, and also co-authored two books. Her Ph.D. in Economics is from the Indian Statistical Institute.

Chanda Gurung Goodrich is currently Executive Director, South Asia Consortium for Interdisciplinary Water Resources Studies (SaciWaters), Hyderabad. She has 15 years' experience in gender and participatory research and development, having worked as a researcher and consultant in the not-for-profit sector, specialising in integrating social and gender equity into development programmes and projects. Her interests are related to natural resource management, sustainable agriculture and livelihoods research, project management, capacity building, training, and documentation. She holds M.Phil. and Ph.D. degrees from the School of International Studies, Jawaharlal Nehru University, New Delhi.

Ritupan Goswami is a research associate at the Council for Social Development, New Delhi. His doctoral thesis at the Centre for Historical Studies, Jawaharlal Nehru University, New Delhi, was a study of the changing relations between Assam's agrarian society and the Brahmaputra river in the last two centuries. His research interests include questions related to agrarian history, social transformation, Marxism, revolutionary communist movements, and national liberation struggles in South Asia.

D. K. Hore is currently the Chief Germplasm Botanist, Research and Development, Krishichan Seeds Ltd., Jalna, Maharashtra. Earlier, he was Principal Scientist and Head of the National Bureau of Plant Genetic Resources (NBPGR) of the Indian Council of Agricultural Research at Barapani, near Shillong, in Meghalaya. At NBPGR he led the collection of important plant genetic resources from the northeastern region, particularly upland rice germplasm and medicinal plants. His research interests include plant germplasm and biodiversity on which he has published a number of scientific articles.

K. M. Jayahari as Programme Officer in the Biodiversity and Conservation group of Winrock International India (WII), has over 10 years' experience in this field and has been pivotal in the success of a rhododendron conservation initiative in Arunachal Pradesh. Jayahari is presently involved in WII's conservation projects in the Eastern Himalaya and Western Ghats. Earlier he served in the Kerala Forest Research Institute and WWF. He has worked on issues related to wildlife biology, conservation, and livelihood enhancement, playing a key role in finalising the Kerala State Biodiversity Action Plan. His doctoral thesis was on the small mammals of the Western Ghats.

Sumi Krishna is an independent scholar and writer based in Bangalore, with 40 years of experience in environment, development and gender at field, programme and policy levels. She has been President of the Indian Association for Women's Studies (2005–08). Her work encompasses development, environment, natural resource management, people's movements, gender, and livelihood issues. She has authored several essays and books such as *Environmental Politics: People's Lives and Development Choices* (1996) and *Genderscapes: Revisioning Natural Resource Management* (2009), and has edited volumes including *Livelihood and Gender: Equity in Community Resource Management* (2004) and *Women's Livelihood Rights: Recasting Citizenship for Development* (2007).

Audrey Laldinpuii is a researcher based in Mizoram and Shillong. She obtained a Ph.D. from the Department of Political Science, NEHU, Shillong. At present she is working on the process of democratisation in the context of Mizoram. Earlier, she served as a project assistant in a LOKNITI project entitled 'Crisis of Governance in North East India'. The project was housed in NEHU under the aegis of the Centre for the Study of Developing Societies, New Delhi, and was funded by the London School of Economics.

Laithangpuii is from Mizoram, and has been a research scholar at the Department of History, NEHU, Shillong. She works on gender concerns in Mizoram. She has published articles related to gender and presented papers at various national seminars.

Deepak K. Mishra is currently Associate Professor of Economics at the Centre for the Study of Regional Development, School of Social Sciences, Jawaharlal Nehru University, New Delhi. He works in the areas of agrarian relations, and gender and livelihood diversification in mountain economies. He has been a South Asian visiting fellow and a Commonwealth visiting fellow at the Department of

International Development, Queen Elizabeth House, University of Oxford. He was Indian Council for Cultural Relations chair professor of Contemporary India Studies at the Russian State University of Humanities, Moscow, in early 2012. He has co-authored *Unfolding Crisis in Assam's Tea Plantations: Employment and Occupational Mobility* (New Delhi: Routledge, 2011) and the *Arunachal Pradesh Human Development Report* (Itanagar: Department of Planning and Statistics, Government of Arunachal Pradesh, 2005).

Melvil Pereira is currently Director of North Eastern Social Research Centre (NESRC), Guwahati, where he was earlier a research associate. He specialises in the gender implications and political dynamics of the tribal customary laws of the northeast. He completed his doctorate at Jawaharlal Nehru University on this theme and was involved in an earlier study on similar gender implications. At present he is guiding a study on 'Climate Change and Food Security in the Brahmaputra Valley' and another study on 'Gender Implications of the Customary Laws of Fourteen Tribes in Seven States of the Northeast'.

Thingnam Anjulika Samom, freelance journalist, Manipuri–English translator and filmmaker, is based in Imphal, Manipur. She writes on conflict, gender, child rights, health, and environmental issues regularly for Panos, Women Features Service, Infochange and *Himal Southasian*, as well as various local publications in Manipur. She has scripted, directed and produced two short films, *Shadow Lives* and *Nokkhigani* (I Will Laugh), based on the lives and conditions of women widowed by the ongoing armed conflict situation in Manipur. She is the coordinator of the Manipur chapter of the Network of Women in Media, India.

Monalisa Sen, Programme Officer in the Biodiversity and Conservation Group of Winrock International India (WII), works on conservation in the eastern Himalaya. She has over 10 years experience and has had a central role in rhododendron conservation initiative in Arunachal Pradesh. Her former work experience and research at the University of Delhi and the International Union for the Conservation of Nature (IUCN) relate to restoration ecology, livelihood enhancement and biodiversity conservation. Her doctoral research is on 'Avifauna and Community Dynamics in the Aravallis'.

U. A. Shimray (1972–2009), a Naga scholar born in Ukhrul district, Manipur, was an assistant professor at the Institute of Social and Economic Change, Bangalore at the time of his untimely death. Earlier, he had studied in Imphal and then gained a Ph.D. from the Centre for the Study of Regional Development, Jawaharlal Nehru University, New Delhi. He was briefly with the North Eastern Social Research Centre, Guwahati, and wrote a book on land relations published by NESRC in 2006. He was actively engaged in researching issues related to political and economic systems, land rights, the inter-relationship between ecology and economic development, etc. In his all too brief academic career, he published three books and many essays. He was also actively involved with and contributed to the public discourse on human rights.

P. K. Viswanathan, Associate Professor, Gujarat Institute of Development Research, Ahmedabad, was earlier with the Rubber Research Institute of India. He has also worked at the School of Environment Resources and Development, Asian Institute of Technology, Bangkok, been a visiting fellow at the Chinese University, Hong Kong, and a Wellcome Trust visiting fellow at Mahidol University, Thailand. His research interests include institutional and governance aspects of water resources development, collective action and sustainable livelihood outcomes in smallholder agriculture, agrarian transformation in Asia, ecological economics and community benefits of mangrove restoration, industrialisation and its impacts on natural resources and ecosystems. His Ph.D. is from the Institute for Social and Economic Change, Bangalore.

Index

For Product Safety Concerns and Information please contact our EU
representative GPSR@taylorandfrancis.com
Taylor & Francis Verlag GmbH, Kaufingerstraße 24, 80331 München, Germany